Bulletproofing the Psyche

Bulletproofing the Psyche

Preventing Mental Health Problems in Our Military and Veterans

Kate Hendricks Thomas, PhD, and
David L. Albright, PhD, Editors

Foreword by Charles R. Figley, PhD

An Imprint of ABC-CLIO, LLC
Santa Barbara, California • Denver, Colorado

Copyright © 2018 by Kate Hendricks Thomas, PhD and David L. Albright, PhD

All rights reserved. No part of this publication may be reproduced, stored in a retrieval system, or transmitted, in any form or by any means, electronic, mechanical, photocopying, recording, or otherwise, except for the inclusion of brief quotations in a review, without prior permission in writing from the publisher.

This book discusses treatments (including types of medication and mental health therapies), diagnostic tests for various symptoms and mental health disorders, and organizations. The authors have made every effort to present accurate and up-to-date information. However, the information in this book is not intended to recommend or endorse particular treatments or organizations, or substitute for the care or medical advice of a qualified health professional, or used to alter any medical therapy without a medical doctor's advice. Specific situations may require specific therapeutic approaches not included in this book. For those reasons, we recommend that readers follow the advice of qualified health care professionals directly involved in their care. Readers who suspect they may have specific medical problems should consult a physician about any suggestions made in this book.

Library of Congress Cataloging-in-Publication Data

Names: Thomas, Kate Hendricks, editor of compilation.
Title: Bulletproofing the psyche : preventing mental health problems in our military and veterans / Kate Hendricks Thomas, PhD, and David L. Albright, PhD, editors ; foreword by Charles R. Figley, PhD.
Other titles: Preventing mental health problems in our military and veterans
Description: Santa Barbara, California : Praeger, an imprint of ABC-CLIO, LLC, [2018] | Includes bibliographical references and index.
Identifiers: LCCN 2017048630 (print) | LCCN 2017055776 (ebook) | ISBN 9781440849770 (eBook) | ISBN 9781440849763 (print : alk. paper)
Subjects: LCSH: Veterans—United States—Mental health. | Veterans—United States—Psychology. | Veterans—United States—Services for. | United States—Armed Forces—Mental health. | Resilience (Personality trait)—United States.
Classification: LCC UB357 (ebook) | LCC UB357 .B85 2018 (print) | DDC 616.89/05088355—dc23
LC record available at https://lccn.loc.gov/2017048630

ISBN: 978-1-4408-4976-3 (print)
   978-1-4408-4977-0 (ebook)

22 21 20 19 18   1 2 3 4 5

This book is also available as an eBook.

Praeger
An Imprint of ABC-CLIO, LLC

ABC-CLIO, LLC
130 Cremona Drive, P.O. Box 1911
Santa Barbara, California 93116-1911
www.abc-clio.com

This book is printed on acid-free paper ∞

Manufactured in the United States of America

Contents

Foreword ix
   Charles R. Figley

Acknowledgments and Editors' Note xiii

Part One	**Framing the Issues**	1
Chapter 1	Introduction to Military-Connected Well-Being Issues *Jennifer E. C. Lee and Sanela Dursun*	3
	Point of View—The Small Bible *Matthew J. M. Hendricks*	18
Chapter 2	Warrior Culture: Ancient Roots, New Meaning *Kyleanne Hunter*	29
	Point of View—Armor Down: The Power of Mindfulness *Ben King*	43
Chapter 3	Mindfulness: The Neurobehavioral Basis of Resilience *Deborah Norris and Aurora Hutchinson*	47
	Point of View—A Shift on the Mat *Laura Westley*	66
Chapter 4	The Theory and Practice of Training for Resilience *Kate Hendricks Thomas and David L. Albright*	69
Chapter 5	Moral Injury and Resilience in the Military *Joseph M. Currier, Jacob K. Farnsworth, Kent D. Drescher, and Wesley H. McCormick*	76

Part Two	Current Mental Fitness Programming for Military- and Veteran-Connected Populations	93
Chapter 6	Department of Defense Resilience Programming *Cate Florenz and Margaret M. Shields*	95
	Point of View—Fostering Veteran-Student Health through Stress Management: Creating Belonging and Success in a College Setting through the Veterans at Ease Program *Robin Carnes and Stephen Kaplan*	111
Chapter 7	Mental Fitness and Military Veteran Women *Kelli Godfrey, Justin T. McDaniel, Lydia Davey, Sarah Plummer Taylor, and Christine Isana Garcia*	116
	Point of View—Fitting In and Finding Me *Jessica Wilkes*	129
Chapter 8	Learning from Example: Resilience of Service Members Who Identify as LGBT *Katharine Bloeser and Heliana Ramirez*	133
Chapter 9	Resilient Military Families *Charles R. McAdams III*	147
Chapter 10	The Promotion of Well-Being in Older Veterans *Kari L. Fletcher, Mariah Rooney O'Brien, and Kamilah A. Jones*	162
Part Three	Collaborating to Provide Mental Fitness Programming for Military-Connected Populations	179
Chapter 11	Faith-Based Programming for Spiritual Fitness *Rev. Sarah A. Shirley, Rev. Elizabeth A. Alders, Howard A. Crosby Jr., Kathleen G. Charters, and Rev. John Edgar Caterson*	181
Chapter 12	The Role of Individual Placement and Support (IPS) in Military Mental Fitness *Lori L. Davis and Richard Toscano*	196
Chapter 13	Adapting the Collective Impact Model to Veteran Services: The Case of AmericaServes *Nicholas J. Armstrong, Gillian S. Cantor, Bonnie Chapman, and James D. McDonough Jr.*	209

	Point of View—Setting the Bar: Mental Fitness and Performance *Kate Germano*	228
Chapter 14	The Way Forward *Kelsey L. Larsen and Elizabeth A. Stanley*	233

About the Editors and Contributors   255

Index   263

Foreword

A long time ago, I was a Marine in Vietnam. My war was different from other conflicts these days (e.g., training, equipment, enemy), but much is the same. Warfighters have a job to do: to win, to kill, and to complete the mission. Self-care is not on their to-do list. Not then and not now. But it should be. We had no idea back then how stress could affect your sleep or how you can get better sleep by controlling your stress. Common behaviors such as drinking alcohol or other self-medicating efforts are flawed but sometimes necessary to restore stasis. Let me return to my experiences later.

This book is about building resilience in military personnel and veterans. It is an alternative to books that focus on the problems these men and women face or that emphasize the negative consequences of military service in the form of mental illness diagnoses. This book is about hope and about the belief that with effort we are able, all of us, to develop and wear a bulletproof psyche just as we wear a bulletproof vest into battle. We can build up our skills, moral compass, integrating honor, mutual support, trust, and the other tools discussed in this book that better prepare men and women for severe conditions that persist for prolonged periods of time.

Kate Hendricks Thomas and David L. Albright know about the need for such skills and resources to enable effective leadership, adaptability, and creativity to get the job done, no matter what. They were able to recruit not only the authors who are scholars, researchers, and practitioners to contribute to this book but also writers who are military veterans, including combat vets. This mixture of voices leads to a harmony of thoughtful creativity and reflection about what is needed to effectively serve as a shield from the horrors of war and its immediate and long-lasting consequences. Such a shield would enable veterans to go through the phases of reentry to society and to be effective and loving family members.

The aim of this book is consistent with its theme: embracing and quickly managing the s*** by taking advantage of the innovations of the mindfulness movement and other alternative and complementary behavioral health practices. However, there is a cautionary note at the end of this book. Despite the best plans and efforts, the military does what it does. New commanders take over and do the best they can. Sometimes new leadership ends a successful program, like the ones described in this book.

The characteristics of bulletproofing are largely the same as the concept of mettle. Mettle is a person's ability to cope well with difficulties or to face a demanding situation in a spirited and resilient way. Bulletproofing the psyche, then, like having the "right stuff," mettle, or resilience, is about decreasing the mental health risk factors and increasing the protective factors. Rather than focusing on a diagnosis (e.g., posttraumatic stress disorder, depression), the focus is on preventing and bouncing back from traumatic events.

This book illustrates how and why resilience can be taught and trained. It is far better than the traditional focus on mental disorders and psychopathology. The focus is on medical prevention as well as rehabilitation toward functioning. This is one of the reasons why many are shifting toward favoring the World Health Organization's nomenclature over that of the *Diagnostic and Statistical Manual*. Focusing on mental illness diagnoses such as posttraumatic stress disorder is a disservice to those who are seeking treatment: these types of diagnoses can trigger further problems, including feelings of shame and of failure, rather than the acknowledgment that one is injured and requires appropriate rehabilitative care. Self-care and social support are vital to building resilience.

Indeed, resilience arguments and evidence are becoming popular among active-duty programs. They are more often focused on preparing warfighters for the mental and emotional toll that are brought about by combat operations.

But no matter their documented success, future military leaders will need to be educated about their value and kept up-to-date on new findings in this field. So, despite the extraordinary contributions made in this book, we cannot count on the lessons being applied in the future. This is in line with the recent analysis Mark Russell (former Navy Commander and the lead psychologist treating Marines) and I published through a series of systematic reviews of military publications and documents (cf., Russell & Figley, 2017a, 2017b, 2017c). We noted that the Department of Defense in general and frontline psychiatry in particular are failing in their responsibility to prevent psychiatric casualties and that there are more *psychiatric* casualties than physical casualties and wartime psychiatric casualties even exceed *combined* totals of personnel physically wounded and personnel killed in action.

When I returned from Vietnam, I had no idea how I had been changed by my experiences leading Marines and fighting in war. I was fortunate that my bulletproof vest was for mental bullets, not just metal ones. I was able to focus my postwar rage generated in Vietnam (1965–1966) on to my academic studies and degrees. My fortune of a loving family, intellectual and social resources, and an emerging hate of war motivated me to try to help other vets find and build their vests. What I have tried to convey is that this book is about helping war fighters, during and following war, build resilience to the war stressors.

The military has dual missions of war: fighting wars and force protection. This requires both protecting those who fight the war and getting them home in one piece with a plan to promote healing mentally and physically from their war injuries.

This book provides a way forward to improve military mental health. Collectively, we can hope that this book will be read by war planners. So far, the war planners have not worried about a bulletproof "vest" for mental injury, just vests to prevent physical injury. Protecting our warfighters during and following battle must be our primary mission on a par with the military mission. This book is an important start.

Charles R. Figley, PhD
Paul Henry Kuzweg, MD, Distinguished Chair and Professor
Tulane University
New Orleans, USA

References

Russell, M. C., & Figley, C. R. (2017a). Do the military's frontline psychiatry/combat and operational stress control doctrine help or harm veterans? Part one: Framing the issue. *Psychological Injury and Law, 10*, 1–23. doi:10.1007/s12207–016–9278-y

Russell, M. C., & Figley, C. R. (2017b). Do the military's frontline psychiatry/combat operational stress control programs benefit veterans? Part two: Systematic review of the evidence. *Psychological Injury and Law, 10*, 24–71.

Russell, M. C., & Figley, C. R. (2017c). Is the military's century-old frontline psychiatry policy harmful to veterans and their families? Part three of a systematic review. *Psychological Injury and Law, 10*, 72–95. doi:10.1007/s12207-016-9280-4

Acknowledgments and Editors' Note

We came to this project after many, many conversations about veterans' well-being issues. Perhaps we work in this space today because our own experiences leaving the Marine Corps and Army were not ideal—it just wasn't as easy to leave and reinvent as we had expected. It is easy to focus on how things aren't optimized for military personnel leaving the active component, but as we chatted, we always turned back to notions of *preventing* some of that transition stress. "If I'd only known to do this" became a familiar refrain. We believe that it doesn't have to be as hard to reintegrate into a civilian community for tomorrow's service members. This project is the first of our attempts to contribute to and extend the prevention, rehabilitation, and training conversation for military personnel navigating that liminal space between service and civilian life and those that support these processes.

First and foremost, we would like to thank the team of contributors who lent their expertise, efforts, and skillful prose to this volume. Without you, there would be no book. The research and personal experiences you shared are an invaluable gift. We would also like to thank Charlotte Brock, a Marine Corps veteran and freelance editor, who helped us turn early chapter drafts into cleaner prose.

Important to mention are our partners, who provide continual support for our activities, and our children whose enthusiasm and energy sustain us. Finally, we are forever thankful to the service members, veterans, and their families and communities.

Many of us return from military service meaningfully changed—physically, mentally, emotionally, and spiritually. These changes encompass the whole person and hold the potential to transcend whole communities. Section one of this anthology will highlight some of these issues and discuss the physiology of stress injury and other barriers to well-being as well as the way that hardship can create growth and even "bulletproof the psyche."

We hope this book contributes to larger community efforts that support healing. We also hope it motivates a new emphasis on mental fitness training for the active duty component. Here, rigorous evaluation of existing outreach efforts provide the foundation upon which savvy programmers must build. We focus in section two of this book on examining resiliency programs making inroads with today's veterans. Our best chance for making a difference in both the postservice and training environments (before a service member faces transition stress) involves designing programs from a baseline of proven success.

To operate in training commands requires great cultural competency, making mental fitness programming relevant to warfighters working to maintain readiness and improve performance. The narrative must become about mission success, not mental health treatment. It means not only trying to understand the veteran experience but also learning the most effective ways to communicate with different subsets of the veteran and military populations. To train is to actively participate, and this is a wellness concept with which service members are already familiar. Framing self-regulatory training as a way to "bulletproof the brain" renders palatable a training opportunity specifically designed to create more effective warriors who possess mental endurance. Framing mental fitness training as promotion of combat fitness, resilience, and mental endurance renders it accessible to the military population. We're interested in building strengths after all.

We have to speak the language of warriors who have been immersed in combat operations for over 15 years when we talk about resiliency-cultivation. PowerPoint presentations simply won't cut it. By establishing mental fitness as another component of optimal combat readiness, we establish such training as a crucial component of mission preparedness and, as a benefit, remove the stigma of such practices for postdeployment troops that may be struggling with stress illnesses of varying degrees. The message can become directive; just as Marines and soldiers learn mission essential skills and train their bodies for arduous combat, we must adopt practices designed to train and promote health in the mind, body, and spirit in a holistic sense. This training doesn't succeed in sustainable fashion in a vacuum. Knowing the importance of social support to well-being and generally wanting to contribute to improved quality of life for service members require a focus on the larger community in which a warrior operates. Social and family fitness is part of mental fitness, and we must consider family readiness programming that is more extensive and progressive than our current offerings.

When we consider how we could apply these basic recommendations to military veterans seeking relief from reintegration stress or to active-duty military preparing for it, we must consider how to make stress management a testable metric. Biofeedback tools exist that can do this. Checking for dehydroepiandrosterone and blood cortisol ratios or conducting periodic blood cortisol checks can be as important as other physical standards are in the military. Biomarkers tell us quickly whether someone is taking time to practice balanced wellness.

Section three of this anthology will highlight the possibility of training an individual to de-escalate his or her nervous system response as a performance metric and discuss methods for rolling such programs out both in the active duty component and the veteran space. This anthology's primary conclusion is a call to action. We can use biofeedback testing to make resilience a performance metric for the active duty component. It turns self-awareness and resilience into standards and motivates learning, training, practice, and performance in our community's culture. Our future work involves delivery and evaluation of a theoretically based, validated training curriculum to bulletproof the brain.

The future is exciting from clinical, training, and prevention perspectives, and these recommendations offer tremendous promise for tomorrow's military personnel. Training to embrace a mental temerity training regimen can make them better at their jobs and more resilient in their lives, both during and after their service to our country.

Kate Hendricks Thomas and David L. Albright

PART ONE

Framing the Issues

CHAPTER 1

Introduction to Military-Connected Well-Being Issues

Jennifer E. C. Lee and Sanela Dursun

Together, the wars in Afghanistan and Iraq are among the most hostile conflicts seen in recent history. Since 2001, over 2.7 million U.S. troops have been deployed in support of these operations, while over 40,000 Canadian Armed Forces (CAF) members have been deployed in support of the mission in Afghanistan (Ramchand, Rudavsky, Grant, Tanielian, & Jaycox, 2015; Zamorski & Boulos, 2014). There have been more than 8,000 military casualties among members of the coalition and over 52,000 U.S. military personnel wounded in action for the conflicts combined (Defence Casualty Analysis System, 2016). Furthermore, it is widely recognized that the impacts of war go beyond the immediate fatalities and injuries. Having faced extreme stress and hostile situations, military personnel are at increased risk of experiencing mental health problems. These "invisible wounds" of war have garnered a great deal of attention in recent years (Tanielian & Jaycox, 2008), with research on the mental health impacts of recent conflicts in Southwest Asia having surged over the past decade and a half. A number of well-designed epidemiological studies have now contributed to a better understanding of the overall burden of postdeployment mental health outcomes, such as post-traumatic stress disorder (PTSD) (Averill, Fleming, Holens, & Larsen, 2015).

From the psychological lens, research has also provided substantial insight into the processes and mechanisms that may explain how exposure to combat stress gives rise to mental health disorders and, ultimately, influence individuals in the longer term. Now that an extensive body of work has developed, there is an opportunity to integrate what is known, identify remaining gaps, and propose promising strategies to address these. The present chapter provides an overview of key findings in this area based on research conducted on U.S. and Canadian military personnel deployed in support of the conflicts in Southwest Asia since 2001, with the aim of providing a more integrative perspective of psychosocial pathways in the course of PTSD and its sequelae.

Burden of Postdeployment Mental Health Problems

Given the traumatic nature of combat, it is not surprising that a great deal of research on the mental health of military personnel has focused on the psychological impacts of trauma exposure. Despite only having been formally recognized as a mental health condition in the third American Psychiatric Association *Diagnostic and Statistical Manual (DSM-III)* in 1980 (Friedman, 2016), PTSD has evolved into one of the most commonly researched impacts of combat exposure. As noted by Friedman (2016), the PTSD concept represented an important shift in psychiatric theory through the acknowledgment that etiologic factors for the disorder were outside of the individual rather than resulting from an inherent weakness.

It is argued that the recent missions in Afghanistan and Iraq have created a unique set of conditions for increased risk of PTSD among military personnel (Schnurr, Lunney, Bovin, & Marx, 2009): in the United States, these wars primarily relied on National Guard and reserve forces and required personnel to go on multiple deployments to meet the demands of the conflict (Galea et al., 2012); tours were longer, with shorter periods between them; and, finally, during the tours themselves, commonly reported stressors included the risk of improvised explosive devices (IEDs), suicide bombers, or handling human remains among several others (Tanielian, Jaycox, Adamson, & Metscher, 2008). In turn, significant efforts have been placed on quantifying the burden of PTSD among military personnel deployed in support of these missions.

In Canada, an estimated 7.7 percent of Regular Force members with an Afghanistan-related deployment reported PTSD in the past year according to a recent survey on mental health in the CAF (Boulos & Zamorski, 2016). Despite its relatively greater abundance, research on the prevalence of PTSD among U.S. military personnel returning from deployment to Afghanistan or Iraq has produced variable results. Indeed, the wide variation in estimates of PTSD across U.S. studies is among the main criticisms of research in this

Introduction to Military-Connected Well-Being Issues 5

area and has been attributed to a number of factors, including differences in the sampling strategy used across studies, inconsistencies in the timing of studies relative to deployments, and variations in the case definition used (Kok, Herrell, Thomas, & Hoge, 2012; Ramchand, Karney, Osilla, Burns, & Caldarone, 2008; Richardson, Frueh, & Acierno, 2010).

Of note, one important factor that has been found to contribute to the varying estimated prevalence of PTSD among service members deployed in support of Operation Enduring Freedom/Operation Iraqi Freedom (OEF/OIF) is the specific population under study (Kok et al., 2012). Kok et al. (2012), for instance, found that the average population-wide prevalence of postdeployment PTSD was 5 percent, while it was estimated at 13.2 percent among operational infantry units, which tend to have greater exposure to ground combat. Some researchers have argued that focusing research on combat troops is problematic because increased combat exposure in these groups may result in inflated estimates of PTSD or depression (Hotopf et al., 2006). Indeed, research that is more generalizable to all deployed personnel is important to assess the burden of disease and to ensure that mental health services and resources are correctly allocated (Ramchand et al., 2008). PTSD is one of many potential postdeployment health outcomes, and it is important to understand its burden within the context of other problems that might require an expansion of services and programs. At the same time, focusing on all deployed personnel without accounting for important subgroups has some disadvantages, as doing so may obscure important phenomena contributing to postdeployment PTSD among those at greatest risk, such as the role of experiential or psychosocial factors that may exacerbate mental health problems after deployment. To fully understand the range of factors and phenomena contributing to PTSD among military personnel, it is also helpful to focus on the specific experiences of those at greatest risk.

Risk Factors for Postdeployment PTSD

Across studies of military personnel deployed in Southwest Asia, the finding that has been most consistent is the relationship between combat exposure and PTSD (Ramchand et al., 2008). Based on a review of medical records, an estimated 8 percent of CAF members who were deployed in support of the Afghanistan mission up to 2008 were diagnosed with PTSD that was attributed to the deployment (Boulos & Zamorski, 2013). In the United States, an early prospective study that followed a cohort from 2001–2003 to 2004–2006 found that the incidence of new PTSD was 1.4 percent among those who were deployed without combat exposure and 7.6 percent among those who were deployed with combat exposure (according to specific screening criteria for PTSD). The odds of new-onset PTSD were between 2.48 and 3.59 percentage points greater among those who were deployed with combat exposure compared to those who were not deployed, depending on the branch of service (Smith et al., 2008). While this last finding demonstrates the persistence of combat exposure as a risk factor for postdeployment PTSD, it also underlines the variation in risk that may occur across individuals.

Epidemiological research on the risk factors for postdeployment PTSD has largely focused on demographic or military characteristics that may contribute to excess risk. Some of the key individual risk factors for PTSD identified in a large population-based survey of U.S. military personnel deployed in support of OEF/OIF included being in the Army or Marine Corps, in the National Guard or reserve, enlisted, and being female and Hispanic (Schell & Marshall, 2008). Among CAF personnel deployed in support of the mission in Afghanistan, risk factors for postdeployment PTSD have included being unmarried, the experience of stressors on the home front, and lower rank (Zamorski & Boulos, 2014). For many of these characteristics, excess risk for PTSD could be explained by differential levels of combat exposure. Indeed, Army, Marine Corps, and enlisted (or lower rank) personnel are most likely to be exposed to combat. However, this explanation is not likely to be sufficient for some of these other risk factors, particularly the experience of stressors on the home front. Psychological research has helped shed light on some of these other factors. Of particular note is the influence of a range of stressors other than those related to combat on postdeployment mental health outcomes, which may span from adverse childhood experiences to stressful life events occurring closer to the time of deployment.

Increasingly, researchers have considered the role of adverse childhood experiences as factors that may increase vulnerability to postdeployment PTSD. Early work, for example, revealed that Vietnam veterans with PTSD reported higher rates of childhood physical abuse than those without PTSD and that this difference existed even when variation in combat exposure between the groups was taken into account (Bremner, Southwick, Johnson, Yehuda, & Charney, 1993). Since then, similar findings have been reported in other military contexts and in relation to a wider set of mental health problems (Cabrera, Hoge, Bliese, Castro, & Messer, 2007; Fritch, Mishkind, Reger, & Gahm, 2010; Iversen et al., 2007). As a potential explanation for these findings, it has been proposed that exposure to adversity predisposes individuals to PTSD by increasing their propensity to be exposed to combat (Iversen et al., 2007). Indeed, exposure to childhood adversity has been linked with lower educational attainment and lower military rank, which could result in a greater likelihood of being involved in the front line during a combat operation (Iversen et al., 2007). A recent longitudinal study of Canadian military personnel returning from deployment in Afghanistan found that service members who had reported more adverse childhood experiences at the time of recruit training reported greater exposure to combat and that this contributed to lower levels of postdeployment mental health (Lee, Phinney, Watkins, & Zamorski, 2016). However, these service members also reported less favorable characteristics on psychological and social attributes that are believed to confer resilience in the face of adversity, such as their levels of mastery and social support (Lee, Sudom, & McCreary, 2011), which contributed to lower postdeployment mental health in turn. Thus, findings provided evidence that were more in line with a stress-sensitization hypothesis, suggesting that childhood adversity may contribute to a greater risk of mental health problems by way of their impact on how individuals interpret or handle stressors (McLaughlin, Conron, Koenen, & Gilman, 2010).

In addition to adverse childhood experiences, psychological research has emphasized the importance of considering the full range of stressors that may be experienced by service members throughout the deployment cycle, over and above those related to combat. In an investigation of gender differences in postdeployment mental health problems, it was found that women reported only slightly less exposure than men to combat-related stressors. However, they reported greater exposure to other types of stressors, including predeployment stressors and sexual harassment (Vogt et al., 2011). Such gender differences were replicated in a more recent analysis, where it was found that male OEF/OIF veterans reported greater exposure to mission-related stressors, while female veterans reported greater exposure to interpersonal stressors (Fox et al., 2016). Differences in these other stressors also underline the importance of considering factors beyond those related to combat itself as risk factors for postdeployment PTSD, including other psychosocial factors. In a prospective longitudinal investigation of U.S. National Guard soldiers, reporting more stressors prior to deployment, feeling less prepared for deployment, and reporting more stressful life events after deployment were associated with greater odds of new-onset probable PTSD. Conversely, greater social support was associated with lesser odds of new-onset probable PTSD (Polusny et al., 2011). In a more recent prospective study of U.S. Marines, the relationship of cohesion among members of the military unit with various mental health outcomes was examined. Two types of cohesion were examined: the average level of cohesion across the unit (unit-level cohesion) and individuals' perceptions of their cohesion relative to this average. It was found that unit-level cohesion was not associated with probable PTSD, but that Marines who perceived higher levels of cohesion relative to the average level in their unit had lower odds of probable PTSD (Breslau, Setodji, & Vaughan, 2016). Thus, beyond identifying risk factors for PTSD among military personnel deployed in support of the missions in Afghanistan and Iraq, psychological research has helped identify factors that may be protective.

In addition, psychological research has helped shed light on which specific aspects of combat are most difficult for individuals. A recent study examining the relationship between enemy combat tactics being used across phases of OIF found evidence that asymmetric tactics (i.e., those in which guerilla-style tactics are used by the enemy rather than conventional warfare similar to those used by coalition forces) were associated with an increased risk for PTSD, even after controlling for levels of combat exposure (Green et al., 2016). Other studies have examined in greater detail which specific types of combat events were most strongly associated with postdeployment PTSD. In one study of Canadian military personnel, specific combat events that were most strongly associated with PTSD were those that were uncommonly experienced, were unexpected, and could be interpreted as reflecting some violation of one's morality (Watkins, Sudom, & Zamorski, 2016). Born and Zamorski (2017) assessed the fraction of the burden of PTSD that could be attributed to a range of combat events and found that, while perceived responsibility for the death of another was reported infrequently, a substantial proportion of mental health disorder could be accounted for by exposure to this type of event.

The detrimental effects of certain combat experiences (e.g., the perceived responsibility for the death of an ally, the inability to respond to threats due to the rules of engagement, and having witnessed atrocities or massacres) on mental health have led clinicians and researchers to recognize that the psychological anguish that many combat veterans experienced was not represented exclusively by the fear- or terror-based trauma that is the traditional basis of a PTSD diagnosis (Drescher & Foy, 2008). Rather, beyond or instead of leading to PTSD, certain experiences may transgress deeply held moral beliefs and result in less predictable reactions to trauma, such as guilt and shame, in what has been recently referred to as "moral injury" (e.g., Litz et al., 2009). Moral injury has been defined as psychological trauma that can result from "perpetrating, failing to prevent, bearing witness to, or learning about acts that transgress deeply held moral beliefs and expectations" (Litz et al., 2009). A consistent theme in moral injury theory and research is its fundamental connection to feelings of guilt and shame, as opposed to the fear, helplessness, or horror that are traditionally associated with PTSD (Dombo, Gray, & Early, 2013; Litz et al., 2009; Steenkamp, Nash, Lebowitz, & Litz, 2013). The manifestations of moral injury may include an array of dysfunctional behaviors such as self-harming (e.g., substance misuse, extreme risk-taking) and self-handicapping (e.g., avoiding positive experiences and emotions), as well as emotions and cognitions, such as demoralization (e.g., feelings of confusion, hopelessness, and self-hatred) (Litz et al., 2009). Bryan, Morrow, Etienne, and Ray-Sannerud (2013), moreover, found the distress caused by moral transgressions to be significantly associated with suicidal ideation beyond the effects of depression and PTSD symptomatology. Thus, the current "standard" evidence-based PTSD treatment approaches might not be completely effective in addressing the needs of those who experienced moral injury.

Going beyond Postdeployment PTSD

Emerging research on moral injury has emphasized the importance of considering a wider range of outcomes in research on the effects of combat exposure among military personnel. Karney, Ramchand, Osilla, Caldarone, and Burns (2008) described postdeployment mental health as akin to a ripple effect, noting that "whereas ripples diminish over time, the consequences of mental health and cognitive conditions may grow more severe, especially if left untreated" (p. 149). Thus, equally important is the need to understand the broader impacts of PTSD on the lives of service members and some of the factors that may influence its course.

One issue elucidated in research on postdeployment PTSD, and that has been found to influence clinical outcomes, is its high level of comorbidity with other mental health disorders. In a survey of OEF/OIF veterans, not only were PTSD and depression highly correlated, but close to two-thirds of those with PTSD had probable depression as well (Schell & Marshall, 2008). Comorbid PTSD and depression are not unique to U.S. OEF/OIF veterans. One study of Canadian veterans examined the latent profiles of PTSD and major depression and found three profiles of PTSD and depression comorbidity. The first was characterized by high levels of symptoms on both disorders, the second by moderate symptoms on both disorders, and the third by low symptoms (Armour et al., 2015). Not surprisingly, the group with high levels of PTSD and depression symptoms reported the least favorable outcomes in terms of health-related functional impairment. In another similar analysis, it was found that the dysphoria factor of PTSD in particular was associated with various depression factors, suggesting that dysphoric mood underlies PTSD psychopathology (Elhai, Contractor, Palmieri, Forbes, & Richardson, 2011).

As competing hypotheses for the high prevalence of comorbid PTSD and depression, it has been proposed that observed comorbidity is the product of extensive symptom overlap between both disorders; or rather, that this comorbidity is indicative of the presence of a trauma-related phenotype (Flory & Yehuda, 2015). Following a review of studies on the etiology of depression comorbidity in combat-related PTSD, evidence was found suggesting that PTSD was a risk factor for subsequent depression (Stander, Thomsen, & Highfill-McRoy, 2014). At the same time, it was recognized that this association was complex and possibly involved common vulnerabilities or risk factors and bidirectional relationships (Stander et al., 2014). Irrespective of the cause, it is widely recognized that comorbid PTSD and depression are difficult to treat and are associated with poorer outcomes, including suicide ideation (Flory & Yehuda, 2015). In one study of U.S. Army personnel, soldiers with both PTSD and depression were found to be almost three times more likely to report suicide ideation in the past year than those with only a single disorder (Ramsawh et al., 2014). Furthermore, it was estimated that, while PTSD and depression each contributed to the overall risk of suicide ideation in this population, having both disorders concurrently contributed to the greatest proportion of risk, followed by having depression alone (Ramsawh et al., 2014).

With PTSD and depression both having been linked with suicide ideation (LeardMann et al., 2013; Ramchand et al., 2015; Ramsawh et al., 2014), some studies have focused on clarifying the different pathways that might explain these associations. In line with findings emphasizing the relationship of noncombat factors, such as other psychosocial stressors or social resources, with PTSD among military personnel returning from combat, a number of these studies have examined the role of social support in the course of PTSD. In one study, it was found that PTSD and depression symptoms were not strongly associated with suicide ideation among OEF/OIF veterans with high postdeployment social support, but that such symptoms were strongly associated with suicide ideation among OEF/OIF veterans who reported low postdeployment social support (DeBeer, Kimbrel, Meyer, Gulliver, & Morissette, 2014).

Other proposed pathways from postdeployment PTSD to suicide ideation have focused on individual psychological processes related to service members' exposure to combat. In line with findings pointing to moral injury as a risk factor for PTSD, one study found that these disorders might be associated with suicide ideation as a result of feelings of guilt experienced by service members after they experience combat (Bryan, Roberge, Bryan, & Ray-Sannerud, 2015). It was suggested that providing OEF/OIF veterans with brief cognitive-behavioral therapy targeting this guilt might help reduce suicide ideation and suicide attempts. Similarly, a more recent study of treatment-seeking OEF/OIF veterans investigated whether trauma-related cognitions and decreased levels of social support related to PTSD and depression might explain why these disorders are associated with suicide ideation. Ultimately, results indicated that the associations of both PTSD and depression with suicide ideation could be explained by trauma-related cognitions. However, decreases in social support related to depression could also explain why this disorder was associated with suicide ideation (McLean et al., 2017).

One major limitation of the studies reviewed previously, however, is that they were based on cross-sectional data. Ramchand et al. (2015) noted the need for more longitudinal research to better understand the temporal sequence of mental and behavioral health problems following return from deployment. While suicide ideation was not examined in their study, James and her colleagues examined the relationship of predeployment stressors, combat exposure, and postdeployment with PTSD and depression at 6, 12, and 24 months postdeployment (James, Van Kampen, Miller, & Engdahl, 2013). Interestingly, they found that while combat exposure was associated with PTSD at 6 months, it was not associated with symptoms at 12 or 24 months postdeployment. On the other hand, postdeployment social support was associated with PTSD at each time point, in addition to depression at 12 and 24 months (James et al., 2013). Taken with the studies reviewed previously, these findings emphasize the importance of considering the psychosocial factors that may influence the risk and consequences of postdeployment PTSD. Indeed, poor mental health after return from deployment can impact the way service members interact with their social environment (Karney et al., 2008). It can strain relationships with family members (Monson, Taft, & Fredman, 2009), who often represent an important source of social support. Because of the role social support can play in "[facilitating] effective treatment, healing, and recovery for service members, veterans, and their families" (Galea et al., 2012, p. 309), this may interfere with the extent or quality of care received.

Integrative Frameworks on Postdeployment Mental Health and Its Course

Thus far, the present chapter has provided a review of the key findings that have emerged from research on PTSD and its impacts among service members deployed in support of the missions in Afghanistan and Iraq. Population-based epidemiological research has helped gain a better understanding of the burden militaries face in relation to postdeployment PTSD and of specific subpopulations that are particularly at risk, while psychological research has shed light on experiential and more dynamic psychosocial processes that might underlie the course of PTSD. In order to further advance theory and practice in this area, approaches are needed that can facilitate the integration of research from both perspectives and allow for the investigation of more dynamic processes and individual variation while adopting the methodological rigor of epidemiological research. The following section describes two approaches—one conceptual approach and one methodological approach—that have recently been described in the literature and may have the potential to do this.

In their integrated framework, Karney et al. (2008) describe some of the consequences of deployment on mental, emotional, and cognitive health and how these might influence service members' and veterans' family or social conditions. From their perspective, postdeployment mental health conditions such as PTSD or depression can be regarded as a source of vulnerability. However, the specific consequences of these conditions are believed to depend on the extent that service members and veterans have other vulnerabilities, such as low social support or poor access to treatment or psychosocial resources that may help them in their recovery. Longer-term outcomes will also depend on whether service members and veterans experience any additional stressful situations that may place further demands on their resources. Furthermore, two mechanisms are believed to account for the manner in which postdeployment mental health conditions exert their ripple effects. First, the conditions may influence the way service members and veterans interact with others around them, possibly straining relationships with individuals who could otherwise provide needed support. Second, changes related to mental health problems may result in an increased risk of additional life events, such as job loss, divorce, or homelessness, that would set boundaries on one's living conditions in the longer term. As new potential sources of vulnerability, these consequences could subsequently influence the course of the mental health conditions.

As demonstrated in several studies reviewed previously, research has generally provided support for the view that mental health conditions can spill over into other life domains and contribute to additional problems. To investigate the dynamic processes through which such conditions contribute to new stressors and produce additional vulnerability adequately, more sophisticated approaches are needed in research in this area. While the need for longitudinal research to better understand the temporality between risk factors and outcomes among service members and veterans returning from deployment has been recognized (Polusny et al., 2011; Ramchand et al., 2015), some have noted the importance of developing approaches that can account for the complexity, multiplicity, nonlinearity, and bidirectionality of relationships between those risk factors and outcomes (De Schryver, Vindevogel, Rasmussen, & Cramer, 2015). As a solution, De Schryver et al. (2015) proposed applying a network approach. This approach could allow for the investigation of differential relationships between particular exposures to war, daily stressors, and symptoms of PTSD by exploring patterns of association at the level of variables, and for the modeling of variables as both predictors and outcomes concurrently, resulting in "a conceptualization and representation of variables and relationships that better approach reality and represent the actual research context" (De Schryver et al., 2015, p. 7). The representation of these relationships within a network can reveal how strongly related variables are to one another, point to important clusters of highly related variables, and show the centrality of a given variable relative to the others in describing a particular phenomenon. If longitudinal data are available, changes in the network over time may also be investigated to understand causal relationships among variables. Ultimately, this information could be used to develop more effective preventative strategies, by ensuring that these focus on the most prominent issues and target those factors that are most likely to produce and sustain negative outcomes.

Concluding Remarks

The body of work on mental health following return from deployment has expanded dramatically since the formal recognition of PTSD as a mental health disorder. Recent epidemiological work has provided valuable insight into the burden of PTSD among military personnel deployed in support of the Afghanistan and Iraq missions and outlined a number of factors that may give rise to greater or lesser risk. At the same time, emerging research has emphasized the vast array of factors that may influence the impacts of combat exposure on the mental health and well-being of OEF/OIF veterans upon their return, beyond PTSD. Researchers are beginning to recognize the need to develop methodological approaches that can account for the complexity and dynamic nature of psychosocial processes that may contribute to PTSD and its course, although these have seldom been applied. To ensure that military organizations have the necessary agility to develop prevention strategies that adequately address postdeployment mental health and its sequelae, it is important that these be based on evidence that reflects the inherent multifaceted nature and complexity of processes involved following the return and recovery from deployment. More integrative conceptual and methodological frameworks, such as those discussed previously, provide promising directions for future research on the well-being of military personnel after their return from deployment to combat missions.

References

Armour, C., Contractor, A., Elhai, J. D., Stringer, M., Lyle, G., Forbes, D., & Richardson, J. D. (2015). Identifying latent profiles of posttraumatic stress and major depression symptoms in Canadian veterans: Exploring differences across profiles in health related functioning. *Psychiatry Research, 228*(1), 1–7.

Averill, L. A., Fleming, C. E., Holens, P. L., & Larsen, S. E. (2015). Research on PTSD prevalence in OEF/OIF Veterans: Expanding investigation of demographic variables. *European Journal of Psychotraumatology, 6.* http://dx.doi.org/10.3402/ejpt.v6.27322

Born, J. A., & Zamorski, M. (2017). *Contribution of traumatic deployment experiences to the burden of mental health problems in Canadian Armed Forces personnel: Exploration of population attributable fractions.* Manuscript submitted for publication.

Boulos, D., & Zamorski, M. A. (2013). Deployment-related mental disorders among Canadian Forces personnel deployed in support of the mission in Afghanistan, 2001–2008. *Canadian Medical Association Journal, 185*(11), E545–E552.

Boulos, D., & Zamorski, M. A. (2016). Contribution of the mission in Afghanistan to the burden of past-year mental disorders in Canadian Armed

Forces personnel, 2013. *The Canadian Journal of Psychiatry, 61*(1 suppl), 64S–76S.

Bremner, J. D., Southwick, S. M., Johnson, D. R., Yehuda, R., & Charney, D. S. (1993). Childhood physical abuse and combat-related posttraumatic stress disorder in Vietnam veterans. *The American Journal of Psychiatry, 150*(2), 235–239.

Breslau, J., Setodji, C. M., & Vaughan, C. A. (2016). Is cohesion within military units associated with post-deployment behavioral and mental health outcomes? *Journal of Affective Disorders, 198*, 102–107.

Bryan, C. J., Morrow, C. E., Etienne, N., & Ray-Sannerud, B. (2013). Guilt, shame, and suicidal ideation in a military outpatient clinical sample. *Depression and Anxiety, 30*(1), 55–60.

Bryan, C. J., Roberge, E., Bryan, A., & Ray-Sannerud, B. (2015). Guilt as a mediator of the relationship among depression and posttraumatic stress with suicide ideation in two samples of military personnel and veterans. *International Journal of Cognitive Therapy, 8*(2), 142–154.

Cabrera, O. A., Hoge, C. W., Bliese, P. D., Castro, C. A., & Messer, S. C. (2007). Childhood adversity and combat as predictors of depression and post-traumatic stress in deployed troops. *American Journal of Preventive Medicine, 33*(2), 77–82.

De Schryver, M., Vindevogel, S., Rasmussen, A. E., & Cramer, A. O. (2015). Unpacking constructs: A network approach for studying war exposure, daily stressors and post-traumatic stress disorder. *Frontiers in Psychology, 6*, 1896.

DeBeer, B. B., Kimbrel, N. A., Meyer, E. C., Gulliver, S. B., & Morissette, S. B. (2014). Combined PTSD and depressive symptoms interact with post-deployment social support to predict suicidal ideation in Operation Enduring Freedom and Operation Iraqi Freedom veterans. *Psychiatry Research, 216*(3), 357–362.

Defence Casualty Analysis System. (2016). U.S. Military Casualties—OCO Casualty Summary by Casualty Type (as of December 29, 2016). Retrieved from https://www.dmdc.osd.mil/dcas/pages/report_sum_reason.xhtml

Dombo, E. A., Gray, C., & Early, B. P. (2013). The trauma of moral injury: Beyond the battlefield. *Journal of Religion & Spirituality in Social Work: Social Thought, 32*(3), 197–210.

Drescher, K. D., & Foy, D. W. (2008). When they come home: Posttraumatic stress, moral injury, and spiritual consequences for veterans. *Reflective Practice: Formation and Supervision in Ministry, 28*, 85–102.

Elhai, J. D., Contractor, A. A., Palmieri, P. A., Forbes, D., & Richardson, J. D. (2011). Exploring the relationship between underlying dimensions of posttraumatic stress disorder and depression in a national, trauma-exposed military sample. *Journal of Affective Disorders, 133*(3), 477–480.

Flory, J. D., & Yehuda, R. (2015). Comorbidity between post-traumatic stress disorder and major depressive disorder: Alternative explanations and treatment considerations. *Dialogues in clinical neuroscience, 17*(2), 141.

Fox, A. B., Walker, B. E., Smith, B. N., King, D. W., King, L. A., & Vogt, D. (2016). Understanding how deployment experiences change over time: Comparison of female and male OEF/OIF and Gulf War veterans. *Psychological Trauma: Theory, Research, Practice, and Policy, 8*(2), 135.

Friedman, M. J. (2016). PTSD History and Overview. Retrieved from http://www.ptsd.va.gov/professional/PTSD-overview/ptsd-overview.asp

Fritch, A. M., Mishkind, M., Reger, M. A., & Gahm, G. A. (2010). The impact of childhood abuse and combat-related trauma on postdeployment adjustment. *Journal of Traumatic Stress, 23*(2), 248–254.

Galea, S., Basham, K., Culpepper, L., Davidson, J., Foa, E., Kizer, K., . . . McCormick, R. (2012). *Treatment for posttraumatic stress disorder in military and veteran populations: Initial assessment*. Washington, DC: National Academies Press.

Green, J. D., Bovin, M. J., Erb, S. E., Lachowicz, M., Gorman, K. R., Rosen, R. C., . . . Marx, B. P. (2016). The effect of enemy combat tactics on PTSD prevalence rates: A comparison of Operation Iraqi Freedom deployment phases in a sample of male and female veterans. *Psychological Trauma: Theory, Research, Practice and Policy, 8*(5), 634–640.

Hotopf, M., Hull, L., Fear, N. T., Browne, T., Horn, O., Iversen, A., . . . & Greenberg, N. (2006). The health of UK military personnel who deployed to the 2003 Iraq war: A cohort study. *The Lancet, 367*(9524), 1731–1741.

Iversen, A. C., Fear, N. T., Simonoff, E., Hull, L., Horn, O., Greenberg, N., . . . Wessely, S. (2007). Influence of childhood adversity on health among male UK military personnel. *The British Journal of Psychiatry, 191*, 506–511.

James, L. M., Van Kampen, E., Miller, R. D., & Engdahl, B. E. (2013). Risk and protective factors associated with symptoms of post-traumatic stress, depression, and alcohol misuse in OEF/OIF veterans. *Military Medicine, 178*(2), 159–165.

Karney, B. R., Ramchand, R., Osilla, K. C., Caldarone, L. B., & Burns, R. M. (2008). Predicting the immediate long-term consequences of posttraumatic stress disorder, depression, and traumatic brain injury in veterans of Operation Enduring Freedom and Operation Iraqi Freedom. In T. Tanielian & L. H. Jaycox (Eds.), *Invisible wounds of war: Psychological and cognitive injuries, their consequences, and services to assist recovery* (pp. 119–166). Santa Monica, CA: RAND Corporation.

Kok, B. C., Herrell, R. K., Thomas, J. L., & Hoge, C. W. (2012). Posttraumatic stress disorder associated with combat service in Iraq or Afghanistan: Reconciling prevalence differences between studies. *The Journal of Nervous and Mental Disease, 200*(5), 444–450.

LeardMann, C. A., Powell, T. M., Smith, T. C., Bell, M. R., Smith, B., Boyko, E. J., . . . Hoge, C. W. (2013). Risk factors associated with suicide in current and former US military personnel. *JAMA, 310*(5), 496–506.

Lee, J. E. C., Phinney, B., Watkins, K., & Zamorski, M. A. (2016). Psychosocial pathways linking adverse childhood experiences to mental health in recently deployed Canadian military service members. *Journal of Traumatic Stress, 29*(2), 124–131.

Lee, J. E. C., Sudom, K. A., & McCreary, D. R. (2011). Higher-order model of resilience in the Canadian forces. *Canadian Journal of Behavioural Science, 43*(3), 222–234.

Litz, B. T., Stein, N., Delaney, E., Lebowitz, L., Nash, W. P., Silva, C., & Maguen, S. (2009). Moral injury and moral repair in war veterans: A preliminary model and intervention strategy. *Clinical Psychology Review, 29*(8), 695–706.

McLaughlin, K. A., Conron, K. J., Koenen, K. C., & Gilman, S. E. (2010). Childhood adversity, adult stressful life events, and risk of past-year psychiatric disorder: A test of the stress sensitization hypothesis in a population-based sample of adults. *Psychological Medicine, 40*, 1647–1658.

McLean, C. P., Zang, Y., Zandberg, L., Bryan, C. J., Gay, N., Yarvis, J. S., . . . Consortium, S. S. (2017). Predictors of suicidal ideation among active duty military personnel with posttraumatic stress disorder. *Journal of Affective Disorders, 208*, 392–398.

Monson, C. M., Taft, C. T., & Fredman, S. J. (2009). Military-related PTSD and intimate relationships: From description to theory-driven research and intervention development. *Clinical Psychology Review, 29*(8), 707–714.

Polusny, M. A., Erbes, C. R., Murdoch, M., Arbisi, P. A., Thuras, P., & Rath, M. B. (2011). Prospective risk factors for new-onset post-traumatic stress disorder in National Guard soldiers deployed to Iraq. *Psychological Medicine, 41*(4), 687–698. doi: 10.1017/s00332291710002047

Ramchand, R., Karney, B. R., Osilla, K. C., Burns, R. M., & Caldarone, L. B. (2008). Prevalence of PTSD, depression, and TBI among returning service members. In T. Tanielian & L. H. Jaycox (Eds.), *Invisible wounds of war: Psychological and cognitive injuries, their consequences, and services to assist recovery* (pp. 35–85). Santa Monica, CA: RAND Corporation.

Ramchand, R., Rudavsky, R., Grant, S., Tanielian, T., & Jaycox, L. (2015). Prevalence of, risk factors for, and consequences of posttraumatic stress disorder and other mental health problems in military populations deployed to Iraq and Afghanistan. *Current Psychiatry Reports, 17*(5), 1–11.

Ramsawh, H. J., Fullerton, C. S., Mash, H. B. H., Ng, T. H. H., Kessler, R. C., Stein, M. B., & Ursano, R. J. (2014). Risk for suicidal behaviors associated with PTSD, depression, and their comorbidity in the US Army. *Journal of Affective Disorders, 161*, 116–122.

Richardson, L. K., Frueh, B. C., & Acierno, R. (2010). Prevalence estimates of combat-related post-traumatic stress disorder: Critical review. *Australian and New Zealand Journal of Psychiatry, 44*(1), 4–19.

Schell, T. L., & Marshall, G. N. (2008). Survey of individuals previously deployed for OEF/OIF. In T. Tanielian & L. H. Jaycox (Eds.), *Invisible wounds of war: Psychological and cognitive injuries, their consequences, and services to assist recovery* (pp. 87–115). Santa Monica, CA: RAND Corporation.

Schnurr, P. P., Lunney, C. A., Bovin, M. J., & Marx, B. P. (2009). Posttraumatic stress disorder and quality of life: Extension of findings to veterans of the wars in Iraq and Afghanistan. *Clinical Psychology Review, 29*(8), 727–735.

Smith, T. C., Ryan, M. A., Wingard, D. L., Slymen, D. J., Sallis, J. F., & Kritz-Silverstein, D. (2008). New onset and persistent symptoms of post-traumatic stress disorder self reported after deployment and combat exposures: prospective population based US military cohort study. *British Medical Journal, 336*(7640), 366–371.

Stander, V. A., Thomsen, C. J., & Highfill-McRoy, R. M. (2014). Etiology of depression comorbidity in combat-related PTSD: A review of the literature. *Clinical Psychology Review, 34*(2), 87–98.

Steenkamp, M. M., Nash, W. P., Lebowitz, L., & Litz, B. T. (2013). How best to treat deployment-related guilt and shame: Commentary on Smith, Duax, and Rauch (2013). *Cognitive and Behavioral Practice, 20*(4), 471–475.

Tanielian, T., & Jaycox, L. H. (Eds.). (2008). *Invisible wounds of war: Psychological and cognitive injuries, their consequences, and services to assist recovery.* Santa Monica, CA: RAND Center for Military Health Policy Research.

Tanielian, T., Jaycox, L. H., Adamson, D. M., & Metscher, K. N. (2008). Chapter one: Introduction. In T. Tanielian & L. H. Jaycox (Eds.), *Invisible wounds of war: Psychological and cognitive injuries, their consequences, and services to assist recovery* (pp. 3–17). Santa Monica, CA: RAND Corporation.

Vogt, D., Vaughn, R., Glickman, M. E., Schultz, M., Drainoni, M.-L., Elwy, R., & Eisen, S. (2011). Gender differences in combat-related stressors and their association with postdeployment mental health in a nationally representative sample of US OEF/OIF veterans. *Journal of Abnormal Psychology, 120*(4), 797.

Watkins, K., Sudom, K., & Zamorski, M. (2016). Association of combat experiences with post-traumatic stress disorder among Canadian military personnel deployed in support of the mission in Afghanistan. *Military Behavioral Health, 4*(3), 285–292.

Zamorski, M. A., & Boulos, D. (2014). The impact of the military mission in Afghanistan on mental health in the Canadian armed forces: A summary of research findings. *European Journal of Psychotraumatology, 5*(1), 23822.

Point of View—The Small Bible

Matthew J. M. Hendricks

What does a world tabernacled with grace look like? . . . Ramadi . . . a field hospital . . . an armless Marine weeping late at night knowing he will never hold his child again? All I know is that such a world cloaked in His love creates a triumph of grace. "For it is by grace you have been saved, through faith—and this is not from yourselves, it is the gift of God."—Ephesians 2:8

Ramadi, Iraq: September 3, 2005

"Ride's here, Sir."

"Roger that, Staff Sergeant. Alright, you take care of the platoon and I'll see you in the Snake Pit in a couple of days. God bless. Oorah!"

The unforgiving sun hit me in the face like an opened oven as I walked out of the large, air-conditioned tent. My blue eyes and Casper-white skin had not yet acclimated to the alien desert environment. It took a few moments for my eyes to adjust to the blinding sunlight. They did, just in time to see a group of five or six Marines walking towards us. They had come to bring us—"green" Lima company lieutenants—the short distance from Camp Ramadi to our new base of operations known as the "Snake Pit." This first meeting would be the beginning of a two-week process known as a relief-in-place, where one military unit gradually switches battlefield responsibilities with another. The Marines who picked us up that afternoon looked thin—

their taut skin darkened by the brutal sun. They were somewhat reticent, but when they did speak, it was with an urgency that hinted at a threat I could not yet see or understand. Some of the Marines seemed to look past us and gave off an unfamiliar, angry vibe. Other than the obligatory "Sir," they paid little attention to garrison etiquette. Their vehicles bore the scars of urban combat: burn marks and missing hunks of metal, the effects of various IED blasts, and small arms fire. We had been briefed on the casualties that their unit had sustained these last seven months. Their company commander had been killed in an IED explosion, and I shuddered when, later, they described how they were forced to use a shovel to scrape his charred body off the melted seat. "He looked like a doggone burnt hot dog," one said sardonically, as if talking about a barbecue fail. I realized that I was actually unnerved, maybe even scared: I was scared of fellow Marines. I could not figure out why. Perhaps I was afraid thinking about what could have possibly made them seem so different from us. If such a transformation had happened to them in such a short time, what would happen to us—to me? With little time to indulge in an existential moment, we loaded into their gun trucks and departed the relative safety of massive Camp Ramadi for the ominous looking streets of the city.

As we began to roll forward, I checked and re-checked my weapons to make sure the magazines of the 9MM pistol and M16-A2 rifle were properly inserted. For months leading up to the deployment, I had had a reoccurring nightmare in which I was engaged in a firefight and every time I pulled the trigger, my magazine either fell out or sprayed a non-lethal barrage of staples. Ludicrous as these dreams were, I felt like I had to ensure they remained just foolish dreams. My throat burned and my hands shook as I fumbled with my weapons, checking they were on "safe," but also ready to unload some double pizza box hell[1] on any potential enemy targets that might spring out. The Humvee jostled across the bridge which spanned the Euphrates River and led us into the combat zone of the legendary, the lethal, Ramadi, Iraq.

Ramadi had once been a beautiful Arabian city with palaces, large mosques, elegant "mansions" and ancient structures serenely nestled between the Euphrates River and a tributary canal. Farm lands on the outskirts of the city and scenic palm trees softening the urban landscape had given Ramadi a charming almost resort-like feel. But in the early fall of 2005, Ramadi was a city ruined by war. As we drove over the bridge, my mouth dropped as I saw the urban landscape in the daylight for the first time. What I saw could have been in a scene from one of those post-apocalyptic, lawless Hollywood worlds, like those in *The Road*, *Mad Max*, or *Terminator*. How could anyone live in this savage place? But as battered as Ramadi looked, I soon discovered that her heart still beat ferociously. We were marked. We were hunted with precision. We blindly hunted for ghosts in return.

The rip of automatic gunfire echoing off the concrete buildings.

Rockets tearing through the air like a jet airliner exploding with earthquake like power.

Mortar rounds whistling like deadly raindrops.

Improvised explosive devices detonating in the distance with deadly precision.

Bullet holes and burn marks scarring the city structures telling the stories of hundreds of engagements between American and "Mujahideen" fighters.

Feral cats and mangy wild dogs running through the trash-filled streets.

Remains of concrete buildings.

Insipid tarns of sewage and foul-smelling standing water festering under 110-degree heat. In the middle of this macabre scene were the civilian survivors, who attempted to navigate the man-made obstacles of war and live their lives—trapped and without the basic municipal services that humans come to expect as basic in a 21st century world. I wanted to leave immediately.

Ramadi, Iraq: October 4, 2005

Another mission, yet another convoy through the city. The early flashes of dawn shimmered through the windshield, encouraging the occupants of the up-armored Humvee to begin to locate their sunglasses. I eyed our route, directed a turn to the Marine driving. Private First Class Bedard's blue eyes met mine for a moment as he responded with a firm "Yes, Sir." He turned our armored Humvee gun truck onto the dirt road. *My God. This road is dirt. This is bad*, my mind screamed. The earth erupted.

Heat.

Twisted metal.

Fire.

Our 12,000-pound vehicle was tossed into the air like a toy truck. In the first moment of the explosion, I lurched forward as if on a fast-moving roller coaster about to make the incline on a loop. This was followed by some time in slow-motion weightlessness. The engulfing shockwave of the detonation took place in a surreal silence as it rippled through metal, blood, and flesh. The pure silence amplified the sharp ping of sand ricocheting off the metal hull of the gun truck's cabin, lightly peppering my face and stinging my eyes. As soon as we crashed back to earth, reality jolted me back to my senses and I felt the full, raw violence of the explosion rush through me. I tried to catch my breath.

Triage.

Don't panic.

Think.

What happened?

We just hit an IED and I am not dead.

Is anyone else?

This is going to really slow our operation down. Captain Quinn is going to be pissed.

How long will it take for them to get me out of here?

I can't take being trapped in small spaces.

I really can't move.

Get me OUT!

(Silence.)

Can't move.

Left leg hurts . . . a lot. Probably broken.

With the cabin of the vehicle collapsed around me, I tried to shout out but could not hear my own voice. My mouth was caked with something. I gasped for air but choked on dust and grains of sand. My panic rose as I fought to suck in a breath of air similar to the sensation of confused fright that a Marine recruit would experience if they attempted to suck in the CS gas of the boot camp gas chamber. I pushed myself up with my legs, but stopped instantly as sharp pain screamed through my left leg and overwhelmed my senses. *Definitely broken and I can't get out of here.* Fear morphed into terrified anguish as the smell of diesel from the ruptured fuel tank seeped into my nose. "We gotta get out of here. Diesel. It's diesel. Get me out!" someone screamed. Thoughts of burning to death in a metallic sepulcher flooded into my mind as visions of my body recoiling, searing flames feeding on my flesh flashed before my eyes. *Jesus, God, GET ME OUT OF HERE!*

Clank! Clank! Clank! I watched, fascinated, as the M16 strapped around my body knocked repeatedly against the side of the hatch and the mangled remains of my seat. *The barrel is bent,* I thought to myself. *That's odd.*

"Take your harness off!" someone bellowed from above. I unsnapped my harness and was jerked free from what was left of the truck. The tugging from behind stopped and I fell to my knees. Unable to stand, I glimpsed the remains of the smoldering truck as I continued to gasp for air and try to find my voice. Lieutenant Watson, the company executive officer, had been riding in the seat behind me and had been able to escape the destroyed Humvee. Once free himself, he began to help the rest of the crew still trapped inside. I tried, and failed, to get off my knees and began to hoarsely bellow for PFC Bedard, the driver of the Humvee—the blue-eyed, blond-haired 19 year-old who had been sitting inches from me before the earth exploded. "Bedard! Bedard!" I croaked. There was no response, and before I knew it, Watson had me under his arms and was dragging me away from the wreckage.

Smoke.

Heat.

Hood of the Humvee immediately behind us in a crater.

Truck bed up ahead.

Plumes of smoke blotting out the warm rays of sunlight.

"Corpsman, up!"

"IED. Two vehicles hit," I groaned over my radio.

Watson helped lift me into the back of a truck and closed the doors to protect me from potential enemy fire. Before I had time to think, the back doors were flung open and Marines lifted our corpsman into the truck beside me. Doc "Leo" had been sitting behind PFC Bedard in our gun truck. "Hey, Sir," Doc Leo exclaimed weakly. His dark brown eyes betrayed the pain he was choking back. Lieutenant Watson and I tried to make Doc as comfortable as possible, holding his hand and giving him sips of water when he asked. Leo's right leg was twisted nearly off below the knee; it held on to his body by a few threads of yellowish skin and sinews of gnarled tissue. A self-administered tourniquet stopped the blood loss from his leg but not from his mouth. "How bad is my leg, Sir? Is it still there, Sir? Can I have some water, Sir?" "DON'T MOVE," ordered Lieutenant Watson. Doc ignored the company XO and proceeded to attempt to treat my wounds, all the while gasping and choking on his own blood.

How are you, Sir? Is that your blood, Sir? Here, take this gauze, Sir. How am I doing? My God, this guy is unbelievable, I thought, my mind racing as my eyes fogged with burning tears. Once Doc Leo was convinced that I was stable, he obeyed Watson's orders to stop moving and softly asked for some more water. Watson gave it to him in slow, deliberate drinks.

My mind raced. How could such an amazing man be wounded so violently? Where were PFC Bedard and Lance Corporal Seeley, the gunner in the vehicle's turret? Had someone said that there was a KIA? Who was it? What should I do? Could I get up and move? Why wasn't I? Why wasn't I even trying to get back up? Unable to make sense of the chaos surrounding me, I simply closed my eyes and prayed as the truck raced toward Ramadi medical. *Please God, help us.*

We arrived at the medical field hospital. The nurses brought Doc Leo in first where he was quickly assessed and brought directly to surgery. I was brought into hospital; became somewhat "snow blind" from being brought out of the piercing sunlight into the relative darkness of the hospital; placed on a medical table; surrounded by medical personnel; stripped down; quickly assessed. I had deep penetrating shrapnel wounds to my left hip and hamstring as well as what appeared to be less significant lacerations on my left hand, under my pointer finger, and under my chin. I remember feeling the deep pains in my left leg, but believed I was dealing with nothing more than a broken leg. A shotgun style blast of shrapnel had entered my left hamstring and penetrated deep into the leg. The entry wound was jagged and portions of tissue and muscle were protruding from the site.

"Ok, Ok, this will definitely be sore for a while. But I think you should be good to go in three months," said the first nurse—before he looked at any X-rays. Another nurse told me that I was probably in shock. "Don't tell him that," said a 3rd nurse. I then felt warm saline flowing through my arm, tingling my face and releasing floods of pain relieving dopamine once it reached my head. I felt like I was being wrapped in a warm blanket. My first experience with morphine left me feeling the temporary opium "veil" of no pain.

"1st Sergeant! That you? Over here. Where's Bedard?"

Silence

"He's gone, Sir."

Gone.

Please God . . . please God . . . be with him.

I was later told that the explosion had blown Bedard out of the driver's seat onto a sand dune several feet away from the vehicle. The marines searching for him had struggled to locate his body. He was covered in a thin layer of sand. He looked as if he had been laid down gently; his arms were folded across his chest as though he were sleeping serenely. The three-hundred-pound Humvee door—his door—was just feet away from him.

Alexandria, Virginia—July 17, 2005

Before leaving for Iraq, I had gone on pre-deployment leave in Virginia and stopped by my Aunt Leslie's house on the outskirts of Old Town, Alexandria. As my Uncle Jim, Aunt Leslie, cousins Taylor and Olivia, and I said our tearful goodbyes, Aunt Leslie handed me a small New Testament Bible. The leather-bound Bible was very small, smaller than an iPhone. As Aunt Leslie choked back tears, she opened the Bible and showed me the inscription on the inside cover: *Read this wherever you are and you will come back the way you are.* Someone had given the Bible to Aunt Leslie's uncle before he went to fight in the Korean War. Struggling to hold back tears and finding it hard to breathe, I took the Bible and put it in my pocket. A month later, as I prepared to deploy with my unit, I put the Bible in a small zip-lock bag and placed it in the breast pocket of my blouse—where it remained the entire time I was deployed.

Ramadi, Iraq—October 3, 2005

The Zippo clicked as I pulled the first comforting drag of blue smoke deep into my lungs. The Marlboro cigarette hung from my lips, the smoke stinging my nostrils as I sat staring at a small laptop in the lieutenants' room of the Snake Pit. "Orientation . . . Situation . . . Mission . . ." my fingers typing out the plan designed to keep the fog of battle at bay for as long as possible. For no reason at all, I stretched and tapped my chest, my fingers noticing the small Bible in my left breast pocket. I pulled it out of my blouse and coincidently flipped to Psalm 23.

The Lord is my shepherd; I shall not want . . .
Yea, though I walk through the valley of the shadow of death, I will fear no evil:
   for thou
art with me; thy rod and thy staff they comfort me . . .
Surely goodness and mercy shall follow me all the days of my life: and I will dwell
   in the
house of the Lord forever.

A sense of calm came over me like a warm embrace; I no longer felt anxious about where I was or the mission we were about to undertake. I had never been much of a Bible reader and was unfamiliar with specific biblical passages, so the fact that I randomly turned to Psalm 23 and had such a calming reaction to the words seemed like more than just a coincidence to me. I felt compelled to share this message with my platoon. I had never prayed with them before—I didn't even know if they were spiritual. But in that moment, I didn't care if they were or not. I wanted to share with them the mollifying message of love that I had just experienced, even if I didn't fully understand it myself.

When I had finished issuing the five-paragraph order to the dimly lit, concrete-walled room full of marines, I "asked" if I could read them something from the Bible. The room became dead quiet. Taking the pristine silence as their collective consent, I read the Psalm. When I was finished, I closed the small Bible and waited for some sort of reaction from my marines. I wondered if anyone would speak. No one did.

Medevac: October, 2005

"You are in Baghdad and we will take care of you."
"Well, looking at these X-rays, you're certainly going home."
"That's right, to The United States of America."
Two six inch incisions were now visible on the front of my left leg. The gaping slits started at my groin and seemed huge—big enough to put a hand into.
"Look at all this shrapnel we took out of your leg—wow."
"We almost lost an intern in your wound!"
I scream into the waist of the doc as he rips something from deep inside my leg.
"STOP! WHAT ARE YOU DOING?"
"We need to pull these bandages out of your leg to take off the dead tissue and ensure that the leg has good blood flow."
"Umm. This is a lot of blood. Let me get a surgeon."
"Are you Catholic? Are you Catholic? Lt. Hendricks, please open your eyes. Are you Catholic? 'Through this holy anointing may the Lord in his love

and mercy help you with the grace of the Holy Spirit. May the Lord who frees you from sin save you and raise you up.'"

Well that was nice.

"I hate this war. I can't find anymore shrapnel to take off your femoral besides these pieces. I know there are still more in there. I just can't get them. They'll help you in the US."

"Where am I?"

May I have another shot of morphine? Please . . ."

"Welcome home. Welcome to the 5th floor of Bethesda. We got you, OK?"

Washington, DC—December, 2005

"Lt. Hendricks? This is Captain Quinn."

After a brief conversation discussing how I was doing, he got to the main point of his call. Several Marines in my old platoon had been severely wounded in a catastrophic series of IED blasts. The survivors were being evacuated to Walter Reed and Bethesda. Captain Quinn wanted to know if I would visit them when they arrived and provide him with periodic updates on their progress. It didn't take long for them to trace the path home that I had and soon after the phone conversation, I found myself meeting with one of those Marines at Walter Reed Medical Center. Cort had been a tall (maybe 6 foot), kind, likeable young man. His affable smile stretched across his dark skinned face as I leaned *down* to give him a hug. His usual gleaming eyes were dulled and hazy—side effect of the narcotic painkillers. My heart truly sank as I looked down at his chair. Both of his legs were gone above the knees. The air sucked from my lungs. A flood of emotion seemed to engulf my head. I stumbled backwards to my chair, using as much bearing as I could muster to keep my composure. As we talked, we recalled the October night when I had read Psalm 23 and had prayed with the men.

"I wish all officers would pray with their marines like that. I felt like nuthin could hurt us after I heard those words," Cort struggled to say. His voice hoarse from the extended incubation period he endured immediately after his IED attack. His emotions still raw from his experience and seeming overwhelmed by his own words, we both struggled with the power of the moment.

Alexandria, VA, Today

I can't understand the indifferent, cold sneer of who lives and who dies in war—Bedard and I were separated by 12 inches. He is dead. I am alive. There is no meaning found here.

Why did I tell Bedard to take that road? Why did *he* have to die? Doc Leo lost his leg and had severe internal injuries; Seeley's body was busted. Did I cause Bedard's death and the injuries to Seeley and Doc Leo in some way?

If a different lieutenant had been sitting in my seat, would they all be OK today? Am I a coward for requesting and agreeing to begin the medical evaluation board process to see if I was qualified to remain in the military?

No therapist was able to answer any of these questions for me. No medication could make the guilt or shame go away. No amount of alcohol could wash the memories from my mind. Not even family members—such as my most beloved wife Lynn—were able to provide me with complete peace. So what was I to do? Those black plumes of smoke that blotted out the sun's rays that fateful morning weren't clearing from my soul. They were beginning to choke me.

"When you pass through the waters, I will be with you; and when you pass through the rivers, they will not sweep over you. When you walk through the fire, you will not be burned; the flames will not set you ablaze." Isaiah 43:2

My spiritual metanoia did not happen over-night. There were many long nights filled with nightmares and mornings of self-doubt that made me question the decisions that I made in Ramadi in the months after I returned. I have questioned and doubted the ultimate "plan" that people kept telling me exists and in which I should have faith. "What plan is that?" I would often think to myself or say to a person attempting to console me.

I have felt the soul-consuming fires of rage, revenge, anger, fear, and the self-destructive pangs of guilt and self-hate. I have felt alone—even after going to a church service or hearing my wife tell me that she loves me. The temptation to mourn, to doubt, to loathe myself or others is always just around the corner. I have doubted the wisdom of God's plan and even scoffed at the power of prayer or point of believing in a God who could allow such things to happen. I have ignored going to church.

The change began for me in small whispers. The fall after I was discharged from the marines, I began working in a Catholic high school and found myself busy, engaged, needed—I'd become part of something bigger than myself. I was surrounded by people of faith and young teenagers filled with hope and optimism. Required to pray with my students before each class and attend mass as a school community once a month. I honored my teaching responsibilities for nearly 5 years before I actually began to understand and believe in the words that I was speaking and hearing.

I was blessed with some very good people who became part of my life and shared their faith stories, thus encouraging me to develop a relationship with Christ. My wife helped me with my spiritual injuries more than anyone else. She never left my side. She never became angry with me. She kept pushing me to continue breathing. She brought me back to church. She is the one who initially helped me to turn to God during those dark moments. She is the partner who took me by the hand and guided me—even when I wanted to let go. With her help and the help of other close mentors, I slowly began to turn to prayer and faith as a path to spiritual recovery.

I soon realized that not all those positive elements in my life were chance; they were not random; they were not luck. They were God's grace. My re-established faith was simply allowing me to see them for what they were: Whispers of God's grace present in my life all the time. I now pray every day: "God forgive me; give me the strength to do what is right; to be a good man; to be a good husband and a good father; to live a worthy life—one that Bedard would be proud of—one that honors the blessings You have bestowed upon me. Give me the strength to accept Your will and faith to understand that I am not in control."

As I pray, I do find solace and comfort. God's love guides me through the darkest moments and helps me to "get up," shake the dust, and ready myself for the goodness sure to be found in that day. I go back to church on Sundays—even if I have had a bad Tuesday or Wednesday or Friday. I go back. On my knees, I thank God for my wife Lynn and our children, Hadley and Sean. I thank him for my parents and sisters. I thank Him for calling me to be a teacher. "My children are angels that deserve a father who is present for them mind, body, and soul. My wife is all that is good in this world. I love them all so much and know that their presence is a miracle that cannot be squandered. They are cornerstones of my life—Your grace personified. Help me to be a good father, a good husband, a good son, a good teacher," I pray. In addition to prayer and attending church, I read the Bible. While reading the inspired words of God, I do believe that I begin to discover who God, who Jesus Christ, and who the Holy Spirit are; I begin to understand the healing power that comes by fostering a relationship with Him.

Ultimately, I must *choose* to have faith and I must *choose* to live a better life. I have learned that my faith must be the center of who I am because when it is, all other aspects of my life flourish. Acknowledging that some readers may find my faith in the healing power of God's grace hard to believe, all I can say is that I hear your doubts. I have lived your doubts. By choosing to live those doubts, I experienced nothing but more anger, more frustration, more fear, and much more sadness. By flipping the script—over time—and choosing to live the life of a believer, I have experienced love, joy, success, and hope. By *choosing* to have faith, I recognize God's grace which has enabled me to become a committed husband, a loving father of two living angels, and a dedicated high school English teacher charged with helping young people achieve their dreams. I am able to thwart the darkness in my life and allow love to guide me with purpose in my heart. My message to anyone, to any veteran, who is struggling to find answers and hurting in the darkness of your personal experiences: Give God's love a chance. You may be surprised by the resulting light that you see in your own life.

While almost nothing else that I was actually wearing on the day that we were hit by the IED explosion—not even the contacts in my eyes—made it back to the US, somehow the small Bible did. I choose to believe that this truth is not a random coincidence. Every day I look down at the deformed wound and jagged scars on my left leg and fully embrace the periodic sharp pains that come from living with a wound of war. I look at the medicine vial filled with chunks of shrapnel that I keep in my family room display hutch. I take the fragments out and roll them between my fingers. My nose cringes as I smell the metallic pong and I am screamed back to that transformative, dark October day. Instinctively, I reach for the small Bible resting next to the vial and continue to read the healing words—embraced by the light of His love.

Note

1. Slang term for the "Marksman" badge, the lowest-scoring of the three rifle and pistol marksmanship proficiency badges.

CHAPTER 2

Warrior Culture: Ancient Roots, New Meaning

Kyleanne Hunter

Throughout all of recorded history, the warrior, or at least the idea of the warrior, has taken center stage in society. Indeed, the history of people is largely a history of war as written by the victor. A strong warrior class is essential for a strong, lasting, and fruitful society. The warrior, quite literally, is one who engages in war. But in a social and political context, the warrior is far more. The warrior is the cornerstone of society. Warriors' toils and blood keep civilians safe, preserving their culture, economy, and political systems for future generations. The warrior is thus conceptualized as the embodiment of a hero. Lauded in parades and celebrations, she is revered as a symbol of strength. The warrior is the ideal citizen, dedicated to the point of being willing to lay down his or her life for the good of the country.

Warriors have traditionally been separated from civilian society. This separation has occurred both formally, through the creation of a distinct warrior class, and informally, through the self-selection out of society of individuals into an all-volunteer force. Whether formal or informal, a distinct warrior culture has emerged as a result of this separation.

Defining Modern Warrior Culture

In both popular and scholarly circles, the Greek and Roman warrior cultures are often held up as an ideal. From the tie between military service and political engagement to the civil rituals around war, ancient societies were inextricably linked with their warrior class. Indeed, the classical view of the warrior permeated ancient society, from the arts to politics and education. Society defined itself by how warriors performed in battle, with military conquest or territorial defense comprising the institutional and social identity of the state and its citizens. Warrior culture was thus not clearly distinct from everyday life, but an integral part of sociopolitical identity. Citizens were forged on the battlefield, and military service paved the way for outsiders to become formally part of culture and society. While modern warrior culture has its roots in these ancient traditions, it is unique in several ways that are particularly important when discussing the resiliency of the modern warrior.

First is the fact that modern societies do not spend the majority of their time or personnel fighting wars. Broadly speaking, war is on the decline. The conduct of war, therefore, is no longer the primary purpose or activity of a state. Though the military still comprises a large portion of a state's resources (especially monetary), it is not the main focus of the state's institutions or personnel. Despite the United States being currently embroiled in its "longest war" with the conflicts in Iraq and Afghanistan, even at its peak, spending in both time and man-hours was less than 1/3 that was spent during World War I and less than 1/8 of World War II. With conquest or even territorial defense no longer being the primary characteristic of international relations, warriors are no longer the centerpiece of a broader cultural identity.

Second, and related, is the transition from conscription to professional, all-volunteer militaries. Historically, military service has been a mandatory condition of (or path to) citizenship, strengthening the ties between military service and civil society. Since the latter half of the 20th century, however, states have been moving toward professional, all-volunteer militaries. Therefore, citizenship and national identity are no longer strongly tied to military service. Concurrently, the percentage of a citizenry that serves in the military has been on the decline, effectively separating those who engage in the conduct of war further and further from their civilian counterparts.

Finally, technology is playing an unprecedented role in (re)shaping modern warrior culture. Much of the classic ideals around warrior culture were forged as a result of having to engage in hand-to-hand combat, coming into close contact with the enemy. Technology, however, has removed a portion of the human aspect from the conduct of war. It has also changed dynamics within military units. From training techniques to unit composition to tactical and strategy doctrine, technology has fundamentally changed what it is to fight a war, and, by extension, be a warrior.

The above changes have had an impact on both the definition of warrior culture and its pervasiveness in society. Rather than becoming diluted, as war is becoming less common and fewer people are required to conduct war, warrior culture has become more intensely concentrated. As such, it is arguably more important to understand modern warrior culture and the ways in which it can both contribute to and hinder resiliency. Additionally, changes in the conduct of war have led to members of the military clinging tighter to traditional vestiges of their military heritage. Thus, the practices of the warrior culture, while not necessarily essential for conducting modern war, are an essential part of connecting modern warriors to their past and provide valuable tools for understanding this community.

How Is Culture Formed?

While much work has been done on defining or identifying specific components of warrior culture, the broader purpose of this chapter is understanding how warrior culture is formed and instilled in individuals and its subsequent relationship to mental health. Modern warrior culture is best understood as a set of semiotic practices. Semiotic practices refer to processes whereby an agent's practices interact with language and other symbolic systems to create a new and distinct meaning. Culture is thus not just a set of beliefs but also practices that reinforce, strengthen, and manifest those beliefs—a connection between what is done and what is believed (Sewell, 2005).

Culture is developed through both formal and informal experiences that focus on a mind-body interaction. As a result, an individual immerses more deeply into a culture through what he or she does. Action and practice in this way also reinforce beliefs.

Focusing on semiotic practices also allows us to understand warrior culture as a culture independent of proximity and location. Several definitions of culture rely on proximity and/or shared space as a condition of cultural unity. However, the warrior culture transcends geography and generations. The ritualized practices of military life mean that a 19-year-old Marine in California may share more cultural similarities with a 70-year-old Army veteran in Oklahoma than those living in his own neighborhood. Indeed, it is a

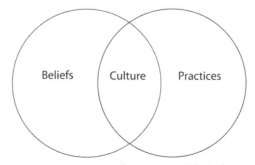

Figure 2.1 Culture as an intersection of practice and belief

reinforcing action-belief cycle that creates a shared culture. The independence from location or proximity is an important distinction to be made about the warrior culture, as it allows for both location-independent resiliency techniques and ability to take advantage of technology to build support networks among geographically dispersed yet culturally linked individuals. As Drs. Thomas and Albright note in this volume, the veteran community is unique in its need for group-support to build resiliency networks. Understanding the transcendent nature of the warrior culture is the foundational building block to crafting effective and innovative strategies to combat troubling trends in veterans' mental health and fitness.

Throughout this volume, the mind-body connection is referenced in order to discuss its impact on mental health and resiliency training. This mind-body connection is also essential to understanding how the warrior culture is developed and thus to discussing where and when resiliency training can best be incorporated.

From a semiotic practice point of view, warrior culture is a result of the practices, language, and symbols used in the training and preparation for or conduct of war. Evaluating and understanding warrior culture in this way is beneficial for three primary reasons. First, it emphasizes culture as a practice, something that is done and can be learned, rather than as an intrinsic component of a person's being. This allows us to better understand how the feeling of belonging to the warrior culture transcends other identities such as race, religion, or gender. The sense of belonging to the warrior culture is created through a conditioned mind-body interaction that not only creates the initial conditions for indoctrination into the culture but also reinforces and strengthens the sense of belonging throughout a warrior's life.

Second, it allows unique meaning to be given to seemingly everyday objects or language, allowing us to better appreciate why certain things impact warriors differently than civilians. A boot may be just a boot to a civilian, but when coupled with specific practices of shining and lacing, it becomes a central component to the formation of modern warrior culture. Taps is not merely notes played on a bugle but the final honor given to a brother in arms. These objects and events become sacred to the warrior.

Third, it allows for an explanation as to why there is variance in the way individuals relate to warrior culture. Members of the military feel a varying degree of association with the warrior culture. Survey data of over 700 veterans show that less than 30 percent are involved with a Veterans' Service Organization (VSO), and only around 50 percent introduce themselves as veterans in public (Hunter & Best, 2017).

The mind-body practice of becoming a part of the warrior culture begins at the early stages of training and continues through various stages in one's military career. There is conflicting evidence as to the impact of combat experiences on one's feeling of connectedness to the warrior culture. Focusing on the warrior culture as a semiotic practice further helps us understand why some veterans try to distance themselves from their warrior identity, while others dive more fully into it. In the following sections, each of the above components—practices, symbols and objects, and variation in identity—are discussed. Grasping mind-body aspects of warrior culture can provide valuable openings for introducing mental-health resiliency practices for adherents.

Practices

From the first day of training, members of the military engage in purposeful, ritualized practices. From lacing boots to making beds to marching in formation to group physical training to responding in unison to the barks of the drill instructor, the practices and actions recruits engage in reinforce specific beliefs about both the definition and the role of the warrior. In a practical sense, the practices and actions of early training are an example of neuroplasticity, the idea that learning from experience or total immersion results in cognitive changes in an individual. Learning-by-doing not only leads to learning new skills but also changes individuals' brain structure. The more one engages in immersive learning-by-doing, the more "sticky" these changes to both brain structure and cognition become (Draganski et al., 2004). Military training is a prime example of such a learning environment. One cannot become an effective soldier by reading books or taking correspondence courses but rather become fully immersed and engaged with the practice of soldiering.

The practices of early recruit training provide fertile ground for taking advantage of the neuroplasticity of young recruits. Indeed, the purpose of recruit training is both to "indoctrinate" new recruits into military life and to "inoculate" them from the potential horrors of their chosen profession (Ricks, 2007). Marching, shooting, and movement under fire are not done merely for the sake of learning these skills. They are simultaneously combined with a set of beliefs about both *why* these actions are necessary and *who* the recruit becomes when doing them.

The cognitive changes that occur through immersive training are accompanied by intense psychological conditioning and indoctrination into this new belief system. As the brain changes, it learns new ways of thinking and new beliefs about self. Hours are not spent on the rifle range merely to make a recruit a better marksman but to transform an individual into a warrior capable of protecting and defending his or her country from those who wish to do it harm. Boots are not polished to a shine to make one look good in uniform but to ingrain the discipline necessary to receive, understand, and execute necessary orders on the battlefield. The conduct of war requires shedding the practices and moral cognition of civilian life, and this early immersive training is essential for laying the foundation for future success.

The combination of neuroplasticity-inducing practice with belief has an extremely powerful impact. Recruit training not only turns civilians into soldiers, but it also has a lifelong impact on the identity of those who have completed such training. These powerful early practices create the foundation of military culture.

It is no accident that military training relies so heavily on intense and repetitive action to create habit. Success as a warrior requires the adoption of a new moral code (Toner, 2013). Individuals are asked to potentially take another human life, and/or sacrifice their own life, for an abstract set of ideas and ideals. Telling a young woman or man to take another human life is no easy affair. Whether due to our social ethical code or biological sense of self-preservation, most individuals do not easily or readily engage in violent combat, putting them at odds with the military mentality (Toner, 2013). Early training thus combines historical lessons of heroism from wars past with practical lessons of movement to contact. While modern training has adapted to new wars, the focus on shaping a new morality, and the means by which it is achieved, has remained.

Examples of the power of the mind-body connection in creating and reinforcing this new culture are plentiful. Recruits respond to drill instructors' demands with cries of "KILL!" as an affirmative response, both desensitizing them to the word and creating a new semantic-based in-group. Young women and men are physically broken down through rigorous training in order to create a new identity around the ideals of honor, duty, and country and a new "family" in those they suffered alongside. Citations of the awards won by service members in battles past are incorporated into hand-to-hand combat training lessons to reinforce the "warrior ethos" as a part of the conduct of violence. Indeed, a culture is created around killing—what is otherwise a heinous and immoral act—for a noble and moral good. From singing cadence to rewarding violence-based heroism, recruits are inoculated against traditional views around death and killing and indoctrinated into a new culture and class.

In his study of Marine Corps Recruit Training, Tom Ricks (2007) asserts that new Marines feel a separation from, and even a disdain for, civilians. These feelings highlight the power of the warrior culture, especially in its infancy. Because of the gravity of the acts around which the warrior culture is formed, a very tight "in-group" results. The strength of these in-group ties creates an opening, early on, for mental fitness training. Indeed, while young recruits learn to engage in a new morality, they are also taught to lay down their lives for one another in a way that is unique and distinct. The relationships forged with other soldiers and recruits overcome much of the sadness and confusion that new recruits feel when learning this new morality. Additionally, some of the practices Norris and Hutchinson highlight in the next chapter, can be introduced in early recruit training. Mindfulness practices need not wait until after trauma is sustained but can be introduced into early training as an essential part of what it is to be a warrior.

Practices also work to maintain the cognitive and psychological aspects of the warrior culture in the years beyond initial training. Though, as mentioned earlier, the actual conduct of war has a mixed impact on reinforcing the warrior culture, practices that reinforce beliefs about one's belonging in the in-group continue throughout one's service and even one's life. These practices are both formal and informal. Formally, units continue to engage in activities that both call on the nature and traditions of the warrior culture. From large-scale training exercises to balls and mess nights, the combination of symbolism and imagery reinforces beliefs and feelings about what it means to belong to the in-group culture. Exercises and participation in traditions bond the modern warrior with his or her traditional roots.

Outside of their units, individuals engage in informal practices that allow them to maintain a connection to the warrior culture. Despite being out of uniform, veterans may continue to shine their shoes, a homage to their days of service and an outward sign of their continued discipline and dedication. Strict physical training regimens and ongoing participation in ceremonies and parades maintain a practical connection to the beliefs about belonging that are essential to warrior culture. The popularity of veterans' organizations, such as Team Red, White, and Blue and Team Rubicon, highlights how continued participation in activities that define military life (physical fitness, service, and crisis response) is an important part of an individual's tie to the warrior culture that extends into postmilitary life.

Inserting resiliency training into the warrior culture post initial training presents more difficulty than it does during initial training. Since neuroplasticity is strongest upon the initial learning, the timing of the introduction of resiliency practices into the warrior culture may explain some of the variation in success that the programs discussed in this volume experience. Habits, skills, knowledge, and beliefs learned early on, especially in recruit training, are among the most "sticky" parts of the military culture.

Unique Meaning to Language and Symbols

Not only do practices, such as those discussed earlier, reinforce the belief structures that give rise to the warrior culture, but they also give unique meanings to language, symbols, and objects that work to strengthen the "in-group" mentality of the warrior culture. While practices are essential for creating the mind-body connection that indoctrinates one into a culture, language, symbols, and objects are necessary for maintaining cultural continuity. The uniqueness of the meanings given to objects and symbols creates exclusivity around any culture, and warrior culture is no exception. They are important for cultural preservation, as the specific and unique meanings are known and appreciated only by those who have participated in the corresponding cultural practices. Knowledge of their existence and the importance of their meaning thus create an automatic cultural connection between otherwise dissimilar individuals.

Much like practices, conveying the understanding of the unique meaning placed on language, symbols, and objects begins during basic training. These unique meanings are in part an extension of, and also a discrete compliment to, the practices necessary for the creation of the warrior culture. While language, symbols, and objects all receive unique meaning as part of warrior culture, each does so in a unique way.

Language is one of the strongest markers for in-group/out-group culture. Unique language marks belonging and signals to other group members that one is a member of the in-group as well. The language of the warrior culture is distinctive in three ways: tone, manner of speaking, and vocabulary. Throughout training and operations, members of the military speak to one another in loud and seemingly aggressive tones. What sounds like anger or disapproval to an outsider communicates a shared sense of urgency and gravity to one within the culture. On the battlefield, terse, strong, and commanding language is necessary to ensure mission accomplishment. Indeed, strong language becomes a comfort to soldiers in times of war and conflict as it portrays assurance in action. A strong, commanding tone thus becomes the way in which members of the warrior culture in-group speak to one another.

Similarly, the warrior culture employs a unique manner of dialogue. It is decidedly blunt and direct, with little filler or flourish. It is also frequently dispassionate, focusing on objectives rather than emotions. Straightforward, simple, and direct phrases are also essential for battlefield success. There is no room for individuals to second-guess the meaning or intent behind language during combat or crisis situations. Even after leaving the military, veterans are frequently characterized by their blunt and direct manner of speaking. While potentially mistaken for lacking social graces, bluntness and directness are, for those in the in-group, a way in which the warrior culture is maintained and practiced.

Finally, particular words contribute to the warrior culture. Some words, such as "bird," "fangs," "hardball," and "moonbeam," are also used in civilian language but carry different meanings for those engaged in the military culture. The special meaning gives a uniqueness that strengthens the in-group identity. They are words that were used during initial training, part of the shedding of the civilian life and indoctrination into a new culture, which begin the formation of the warrior culture and which act as a reinforcing mechanism for that culture in subsequent years. There are also words and phrases, primarily motivational terms such as "ooh-rah," that are unique to the members of the warrior culture. Similarly, these unique words and phrases reinforce the "in-group" culture. They give an otherwise diverse group of individuals a common understanding and bond.

In addition to language, symbols and objects gain unique meaning in the warrior culture. Symbols create the "toolkit" of a culture, the outward building blocks that announce one's culture to the world. Symbols allow an individual to carry his or her culture with him or her to the world and convey the legacy of a culture to future generations.

The military uniform is the most obvious and visible of symbols. It shows to the outside world that one is a member of the military. The uniform transforms an individual in an external manner, identifying him or her as part of a unique "in-group." Cloth thus becomes sometime more than just an outfit, as it emerges as a marker of a greater sense of belonging.

Service crests, flags, and emblems, as well as unit guidons and patches, similarly provide an outward symbol of culture. Displaying the crest signals a belonging to a group. Even after leaving the services, individuals continue to display crests, as well as academy rings or awards won during service as an outward signal to others of their in-group status. License plates, jewelry, stickers, and clothing all transform from everyday objects to important signaling devices when endowed with the symbolic meaning the crests hold.

Participation in the conduct of war strengthens the role of the language, symbols, and objects in the warrior culture. It is the place where they are tested and their importance shown. It is also the time when individuals are most likely to experience trauma and hardship. Combat requires individuals to walk a tightrope, constantly deciding whether to take or spare lives. And while speech, uniforms, and symbolic attachment help in facilitating the decisions and performance of actions required during war, they often fall short in imparting the importance of resilience in the face of the actions required during war. The use of language, symbols, and objects in post-trauma healing and future resiliency building can strengthen these practices by making them part of a unique and far-reaching culture.

Variation in the Warrior Culture

Understanding the warrior culture as a semiotic practice also helps explain the variation in the way in which individuals feel connected (or a part of) the warrior culture. Though, as shown previously, there is much that is universal about the warrior culture, not every service member or veteran experiences it the same way or to the same degree. There is great variation in the degree to which the warrior culture "sticks" to individuals. Even individuals may experience a variation in their own feelings of belonging to the warrior culture. While all members of the military undergo the same initial training, the feeling of being a part of the culture is not identical.

That a mind-body process is required to create the warrior culture can help explain these variations. While the mind-body connection forms the warrior culture, it requires continual practices to reinforce the belief system on which the culture is built. Due to the diverse backgrounds or belief systems individuals recruited into the military, they "buy into" the foundational beliefs of the warrior culture in different ways. Individuals with a greater adherence to the values of the military are more likely to develop a stronger bond to the culture. While scholarly work on military values shows mixed results on whether one's adherence to these values is dependent on pretraining beliefs or if they can be internalized during the time of military service, it is clear that the durability of the culture will be stronger in those with a stronger buy-in to the ideas and practices of the warrior culture when they leave the service.

Similarly, the amount of time spent around the unique language, symbols, and objects may explain the variance in adherence to the warrior culture. The amount of time, or the intensity of time, that one is immersed in a semiotic practice impacts the degree to which one is immersed into the resulting culture. Therefore, individuals serving an entire career, or serving during an intense period of conflict, may be more apt to be adherent to the warrior culture than those who served one tour during peacetime.

What one does after leaving the military can also explain variation in adherence to culture. Those individuals who engage in postmilitary careers or activities that mimic or engage with the military continue some of the same practices and surround themselves with the language, symbols, and objects that reinforce the foundational beliefs of the warrior culture. From working with defense contractors or in veterans service organizations to maintaining military-regulation haircuts and physical training regimes, the warrior culture can be maintained through deliberate practices and engagement in those practices learned during indoctrination. Conversely, individuals who choose to disengage with these practices after leaving the service can lessen their affiliation with the warrior culture. Many veterans take on civilian jobs that replace the practices of the warrior culture with other rituals and practices, allowing them to distance themselves or disengage with the warrior mentality. It is therefore often upon retirement from a civilian career that veterans begin to feel an affinity once again for the warrior culture of their youth.

Understanding this variation can help those seeking to engage in resiliency training meet veterans where they are. A 2014 Centers for Disease Control and Prevention report found that Vietnam veterans are the fastest-growing group of suicide victims. A majority of those whose families agreed to disclose suicide notes made mention of their military past and a feeling of loss of belonging as a driver in their decision to take their own life (Centers for Disease Control and Prevention, 2014). It is thus not just in young veterans that resiliency must be built but in those too who have left the culture and are returning in search of a sense of belonging and purpose.

Warrior Culture and the Practices of Mental Health

Discussion of mental health and the warrior culture frequently focuses on the culture's negative impact on obtaining the necessary resources for mental health resiliency. Indeed, there are several aspects of the warrior culture that hinder proper treatment for mental health ailments. However, the semiotic nature of how the warrior culture is formed also allows for openings for practices of resiliency to be inserted into the culture.

Beliefs about Mental Health Resultant from the Current Warrior Culture

As noted earlier, many of the practices in the warrior culture exist to establish a mind-body connection that allows individuals to separate from what society deems normal moral human activities. It allows individuals to distance themselves both from the humanity of potential enemy combatants as well as from the rest of civilian society. To this end, "strength" is highly privileged, as it is believed that it creates mental fortitude necessary to do things that are unnatural and otherwise inhumane.

Physical strength, in particular, is emphasized as central to the warrior culture. During combat, awards are given for physical bravery and strength. Soldiers are praised for putting their life on the line, often accomplishing seemingly superhuman feats. There is no place for physical weakness in combat.

Unfortunately, the idea of strength, and the practices creating it, has resulted in it being translated from the physical to the mental in a nonequivalent (and potentially dangerous) manner. Just as superhuman physical feats are frequently praised, soldiers often see human emotion or mental reactions as a sign of weakness. In a culture that privileges physical strength, lack of outward display of "weak" emotions can be easily mistaken as also praiseworthy. The emphasis on strength can, in extreme cases, create a practice of refusing mental health treatment, as it is seen as a sign of weakness.

This cultural prioritizing of strength has had an impact on the resources committed to mental health care. Both for active-duty soldiers and veterans, resources have been diverted away from mental health and toward other personnel programs. This reality reinforces the cultural rejection of mental health care, at the expense of those suffering the most.

A Space for Resiliency Practice

Current practices in military culture do not prefer mental health; the neuroplastic aspects of the warrior culture offer a space for the introduction of practices that reinforce mental resiliency. A growing body of work highlights how physical training and task-based unit cohesion have a positive impact on individuals' mental state. Indeed, the physical and the mental are inextricably linked. Shaping the physical aspects of military training in such a way that they acknowledge the importance of emotional responses to physical stimuli is important not just for immediate success in battle but also for the longevity of both the physical and mental well-being that allows an entry point for resiliency.

Similarly, injecting mental resiliency into the culture taught during recruit training, when recruits are first being "broken down" to be built back up as part of the warrior culture, would leverage the neuroplasticity of young adults in a positive way. Mental health in general, and fortifying oneself against harsh situations, is not central to the civilian identity. As seen in this volume, the integration of mindfulness into military culture provides powerful inroads to making resiliency part of the practices that reinforce one's in-group identity and status. A greater understanding of the impact each of these has on an individual will allow for better mental resiliency and mental health "best practices" to be integrated into a recruit's new identity as part of the warrior culture.

Culture is a power force on an individual's life. By understanding it as a semiotic practice, the warrior culture can become a powerful ally to the building of resiliency practices. Despite the negative influence culture has had on the willingness of individuals to seek mental health treatment, it can also be a powerful tool to introduce resiliency and help veterans internalize the strength that comes from bulletproofing the psyche as well as the physical self.

References

Aaker, J. L., Benet-Martinez, V., & Garolera, J. (2001). Consumption symbols as carriers of culture: A study of Japanese and Spanish brand personality constructs. *Journal of Personality and Social Psychology, 81*(3), 492.

Archer, E. M. (2014). Crossing the Rubicon. *The European Legacy, 19*(5), 606–621.

Boëne, B. (1990). How "unique" should the military be? A review of representative literature & outline of a synthetic formulation. *European Journal of Sociology, 31*(01), 3–59.

Bryan, C. J., & Morrow, C. E. (2011). Circumventing mental health stigma by embracing the warrior culture: Lessons learned from the Defender's Edge program. *Professional Psychology: Research and Practice, 42*(1), 16.

Centers for Disease Control and Prevention. (2014). Deaths: Final Data for 2014. Retrieved from https://www.cdc.gov/nchs/data/nvsr/nvsr65/nvsr65_04.pdf

Coker, C. (2007). *The warrior ethos: Military culture and the war on terror.* New York, NY: Routledge.

Cone, R. W. (2006). The changing National Training Center. *Military Review, 86*(3), 70–79.
Council, N. R. (2008). *Human behavior in military contexts*. Washington, DC: National Academies Press.
Daggett, S. (2010). *Costs of major U.S. wars*. Washington, DC: Congressional Research Service.
Doyle, M. E., & Peterson, K. A. (2005). Re-entry and reintegration: Returning home after combat. *Psychiatric Quarterly, 76*(4), 361–370.
Draganski, B., Gaser, C., Busch, V., Schuierer, G., Bogdahn, U., & May, A. (2004). Neuroplasticity: Changes in grey matter induced by training. *Nature, 427*(6972), 311–312.
Dunivin, K. O. (1994). Military culture: Change and continuity. *Armed Forces & Society, 20*(4), 531–547.
Farrell, T. (2002). *The sources of military change: Culture, politics, technology*. Boulder, CO: Lynne Rienner Publishers.
Franke, V., & Heinecken, L. (2001). Adjusting to peace: Military values in a cross-national comparison. *Armed Forces & Society, 27*(4), 567–595.
Goldstein, J. S. (2011). *Winning the war on war: The decline of armed conflict worldwide*. New York, NY: Penguin Press.
Goodwin, R. D. (2003). Association between physical activity and mental disorders among adults in the United States. *Preventive Medicine, 36*(6), 698–703.
Gupta, A., & Ferguson, J. (1992). Beyond "culture": Space, identity, and the politics of difference. *Cultural Anthropology, 7*(1), 6–23.
Higate, P. R. (2001). Theorizing continuity: From military to civilian life. *Armed Forces & Society, 27*(3), 443–460.
Holdeman, T. C. (2009). Invisible wounds of war: Psychological and cognitive injuries, their consequences, and services to assist recovery. *Psychiatric Services, 60*(2), 273.
Hunter, K., & Best, R. (2017) *Veterans, transitions, and self-identity in public spaces*. Presented at the Peace Science Society International Annual Conference, Tempe, Arizona.
Janowitz, M. (1975). The all-volunteer military as a "sociopolitical" problem. *Social Problems, 22*(3), 432–449.
Jessop, B. (2004). Critical semiotic analysis and cultural political economy. *Critical Discourse Studies, 1*(2), 159–174.
Knight, J. P. (1990). Literature as equipment for killing: Performance as rhetoric in military training camps. *Text and Performance Quarterly, 10*(2), 157–168.
Krebs, R. R. (2006). *Fighting for rights: Military service and the politics of citizenship*. Ithaca, NY: Cornell University Press.
Lazear, E. P. (1999). Culture and language. *Journal of Political Economy, 107*(S6), 95–126.
Lendon, J. E. (1999). The rhetoric of combat: Greek military theory and Roman culture in Julius Caesar's Battle Descriptions. *Classical Antiquity, 18*(2), 273–329.

Lyall, J., & Wilson, I. (2009). Rage against the machines: Explaining outcomes in counterinsurgency wars. *International Organization, 63*(01), 67–109.

Marlantes, K. (2011). *What it is like to go to war.* New York, NY: Grove/Atlantic, Inc.

Münte, T. F., Altenmüller, E., & Jäncke, L. (2002). The musician's brain as a model of Neuroplasticity. *Nature Reviews Neuroscience, 3*(6).

Pietrzak, R. H. (2009). Perceived stigma and barriers to mental health care utilization among OEF-OIF veterans. *Psychiatric Services, 60*(8), 1118–1122.

Ricks, T. E. (2007). *Making the Corps.* New York, NY: Simon and Schuster.

Rostker, B. D., & Yeh, K. C. (2006). I Want You! The Evolution of the All-Volunteer Force. Rand Corporation. Retrieved from http://www.rand.org/content/dam/rand/pubs/monographs/2007/RAND_MG265.pdf

Schwartz, J., & Begley, S. (2003). *The mind and the brain: Neuroplasticity and the power of mental force.* New York, NY: Harper Perennial.

Segal, M. W. (1995). Women's military roles cross-nationally past, present, and future. *Gender & Society, 9*(6), 757–775.

Sewell, W. H., Jr. (2005). The concept(s) of culture. In Spiegell, G. (Ed). *Practicing history: New directions in historical writing after the linguistic turn.* New York, NY: Routledge.

Skelton, W. B. (1996). Samuel P. Huntington and the roots of the American military tradition. *The Journal of Military History, 60*(2), 325.

Swidler, A. (1986). Culture in action: Symbols and strategies. *American Sociological Review, 51*(2), 273–286.

Toner, J. H. (2013). *True faith and allegiance: The burden of military ethics.* Lexington, KY: University of Kentucky Press.

Turner, B. S. (1990). Outline of a theory of citizenship. *Sociology, 24*(2), 189–217.

Woolf, G. (1994). *Becoming Roman, staying Greek: Culture, identity and the civilizing process in the Roman East.* Proceedings of the Cambridge Philological Society.

Yi, J. (2004). MCMAP and the marine warrior ethos. *Military Review, 17*(1), 17–24.

Point of View—Armor Down: The Power of Mindfulness

Ben King

In 2006, I deployed to Iraq as a psychological operations specialist for the United States Army. My job was to build rapport and gather soft intelligence from key communicators or local Iraqis within an area of operations known as Zaphrania. Before building those relationships however, we had to deal with the IEDs.

Two months before my deployment I began getting classes on how to deal with Improvised Explosive Devices. "These new shape charges can penetrate every form of armor we have," an instructor shared. "Notice how the 50 ton Bradley fighting vehicle is completely destroyed by the IED. Here you will notice in the highlighted circles the body parts of the men flying through the air."

How many times are they going to show us how and why we are screwed before they show us how to do anything about it?

There are terrorists and IEDs everywhere!

"Always change your routine. Keep Vigilant. Look for anything suspicious."

We touched down in Iraq in late April 2006. Our first briefing was about our Area of Operations. All they talked about were IEDs. "Beware of everything," we heard over and over.

What was terrifying was the head game of the IED. You know they are out there, but you don't know where. You know they can kill you, and have been killing warriors by the hundreds, but there is very little you can do about it.

My first convoy, I got into the back right side of an up-armored HMMWV. I remember feeling very nervous but wanting to put on a good face. We were part of a small Civil Affairs convoy and when we started moving, I started to feel worried.

If an IED can be anything and anywhere, how in the world do you prepare for it?

When we passed through the main gate I started scanning my area looking for IEDs. I saw them everywhere. That curb, that piece of trash, that mound of dirt. What I didn't notice was that my body was also reacting. I was shaking so much that the convoy commander looked back at me and said, "Relax Corporal King, we haven't even left the green zone yet."

When we did finally leave the green zone and drive into the flow of Baghdad I realized that all my IED training was futile. Outside my window was a bustling city with people and cars and donkeys and trash and a thousand million things that could be an IED. In that moment I surrendered myself to fate and drove on.

On December 31st, 2006 my vehicle was hit by an IED on a convoy. Here is what I wrote in an email home:

January 3, 2007

>It is being called the New Year's Eve miracle.
>I'm not really sure how I am handling it because I feel like I have moved on. I truly do. I went by the truck today, took some pictures said a prayer and told the truck goodbye. I know there are going to be a lot of stories being told from lots of different angles, there are going to be more nut and ball jokes than you or I can imagine and then it will be over with. What an experience. . . . ok next.
>I don't know. Maybe it will hit me later on and I'll go holy shit I can't believe I didn't die, but what's the point. I didn't die, it's as simple as that. Yes the what if and maybe game is one that could be played all day long, but why?
>It is completely amazing that I survived the attack. It was an EFP IED, those are the special ones sent in from the Iran, that send molten copper at the truck at a staggering rate of speed, 10,000 feet per second I believe. At the very least I should have lost a leg, a hand, there should be a hole through me the size of a soft ball, yadda yadda yaddda etc, etc etc. But again, there is not. My body, including the twins, is perfectly fine. I also have no reason to believe that the same thing can't be said for my mind.

I got a purple heart for injuries sustained and moved on. Or so I thought.

In the bowels of my darkest self a sinking hole forms beneath my heart. Its pulses with emptiness and my mind goes blank and just buzzes like a broken fluorescent light bulb twitching and sputtering. When this happens sleep is impossible. I called them white nights because every time I close my eyes, no matter how tired I was, all I saw was white light. Night after night it would be the same thing.

After returning home I couldn't seem to turn off. Almost anything triggered my mind into overdrive. The nights were the worst because I couldn't sleep. Not sleeping meant that my days were cloudy and foggy with fatigue.

My girlfriend (now my wife) created my first experience of peace following a melt-down. It was a particularly bad night for me and I called her at four in the morning sobbing that I hadn't slept in days and I had a big day and how was I going to handle it. She told me to come to her house. She put me in a bath, of all things. I wasn't aware of this at the time but that warm water created an experience for my body that was big enough—sensational enough—to override the storm in my mind.

I struggled and stumbled along, self-medicating and not knowing why I could never sleep. I was a personal trainer at the time. The gym had been a safe space for most of my life, but after Iraq I was lost. Climbing the stairs from the weight room one day, one painful step after another, I saw a gym yoga class beginning. Out of desperation, I decided to try it. A yoga teacher named Jewel helped me find a spot. About ten minutes into the practice Jewel encouraged the class to breathe and move our shoulder blades at the same time. I remember looking up to see what she meant and as I started to breathe and move I felt something weird. The feeling was warm and fluid—I felt it spread through my neck and shoulders. I liked it! That night I slept for the first time in days.

I kept going back to yoga. The novelty of moving my body in a smooth, connected way was such a foreign concept to me. Up to that point in my life, my relationship to my body was "No Pain No Gain," "Harder, Faster, Stronger." To move my body with ease was totally new, and as I moved, analysis and self-talk dropped away. All I noticed was the sensation.

It wasn't until Mindfulness however that things really started to make sense. It showed up like a gift from a long-lost acquaintance when I was invited to a class at the Washington DC VA. About 15 minutes into my first class, I noticed a change in my mind—I felt it get quieter and farther away. Being in my mind when things were bad was a bright and irritating experience. Being in my mind during mindfulness training was quiet and comfortable. I experienced not being in a hurry. I watched myself being still. I remember feeling a sense of awe and wonder, I clearly wasn't asleep but I wasn't what I understood to be awake either.

I went back to training every Thursday, and each time I felt the draw to return. Over the weeks I began recognize my mind as a tool that could be tamed and trained instead of a body part to be dominated. I began to recognize that in any moment that I had a choice. I could either put my brain power into my thoughts or I could put my brain power into my body. During my darkest days, my body would be doing all kinds of things, but I would only be focused on my thoughts. I ignored the body because that is what I had always done and had trained to do in the Army. After mindfulness training I began to recognize that in any situation I had the choice of what to pay attention to.

Now here is the kicker—I still feel the same bodily sensations that I used to feel during the bad times. The sinking feelings around my heart that used to send my mind into "here we go again" still happen. The difference now however is that when I feel the feeling, I have a choice of where to put my thoughts. *Choice is everything.*

CHAPTER 3

Mindfulness: The Neurobehavioral Basis of Resilience

Deborah Norris and Aurora Hutchinson

The role of mindfulness meditation as a therapeutic health care modality is becoming established in the medical literature and in military hospitals. Advances in the medical standard of care have encouraged the use of meditation and other mind-body practices for the treatment of pain (Wells, Smitherman, Seng, Houle, & Loder, 2014), depression (Srivastava, Talukdar, & Lahan, 2011), anxiety (Hart, 2013), posttraumatic stress disorder (PTSD) (Kim, Schneider, Kravitz, Mermier, & Burge, 2013), and numerous other mental health care concerns (Joy, 2014). Mindfulness practices are taught widely throughout the Department of Veterans Affairs, including many Veterans Affairs medical centers, and recent research is beginning to evaluate the clinical benefits of these mindfulness programs (Nassif et al., 2015). In addition to providing clinical health benefits, mindfulness practices are also identified as helping to overcome stress and improve quality of life, sleep quality, cognitive performance, and many other enhancements in physical and psychological function. Furthermore, perhaps as a result of the health-regulating effects of meditation practices, evidence supports the possibility that mindfulness may be one of the trait characteristics mediating resilience and the capacity to adaptively overcome stress and/or other life traumas.

If mindfulness can be shown to mediate resilience, and the neurobehavioral mechanisms of action can be identified, then perhaps specific behavioral elements of the practice can be identified and targeted to both prevent and treat mental health problems in the military. Several studies have already begun to explore the impact of mindfulness training on resiliency in military forces, and programs are currently being implemented on the basis of the assumption that meditation may enhance resiliency traits. Indeed, mindfulness practices have been a component of martial arts training for thousands of years to improve military performance. This chapter will explore the ancient wisdom of mindfulness practices as way to bulletproof the psyche of our armed forces from the perspective of modern, evidence-based scientific research.

Resilience is broadly defined as the ability to bounce back from adversity (Ledesma, 2014; Southwick, Bonanno, Masten, Panter-Brick, & Yehuda, 2014) and more specifically as growth after disruption (Richardson, 2002). Key elements of such growth involve an element of introspection and an opportunity for change. Introspection and transformation are also recognized as defining elements of mindfulness meditation (Fox et al., 2012), suggesting that there may be a relationship between the practice of meditation and the trait of resilience. Werner and Smith (2001) similarly identified resilient individuals as those having an "internal locus of control" and "a more positive self-concept," which are also defining characteristics of those who practice mindfulness meditation (Crescentini & Capurso, 2015).

Both resilience and mindfulness are also defined by their association with stress. The ability to maintain biochemical balance without stress activation is referred to as homeostasis. The stress response occurs when there is a real or perceived threat to homeostasis. Stress activation of the hypothalamic-pituitary-adrenal (HPA) axis involves a cascade of hormonal changes that correspond with a heightened state of arousal. The dynamic process by which the body is able to respond to stress activation of the HPA axis and return to a biochemically balanced state is referred to as allostasis. Researchers have defined "resilience" as either the ability to maintain homeostasis following an experience of stress or enhanced allostasis (Alim et al., 2012).

Mindfulness mediates the stress response in two ways. Greater indices of mindfulness are associated with (1) lower levels of response to typical stressors (maintaining homeostasis) and (2) a more rapid return to the relaxed state when stress is activated (improved allostasis; Herman et al., 2016). Resilience is also associated with both lower levels of response to typical stressors and the ability to bounce back to a normal state after stress activation (Sinha, Lacadie, Constable, & Seo, 2016). Resilient individuals are more likely to maintain homeostasis and, when disrupted by stress, have a faster rate of allostasis to normal function. Studies exploring the role of training in mindfulness meditation as a way to improve resilience in the military suggest that mindfulness training may indeed enhance resilience in the armed forces (Johnson et al., 2014). Studies of the physiological basis of mindfulness and resilience show that the underlying brain mechanisms that are altered by mindfulness training provide a physiological foundation that characterizes emotional resilience (Haase et al., 2016).

Physiological Foundations of Resilience May Be Mediated by Meditation

Researchers have sought to identify a number of physiological mechanisms that may underlie characteristics of resiliency. These physiological foundations of resilience are located in the brain and include changes in both brain neurochemistry and neural structures (Feder, Nestler, & Charney, 2009). Mindfulness exercises have also been identified that are associated with these same neurochemical and structural characteristics by which we identify resiliency.

The Biochemistry of Stress Resiliency and Mindfulness Outcomes

In a review by Charney (2004), 11 biochemical correlates that may underlie resiliency and vulnerability were identified to mediate the psychobiological response to extreme stress. These biochemicals associated with stress and resiliency include the hormones cortisol, dehydroepiandrosterone (DHEA), corticotrophin-releasing hormone (CRH), testosterone, and estrogen; neurotransmitters (neurohormones) of norepinephrine, dopamine, serotonin, and gamma-aminobutyric acid (GABA; benzodiazepine receptor reactivity); and neuropeptides Y (NPY) and galanin.

Hormones Associated with Resilience and Mindfulness (Cortisol, DHEA, CRH, Testosterone, and Estrogen)

Cortisol, DHEA, and CRH are normal parts of the HPA activation that characterize the stress response. A study of soldiers performing the U.S. Army Survival Course found that those who completed the training had dramatically increased cortisol levels and that these levels of cortisol did not return to normal baseline levels following a period of recovery (Morgan et al., 2001).

Numerous studies on the mechanism of action of mindfulness practices have found that meditation is associated with a rebalancing of essential hormones and in particular can rebalance those hormones associated with the stress response, PTSD, and resiliency. For example, following a mindfulness meditation intervention, resilient medical students had lower levels of cortisol, DHEA, and CRH reaction relative to baseline than nonresilient cohorts (Turakitwanakan, Mekseepralard, & Busarakumtragul, 2013). Resilient subjects also returned more quickly to homeostatic levels of these hormones after a stress-eliciting event. Just as research has shown that resilience is defined as the ability to maintain lower levels of cortisol, DHEA, and CRH in the face of stressors, mindfulness exercises are proving to be a behavioral intervention that controls cortisol, DHEA, and CRH levels (Matousek, Dobkin, & Pruessner, 2010). The more practice one has in mindfulness meditation, the lower the increase in cortisol and CRH in response to stressful events, improving the ability to return to homeostasis following a stress or trauma that activates the HPA axis (Castro et al., 2012). Again, mindfulness exercises have been found to hasten the return to equilibrium following activation of the HPA axis and release of cortisol, DHEA, and CRH (Carlson, Speca, Patel, & Goodey, 2004). These data suggest that mindfulness practices can enable self-regulation of neurohormonal balance and that this neurohormonal balance is the foundation of the behavioral state we are defining as resilience.

The stressful experience of Army survival testing was also found to significantly decrease testosterone (Morgan et al., 2001). Low levels of testosterone are associated with depression, PTSD, and other indices of declining mental health (Yeap, 2014). Resilience, however, is defined by higher levels of testosterone, which in turn is related to higher social rank, competitive success, and greater feelings of personal success and connectedness within social groups (Russo, Murrough, Han, Charney, & Nestler, 2012).

Similarly, estrogen levels are also recognized as a relevant determinant of resilience. A study by Bredemann and McMahon (2014) found that animals pretreated with estrogen (17β estradiol) before being exposed to inescapable shock were less likely to exhibit symptoms of learned helplessness during the shock. Learned helplessness is associated with, and used as a model of, depression (Seligman, 1972). Furthermore, treatment with estrogen was able to reverse previously established learned helplessness behaviors. These findings suggest that homeostatic levels of estrogen may play a protective role in preventing depression and that balancing levels of estrogen may be associated with resilience (Bredemann & McMahon, 2014).

Meditation practices may also provide a prophylactic effect on stress-induced disruptions in testosterone and estrogen, serving as a behavioral intervention for rebalancing of these critical hormones associated with resiliency. Given that mindfulness practices modulate the biomarkers associated with stress (Carlson et al., 2004; Matousek et al., 2010; Walker, Pfingst, Carnevali, Sgoifo, & Nalivaiko, 2017), and stress affects levels of testosterone and estrogen, meditation may also impact the hormonal mechanisms that are fundamental to resilience.

Neurotransmitter Mechanisms of Action

Changes in neurotransmitter systems also appear to mediate the relation between mindfulness practices and resiliency. Specifically, changes in norepinephrine, dopamine, serotonin, and NPY have been identified as characterizing resilience (Krystal & Neumeister, 2009). Stressful events can cause a significant increase in levels of excitatory neurotransmitters such as norepinephrine and dopamine, can disrupt serotonin homeostasis, and can diminish brain levels of inhibitory neurotransmitters such as GABA, consequently influencing the function of specific brain regions and associated behavioral outcomes. Resilient individuals are identified as maintaining a more balanced state of these neurotransmitters in the face of stress or traumatic events and as returning to a balanced state when disruption of these biochemicals does occur (Bowirrat et al., 2010).

Norepinephrine

The greatest concentration of norepinephrine in the brain is in the region of the locus coeruleus in the brain stem. When activated by stress, the locus coeruleus releases norepinephrine into the brain, activating the HPA axis and influencing the balance of stress-related hormones. Elevated levels of the catecholamine norepinephrine are identified in individuals who suffer from anxiety. Animals who were treated in such a way as to block norepinephrine release were not able to respond in an anxious way to a fear-inducing stimulus, supporting the role of norepinephrine in anxious behavior (Peng et al., 2016). Several studies have found that individuals who practice meditation are able to maintain significantly lower levels of norepinephrine compared to control subjects who do not meditate. Change in the stability of norepinephrine levels has been found to correlate with improved quality of life and other indices of health (Curiati et al., 2005). Those who practiced meditation had lower levels of norepinephrine, higher scores on quality of life, and lower levels of concern for heart disease. These findings suggest that mindfulness practices may help to mediate resiliency through a catecholaminergic mechanism involving norepinephrine.

Dopamine

Experiencing stressful events is also associated with elevated levels of dopamine in the brain. Dopamine, like norepinephrine, is a catecholamine neurotransmitter that initiates cortisol release through activation of the stress response. Activation of the stress response is an adaptive mechanism in response to an environmental situation that requires activation of the arousal system—basically physical exertion, such as competitive sports or fighting for your life. Elevated levels of dopamine may not only be appropriate but also actually adaptive in certain stressful situations. Dopamine is known to activate the nucleus accumbens, the reward center of the brain, and is associated with reward-motivated behaviors. For example, it is the activity of dopamine on the nucleus accumbens that prompts people to abuse cocaine. Cocaine stimulates dopamine receptors in the nucleus accumbens causing rewarding feelings of intense pleasure. Similarly, some stressful situations may be motivating (e.g., competitive sports) in that they stimulate dopamine release and activate the nucleus accumbens. There are emotional rewards for engaging in some types of competitively stressful situations and succeeding. Other situations, however, may be traumatizing—such as fighting for your life. In life-threatening instances, the initial stressor activates both the stress response (the HPA axis) and the nucleus accumbens, providing motivation for action. However, after the stressor is gone, the stress response (fear) persists, while dopamine activation subsides. Other brain mechanisms may regulate whether dopamine release and related heightened arousal are associated with negative or positive outcomes.

Understanding the dual effects of dopamine—both activating the arousal system and regulating feelings of motivation and reward—can help us understand the role of dopamine in resiliency. Returning to the definition of resilience, we are reminded that resilience involves experiencing a stressful event or opportunity, being disrupted by it, and then returning to homeostasis, becoming even stronger in the process. This effect can be compared to the consequences of weight-lifting exercises that work out the muscles. The muscles are stressed by the exercise of lifting weights, which is followed by a period of recovery. The result of this exercise is that one becomes physically stronger and better able to cope with muscle exertion in the future.

In the case of resiliency, individuals are working out their brains to become more resilient; stress followed by a period of introspection and recovery eventually yields greater mental strength/resilience. Evidence suggests that mindfulness meditation practices involving introspective awareness are the mental exercises that can enhance resiliency through an underlying mechanism involving dopamine and related catecholamine actions in the brain (Rees, 2011). Mindfulness meditation activates dopamine receptors in the nucleus accumbens, without activating the HPA axis, resulting in greater feelings of motivation, inspiration, and pleasure.

Gamma-Aminobutyric acid (GABA)

Studies of the neurobiology of resilience suggest that GABA also plays a role in the ability to bounce back from adversity and regain equilibrium. Numerous studies have shown that lower levels of GABA and fewer GABA receptors are associated with higher levels of anxiety (Krishnakumar, Hamblin, & Lakshmanan, 2015). GABA modulates cortical excitability and neural plasticity. Since GABA is an inhibitory neurotransmitter, decreasing excitation in the brain, higher levels of GABA are associated with calmness, serenity, and even sedation—hence, the use of GABAergic pharmacotherapies such as Valium (diazepam) as anxiolytics and sedatives. Restoring homeostatic levels of GABA in the brain is associated with a more stable emotional state and greater resilience. Meditation has been shown to increase GABA levels in the brain and consequently decrease hyperexcitability and excess brain activation. Recent reports provide evidence that the practice of meditation results in production of higher levels of GABA and thus may serve a role in more resilient adaptation to normal brain biochemistry following a stressful experience.

Neuropeptide Y (NPY)

Neuropeptide Y (NPY) is abundant in the hypothalamus and other regions of the brain and plays a role in processing stress, anxiety, the perception of pain, blood pressure, food intake, and energy homeostasis. Researchers evaluated the effects of mindfulness-based mind fitness training (MMFT) on NPY levels of Marines preparing for deployment and being put through a series of stressful training operations. Blood levels of NPY at the beginning of the study did not differ in Marines who received eight weeks of MMFT and those who only received training as usual. Nor was there a difference in NPY levels after eight weeks of training. However, following the stressful operations, Marines who had undergone mindfulness training had significantly lower levels of NPY than Marines who had only standard training. These differences in NPY levels correlated with faster heart rate recovery and faster rates of recovery from brain activation in the insula associated with greater emotion regulation.The authors in this study conclude that mindfulness training facilitates resiliency as measured by a quicker recovery and more adaptive response to NPY levels following stress. Specifically, MMFT was found to modulate NPY mechanisms underlying recovery from stress in active-duty military personnel when taught along with standard training for deployment (Johnson et al., 2014).

Galanin

Galanin is a neuropeptide that plays a role in both the central nervous system (CNS) and gastrointestinal tract. Galanin regulates neural activity in the hypothalamus, locus coeruleus, cortex, and brain stem and alters the plasticity of neurons, including promoting neurogenesis in these regions of the brain that mediate resilience. Galanin is found to modulate the monoamines of serotonin, dopamine, and norepinephrine as well as NPY in these stress-responsive areas of the brain. Although research is yet to evaluate the effects of meditation on galanin activity, several studies have found that exercise activates gene expression of galanin, thus preventing activation of neural stress pathways. Similarly, it would be worth evaluating the role of meditation in releasing galanin's neuromodulatory mechanisms to relieve stress and enhance resiliency.

Resiliency Mechanisms

Allostasis and homeostasis appear to be physiological mechanisms that can be enhanced through behavioral strategies involving mindfulness practices (Alim et al., 2012; Bowirrat et al., 2010; Goodyer, 2006; Sinha et al., 2016). Given that mindfulness exercises are proving to be a behavioral intervention that can be used to modulate cortisol, DHEA, and CRH levels, enhance allostasis, and restore homeostasis (Bränström, Kvillemo, & Åkerstedt, 2013), meditation may rebalance essential biochemicals to include those associated with the stress response, PTSD, and other mental health indices. The more practice one has in mindfulness meditation, the higher the measures of mindfulness, and the lower the increase in cortisol, DHEA, and CRH in response to stressful events. To that end, mindfulness decreases the allostatic load.

By definition, the psychological profile of the nonresilient individual is one who is easily affected by stress and is slow to return to a normal or functional state following a stressor (e.g., remains traumatized). Alternatively, the resilient individual is both able to maintain homeostasis during a stressful experience and is able to regain homeostasis when he or she is disrupted by the challenge of a stressful experience. These psychological traits have a physiological basis reflected in the biochemical mechanisms that have been described. Meditation is the practice that impacts the neurobehavioral mechanisms that are the foundation of resilience (Wang, Xu, & Luo, 2016).

Taken together, the results of numerous studies suggest that a certain biochemically balanced state may characterize resilient individuals and that these physiological mechanisms for establishing and maintaining biochemical balance may be the foundation of the psychological traits of resiliency. Furthermore, these physiological mechanisms for rebalancing can be activated through behavioral strategies. Research suggests that these behavioral strategies are the active ingredients of the practice of mindfulness meditation.

Behavioral Strategies of Mindfulness Practices and Their Neurological Correlates

There are many forms of meditation; the difference in the various practices is the element of the focus. Mindfulness practices are defined by a focus on interoceptive experiences. Also referred to as somatic sensing or body scanning, interoceptive awareness is the practice of attending to all forms of sensory experience as they arise. For example, in a body scan, one may begin with a focus on the toes (or the head) and gradually move through the body, exploring the sensations arising in an ascending (or descending) order. Somatic sensing refers to any sensations arising from the body. In mindfulness meditation, one explores the sensations that arise within the body. In addition to the body scan, the movement of the breath is a common point of focus as an interoceptive experience, though there are many others. The breath is a useful point of focus, in that the exhale of the breath naturally activates the parasympathetic relaxation response and can contribute to allostasis and homeostasis in the presence of a perceived potential threat. The use of the breath as a point of focus is characteristic of many mindfulness practices, including seated meditation as well as yoga, tai chi, and qigong.

When one directs his or her point of focus toward sensations arising from the body, afferent nerve pathways are activated to send information through the vagus nerve into the brain stem. It is here in the brain stem that the norepinephrine pathway arising in the nucleus called the locus coeruleus relays information to the thalamus for processing (Aston-Jones, Shipley, & Grzanna, 1995; Berridge & Waterhouse, 2003; Hurley, Devilbiss, & Waterhouse, 2004). The thalamus serves to modulate, amplify, or inhibit sensory information transmission to the cerebral cortex where it is processed as part of the consciousness. Sensory information including seeing, hearing, tasting, touch, and somatic sensations arising from the viscera, the heart, and elsewhere are gated through the brain region of the thalamus. Only olfactory information coming through the nasal epithelium is able to bypass the thalamic gates and goes directly into the sensory cortex. Sensations of pain (nociception) are also transmitted via the vagus nerve and gated by the thalamus. This thalamic gating mechanism (Norris, 2016) is dependent upon the state of arousal and attention of the organism (Price, 1995; Simpson et al., 1997; Simpson, Waterhouse, & Lin, 1999). In addition to afferent input from the sensory receptors, other input to the thalamus is received from the hypothalamus. Hypothalamic activation of the thalamus is associated with selective closing of thalamic gates, particularly those providing somatosensory information from the periphery of the body. Selective thalamic gating translates into enhanced ability to focus on visual or auditory information and suppressed awareness of bodily sensations.

Ignoring somatosensory input during traumatic stressful situations may be adaptive in that somatosensory pain is often associated with these situations. In a fight-or-flight situation, attending to pain could be distracting from attending to other more relevant stimuli that could be critical for survival. For example, during stress or trauma, people often do not notice a wound or an injury. The focus remains on the battle at hand. It is not until later, once the battle is over, that one may notice an injury and the pain associated with it. Stress activation of the hypothalamus, in addition to activating the pituitary and adrenal cascade, simultaneously activates the gating mechanisms of the thalamus, blocking somatosensory input to the sensory cortex, and enabling the critical decision-making cortical region of the brain to remain focused on the external environment. Breath-holding facilitates sympathetic activation of the hypothalamus and is something that most individuals do when they are startled, afraid, tense, or dealing with a traumatic fight-or-flight situation. Dealing with stress or trauma activates the HPA axis, closes the thalamic gates to somatosensory processing, and heightens focus on selective external stimuli. The thalamic gating of somatosensory information allows the cortical regions of the brain to hyperfocus on processing only sensory information critical for survival.

The first key to reopening the thalamic gates is deactivation of the stress response. Once the HPA axis is deactivated, the thalamic gates are free to reopen. Mindfulness practices that focus on somatic sensing can hasten restoration of flow of sensory messages from the body. By intentionally directing the focus of awareness on the body, the thalamic gates are invited to reopen to receive somatosensory input. By intentionally focusing on the breath, breathing patterns may become normalized, and parasympathetic activity may facilitate thalamic opening. Here is where experienced practitioners issue warnings to proceed with caution. When these gates open, a flood of suppressed experience is invited into the consciousness and can overwhelm the inexperienced practitioner. For an inexperienced mindfulness practitioner who suffers visceral or other pain or trauma to the body, the rehearsed reaction to this experience has been to divert the awareness elsewhere, close the thalamic gates, and suppress any pain that may have started to arise—what psychologists refer to as denial or repression. Ignoring the pain, or repressing it, has become a conditioned coping strategy. Mindfulness is not a coping strategy—it is a healing strategy. In a safe environment, perhaps with support, mindfulness practices can gradually train the practitioner to open to somatic experiences, reopen the thalamic gates, release stored trauma, and gradually release and recover from a state of blocked feelings and emotional numbness. Continuing to focus on respiratory processing will continue to normalize breathing patterns and facilitate the release of suppressed experiences coincident with parasympathetic activity as opposed to stress.

In this author's research with veterans who suffer from chronic pain, as they begin a mindfulness practice, the first thing that they note is that they become more aware of the pain (Nassif et al., 2015). They might report that they feel the pain more, but their explanations reveal that they are simply more conscious of the pain; that is, it has always been present, but that they had been ignoring it, resisting letting their awareness notice the pain. As a result, in their mindfulness practice, when they pay attention to pain, it seems more present. This mindfulness practice of interoceptive awareness is the active process of opening the thalamic gates to allow the nociceptive experience to flow from vagal afferents through the brain stem nucleus of the locus coeruleus and then through the thalamus into the insular and sensory cortices where awareness is perceived. In the relaxed state, with the thalamic gates open, bodily states associated with feelings are transmitted to the insular cortex and give rise to consciousness of emotional experiences. Releasing resistance by opening the thalamic gates allows the flow of information into the brain and restores the flow of neural processing involving multiple transmitter systems and related biochemicals. Homeostatic states can again be achieved.

Hölzel et al. (2011) identify several behavioral activities associated with mindfulness practices: (1) attention regulation; (2) body awareness; (3a) emotion regulation and reappraisal; (3b) emotion regulation: exposure, extinction, and reconsolidation; and (4) change in perspective on self. Correlated with these behavioral activities are changes in the underlying neural substrates of the behavior.

As mentioned previously, nociceptive experience is received from vagal afferents through the thalamus. These bodily sensations are then processed in the insula, which is located deep within the cerebral cortex of the brain. Several studies have demonstrated that the insula regulates interoceptive awareness (Craig, 2003, 2009; Critchley et al., 2004; Hölzel et al., 2011) and processing of social-emotional behaviors as well as pain and other sensorimotor experiences (Chang, Yarkoni, Khaw, & Sanfey, 2013). Specifically, the anterior insula is associated with awareness of the visceral states associated with emotions (Craig, 2003.)

Information from the insula is further processed in the anterior cingulate cortex (ACC), which is the area of the brain associated with attention regulation and emotional processing and is known to be the locus of self-regulatory behavior (Etkin, Egner, & Kalisch, 2011). The cingulate cortex is situated above and adjacent to the corpus callosum, in the medial wall of each cerebral hemisphere. It is unique in that it has connections to both the limbic system and the prefrontal cortex, connecting emotional processing with cognitive processing. Studies using functional neuroimaging have shown that PTSD is associated with reduced activation of the cingulate cortex. Similarly, depression and related forms of emotional suppression and emotional numbing such as substance abuse and suicidal ideation are also associated with decreased response in the cingulate cortex following an emotional experience (Stevens, Hurley, & Taber, 2011).

Physical or emotional trauma, which may lead to depression or numbness, blocks somatic sensation by closing thalamic gating mechanisms. Conditioning causes them to remain closed, and continual activation of the HPA axis becomes a habit. Resilient individuals, however, have learned to reopen these subcortical gating mechanisms following a stress or trauma, thus allowing information about the somatic state to enter the ACC. Studies of resiliency show that resilient individuals have larger volumes and greater gray matter density of the ACC (Kasai et al., 2008; Rauch et al., 2003; Woodward et al., 2006). Using functional magnetic resonance imaging or functional MRI (fMRI), Hölzel et al. (2007) found that the practice of focused attention meditation leads to greater activation of the ACC.

Meditation instructions to maintain focus on interoceptive processing can improve ACC function. Meditators' self-reports indicate that with practice, it becomes easier to maintain focus on a single interoceptive sensation. Meditation practice also correlates with growth in the ACC region of the brain (Hölzel et al., 2007). The meditative practice of directing, and redirecting if necessary, one's focus to his or her somatosensory experience may serve to enhance the capacity for emotional regulation and self-control through neuroplastic developments of the ACC, leading to greater levels of resiliency (Thomas & Plummer Taylor, 2015). Taken together, these data suggest common neural substrates and circuitry underlying resilience and meditation. Given this common physiological substrate, meditation practice may provide a behavioral mechanism for increasing resilience.

As mentioned earlier, the ACC is connected to both the limbic system and the prefrontal cortex. This connection is part of a network of brain areas that are implicated in self-referential processes. Known as the default mode network (DMN), these cortical and subcortical areas are active when the brain is at rest (Greicius, Krasnow, Reiss, & Menon, 2003; Mason et al., 2007; Raichle et al., 2001). When disengaged from attentional control or specific goal-directed behavior, neuroimaging studies of the brain's resting state have shown activity in the medial prefrontal cortex (mPFC), posterior cingulate cortex (PCC), the ventral anterior cingulate cortex (a subregion of the ACC), hippocampus, and amygdala, which are areas associated with self-perception, emotion, memory processing and integration, and planning. Thus, activity in the DMN may serve as a baseline of cognitive activity that is self-referential, providing a narrative for a self across time that assesses the salience of internal and external information and attributing meaning and context among disparate, subjective experiences (Farb et al., 2007; Mason et al., 2007). While DMN activity may be adaptive in underlying the establishment of a narrative, consistent sense of self that can plan future activity, engage in introspection, recall important details, and attend to multiple, concurrent tasks, this default mode is also characterized by stimulus-independent thought, or mind-wandering, and may also subserve automatic and ruminative thought processes. For example, increased DMN connectivity, particularly in the mPFC and ACC, which are brain areas implicated in self-referential and emotional processes, is correlated with major depression, excessive rumination, and anxiety (Coutinho et al., 2016; Sheline et al., 2009).

In contrast, goal-directed tasks or shifts in attentional control appear to dampen or inhibit DMN activity. For example, mindfulness meditation shifts attention away from a narrative, self-referential focus to present-moment awareness. Neuroimaging studies have shown that this attentional shift activates corresponding brain structures that are involved in attention, interoception, and sensory processing (Farb et al., 2007; Hölzel et al., 2011; Lazar et al., 2005), areas of the brain that are distinct from the DMN and when activated serve to attenuate or disengage DMN associated activity. Meditation can attenuate activation of the DMN, particularly in the mPFC and PCC, while facilitating a stronger connection between the PCC, dorsal ACC, and dorsolateral prefrontal cortices. This may indicate greater cognitive control and self-monitoring as well as greater attentional focus (i.e., decreased mind-wandering; Brewer et al., 2011). In addition, these areas of the cingulate cortex (i.e., PCC and ACC) are connected to the nucleus accumbens and hypothalamus, which may provide an important link between higher cognitive control processes and more basic, emotional processes perhaps by modulating affective and autonomic states (Greicius et al., 2007). This connection and modulation among cognitive, sensory, and emotion cortices supported by meditation may allow for more adaptive, skillful responses to stressful or emotionally salient experiences, providing a neurobehavioral basis for the effectiveness of meditation in attenuating depression, anxiety, and stress, thus building resiliency.

Actively practicing body sensing/interoceptive awareness during the mindfulness exercise is a critical ingredient of the practice that enables recovery from pain. One of the key elements of interoceptive awareness is the sensation of the breath moving into, through, and out of the body. Since exhalation of the breath is associated with parasympathetic activation of the relaxation response, mindfulness practices that use the breath as an element of interoceptive focus may be particularly helpful in attenuating hypothalamic activity associated with hyperfocus, allowing the thalamic gates to reopen and reestablishing somatic processing all at once. To the practitioner, it intuitively makes sense that focusing on the breath enables coping and management of pain. It also allows the healing mechanisms of the brain to engage.

When we pause to consider pain from an evolutionary perspective, it makes sense that pain serves an adaptive function. When there is an injury to the body, the brain should become aware of the injury in order to move the body away from the source of the pain and to coordinate the healing response. By definition, what the brain perceives as an injury must be a "negative" experience, in this case what we refer to as pain. The sensation is *intended to draw our awareness to the sensation.* In this awareness, the CNS (brain) can coordinate the healing mechanisms needed to preserve, restore, and regenerate the injured body. With this neural integration of awareness of the entire physical being, the dynamic activity of healing can occur.

A later evolutionary mastery in the phylogenetic development of the nervous system is the ability to override awareness and ignore pain. This ability to suppress awareness may also have served an adaptive function. Indeed, this is an ability taught in military training and practice. The ability to close the thalamic gates and "good-soldier" through all forms of trauma is a recognized quality of the so-called good soldier. Abandoned in this closed condition, however, the brain's ability to integrate with the periphery of the body and coordinate internal healing mechanisms is blocked. The soldier remains in a hyperfocused state, attending primarily to visual and auditory stimuli and suffering from chronic activation of the HPA axis. The experience is described as one of feeling hypersensitive to sounds and sights and constant or chronic experience of stress and anxiousness. It is also described as a sense of emptiness or numbness of the body (including the heart) and a lack of sensate awareness of the body—an inability to feel, literally. In this state, serious physical and emotional conditions can begin to develop and are left unattended by the brain and related CNS coordination.

Mindfulness is the antidote to this training and can allow the soldier to heal. Moreover, it is a tool that can be used in advance of exposure to trauma to build resilience by training the soldier to stay present to a broader range of sensorial experience. Just as we train soldiers to build muscular strength and capacity, we can use mindfulness exercises to train our soldiers to build mental strength and capacity, reflected in neuroplastic growth in the brain. The field of mindfulness would suggest that the soldier can be trained to stay present to a fuller degree of conscious awareness and, when stressful or traumatic distractions are encountered, to use mindfulness strategies to return to homeostasis and present-moment awareness, thus enhancing resilience and preventing and treating mental health problems in the military.

References

Alim, T. N., Lawson, W. B., Feder, A., Iacoviello, B. M., Saxena, S., Bailey, C. R., Green, A. M., & Neumeister, A. (2012). Resilience to meet the challenge of addiction: Psychobiology and clinical considerations. *Alcohol Research: Current Reviews, 34*(4), 506–515.

Aston-Jones, G., Shipley, M. T., & Grzanna, R. (1995). The locus coeruleus, A5 and A7 noradrenergic cell groups. In G. Paxinos (Ed.), *The rat nervous system* (pp. 183–214). Boca Raton, FL: Academic Press.

Berridge, C. W., & Waterhouse, B. D. (2003). The locus coeruleus-noradrenergic system: Modulation of behavioral state and state-dependent cognitive processes. *Brain Research. Brain Research Reviews, 42*, 33–84.

Bowirrat, A., Chen, T. H., Blum, K., Madigan, M., Bailey, J. A., Chuan Chen, A. L. M. (2010). Neuro-psychopharmacogenetics and neurological antecedents of posttraumatic stress disorder: Unlocking the mysteries of resilience and vulnerability. *Current Neuropharmacology, 8*(4), 335–358.

Bränström, R., Kvillemo, P., & Åkerstedt, T. (2013). Effects of mindfulness training on levels of cortisol in cancer patients. *Psychosomatics: Journal of Consultation and Liaison Psychiatry, 54*(2), 158–164.

Bredemann, T. M., & McMahon, L. L. (2014). 17β Estradiol increases resilience and improves hippocampus synaptic function in helpless ovariectomized rats. *Psychoneuroendocrinology, 42,* 77–88.

Brewer, J. A., Worhunsky, P. D., Gray, J. R., Tang, Y.-Y., Weber, J., & Kober, H. (2011). Meditation experience is associated with differences in default mode network activity and connectivity. *Proceedings of the National Academy of Sciences of the United States of America, 108*(50), 20254–20259.

Carlson, L. E., Speca, M., Patel, K. D., & Goodey, E. (2004). Mindfulness-based stress reduction in relation to quality of life, mood, symptoms of stress and levels of cortisol, dehydroepiandrosterone sulfate (DHEAS) and melatonin in breast and prostate cancer outpatients. *Psychoneuroendocrinology, 29*(4), 448–474.

Castro, J. E., Diessler, S., Varea, E., Márquez, C., Larsen, M. H., Cordero, M. I., & Sandi, C. (2012). Personality traits in rats predict vulnerability and resilience to developing stress-induced depression-like behaviors, HPA axis hyper-reactivity and brain changes in pERK1/2 activity. *Psychoneuroendocrinology, 37*(8), 1209–1223.

Chang, L. J., Yarkoni, T., Khaw, M. W., & Sanfey, A. G. (2013). Decoding the role of the insula in human cognition: Functional parcellation and large-scale reverse inference. *Cerebral Cortex, 23*(3), 739–749.

Charney, D. S. (2004). Psychobiological mechanisms of resilience and vulnerability: Implications for successful adaptation to extreme stress. *American Journal of Psychiatry, 161,* 195–216.

Coutinho, J. F., Fernandesl, S. V., Soares, J. M., Maia, L., Gonçalves, Ó. F., & Sampaio, A. (2016). Default mode network dissociation in depressive and anxiety states. *Brain Imaging and Behavior, 10,* 147–157.

Craig, A. D. (2003). Interoception: The sense of the physiological condition of the body. *Current Opinion in Neurobiology, 13*(4), 500–505.

Craig A. D. (2009). How do you feel—now? The anterior insula and human awareness. *Nature Reviews Neuroscience, 10,* 59–70.

Crescentini, C., & Capurso, V. (2015). Mindfulness meditation and explicit and implicit indicators of personality and self-concept changes. *Frontiers in Psychology, 6,* doi: 10.3389/fpsyg.2015.00044

Critchley, H. D., Wiens, S., Rotshtein, P., Ohman, A., & Dolan, R. J. (2004). Neural systems supporting interoceptive awareness. *Natural Neuroscience 7,* 189–195.

Curiati, J. A., Bocchi, E., Freire, J. O., Arantes, A. C., Braga, M., Garcia, Y., Guimaraes, G., & Fo, W. J. (2005). Meditation reduces sympathetic activation and improves the quality of life in elderly patients with optimally treated heart failure: A prospective randomized study. *Journal of Alternative and Complementary Medicine, 11*(3), 465–472.

Etkin, A., Egner, T., & Kalisch, R. (2011). Emotional processing in anterior cingulate and medial prefrontal cortex. *Trends in Cognitive Sciences, 15*(2), 85–93.

Farb, N. A. S., Segal, Z. V., Mayberg, H., Bean, J., McKeon, D., Fatima, Z., & Anderson, A. K. (2007). Attending to the present: Mindfulness meditation reveals distinct neural modes of self-reference. *Social Cognitive and Affective Neuroscience, 2*(4), 313–322.

Feder, A., Nestler, E. J., & Charney, D. S. (2009). Psychobiology and molecular genetics of resilience. *Nature Reviews Neuroscience, 10*(6), 446–457.

Fox, K. C., Zakarauskas, P., Dixon, M., Ellamil, M., Thompson, E., & Christoff, K. (2012). Meditation experience predicts introspective accuracy. *PLoS ONE, 7*(9), e45370.

Goodyer, I. M. (2006). The hypothalamic-pituitary-adrenal axis: Cortisol, DHEA, and psychopathology. In M. E. Garralda & M. Flament (Eds.), *Working with children and adolescents: An evidence-based approach to risk and resilience* (pp. 45–66). Lanham, MD: Jason Aronson.

Greicius, M. D., Flores, B. H., Menon, V., Glover, G. H., Solvason, H. B., Kenna, H., Reiss, A. L., & Schatzberg, A. F. (2007). Resting-state functional connectivity in major depression: Abnormally increased contributions from subgenual cingulate cortex and thalamus. *Biological Psychiatry, 62*(5), 429–437.

Greicius, M. D., Krasnow, B., Reiss, A. L., & Menon, V. (2003). Functional connectivity in the resting brain: A network analysis of the default mode hypothesis. *Proceedings of the National Academy of Sciences of the United States of America, 100*(1), 253–258.

Hart, J. (2013). Mind-body therapies for treating anxiety. *Alternative and Complementary Therapies, 19*(6), 306–309.

Haase, L., Thom, N. J., Shukla, A., Davenport, P. W., Simmons, A. N., Stanley, E. A., Paulus, M. P., & Johnson, D. C. (2016). Mindfulness-based training attenuates insula response to an aversive interoceptive challenge. *Social Cognitive and Affective Neuroscience, 11*(1), 182–190.

Herman, J. P., Mcklveen, J. M., Ghosal, S., Kopp, B., Wulsin, A., Makinson, R., Scheimann, J., & Myers, B. (2016). Regulation of the hypothalamic-pituitary-adrenocortical stress response. *Comprehensive Physiology, 6*, 603–621.

Hölzel, B. K., Lazar, S. W., Gard, T., Schuman-Olivier, Z., Vago, D. R., & Ott, U. (2011). How does mindfulness meditation work? Proposing mechanisms of action from a conceptual and neural perspective. *Perspectives in Psychological Sciences, 6*(6), 537–559.

Hölzel, B. K., Ott, U., Hempel, H., Hackl, A., Wolf, K., Stark, R., & Vaitl, D. (2007). Differential engagement of anterior cingulate and adjacent medial frontal cortex in adept meditators and non-meditators. *Neuroscience Letters, 421*, 16–21.

Hurley, L. M., Devilbiss, D. M., & Waterhouse, B. D. (2004). A matter of focus: Monoaminergic modulation of stimulus coding in mammalian sensory networks. *Current Opinions in Neurobiology, 14*, 488–495.

Johnson, D. C., Thom, N. J., Stanley, E. A., Haase, L., Simmons, A. N., Shih, P. B., . . . Paulus, M. P. (2014). Modifying resilience mechanisms in at-risk individuals: A controlled study of mindfulness training in marines preparing for deployment. *American Journal of Psychiatry, 171*(8), 844–853.

Joy, S. D. (2014). Meditation for anxiety, depression, and pain. *American Journal of Nursing, 114*(4), 58.

Kasai, K., Yamasue, H., Gilbertson, M. W., Shenton, M. E., Rauch, S. L., & Pitman, R. K. (2008). Evidence for acquired pregenual anterior cingulate gray matter loss from a twin study of combat-related posttraumatic stress disorder. *Biological Psychiatry, 63*, 550–556.

Kim, S. H., Schneider, S. M., Kravitz, L., Mermier, C., & Burge, M. R. (2013). Mind-body practices for posttraumatic stress disorder. *Journal of Investigative Medicine, 61*(5), 827–834.

Krishnakumar, D., Hamblin, M. R., & Lakshmanan, S. (2015). Meditation and yoga can modulate brain mechanisms that affect behavior and anxiety: A modern scientific perspective. *Ancient Science, 2*(1), 13–19.

Krystal, J. H., & Neumeister, A. (2009). Noradrenergic and serotonergic mechanisms in the neurobiology of posttraumatic stress disorder and resilience. *Brain Research, 1293*, 13–23.

Lazar, S. W., Kerr, C. E., Wasserman, R. H., Gray, J. R., Greve, D. N., Treadway, M. T., . . . Fischl, B. (2005). Meditation experience is associated with increased cortical thickness. *Neuroreport, 16*(17), 1893–1897.

Ledesma, J. (2014). Conceptual frameworks and research models on resilience in leadership. *SAGE Open, 4*(3), 1–8.

Mason, M. F., Norton, M. I., Van Horn, J. D., Wegner, D. M., Grafton, S. T., & Macrae, C. N. (2007). Wandering minds: The default network and stimulus-independent thought. *Science* (New York, N.Y.), *315*(5810), 393–395.

Matousek, R. H., Dobkin, P. L. & Pruessner, J. (2010) Cortisol as a marker for improvement in mindfulness-based stress reduction. *Complementary Therapies in Clinical Practice, 16*, 13–19.

Morgan, C. I., Wang, S., Rasmusson, A., Hazlett, G., Anderson, G., & Charney, D. S. (2001). Relationship among plasma cortisol, catecholamines, neuropeptide Y, and human performance during exposure to uncontrollable stress. *Psychosomatic Medicine, 63*(3), 412–422.

Nassif, T. H., Chapman, J. C., Sandbrink, F., Norris, D. O., Soltes, K. L., Reinhard, M. J., & Blackman, M. (2015). Mindfulness meditation and chronic pain management in Iraq and Afghanistan veterans with traumatic brain injury: A pilot study. *Military Behavioral Health, 4*(1), 82–89.

Norris, D. O. (2016). *In the flow: Passion, purpose and the power of mindfulness.* Charleston, SC: CreateSpace Independent Publishing Platform.

Peng, S., Zhuang, Q., Zhang, Y., Zhang, X., Wang, J., & Zhu, J. (2016). Excitatory effect of norepinephrine on neurons in the inferior vestibular nucleus and the underlying receptor mechanism. *Journal of Neuroscience Research, 94*(8), 736–748.

Price, J. L. (1995). Thalamus. In G. Paxinos (Ed.), *The rat nervous system* (pp. 629–648). London: Academic Press.

Raichle, M. E., MacLeod, A. M., Snyder, A. Z., Powers, W. J., Gusnard, D. A., & Shulman, G. L. (2001). A default mode of brain function. *Proceedings of the National Academy of Sciences of the United States of America, 98*(2), 676–682.

Rauch, S. L., Shin, L. M., Segal, E., Pitman, R. K., Carson, M. A., McMullin K., & Makris, N. (2003). Selectively reduced regional cortical volumes in post-traumatic stress disorder. *Neuroreport, 14,* 913–916.

Rees, B. (2011). Overview of outcome data of potential meditation training for soldier resilience. *Military Medicine, 176*(11), 1232–1242.

Richardson, G. E. (2002). The metatheory of resilience and resiliency. *Journal of Clinical Psychology, 58*(3), 307–321.

Russo, S. J., Murrough, J. W., Han, M., Charney, D. S., & Nestler, E. J. (2012). Neurobiology of resilience. *Nature Neuroscience, 15*(11), 1475–1484.

Seligman, M. E. P. (1972). Learned helplessness. Annual Review of Medicine, 23, 407–412.

Sheline, Y. I., Barch, D. M., Price, J. L., Rundle, M. M., Vaishnavi, S. N., Snyder, A. Z., . . . Raichle, M. E. (2009). The default mode network and self-referential processes in depression. *Proceedings of the National Academy of Sciences, 106,* 1942–1947.

Simpson, K. L., Altman, D. W., Wang, L., Kirifides, M. L., Lin, R. C. S., & Waterhouse, B. D. (1997). Lateralization and functional organization of the locus coeruleus projection to the trigeminal somatosensory pathway in rat. *Journal of Comprehensive Neurology, 385,* 135–147.

Simpson, K. L., Waterhouse, B. D., & Lin, R. C. S. (1999). Origin, distribution, and morphology of galaninergic fibers in the rodent trigeminal system. *Journal of Comprehensive Neurology, 411,* 524–534.

Sinha, R., Lacadie, C. M., Constable, R. T., & Seo, D. (2016). Dynamic neural activity during stress signals resilient coping. *Proceedings of the National Academy of Sciences, 113*(31), 8837–8842.

Southwick, S. M., Bonanno, G. A., Masten, A. S., Panter-Brick, C., & Yehuda, R. (2014). Resilience definitions, theory, and challenges: Interdisciplinary perspectives. *European Journal of Psychotraumatology, 5,* 241–245.

Srivastava, M., Talukdar, U., & Lahan, V. (2011). Meditation for the management of adjustment disorder anxiety and depression. *Complementary Therapies in Clinical Practice, 17*(4), 241–245.

Stevens, F. L., Hurley, R. A., & Taber, K. H. (2011). Anterior cingulate cortex: Unique role in cognition and emotion. *The Journal of Neuropsychiatry and Clinical Neurosciences, 23*(2), 121–125.

Thomas, K. H., & Plummer Taylor, S. (2015). Bulletproofing the psyche: Mindfulness interventions in the training environment to improve resilience in the military and veteran communities. *Advances in Social Work, 16*(2), 312–322.

Turakitwanakan, W., Mekseepralard, C., & Busarakumtragul, P. (2013). Effects of mindfulness meditation on serum cortisol of medical students. *Journal of the Medical Association of Thailand = Chotmaihet thangphaet, 96,* S90–S95.

Walker, F. R., Pfingst, K., Carnevali, L., Sgoifo, A., & Nalivaiko, E. (2017). In the search for integrative biomarker of resilience to psychological stress. *Neuroscience & Biobehavioral Reviews, 74*(Pt B), 310–320.

Wang, Y., Xu, W., & Luo, F. (2016). Emotional resilience mediates the relationship between mindfulness and emotion. *Psychological Reports, 118*(3), 725–736.

Wells, R. E., Smitherman, T. A., Seng, E. K., Houle, T. T., & Loder, E. W. (2014). Behavioral and mind/body interventions in headache: Unanswered questions and future research directions. *Headache: The Journal of Head and Face Pain, 54*(6), 1107–1113.

Werner, E. E., & Smith, R. S. (2001). *Journeys from childhood to midlife: Risk, resilience, and recovery.* Ithaca, NY: Cornell University Press.

Woodward, S. H., Kaloupek, D. G., Streeter, C. C., Martinez, C., Schaer, M., & Eliez, S. (2006). Decreased anterior cingulate volume in combat-related PTSD. *Biological Psychiatry, 59,* 582–587.

Yeap, B. B. (2014). Hormonal changes and their impact on cognition and mental health of ageing men. *Maturitas, 79*(2), 227–235.

Point of View—A Shift on the Mat

Laura Westley

A friend invited me to my very first yoga class three years after I left the Army. Sarah and I had known each other at West Point, served together during the Iraq invasion, and were stationed at Fort Rucker, Alabama. She warned me that we were going to something called Bikram yoga, and it would be intense and hot. Since I excelled physically at both West Point and in the Army, she felt it might be right up my alley. She explained that the instructor would lead us through 26 different postures.

How hard can that be?

That confidence was before the stench overtook *all* of my senses. The Oregon studio contained wall-to-wall carpet which absorbed the sweat of every class attendee. The 104-degree temperature served like a crock pot, marinating a unique stew I would classify as "Portlandia Yogi." Then the instructor literally marched front and center in his tiny, barely-bigger-than-Speedos shorts and began to lecture us.

"I will lead you through the 26 poses today," he chimed robotically. "And when you go through the introductory sequence, you need to refrain from drinking water."

What the hell? Not even the Army would suggest the preposterous notion of not consuming water if needed. Our old mantra, "Hydrate or Die!" came to mind as I wondered if I could survive even three minutes of this hot and smelly studio without a swallow of water to cool my throat.

Thankfully, I made it through the dehydrating introduction and proceeded well through the poses. Or at least I thought I was performing well. The instructor called me out more than a few times. "Laura, tilt more to the right." "Laura, stretch your left arm more!"

Afterward, Sarah asked what I thought. I carefully crafted my response before verbalizing it. "Sarah, you're my dear friend, and I've known you for ages. We've been through a lot of shit together, and I say this as a friend who really cares about you."

I could tell she braced for rough criticism as I paused.

"We are not West Point cadets anymore. This class felt like a DPE (Department of Physical Education) hazing. You don't need to be hazed anymore in order to derive physical benefits from exercise!" We both erupted into laughter. "And the guy leading it was such an ass! He reminded me of my Advanced Close Quarters Combat instructor. He belongs at West Point, not in a Portland yoga studio."

"You're so right," she agreed, "but I love being challenged this way."

"Whatever floats your boat, but I will politely decline all future invitations to Bikram," I teased.

Three years later, my chiropractor told me that I needed to start practicing yoga. "You won't need as many adjustments from me if you go to yoga," he promised. I had been receiving consistent chiropractic care since my time in the Army to manage chronic pain originating from injuries and overuse at West Point. I discovered that regular chiropractic adjustments were far more effective than downing the Army's cure-all of 800mg of Ibuprofen that irritated my increasingly sensitive stomach. My chiropractor suggested the studio down the street, Baptiste Power Vinyasa Yoga, and assured me that it had no "militant vibe."

The bubbly instructor introduced herself—Jane—and told us it was her birthday. During some of the poses she cracked jokes and admitted that her birthday was making her extra giddy. I soaked in her personality and nurturing guidance: "Remember, it's all about your unique expression of the pose. Only do what feels right. You can modify anything to suit what works best for you." At the end of class, I was hooked.

Yoga got me through what would become the most tumultuous two years of my life, far worse than war—where I decided to end my marriage and allow everything else to completely unravel. Life could look and feel like hell, but on my yoga mat it was safe, nurturing and supportive. On days when I couldn't take it anymore, sometimes I would rest in "Child's Pose" and weep. Yoga gave me permission to express whatever needed to come pouring out of my body, mind and soul.

Alternative treatments (which I discuss in detail in my memoir, *War Virgin*) have become paramount in my healing—not just physically, but emotionally as well.

Many people claim that metaphysical tools are hoaxes. I was initially a skeptic, until I personally witnessed a dramatic improvement in my happiness and well-being. So whether or not something "actually works," I believe it's still beneficial to meditate and focus upon the healing benefits of any number of methods that promote feeling calm and centered.

Yoga helps bring balance and alignment to my body and has come to feel important, almost mandatory. Gone are the days of half marathons, cross-fit, tearing it up in the gym and not stretching. If I push myself to my physical limits, like I became so accustomed to in the past, my body suffers from inflammation and pain that take days to dissipate. Now I have to pay close attention to the signals my body is sending me, and it's a delicate balance of how I can become stronger and faster without overdoing it. My focus is on the flow of positive energy and doing what I can to ensure that which flows into me is good and healthy.

CHAPTER 4

The Theory and Practice of Training for Resilience

Kate Hendricks Thomas and David L. Albright

Behavioral change theories apply what we know about human psychology, sociology, physiology, and culture to health programming (Hayden, 2009), and any good program designed to help train military personnel in mental fitness needs a theoretical underpinning (Malmin, 2013). Unlike too many of the offerings trying to do this work today, such a training program must follow evidence-based practice, paying attention both to what has worked historically and to cultural competency. This saves well-meaning professionals from misdirecting resources in attempts to "speak military mental fitness" that simply miss the mark (Thomas, Haring, McDaniel, Fletcher, & Albright, 2017).

One commonality that behavioral health models share is a focus on the audience as specific, with any priority population requiring targeted interventions. The personality of the military and veteran subpopulation is unique, and working here, one must be mindful of culture and the warrior ethos that render a focus on assets and resources more useful than one focused on susceptibility or recovery (Malmin, 2013; Thomas et al., 2015).

Resiliency has been most frequently defined as positive adaptation despite adversity, innately occurring in some people, able to be cultivated in others (Heavy Runner & Marshall, 2003). Few theories are more appropriate for working with the military groups than resiliency theory. Resilience can be trained and taught and is useful for both military trauma survivors and individuals training prestressor exposure (Fletcher & Sarkar, 2013). The dialogue surrounding resilience-cultivation is uniquely appealing to veterans (Thomas, Plummer Taylor, Hamner, Glazer, & Kaufman, 2015) and involves identifying the protective personality traits and behaviors that promote growth. Mental fitness training seeks practical ways to encourage accessing such traits (Richardson, 2002).

Original research on resiliency theory came out of the fields of social work and social psychology, but unlike more problem-oriented theories, it came about after inquiry into characteristics demonstrated by survivors of trauma. Researchers began first by asking the question of why some survivors fared better after difficulty than others who experienced the same events (Werner & Smith, 1982). Such studies spent three decades studying children labeled "at-risk." In reality, the stories and backgrounds of these children would break anyone's heart. They came to social workers from abject poverty and abusive homes. Some had parents suffering from mental illness, and others were orphans without relatives or resources to take them in. Early resiliency research teams studied over 700 children to look for common traits in the ones who managed to rise above their "at-risk" status (Werner & Smith, 1982). Rising above simply meant becoming an independent and functional adult, avoiding law enforcement involvement, institutionalization for mental health problems, or substance abuse. Teams discovered that about one-third of those at-risk children were thriving and achieving success in schools, professions, and relationships against all odds (Bernard, 1997). They self-reported high levels of happiness and quality of life, and all displayed key, similar qualities and personality indicators, and researchers codified these as resilient traits. Kids who tested as socially responsible, adaptable, tolerant, and achievement-oriented seemed to thrive, especially if they also had excellent communication skills and high self-esteem (Fleming & Ledogar, 2008). Follow-on studies demonstrated important resilient traits in other countries and populations, with marked similarities in high levels of something called self-efficacy in thriving survivors (Rutter, 1985).

Self-efficacy is the belief that you can accomplish something, and it predicts performance as well as the ability to connect with others. Efficacious people are more likely to engage in preventive behaviors, adhere to desired changes, and view new challenges as eustress rather than distress. Efficacy is built several ways. Mastery experience builds confidence, as past success makes an individual feel like achievement can be repeated. Vicarious experience contributes as well; efficacious people have seen success in action modeled for them. Typically supported people, individuals with high self-efficacy receive verbal persuasion from respected social connections (Garmenzy, 1991; Hayden, 2009).

Interestingly, a person's emotional state also contributes to efficacy. Stress researchers have empirically proven that fear, stress, and anxiety set off hormonal chain reactions in the body that elevate blood cortisol and adrenaline. This response limits upper-level cognition, impairs physiology, and reduces feelings of efficacy (Thomas et al., 2016). A person with high self-efficacy typically knows how to manage his or her stress. Numerous studies validate self-efficacy as a tool to promote positive health behaviors, and cultivating efficacy builds traits that define resilience (Garcia & Petrovich, 2011).

Resiliency has been extensively studied, and key traits make a person more resilient. Most of these traits are related to one's ability to demonstrate self-awareness, adapt, and communicate across difference. Researchers repeatedly found in numbers both practically and statistically significant that the ability to self-correct, demonstrate confidence, and exude sociability helped individuals thrive despite dire circumstances and trauma histories (Bernard, 1997). By 1995, such study had clearly demonstrated a case for the existence of key, identifiable traits that make a person resilient (Richardson, Neiger, Jensen, & Kumpfer, 1990).

Interestingly, these identifiable traits can be developed. Service members can train themselves to be resilient for those times when hardship comes unexpectedly (Thomas & Plummer Taylor, 2015). Controlled pressure followed by specific exercises to de-escalate the body's reaction creates the ability to handle more pressure next time. Cultivation is core to the theory's concept; the resiliency model was developed to highlight the process whereby an individual moves through stages of biopsychospiritual (holistic, whole-person) homeostasis. Simple studies have consistently highlighted the model's central premise that disruption followed by time and self-care aimed at reintegration actually cultivates resilient traits (Rankin, 2002).

Researchers interested in psychological and social determinants of health picked up the concept of resilience and have gradually extended its use from the domain of mental health to health in general. Early work on resilience was concerned with the individual, but more recently, researchers have become interested in resilience as a feature of whole communities (Richardson, 2002). Resilient traits can be taught, but this does not happen in a vacuum. Cultural analysis to ensure applicability of the program concept to the intended participants is vital (Malmin, 2013; Thomas, 2016).

Such cultural consideration defines modern resiliency theory; this third wave builds upon existing ecological theory work in behavioral health fields to consider the multiple layers that impact us as individuals (Whiting, Kendall, & Wills, 2012). Ecological theories explain the way that the push and pull of one's environment yields tremendous influence on choices and behaviors. Third-wave resiliency theory works to apply questions of environment and culture to any study of individual resilient traits, with the goal being more effective cultivation of those traits by focusing on building them within supportive communities invested in doing the same (Richardson, 2002). At the individual level, assets and traits matter and interact with the structural and social resources the environment and community offer. This wave is influenced by postmodern, multidisciplinary efforts to identify motivational forces in individuals, groups, and larger communities while simultaneously analyzing context and group experience.

Resiliency theory as it applies to health behavior change is a powerful paradigm from which to approach research and programming for military personnel and veterans, primarily because it promotes a model of agency and participant control. The military already understands that hard training produces results and stress can forge strength. A confrontation with adversity can lead to a new level of growth, as resilience is something innate that needs only to be properly awakened (Calhoun & Tedeschi, 2014).

Trying to help military veterans using this theory involves asking them to get involved in their own training or healing processes (Thomas & Plummer Taylor, 2015). It actively discourages victim-identities and speaks to warrior culture much differently than the highly stigmatized clinical intervention model does (Libby, Corey, & Desai, 2012). Behavioral health education and prevention professions are in the midst of a philosophical revolution, attempting to build upon negative risk reduction programs driven by the medical model and move toward competency models (Richardson, 2002). This philosophical revolution is also leading to alternate models and approaches in the behavioral sciences toward resilience—certainly psychologically and also spiritual—and individuation (Foley, Albright, & Fletcher, 2016).

Particularly in insular communities like the military, capacity assessments emphasizing positive assets can be powerful (Foran, Adler, McGurk, & Bliese, 2012). Mental health professionals working with resiliency-based programs have suggested that competency and resiliency characteristics offer more protective effect than risk reduction efforts when it comes to depression (Thomas, Turner, et al., 2015). Tested specifically for validity in military communities, programs to help participants build protective traits often emphasize adaptability (Michaud & Thomas, 2015).

Postservice, some individuals are more psychologically resilient when faced with reintegration stresses, but the Department of Defense can help train everyone to that standard. For example, studies of returning Canadian and U.S. soldiers completing their deployment to Iraq demonstrated that high levels of resilient characteristics fully mediated the likelihood of self-reported depressive symptoms (Lee et al., 2013). If soldiers were categorized as having resilient traits, they did not also report mental health issues. The results demonstrated the importance of resilient traits in predicting better mental health in veterans and emphasized the protective nature of conscientiousness, emotional stability, and positive social interactions. The more prominent traits indicating resilience that a soldier held, the better their mental health after returning from combat (Pietrzak, Johnson, Goldstein, Malley, & Southwick, 2009).

The process of psychological reintegration is the ability to learn new skills from a disruptive experience and put life's perspective back in a way that will increase abilities to negotiate life events. This is in some ways related to meaning-making, as individuals cope with adverse life events by reconstructing and transforming the meaning of the event and incorporating this reappraised meaning into their larger self-narrative (Holland, Currier, Neimeyer, 2006; Park & Folkman, 1997). Serving in the military (whether one went to war or remained in garrison) is a significant disruption to life in an era where so few Americans do so. Military personnel are a minority, and during the return to civilian life, they are faced with disruptive stressors socially, professionally, mentally, and emotionally (Friedman, 2006).

To optimally reach veterans struggling with transition requires reaching out to teach resilience well before that transition begins. There is value in learning to manage stress, hardship, and challenge, and buttressing specific areas can operate as behavioral medicine (Hendricks, Turner, & Hunt, 2014). The challenge for health professionals looking to improve military mental fitness lies in shifting the paradigm away from a focus on problems and toward theories and methods of resiliency cultivation and preparation (Libby, Corey, & Desai, 2012).

Both cultural analysis and examination of ecologically focused resiliency theory suggest that military wellness programs must emphasize both assets and agency (Nassif et al., 2016). Three decades of evidence provide us with a roadmap to success—the best method for building resilience is to learn and regularly employ techniques to improve social support and self-regulation (Lehavot, Simpson, Der-Martirosian, Shipherd, & Washington, 2013).

References

Bernard, B. (1997). *Turning it all around for youth: From risk to resilience*. Launceston, Tasmania: Resiliency Associates and Global Learning Communities.

Calhoun, L. G., & Tedeschi, R. G. (2014). *Handbook of posttraumatic growth: Research and practice*. New York, NY: Routledge.

Currier, J. M., Holland, J. M., & Neimeyer, R. A. (2006). Sense-making, grief, and the experience of violent loss: Toward a mediational model. *Death Studies, 30*(5), 403–428.

Fleming, J., & Ledogar R. J. (2008). Resilience, an evolving concept: A review of literature relevant to aboriginal research. *Pimatisiwin: Journal of Aboriginal and Indigenous Community Health, 6*(2), 7–23.

Fletcher, D., & Sarkar, M. (2013). Psychological resilience: A review and critique of definitions, concepts, and theory. *European Psychologist, 18*(1), 12–23.

Foley, P. S., Albright, D. L., & Fletcher, K. L. (2016). Navigating the minefield: A model for integrating religion and spirituality in social work practice with service members and Veterans. *Social Work and Christianity, 43*(3), 73.

Foran, H. M., Adler, A. B., McGurk, D., & Bliese, P. D. (2012). Soldiers' perceptions of resilience training and postdeployment adjustment: Validation of a measure of resilience training content and training process. *Psychological Services, 9*(4), 390–403.

Friedman, M. J. (2006). Posttraumatic stress disorder among military returnees from Afghanistan and Iraq. *American Journal of Psychiatry, 163*(4), 586–593.

Garcia, B., & Petrovich, A. (2011). *Strengthening the DSM: Incorporating resilience and cultural competence.* New York, NY: Springer.

Garmenzy, N. (1991). Resiliency and vulnerability to adverse developmental outcomes associated with poverty. *American Behavioral Scientist, 34,* 416–430.

Hayden, J. (2009). *Introduction to health behavior theory.* Boston, MA: Jones and Bartlett Publishers.

Heavy Runner, I., & Marshall, K. (2003). Miracle survivors: Promoting resilience in Indian students. *Tribal College Journal, 14*(4), 14–18.

Hendricks, K., Turner, L., & Hunt, S. (2014). Integrating yoga into stress-reduction interventions: Application of the health belief model. *Arkansas Journal of Health Promotion, 49,* 55–60.

Lee, J. H., Nam, S. K., Kim, A., Kim, B., Lee, M. Y., & Lee, S. M. (2013). Resilience: A meta-analytic approach. *Journal of Counseling & Development, 91*(3), 269–279.

Lehavot, K., Simpson, T. L., Der-Martirosian, C., Shipherd, J. C., & Washington, D. L. (2013). The role of military social support in understanding the relationship between PTSD, physical health, and healthcare utilization in women veterans. *Journal of Traumatic Stress, 34,* 111–117.

Libby, D., Corey, E., & Desai, R. (2012). Complementary and alternative medicine in VA specialized PTSD treatment programs. *Psychiatric Services, 63*(11), 1134–1136.

Malmin, M. M. (2013). Warrior culture, spirituality, and prayer. *Journal of Religion and Health, 52*(3), 740–758.

Michaud, C., & Thomas, K. H. (2015). Military and veteran community help-seeking behaviors. *Bowen Group Report White Paper, 1*(1), 1–13.

Nassif, T. C., Chapman, J., Sandbrink, F. O., Norris, D. L., Soltes, K. J., Reinhard, M., & Blackman, M. (2016). Mindfulness meditation and chronic pain management in Iraq and Afghanistan veterans with traumatic brain injury: A pilot study. *Military Behavioral Health, 4*(1), 82–89.

Park, C. L., &Folkman, S. (1997). Meaning in the context of stress and coping. *Review of General Psychology, 1*(2), 115.

Pietrzak, R. H., Johnson, D. C., Goldstein, M. B., Malley, J. C., & Southwick, S. M. (2009). Psychological resilience and postdeployment social support protect against traumatic stress and depressive symptoms in soldiers returning from Operations Enduring Freedom and Iraqi Freedom. *Depression and Anxiety, 26*(8), 745–751.

Rankin, L. (2013). *Mind over medicine: Scientific proof you can heal yourself.* Carlsbad, CA: Hay House, Inc.

Richardson, G. (2002). The metatheory of resilience and resiliency. *Journal of Clinical Psychology, 58*(3), 307–321.

Richardson, G., Neiger, B., Jensen, S., & Kumpfer, K. (1990). The resiliency model. *Health Education, 21*(6), 33–39.

Rutter, M. (1985). Resilience in the face of adversity: Protective factors and resistance to psychiatric disorder. *British Journal of Psychiatry, 147,* 598–611.

Thomas, K. H. (2016). Warrior culture. *O Dark Thirty, 4*(2), 47–61.

Thomas, K. H., Albright, D. L., Shields, M. M., Kaufman, E., Michaud, C., Taylor, S., & Hamner, K. (2016). Predictors of depression diagnoses and symptoms in United States female veterans: Results from a national survey and implications for programming. *Journal of Military and Veterans Health, 24*(3), 6.

Thomas, K. H., Haring, E., McDaniel, J., Fletcher, K., & Albright, D. L. (2017). Belonging and support: Women veterans' perceptions of veteran service organizations. *Journal of Veterans Studies, 2*(2), 1–12.

Thomas, K. H., & Plummer Taylor, S. (2015). Bulletproofing the psyche: Mindfulness interventions in the training environment to improve resilience in the military and veteran communities. *Advances in Social Work, 16*(2), 312–322.

Thomas, K. H., Plummer Taylor, S., Hamner, K., Glazer, J., & Kaufman, E. (2015). Multi-site programming offered to promote resilience in military veterans: A process evaluation of the Just Roll With It bootcamps. *Californian Journal of Health Promotion, 13*(2), 15–24.

Thomas, K. H., Turner, L. W., Kaufman, E., Paschal, A., Knowlden, A. P., Birch, D. A., & Leeper, J. (2015). Predictors of depression diagnoses and symptoms in veterans: Results from a national survey. *Military Behavioral Health, 3*(4), 255–265.

Werner, E., & Smith, R. (1982). *Vulnerable but invincible: A longitudinal study of children and youth.* Ithaca, NY: McGraw Hill.

Whiting, L., Kendall, S., & Wills, W. (2012). An asset-based approach: An alternative health promotion strategy. *Community Practitioner, 85*(1), 25–37.

CHAPTER 5

Moral Injury and Resilience in the Military

Joseph M. Currier, Jacob K. Farnsworth, Kent D. Drescher, and Wesley H. McCormick

Serving in the military can promote well-being and resilience via seemingly innumerable pathways. When compared to civilians, military service members typically have opportunities to cultivate close personal relationships, self-confidence, maturity, strength of character, and a sense of purpose in life. However, particularly during periods of wartime, military service can require men and women to cope with stressful and potentially traumatic conditions that might engender a complex array or emotional, social, and spiritual problems. In some cases, these difficulties may entail serious moral challenges that threaten resilience by undermining veterans' values and fundamental sense of humanity.

Introduction to Mr. Jones

Mr. Jones was a 41-year-old Caucasian male who was referred to a Veteran Affairs (VA) medical center posttraumatic stress disorder (PTSD) clinic due to unremitting posttraumatic symptoms related to a war-zone deployment that ended prematurely two years earlier. Per his report, his mother passed away from a drug overdose in early childhood and his father's caregiving role fluctuated between abusive and altogether disconnected. As a result, he was primarily raised in the foster care. Due to an undiagnosed learning disability,

Mr. Jones struggled to progress academically and dropped out of formal schooling before graduating high school. However, prior to deploying in Operation Iraqi Freedom (OIF), Mr. Jones had served with the Army National Guard for two decades and supported himself and two teenage children via a variety of blue-collar jobs. In OIF, Mr. Jones was part of an active-duty unit that suffered major casualties in the early years of the war. Although the initial purpose of Mr. Jones's Guard unit was to provide transportation and other support duties, many unit members directly participated in combat-related activities.

In addition to these contextual factors, Mr. Jones experienced a number of unexpected traumas while deployed. For example, after sleeping on the roof of his vehicle due to lack of secure accommodations, he was violently awoken one morning by shouting in Arabic and held at gunpoint by a local militia faction. Mr. Jones was troubled by the extreme poverty of Iraqi children and his inability to provide them relief. The event that caused Mr. Jones the most distress was when he ran over an Iraqi boy during a convoy when traveling through a region with documented terrorist activity. Although he tried to signal the boy to leave the middle of the road, he upheld orders by not stopping or veering his vehicle away. Following this incident, Mr. Jones was sent home early due to emotional distress, was discharged from the National Guard shortly thereafter, and had been relying on friends to provide housing and food for the past year. While discussing his mental health history and treatment expectations, Mr. Jones reported he had intentionally missed three earlier intake sessions in the PTSD clinic. Asked about reasons for not following through with appointments, Mr. Jones grew agitated and stated intense discomfort about needing to revisit the memory of the Iraqi boy in any substantive depth.

Defining Moral Injury in Military Populations

Moral injury (MI) is an emerging construct that clinicians and researchers utilize to conceptualize cases, such as that of Mr. Jones, in which difficulties extend beyond PTSD and other prominent conditions in military populations (e.g., major depressive disorder [MDD]). When considering prominent models of MI, Litz et al. (2009) defined the construct as a "disruption in an individual's confidence and defined the construct about one's own or others' motivation to behave in a just and ethical manner . . . brought about by perpetrating, failing to prevent, bearing witness to, or learning about acts that transgress deeply held moral beliefs and expectations" (p. 700). Likewise, Drescher et al. (2011) have emphasized the effects of military-related events that are perceived as "inhumane, cruel, depraved, or violent, bringing about pain, suffering, or death to others" (p. 9). Focusing on the role of leadership malpractice, Shay (2014) suggested that MI may occur in cases of "(a) a betrayal of 'what's right'; (b) by someone who holds legitimate authority; (c) in a high stakes situation" (p. 183). As in Mr. Jones's sense of being morally damaged by his role in the incident with the boy, MI models assume (1) that the precipitating event has been appraised as being morally wrong and (2) that the veteran is aware of a painful discrepancy between the immediate meaning of this stressor and cherished aspects of his or her more global meaning system.

MI can be defined in terms of both precipitating events and their emotional, social, and behavioral sequelae. Stress injury focuses on the loss of a sense of physical safety due to being the victim or witness of an event that held the threat of death or serious injury. In contrast, whether through perpetrating a trauma on others, witnessing others commit immoral acts, or being unable to act in congruence with one's beliefs/values, MI emphasizes a fundamental loss of trust and disruption of social bonds. For example, research suggests that potentially morally injurious events (PMIEs) include betrayals by peers, leadership, trusted civilians, acts of extreme violence inflicted on others, incidents involving death/harm to civilians, acts of violence or harm committed within military ranks, inability to prevent suffering or death of others, and ethical dilemmas or moral conflicts (Currier et al., 2015b). Similar to Mr. Jones's risk of dying or being taken captive, morally injured veterans might also encounter life-threatening events that cause anxiety. However, as in the case of the Iraqi boy he ran over, PMIEs are primarily characterized by moral violations, regardless of the presence of fear/life-threat. At present, two psychometrically validated instruments are available to assess levels of engagement in and exposure to MI events: the Moral Injury Questionnaire—Military Version (MIQ-M; Currier et al., 2015a) and Moral Injury Events Scale (MIES; Nash & Litz, 2013). When accounting for exposure to other military traumas, a number of studies have supported the negative mental health impacts of PMIEs (for example reviews, see Farnsworth, Drescher, Nieuwsma, Walser, & Currier, 2014; Jinkerson, 2016; Litz et al., 2009).

Human morality is inherently social in that it focuses on proper conduct with respect to a larger social group. MI expressions can thus be directed at both the self and others. In keeping with existing theoretical/empirical work (e.g., Farnsworth et al., 2014; Jinkerson, 2016; Litz et al., 2009), these warning signs can be manifested in beliefs/attitudes, emotions, and behaviors. Self-directed expressions can include beliefs/attitudes that reflect a sense of low self-worth, being fundamentally flawed, unforgiveable, or unworthy of being loved. In such cases, morally injured individuals might experience pervasive shame and guilt and engage in self-handicapping behaviors that highlight this sense of contempt for self. In contrast, veterans characterized by other-directed MI might present a profound sense of mistrust in other people, authority figures, and social contracts and/or institutions. In addition, they might experience anger and disgust about others' roles in MI events and act out with hostility or aggression toward others. Notably, research suggests that these patterns of expressions are not mutually exclusive and will frequently co-occur with PTSD, MDD, and other commonly diagnosed conditions in military populations (Farnsworth et al., 2014; Jinkerson, 2016; Litz et al., 2009). However, unlike well-validated instruments for PTSD and MDD, there are currently no stand-alone assessments for clinicians and researchers to utilize in gauging MI expressions in their work with veterans and military personnel.

From a diagnostic standpoint, Mr. Jones met the full criteria for PTSD with depressive symptoms. In particular, he reported nightmares related to taking the life of the Iraqi boy most nights and intrusive thoughts and hallucinatory experiences of the boy visiting him during the daytime hours. He avoided connection with most previously meaningful relationships and activities in order to be spared discussing his war-zone experiences, which he found both distressing and confusing. His avoidance, which was aided by heavy daily alcohol use, further contributed to profound feelings of alienation and detachment from the world. Mr. Jones was also struggling with insomnia, feeling "on edge" most of the time, and refraining from losing his temper with friends and loved ones. However, he also reported issues that did not fit neatly into diagnostic categories. For example, Mr. Jones experienced a pervasive sense of shame about his role in taking the Iraqi boy's life, along with self-directed beliefs about being unforgivable and no longer worthy of human connection. He reported a cycle of self-defeating behavior that suggested an intense contempt for himself (e.g., not following through with job interviews). Mr. Jones also disclosed mistrust in authority figures in general and intense anger both toward the officer who ordered him to drive over the Iraqi boy and about perceiving that the U.S. government had betrayed/abandoned him by medically discharging him.

Defining Resilience in Military Populations

Despite the recognized need for preventative interventions to alleviate the burden of trauma exposure in military personnel such as Mr. Jones, the study of trauma has historically focused on pathology. Although this research has yielded important information about symptom patterns such as PTSD and common co-occurring disorders (e.g., MDD), this empirical focus has generated less clarity about the meaning of resilience in the aftermath of trauma. In the *Oxford English Dictionary*, "resilience" is defined as "the activity of rebounding or springing back; to rebound; to recoil," suggesting an ability to return to an original state after being temporarily altered by an external force. Bonanno (2004) defined "resilience" for adults exposed to single-incident traumas as "the ability to maintain relatively stable, healthy levels of psychological and physical functioning . . . as well as capacity for generative experiences and positive emotions" (pp. 20–21). Likewise, the APA Task Force on Promoting Resilience in Response to Terrorism defined "resilience" as "the process of adapting well in the face of adversity, trauma, tragedy, threats or even significant sources of stress." Embracing elements of these definitions, Mancini (2014) suggested that at its core, resilience represents the capacity to adapt to, cope with, and recover from challenging situations. When considering the trauma-related challenges of cases such as Mr. Jones, central to these definitions is the shared recognition that (1) resilience reflects a process of adaptation to challenging circumstances and (2) resilient individuals who are exposed to PMIEs will still experience transient stress reactions that are mild and moderate in degree but not significantly disruptive to their functioning.

Adapting to the Moral Environment of Deployment

Definitions of resilience therefore suggest that a central part of moral resilience for military personnel involves adapting to the context of military deployment. The contexts of military traumas, including PMIEs like Mr. Jones's decision to run over the Iraqi boy, are distinct from other events in a number of important ways that might influence an individual's capacity for resilience. Deployments require social adaptations that typically are not present in nonmilitary traumas. Whereas many traumas take place in relative isolation, military training explicitly focuses on the formation of tight-knit fighting groups by promoting moral beliefs, identities, emotions, and obligations that serve to increase cohesion, thereby promoting the overall combat effectiveness and survival of group members. As a result, service members learn to adapt to the moral context of deployment in a number of ways. Survival of the unit depends crucially on the cooperative functioning of its members, and thus, individual roles and responsibilities are given strong emphasis in order to build trust among their fellow service members. In contrast, the constant possibility of covert attacks or betrayals from civilian-clothed insurgents or civilian sympathizers requires that service members be suspicious of strangers who might serve as lethal threats to the group. As such, deployments can promote a strong sense of moral responsibility to the group while also promoting mistrust of outsiders.

Through their training, service members also adapt to exist within larger organizations where opportunities for moral autonomy and reflection can be quite limited. For example, during deployments, rules of engagement (ROEs) provide restrictions on the use of force. Importantly, these ROEs can range from giving large levels of discretion to the service member to tightly controlling when, or even if, they can use lethal force. Furthermore, during some periods, ROEs might evolve based upon changing field conditions or political climate, forcing service members to adapt to the uncertainty of having leadership dictate whether they will be able to defend themselves in highly dangerous situations. Finally, the perpetual flow of stressors/objectives during deployment means that service members must adapt to being constantly mission-focused, regardless of the events they encounter. For example, just moments after a PMIE like the one Mr. Jones experienced during his convoy, service members can be required to suppress moral reactions and simply "drive on" to complete the mission at hand. This is often accomplished by suppressing natural emotions and becoming mission-focused via distracting oneself entirely with the objectives in front of them.

Such adaptations are beneficial, and even necessary to functioning in an active war zone, but come with potential costs from a moral and/or psychological standpoint. In increasing a sense of individual responsibility and obligation to the larger group, service members might also be placed at risk to overestimate their control over situations that affect the safety and well-being of others, thereby increasing risk of excessive guilt and self-blame should any harm occur. For example, Mr. Jones appraised the situation with the Iraqi boy's death in a manner that led him to blame himself rather than considering the many contextual factors that affected the situation. Conversely, what may begin as suspiciousness regarding strangers may, after repeated attacks and betrayals by civilian-insurgents, evolve into stronger attitudes of cynicism, contempt, and even hatred of both the enemy and their broader culture and ethnic group. In all of these ways, adaptations that are initially useful in the context of war may, if left unchecked, also create risk for greater suffering as the service member transitions into new moral contexts.

The limitations to moral autonomy and self-reflection imposed upon service members might likewise be both protective and potentially maladaptive. Variations in levels of latitude and oversight for ROEs can present a number of moral issues. For instance, in the Vietnam conflict, mission success was sometimes measured in body counts and service members were at times given full discretion to designate their targets. This broad moral autonomy, mixed with the constant threat of death, led some Vietnam veterans to adapt to war by losing touch with prior moral values, resulting in abuses of power that they would later regret in transitioning back into the civilian world. In contrast to a lack of moral guidance, there are also times when restrictions in autonomy can create moral distress. Military efforts to win hearts and minds of native populations of war zones through humanitarian aid can lead service members to feel cynical, resentful, and bitter if those efforts are exploited by members of those same populations.

In keeping with Shay's definition of MI (2014), such cynicism can likewise extend up through the military chain of command if frontline service members perceive that senior officers and politicians are exposing them to risk for professional or political gain. Service members who experience the life-and-death consequences of such seemingly arbitrary or bureaucratic moral indifference might adapt to these betrayals by developing a sense of moral relativism as they lose faith in human morality. In other cases, such as Mr. Jones's sense of anger toward and mistrust of authority figures, service members might develop moral sensitivity due to increased awareness of the moral failings of others and unresolved anger as they continue to experience the long-term consequences of their leadership's decisions. Thus, in the course of adapting to extreme variations in moral autonomy, service members may sometimes engage in moral abuses or develop skeptical or highly sensitive attitudes toward their authority figures or morality in general.

Lastly, the need to create psychological distance between PMIEs and one's moral and emotional reactions also presents an adaptation that is both helpful and potentially problematic. Although some levels of disengagement can be necessary to carry out essential functions during a mission, the repeated use of these psychological coping strategies might lead them to eventually become habitual and nonconscious in their application. When such a process occurs, service members can find it difficult to reconnect with their emotions and moral reactions to an event, even when provided the time to do so.

Finally, along with the numbing of painful moral emotions, psychological distancing also creates the risk of losing touch with other-oriented moral emotions, such as elevation, gratitude, and compassion, that affirm one's sense of resilience in psychologically challenging circumstances. In turn, the absence of these emotions increases the probability that enemy combatants will be dehumanized, further increasing the risk of abusive violence and the development of anger, contempt, and hatred for the enemy's ethnic group and culture.

Adapting to the Moral Environment of Home

Importantly, the adverse effects of these adaptations might not be apparent until the service member returns from deployment and attempts to transition to civilian life. While on deployment, such adaptations can increase combat effectiveness by shielding service members from emotional pain and moral uncertainty that might create hesitation and expose them and their units to additional risk. However, the concept of adaptation is inherently context-sensitive in that it speaks to an organism's ability to exist in a specific context. When that context changes, what was once adaptive may become maladaptive in the new environment. Mr. Jones could not imagine civilian counterparts understanding or accepting his role in the Iraqi boy's death, which led to a deep sense of alienation and emotional detachment with persons who had previously been sources of love and joy in life.

Mismatches between deployment adaptations and a civilian social context can occur when service members encounter a civilian society that has both comparatively lax standards of personal responsibility and high expectations of tolerance and cultural and moral diversity. Namely, the transition from a strict culture of personal honor and responsibility to civilian life may lead service members to view civilians with contempt, further hindering their social reintegration. In other cases, the relative abundance of time provided following deployment can create a space in which service members analyze and reanalyze their own guilt and shame over perceived moral failings. In Mr. Jones's case, the lack of constant distraction that was previously available on deployment left his mind free to repeatedly review the incident with the Iraqi boy and question whether there might have been something else he could have done to save his life.

Furthermore, whereas on deployment service members possibly learned to trust a relatively small subset of comrades and to distrust the local population as potential threats, they are now expected to peacefully coexist with a wide array of strangers with differing political, cultural, and ethnic backgrounds. The psychological distance created between PMIEs and self- and other-directed moral reactions may create challenges at home when service members find it difficult to emotionally connect with experiences of family members. In other cases, avoidance strategies for creating distance from powerful moral emotions and reactions, such as substance use, risk-taking, or aggression, might have significant collateral legal, health, and professional costs to the veterans and their families.

Finally, veterans can struggle to adapt to the civilian moral context due to a disconnection with the U.S. population's general awareness of war-zone morality. The rift between military and civilian populations was highlighted by a recent Pew study that documented that less than one-half of 1 percent of the general U.S. population had served in the armed forces since 9/11 (as cited in Taylor et al., 2011). Because of this separation, veterans like Mr. Jones can feel sharply disconnected from a civilian population that seems to be ignorant of the moral and ethical dilemmas of war. During the Vietnam conflict, this civilian-military divide took on a more adversarial tone as antiwar protesters targeted returning veterans as "monsters" for their involvement in the conflict. Veterans in more recent conflicts who grapple with moral guilt and confusion following PMIEs may feel profoundly misunderstood when they are greeted by a national narrative describing their behavior as heroic.

Promoting Resilience to Moral Injury

The preceding discussion has made two central points regarding resilience with respect to MI. The first is that service members must morally adapt to the context of deployment in order to increase combat effectiveness and improve the chances of survival for themselves and their comrades. The second point is that these same adaptations, though potentially useful for promoting combat effectiveness in the context of the military, might increase service members' risk of engaging in and being detrimentally effected by a PMIE. Resilience to PMIEs can therefore be thought of as a complex process of balancing these adaptations so as to facilitate a service member's transition between both deployment and civilian moral contexts. In so doing, service members need to adapt enough to deployment to survive and function effectively but not so much that they are unable to adapt upon returning home.

As pointed out earlier, resilience does not mean the absence of struggle and pain. Rather, pain provides important feedback to a person regarding his or her relationship to the environment that can promote further adaptation to challenging circumstances. Indeed, as with psychological numbing in deployment, the absence of pain might indicate that an individual has over-adapted to his or her context and is at risk by no longer being sensitive to environmental feedback that indicates something might be emotionally wrong. In a similar way, resilience to PMIEs could require service members to also maintain awareness of painful moral thoughts and emotions as a way to continue navigating and adapting to their social moral contexts, both during and after serving in the military. In fact, as the wars in Iraq and Afghanistan dragged on beyond a decade, one of the lessons learned was the need for the U.S. military to strengthen both its institutional and individual adaptability in such contexts (Defense Science Board, 2011). For example, one of the unofficial mantras of the Marine Corps has long been "improvise, adapt, and overcome." That mantra speaks of flexibility and resourcefulness as an important component of military training. Given the life-and-death nature of military combat and war, failure to adapt successfully can be lethal for the individual service member as well as members of his or her unit.

Psychosocial research has identified several factors that can increase resilience in the face of PMIEs. Not surprisingly, one of these protective factors has been called "adaptive flexibility" (Westphal & Bonanno, 2007). This flexibility entails use of cognitive, emotional, and behavioral flexibility in the face of challenging experiences that might lead to a sense of moral violation. Among psychosocial factors associated with resilience, Southwick and Charney (2012) describe cognitive flexibility as the ability to view adversity in a more positive light. Emotion theorists have suggested that positive adaptation requires the ability to flexibly regulate one's emotions to match the demands of a particular situational context. This ability includes being able to choose to either express or suppress one's emotional reactions depending on immediate contextual need (Westphal, Seivert, & Bonanno, 2010). From a behavioral perspective, having a flexible repertoire of coping strategies is also adaptive in stressful situations that commonly occur in military service (Cheng, 2001).

"Psychological flexibility" is another term utilized to encompass the ability to flexibly engage within these domains. Hayes et al. (1999) define "psychological flexibility" as "the ability to contact the present moment more fully as a conscious human being, and to change or persist in behavior when doing so serves valued ends." Kashdan and Rottenberg (2010) describe psychological flexibility as having three important components: (1) the ability to shift one's thinking or behaviors when one's usual approach to a situation are compromising personal and relational functioning; (2) the ability to balance sometimes competing and important life domains; and (3) a commitment to behaviors that are congruent with core values even in the face of stress and emotional discomfort.

In the case example of MI, Mr. Jones struggled to attend therapeutic appointments designed to improve his mental health condition. When pressed upon this avoidance-based coping, he noted intense emotional distress that would arise when he contemplated discussing his morally injurious event and subsequent cognitive and emotional reactions. Unable to tolerate this distress, he would behaviorally avoid attending therapeutic sessions so as to not experience this emotional discomfort. This lack of psychological flexibility, evidenced by avoidance of situations that might elicit emotional distress, left him unable to move forward and compromised his ability to function adequately in his present life.

With regard to MI, flexibility in philosophical/religious views might also be an asset to resilience. Military combat requires rapid decision making in a high-stakes environment. Wars fought in urban environments, wherein enemy combatants hide and attack in the midst of innocent civilians, intentionally placing them at risk, can create painful moral conflicts for service members. When considering Mr. Jones's MI event, travel on the roads in Iraq was fraught with hazard from roadside bombs and risk of enemy ambush. Vehicle drivers were often instructed not to stop lest the whole convoy be placed at risk of enemy ambush. For vehicle drivers, moral dilemmas were sometimes created when enemy insurgents would force innocent civilians onto the roadway in an attempt to force the convoy to stop. On one hand, Mr. Jones therefore had a moral responsibility to protect the innocent, and on the other hand, he had military commands and moral responsibilities to ensure the safety of multiple vehicles that were following him. The inability to accomplish both objectives created enduring moral pain given the young boy's death. Individuals with the ability to acknowledge their moral pain but simultaneously acknowledge the moral value that was protected by their actions will be more likely to be resilient. Philosophical and religious perspectives able to assimilate such complex challenges without additional moral judgment are likely to aid in resilience.

Research evidence has also accumulated in recent decades indicating that social support is positively (and causally) related to physical and mental health and that such support buffers the health consequences of stress exposure (Thoits, 2011). Thus, it is no surprise that social support is often noted as an important resilience factor (e.g., Southwick & Charney 2012). Entry into military service ushers most service members into a new culture and community with its own unique values, hierarchy, and structure. Basic training begins the integration of the individual into that supportive social system. Small-unit cohesion is a key element of early military training that provides the basis for enduring social support. Both "rule-based" and "values-based" moral and ethical training has been incorporated into military settings to support officers as well as enlisted service members (Rowell, 2013). When moral conflict arises, such training can supply useful guidance for action.

Following stressful missions, units can engage in after-action reviews with key leaders to examine and evaluate their performance, thereby providing lessons learned for future actions. The military chain of command also provides opportunities to receive guidance and support. In such contexts, military chaplains play a unique role in the command structure, in that they have full confidentiality for conversations with service members of all ranks. That confidentiality, as well as the more extensive moral and ethical training they receive, might allow them to engage in helpful conversations with service members who might be otherwise reticent to discuss issues related to PMIEs with other mental health providers. The hierarchical structure of the military ensures that there is a broad range of experience within the ranks. As such, mature leaders whose lives embody military core values can become important exemplars for moral behavior for younger, less experienced service members and can help them navigate morally conflicting events.

Mr. Jones's case illustrates the role that social support can play in maintaining resilience. Having lost his mother, Mr. Jones experienced a relationship with his father that varied between punitive and detached and grew up feeling that no one was in his corner. Upon entering the war-zone environment during OIF, Mr. Jones's unit was attached to another unit that had experienced heavy losses. Entering into this new unit and having to function in combat roles for which he was not prepared left Mr. Jones with a greater sense of disconnection. An after-action review might therefore have provided a broader context for understanding his decision not to stop his vehicle and increased his awareness of ways that this decision had protected members of his unit from potential ambush and injury. Supportive leaders who had been through similar experiences might have helped him to process that event more fully in the field, which might then have promoted resilience in the face of increased psychological distress. Ultimately, the decisions to send him home and later to discharge him from the military significantly reduced the social support available to him. In turn, this lack of support contributed to his intensely painful memories of the event and his resulting behavioral avoidance of reminders of that experience.

Interventions for Moral Injury

Interventions for MI should focus both on preventing the occurrence of PMIEs and on targeting factors that might contribute to the development/maintenance of MI. Within the context of military service, improvements in moral and ethical training for all ranks might prevent the occurrences of PMIEs in some cases. However, going beyond the military community, better community education about the moral challenges of war can potentially provide a better climate for veterans returning from deployments and attempting to reenter their lives and relationships within local communities that might be characterized by differing beliefs/values. In cases where MI occurs, health provider training (including clergy and ministry workers) can better prepare those professionals who may be sought out by veterans when moral repair is needed. Within the mental health fields in particular, there are now a number of innovative therapeutic approaches for the treatment of MI. Expanding the possible avenues for the treatment of MI demonstrates positive movement in the field for cases such as Mr. Jones. Specifically, recent attempts at this worthy goal include adaptive disclosure (AD; Litz, Libowitz, Gray, & Nash, 2015), trauma informed guilt reduction therapy (TrIGR; Norman, Wilkins, Myers, & Allard, 2014), Acceptance Commitment Therapy (ACT) for MI (Nieuwsma et al., 2015), and cognitive processing therapy (CPT; Resick & Schnicke, 1993). We will now briefly summarize each of treatment model.

- Among these emerging treatments, AD has received the most empirical evaluation. AD is a brief (six to eight sessions) cognitive-behavioral intervention that targets PTSD, grief and loss, and/or MI. This treatment was first evaluated in an open trial with 44 active-duty Marines and Navy corpsmen (Gray et al., 2012). Pilot results indicated significant reductions in PTSD symptomatology, depression, and other variables. AD utilizes elements of prolonged exposure therapy incorporated with techniques drawn from other therapeutic traditions (e.g., emotion-focused therapy). A randomized controlled trial of AD has been funded and is currently underway.
- TrIGR is another emerging therapeutic approach with potential to help those with MI (Norman et al., 2014). The approach was developed to help veterans examine trauma-related guilt and to identify and engage with important personal values. The treatment is based on the work of Kubany and Watson (2003) who identified four different types of cognitive errors often present in individuals with trauma-related guilt. TrIGR is a four- to seven-session intervention that thus far has been examined in a small pilot study to evaluate feasibility and acceptability. Results of this study suggested potential reductions in trauma-related guilt and associated distress, thereby warranting further research.

- ACT is a transdiagnostic behavioral approach designed to improve psychological flexibility (Hayes, 2016). ACT uses acceptance and mindfulness techniques, values clarification, and behavioral commitments to assist clients in responding flexibly to life events and making active behavioral choices that live out their highest values. At the core of MI is a values violation either by self or others. Because of this, ACT may be particularly well suited to help individuals identify and begin to live those previously violated values in the present moment. A pilot trial of ACT for MI examining its feasibility and acceptability is currently underway.
- CPT is a cognitive-behavioral treatment recently rolled out in the VA as an evidence-based approach for PTSD (Resick & Schnicke, 1993). This approach focuses on trauma's potential impact on aspects of a veteran's global meaning system and the necessary adjustments that must occur to adaptively reconcile situational meanings with prior beliefs and values. According to Resick and Schnicke, PTSD sufferers can become stuck in the recovery process when the trauma is not readily assimilated or when the event becomes too integrated and there is an overaccommodation of maladaptive global beliefs. In turn, CPT emphasizes a survivor's appraisals of the trauma and "manufactured emotions," such as shame, guilt, and anger, which are generated when higher-order cognitive processes go awry.

Given the severity of Mr. Jones's posttraumatic symptoms, evidence-based therapies that had been disseminated in the VA health care system were discussed, and he opted to participate in CPT. Following a psychoeducational session about a social-cognitive model of PTSD and rationale for the treatment, Mr. Jones completed a narrative exercise aimed at clarifying how the incident with the Iraqi boy had affected his beliefs about self/others with respect to safety, trust, esteem, power/control, and intimacy. In reviewing his stuck points, he was principally struggling with a diminished sense of self-worth and a belief that he was not forgivable and no longer able to make moral decisions. Upon articulating these beliefs, treatment focused on revisiting the MI event via another narrative writing exercise that prompted in-session imaginal exposure activities over the next two sessions. These activities were particularly challenging for Mr. Jones, and he benefited from brief phone calls from the therapist over interim periods for emotional support and problem-solving barriers to completing the narrative exposure portion of CPT. In addition, in spite of the therapist's urging, Mr. Jones increased his alcohol consumption as a way to modulate his distress about revisiting painful emotions/thoughts about the trauma. However, Mr. Jones established and maintained his sobriety as therapeutic tasks shifted into cognitive therapy strategies for systematically revising unhelpful beliefs that were interfering with his capacity for resilience over recent years.

Notwithstanding his open-mindedness and commitment to engaging with the CPT protocol, Mr. Jones indicated clinical levels of PTSD/MDD symptomatology post treatment. In particular, he was quite emotionally reactive when discussing the incident with the Iraqi boy (e.g., crying easily) and still struggled with behavioral avoidance of potentially meaningful relationships/activities and sense of inner emptiness and being morally troubled. Weekly sessions continued with a focus on targeting these concerns. For example, in keeping with emotion-focused exercises in Litz et al.'s (2015) AD, Mr. Jones engaged in imaginal dialogues that facilitated processing of painful self-conscious emotions. On one such occasion, Mr. Jones completed an unfinished business chairing exercise in which he communicated with the Iraqi boy. In so doing, Mr. Jones initially expressed a range of emotions about his state at the time and reasons for following orders, ultimately asking the boy for forgiveness. Upon switching roles to respond to this request from the boy's position, Mr. Jones verbalized compassion and acceptance for their tragic encounter and then went on to share about his own experiences of trauma as a child upon further switching of roles in the dialogue. In so doing, he reported an internal shift from guilt/shame to sadness over this process, which then allowed him to grieve for himself and the boy in an adaptive manner over subsequent weeks. Drawing on other emotion-focused strategies for promoting self-compassion (e.g., self-evaluative spit; Greenberg, 2015), the final sessions supported this adaptive process along with other steps for moral repair and reestablishing meaningful relationships and values.

Conclusion

Mr. Jones's case exemplifies complex issues related to MI and strategies for working through guilt/shame and promoting recovery of a functional meaning system that might guide his social and moral behavior in the civilian world. Just as military service personnel and veterans will do well to cultivate psychological flexibility, therapists similarly need to assume a patient-centered posture in which different treatment approaches might be indicated over the therapeutic process. Health and pastoral professionals working with military populations should be prepared to support morally injured patients along these lines. Particularly as research continues to illuminate effective strategies for preventing PMIEs and treating MI, we will be better prepared to address the moral and ethical challenges of war.

References

Bonanno, G. A. (2004). Loss, trauma, and human resilience: Have we underestimated the human capacity to thrive after extremely aversive events? *American Psychologist, 59,* 20–28. doi:10.1037/0003–066X.59.1.20

Cheng, C. (2001). Assessing coping flexibility in real-life and laboratory settings: A multimethod approach. *Journal of Personality and Social Psychology, 80*, 814–833.

Currier. J. M., Holland, J. M., Drescher, K., & Foy, D. (2015a). Initial psychometric evaluation of the Moral Injury Questionnaire—Military Version. *Clinical Psychology & Psychotherapy, 22*, 54–63.

Currier, J. M., McCormick, W., & Drescher, K. D. (2015b). How do morally injurious events occur? A qualitative analysis of perspectives of Veterans with PTSD. *Traumatology, 21*, 106–116.

Defense Science Board. (2011). Enhancing Adaptability of U.S. Military Forces (pp. 1–296). Washington, DC: Office of the Under Secretary of Defense.

Drescher, K. D., Foy, D. W., Kelly, C., Leshner, A., Schutz, K., & Litz, B. (2011). An exploration of the viability and usefulness of the construct of moral injury in war veterans. *Traumatology, 17*, 8–13. doi:10.1177/1534765610395615

Farnsworth, J. K., Drescher, K. D., Nieuwsma, J. A., Walser, R. B., & Currier, J. M. (2014). The role of moral emotions in military trauma: Implications for the study and treatment of moral injury. *Review of General Psychology, 18*, 249–262.

Gray, M. J., Schorr, Y., Nash, W., Lebowitz, L., Amindon, A., & Litz, B. T. (2012). Adaptive disclosure: An open trial of a novel exposure-based intervention for service members with combat-related psychological stress injuries. *Behavior Therapy, 43*, 407–415.

Greenberg, L. S. (2015). *Emotion-focused therapy: Coaching clients to work through their feelings*, 2nd ed. Washington, DC: American Psychological Association.

Hayes, S. C. (2016). Acceptance and commitment therapy, relational frame theory, and the third wave of behavioral and cognitive therapies—republished article. *Behavior Therapy, 47*(6), 869–885. http://doi.org/10.1016/j.beth.2016.11.006

Hayes, S. C., Strosahl, K., & Wilson, K. G. (1999). *Acceptance and commitment therapy: An experimental approach to behavior change*. New York, NY: Guilford Press.

Jinkerson, J. D. (2016). Defining and assessing moral injury: A syndrome perspective. *Traumatology, 22*, 122–130.

Kashdan, T. B., & Rottenberg, J. (2010). Psychological flexibility as a fundamental aspect of health. *Clinical Psychology Review, 30*(7), 865–878. http://doi.org/10.1016/j.cpr.2010.03.001

Kubany, E. S., & Watson, S. B. (2003). Guilt: Elaboration of a multidimensional model. *The Psychological Record, 53*, 51–90.

Litz, B. T., Lebowitz, L., Gray, M. J., & Nash, W. P. (2015). *Adaptive disclosure: A new treatment for military trauma, loss, and moral injury*. New York, NY: Guilford Press.

Litz, B. T., Stein, N., Delaney, E., Lebowitz, L., Nash, W. P., Silva, C., & Maguen, S. (2009). Moral injury and moral repair in war veterans: A preliminary model and intervention strategy. *Clinical Psychology Review, 29*, 695–706.

Mancini, A. D. (2014). Resilience and other reactions to military deployment: The complex task of identifying distinct adjustment trajectories. *Journal of Clinical Psychiatry, 75*, 956–957. doi: 10.4088/jcp.14com09452

Nash, W. P., Carper, T. L. M., Mills, M. A., Au, T., Goldsmith, A., & Litz, B. T. (2013). Psychometric evaluation of the Moral Injury Events Scale. *Military Medicine, 178*, 646–652.

Nash, W. P., & Litz, B. T. (2013). Moral injury: A mechanism for war-related psychological trauma in military family members. *Clinical Child and Family Psychology Review, 16*, 365–375.

Nieuwsma, J. A., Walser, R. D., Farnsworth, J. K., Drescher, K. D., Meador, K. G., & Nash, W. P. (2015). Possibilities within acceptance and commitment therapy for approaching moral injury. *Current Psychiatry Reviews, 11*, 193–206.

Norman, S. B., Wilkins, K. C., Myers, U. S., & Allard, C. B. (2014). Trauma informed guilt reduction therapy with combat veterans. *Cognitive and Behavioral Practice, 21*(1), 78–88. doi:10.1016/j.cbpra.2013.08.001

Resick, P. A., & Schnicke, M. K. (1993). *Cognitive processing therapy for rape victims: A treatment manual.* Newbury Park, CA: Sage.

Rowell, G. B., IV. (2013, April 2). *Marine Corps values-based ethics training: A recipe to reduce misconduct.* U.S. Army War College. *Washington D.C.*

Shay, J. (2014). Moral injury. *Psychoanalytic Psychology, 31*, 182–191. doi:10.1037/a0036090

Southwick, S. M., & Charney, D. S. (2012). The science of resilience: Implications for the prevention and treatment of depression. *Science, 338*(6103), 79–82. http://doi.org/10.1126/science.1222942

Taylor, P., Morin, R., Parker, K., Cohn, D., Funk, C., & Mokrzycki, M. (2011). The military-civilian gap: War and sacrifice in the post-9/11 era. Retrieved from http://www.pewsocialtrends.org/2011/10/05/war-and-sacrifice-in-the-post-911-era/

Thoits, P. A. (2011). Mechanisms linking social ties and support to physical and mental health. *Journal of Health and Social Behavior, 52*(2), 145–161. http://doi.org/10.1177/0022146510395592

Westphal, M., & Bonanno, G. A. (2007). Posttraumatic growth and resilience to trauma: Different sides of the same coin or different coins? *Applied Psychology, 56*(3), 417–427. http://doi.org/10.1111/j.1464-0597.2007.00298.x

Westphal, M., Seivert, N. H., & Bonanno, G. A. (2010). Expressive flexibility. *Emotion, 10*(1), 92–100. http://doi.org/10.1037/a0018420

PART TWO

Current Mental Fitness Programming for Military- and Veteran-Connected Populations

CHAPTER 6

Department of Defense Resilience Programming

Cate Florenz and Margaret M. Shields

Introduction

Both the academic community and the Department of Defense (DoD) have recognized the toll that military service, including deployments, relocations, family separation, and other stressors, takes on individual service members. Studies in military and academic environments have worked to quantify this toll and to assess existing prevention and intervention efforts (Pietrzak, Johnson, Goldstein, Malley, & Southwick, 2009). Prevention and resilience training are generally considered worthwhile undertakings by DoD, both for the sake of service members' well-being and for cost savings in the military (Vyas et al., 2016). However, there are inconsistencies in the definition of "resilience" and a lack of consistent implementation of prevention programs across military services.

Previous chapters have discussed the clinical case for teaching individuals to regulate their own nervous system. Such somatic practices use a variety of bio-individual techniques but often involve physical movement, attention to breath, or mindfulness protocols (Van der Kolk, 2014). Somatic practices are proven to positively lower stress hormone levels in the bloodstream, increase working memory capacity, and improve heart rate variability (Teng et al., 2013; Vasterling et al., 2006). Such changes are physiological indicators of a psychologically resilient state (Thomas, Turner, et al., 2015). However, not all existing resilience programs emphasize somatic protocols, and some do not incorporate them at all (Thomas & Plummer Taylor, 2015). The programming space, particularly as it relates to rigorous evaluation of training protocols, is diverse in terms of curriculum and semantics. Programs with similar intent use terms like "resilience," "combat stress," and "mental fitness" interchangeably and without a central, codified understanding of core content (Thomas, Plummer Taylor, Hamner, Glazer, & Kaufman, 2015).

While clinical mental health services for returning veterans are well established, programs that address psychological resilience in training environments are in their relative infancy (Weinick et al., 2011). The concept of psychological resilience was developed in the 1970s with a focus on developmental psychology and childhood psychopathology (Bonanno & Mancini, 2008). However, it was not until 2007 that the Defense Centers of Excellence (DCoE) for Psychological Health and Traumatic Brain Injury Resilience Program was created (Meredith, Sherbourne, Gaillot, Hansell, Ritschard, Parker, & Wrenn, 2011). Since this time, psychological resilience programming in the military has evolved into a conglomeration of programs military-wide.

Summary of Current DoD Resilience Programs

The DoD has undertaken considerable efforts in the past decade toward preventing suicide, increasing resilience, and reducing stigma related to mental health treatment. In 2009, the department convened the DoD Task Force on Prevention of Suicide by Members of the Armed Forces under section 733 of the National Defense Authorization Act (Berman et al., 2010). At the recommendation of that task force, the Defense Suicide Prevention Office (DSPO) was established in 2011, within the Office of the Under Secretary of Defense for Personnel and Readiness.

Additionally, the office of Force Resiliency was established to provide policy guidance for DSPO as well as for offices and programs covering sexual assault prevention and response, diversity management, equal opportunity, drug demand reduction, and other personnel risk reduction efforts. While Force Resiliency provides policy guidance for suicide prevention programs, DSPO falls operationally under the DoD Human Resources Activity. The establishment of the Force Resiliency office and its alignment to DSPO indicates recognition on the part of DoD of the importance of resilience. Despite that recognition, large-scale resilience programs have been implemented somewhat unevenly among the military services, and outcome measures of these programs are in most cases not yet available (Meredith et al., 2011).

What Is a Resilience Program?

Although the DoD established DSPO in 2011 and Force Resiliency soon thereafter, the definition of "resilience" remains murky and is often confused with conversations about posttraumatic growth (Thomas et al., 2016). The literature abounds with research citing sets of factors that promote resilience, some of which are listed here:

- Positive command climate (Connor, 2006)
- Cohesion (Rutter, 1985)
- Communication (Longstaff & Yang, 2008)
- Teamwork (Meredith et al., 2011)
- Connectedness (Cacioppo, Reis, & Zautra, 2011)
- Positive thinking (Bartone, 2006)
- Support (Pietrzak et al., 2009)
- Cohesion (Bartone, 2006)
- Collective efficacy (Hardy et al., 2010)
- Realism (Meredith et al., 2011)
- Closeness (Meredith et al., 2011)
- Behavioral control (Meredith et al., 2011)
- Nurturing (Denning, Meisnere, & Warner, 2014)
- Belongingness (Meichenbaum, 2012)
- Physical fitness (Cornum, Matthews, & Seligman, 2011)
- Altruism (Meichenbaum, 2012)

Physical fitness programs, chaplain services, counseling services, and many more could be considered "resilience programs," as they address the factors widely accepted as supporting resilience among service members. It would be a large task to address each military program that supports one or more of the above factors. Instead, for the purpose of this chapter, a "resilience program" is a DoD program specifically developed to support resilience as whole. The summary that follows is not a comprehensive catalog of current programs but rather a summary of service-level and other types of programs, which manifest in different ways in different military units, locations, and delivery methods.

Summary

The following chapter provides a summary of current resilience policy in DoD and programs of each military service, categorized by level (service-wide versus unit-level), and measures of effectiveness, when available. Though religious affiliation is correlated with resilience (Meredith et al., 2011), this chapter will not address military chaplain services' impact and program specifics. Chaplain services' role in resilience is addressed in this anthology's section on spiritual fitness.

DoD Strategy for Suicide Prevention

In December 2015, the Defense Department published its Strategy for Suicide Prevention (U.S. Department of Defense, 2015). The document is said to be aligned with the 13 goals and 60 objectives of the National Strategy for Suicide Prevention, as published by the Department of Health and Human Services, Office of the Surgeon General, in 2012.

The strategy lays out four strategic directions, each with several associated goals, for a total of 13 goals. The four strategic directions are:

1. Health and Empowered Individuals, Families and Communities
2. Clinical and Community Preventive Services
3. Treatment and Support Services
4. Surveillance, Research and Evaluation

Within strategic direction 2, Goal 5 is "Develop, implement, and monitor effective Department of Defense programs that promote resilience, and prevent suicide and related behaviors." The three objectives associated with this goal are:

1. Strengthen the coordination, integration, and evaluation of comprehensive suicide prevention programming across all DoD components.
2. Promote the use of military community-based settings to implement effective programs and educate Military Community members on resilience and preventing suicide and related behaviors.
3. Promote effective, evidence-based interventions to reduce suicidal thoughts and behaviors in Military Community populations with suicide risk.

While this strategy, and particularly the objectives associated with Goal 5, indicates an understanding among Defense Department leaders of the importance of resilience and prevention efforts, it does not go so far as to establish resilience, or mental fitness, training for all personnel, either at the entry level or at periodic intervals. The strategy focuses more on clinical intervention, particularly focusing on at-risk subgroups of the military. While this approach is entirely appropriate, it falls short of establishing DoD-wide prevention efforts in the form of mental fitness, or resilience-focused, training.

Types of Resilience Programs

Defense Department resilience programs fall into two main categories, namely:

- implementation of an integrated social service model, which includes a general scope of the issues faced by both service members as well as family members; and
- implementation of focused resilience training for service members, which are often military service specific.

Integrated Social Service Model

An integrated social service model is a broad concept cultivating the factors in an individual's life that can promote resilience. According to Meredith et al. (2011), this includes the individual at the center with family, unit, and community building that framework from the epicenter to the global picture. This model not only includes the service member but also offers a place to the family members and surrounding community to build a support network. During deployment, the separation can impact the military mission and influence service member retention (Drummet, Coleman, & Cable, 2003), but the experience of separation can also strengthen military couples and families by increasing their resiliency (Wiens & Boss, 2006). The strategies that encompass this include preparedness training for the family, having a "buddy" for the family and the soldier that can create an understanding network, unit-specific support during various "phases of deployment," and reintegration or reunion events (Meredith et al., 2011).

The integrated social service model manifests in the military environment as an effort to (1) understand each service member's wellness as being part of a larger unit, family, and community picture and (2) establish and fortify connections between social services, encouraging social service providers to refer to one another and provide a network of support. In this model, a service member seeking mental health counseling may also be referred to a financial advisor or a service member seeking weight-loss tips to a medical facility. When each service provider views the service member as a whole, he or she can treat and refer the service member to the appropriate services.

Integrated Social Service in the DoD

Total Force Fitness (DoD-wide)

Total Force Fitness is a framework established by the chairman of the Joint Chiefs of Staff in September 2011 (Mullen, 2011). The chairman's directive describes Total Force Fitness (TFF) as "a methodology for understanding, assessing, and maintaining service members' well-being and sustaining their ability to carry out missions." It further states "the TFF framework and its tenets are designed to keep Service members resilient and flourishing in the current environment of sustained deployment and combat operations."

The TFF framework acknowledges eight domains, namely, physical fitness, environmental fitness, medical and dental fitness, nutritional fitness, spiritual fitness, psychological fitness, behavioral fitness, and social fitness. Equally important is the balance the warrior feels surrounding him or her in the environment defined by his or her family, organization, and community (Rounds, 2010).

Despite its recognition of these domains, the TFF framework does not go so far as to establish or require any programming by any service branch. It simply calls for "inclusive, innovative, and preventive" strategies. The respective total fitness programs of the air force, Army, and Navy actually predate TFF, and the establishment of this DoD-wide framework appears simply to serve to validate and codify efforts already being taken in those service branches. Many of these programs work to target the individual while promoting the organization and community levels with the challenge of targeting all of the levels through a holistic approach (Rounds, 2010).

Human Performance Resource Center (DoD-wide)

Force Health Protection is not a new concept to the military. In fact, the program came into fruition in the late 1990s at the end of the Gulf War (U.S. Department of Defense, 1999). This varied from previous efforts, which focused on conventional combat medicine and casualty care to increase the efforts to incorporate family members and social networks (Trump, 2002). As this program evolved, it was recognized for the improvements in communication, health surveillance and risk assessment, health records, biomedical research, and interagency coordination.

Under a DoD initiative for the Force Health Protection and Readiness Program, the Human Performance Resource Center (HPRC) acts as a wheelhouse for a variety of therapies for those in service as well as their families to keep in optimal health or human performance optimization (Human Performance Resource Center, 2016). This sector of the initiative aligns itself under the Force Health Protection and Readiness Program to advocate for holistic health including that of the mind and resilience.

The Family Readiness System (DoD-Wide)

DoD Instruction 1342.22 (2012) provides policy guidance for the Family Readiness System (FRS), the mission of which is to "help Service members and their families manage the challenges of daily living experienced in the unique context of military service" (U.S. Department of Defense, 2012). Among other requirements, the policy states that the FRS shall "link formal and informal networks to promote a sense of community and optimize Service member and family strengths and capacity to demonstrate resilience"

(U.S. Department of Defense, 2012). As with the other frameworks and programs described in this chapter, the FRS policy does not dictate new programming but rather focuses on creating and maintaining networks among existing programs and services, ensuring service members and families have knowledge of and access to the services they need. Services in the FRS include but are not limited to religious or spiritual support, medical services, child and youth services, psychological services, sexual assault prevention and response services, suicide prevention services, and children's educational services (U.S. Department of Defense, 2012). The FRS includes both DoD-sponsored programs, including medical, legal, spiritual, recreational, educational, and other programs, and community resources available to military members. By envisioning the FRS as a network of services and being inclusive of community resources, the DoD has attempted to create an integrated model where support options are virtually limitless. Access to both military and community support can be in-person on or off of a military installation or online or by phone through the DoD-sponsored Military One-Source website and call center.

The Military OneSource program, in addition to being the primary referral mechanism for FRS programs, also offers free counseling for service members and families on nonclinical issues. This counseling is described as "an effective and well-established strategy for finding answers to common emotional and interpersonal difficulties (such as adjustment after a deployment, marital conflicts, stress management, parenting challenges, and coping with a loss)" and "an important first step for many people to prevent problems from developing into more serious issues" (Military One Source, 2016).

Early Programs (Service-Specific)

Early programs were operationalized from a variety of planning group levels. An early example includes *Resilient Airmen* (Gravitt, Long, & Hutchison, 2015) and the Army's BATTLEMIND initiative (Denning et al., 2014) rolled out in 2007 from the Walter Reed Army Institute of Research (WRAIR) Land Combat Study Team to help service members' transition from the "*combat*-zone to the *home*-zone" (WRAIR Land Combat Study Team, 2006). These programs were precursors to more comprehensive service-wide initiatives, outlined next.

Comprehensive Airman Fitness (Air Force)

The air force boasts a mature service-wide resilience program, namely, Comprehensive Airman Fitness (CAF). The program's goal is to build and sustain a thriving and resilient air force community that fosters mental, physical, social, and spiritual fitness (U.S. Air Force, 2014a). With emphasis on well-being and self-care, CAF is described as an integrated framework that encompasses many cross-functional education activities and programs such as mental and physical wellness; social activities; family, peer, and mentor support; and spiritual health (Leslie, 2014).

The CAF model represents a shift in the perception and integration of available resources and programs. In such an integrated social service model, each program and service provider is interconnected with the others, and referrals among programs and providers are meant to ensure each person receives the type of support he or she needs. In this way CAF is not a novel program but a new way of thinking about the connections between existing programs and services.

CAF mandates resilience training for all service members at the entry level (U.S. Air Force, 2014a), calling for "basic foundational training on CAF and resilience principles in accession training for enlisted members and officers. Content will cover basic CAF concepts and resilience skills that are desired for the Total Force." CAF also requires resilience training for all personnel at the base/unit level, at each service member's first duty station, and in all levels of professional military education (U.S. Air Force, 2014a). These trainings are conducted by Master Resilience Trainers (MRT), a cadre of trained resilience professionals.

MRTs complete 10 two-hour courses and return to their respective units to serve by providing unit training, group discussions, and referring airmen to appropriate resources (U.S. Air Force, 2014a). The application of the "train the trainer" model intends to ensure all personnel have access to the CAF network of services through their units' MRTs. Resilience Training Assistants, who undergo shorter three-day training, also serve to support this need at the unit level. The air force recently increased the proportion of MRTs, from one trainer per 1,000 airmen to one trainer per squadron, with the goal of enhancing resilience for all airmen and their families (U.S. Air Force, 2014b).

Comprehensive Soldier and Family Fitness (Army)

Comprehensive Soldier Fitness (CSF) was established in August 2008 and launched in 2009 (Denning et al., 2014) in an effort to increase focus on prevention efforts in a military with frequent deployments and increased stress on service members. CSF resilience training was created to build resilience in soldiers, increasing their ability to cope with adversity, and is based on four main components: master resilience training, comprehensive resilience modules, a global assessment tool (GAT), and institutional resilience training (Denning et al., 2014). GAT is integrated into CSF to assess the psychosocial well-being of the individual based on emotional fitness, social fitness, family fitness, and spiritual fitness (Peterson, Park, & Castro, 2011). This creates an inventory of the individual that is immediately available for evaluation and feedback of needed behavior change through commonly used military vernacular and a safe space of reduced stigma (Peterson et al., 2011). While the reviews of this program vary greatly (Harms, Herian, Krasikova, Vanhove, & Lester, 2013; Smith, 2013; Steenkamp, Nash, & Litz, 2013), one study indicated improvement in emotional fitness and social fitness (Lester, Harms, Herian, Krasikova, & Beal, 2011).

In 2012, the program was renamed Comprehensive Soldier and Family Fitness (CSF2) and modified to include a focus on resilience of the Army family—soldiers, their families, and Army civilians. The three main components of CSF2 are online self-development, training, and metrics and evaluation.

The Army CSF2 program also follows an integrated social service and train-the-trainer model. As in the air force model, Army MRTs complete training and return to share their knowledge, train others, and make referrals for personnel in their units.

According to a 2014 Army Medicine fact sheet, the Army requires one MRT per company, an even smaller ratio than the air force's one per squadron (U.S. Army, 2014). However, it is unclear whether required resilience training has been implemented as part of Army entry-level training or at regular intervals in a soldier's career.

Total Sailor Fitness (Navy)

Like other branches of military, the U.S. Navy has changed the focus of health from the individual to the fleet and family (U.S. Navy, 2016a). The group of N170 programs consists of individual and fleet programs known as Navy Alcohol and Drug Abuse Prevention (NADAP) (N170A), Physical Readiness (N170B), and Family Readiness (N170C) (U.S. Navy, 2016a). As a whole, these programs are known as Total Sailor Fitness (TSF).

As one of the progressive programs used, TSF continues to develop the program for the individual and family, including subprograms like "21 Days of Total Sailor FITmas," which spanned from December 14, 2016, until January 3, 2017, to help sailors and their families tackle the stress and strain of the holidays while following the areas of TSF such as physical, psychological, family, behavioral, and spiritual fitness (U.S. Navy, 2016b).

Naval Center Combat and Operational Stress Control (Navy/Marine Corps)

Established by Navy Medicine as a department of the U.S. Department of the Navy, the Naval Center Combat and Operational Stress Control (NCCOSC) was developed in 2008 after the results of research completed in 2007 by the Departments of Defense and Veteran Affairs (U.S. Navy, 2014).

Different from some of the other branch programs, this was developed by Navy medical personnel to improve the rates of traumatic brain injury and posttraumatic stress disorder (PTSD) in service members of the U.S. Navy and Marine Corps.

The NCCOSC operates on three guiding goals:

- "Create a culture of psychological health to strengthen the ready fighting force;
- Advance the quality and delivery of mental healthcare; and
- Optimize the impact of programs and projects through evaluation and process improvement" (U.S. Navy, 2014).

COSC aids in identifying levels of stress based on a continuum (Denning et al., 2014). This includes those who are "ready" with optimal functional growth and wellness; "reacting" indicating mild stress or impairment that is low risk; "injured" which is higher risk with a persistent distress or impairment that often leaves a mark on the individual; and "ill" indicating those who are clinically diagnosed with life impairment to include PTSD, depression, anxiety, or substance abuse (Denning et al., 2014).

Operational Stress Control and Readiness (Navy/Marine Corps)

The Operational Stress Control and Readiness (OSCAR) program was launched in 2011 to help marine and navy officers train mentors within battalions to aid in peer-led resilience. Peer-led resilience involves Marine-led training to help leaders and medical and religious ministry personnel to identify and address stress-related problems as early as possible (U.S. Marine Corps, 2011a). While this is not a personnel intervention, it is a way to use "trained professional and leadership teams that promote healthy social norms and facilitate access to treatment" (Denning et al., 2014).

Multiple levels of OSCAR certification require varied levels of training. Basic OSCAR team certification requires six hours of training and covers the knowledge, skills, and attitudes that are desired of OSCAR mentors, extenders, and mental health professionals among the battalion. Advanced OSCAR team member certification entails four days of training, which prepares the basic OSCAR-certified member to be able to teach the material upon qualification. OSCAR trainer certification entails five days of master instruction with further role-playing, simulated discussions, and supervised hands-on training with a unit. OSCAR master trainer certification is conducted by COSC and requires seven days of training. This allows the trainer to train others (U.S. Marine Corps, 2011a). Each of these levels includes and builds on the last level of training.

DSTRESS (Marine Corps)

The relatively new, established in 2011, Marine Corps DSTRESS call center offers a proactive coaching approach to active-duty, retired, reserve, and veteran Marines as well as their family members (U.S. Marine Corps, 2011b). The "DSTRESS Line's goal is to help callers improve total fitness and develop the necessary skills required to cope with the widely-varying challenges of life in the Corps" (U.S. Marine Corps, 2016). In recognition of the unique culture of the Marine Corps, the call center is staffed with "veteran Marines, Fleet Marine Force Navy Corpsmen who were previously attached to the Marine Corps, Marine spouses and other family members, and licensed behavioral health counselors specifically trained in Marine Corps culture."

Discussion

Barriers

A 2011 RAND study reported that the most commonly cited barrier to resilience program implementation was gaining buy-in from military commanders (Meredith et al., 2011). Other barriers included problems with logistics, limited funding, poor fit within the military, and mental health stigma. Together these factors make clear that programs that support psychological resilience must be enthusiastically supported at the highest levels in order to ensure leadership support and appropriate funds and resources and generally ensure the programs are a priority rather than ancillary, optional, or unnecessary additions.

Assessment of DoD Suicide Prevention Processes

The Office of the DoD Inspector General conducted a review, beginning in November 2014, and published a report in September 2015, titled "Assessment of DoD Suicide Prevention Processes." The report cites a lack of clear governance for suicide prevention and lack of clear processes for planning, implementation, and measurement of suicide prevention programs (U.S. Department of Defense, 2015).

The lack of clear governance is also demonstrated in this chapter: each military service offers several resilience-related models, frameworks, and/or programs, but the name and relative scope of each one varies, and the lines of demarcation between programs are murky at best. Where does BATTLEMIND end and CSF2 begin? How does DSTRESS fit into OSCAR? How does the office of Force Resiliency provide oversight to DSPO when it is not in the same chain of command?

Despite this lack of consistency in governance and implementation, it is clear that considerable strides have been taken by DoD to implement resilience programming. What is less clear is the effectiveness of those efforts.

Effectiveness

Formal evaluation of program effectiveness varies, yet several studies show promising indications that resilience programming can reduce incidences of PTSD and health care costs.

The Army conducts research through an Army research evaluation team, internal inspections of CSF2 implementation, and Army-wide resilience training unit status reporting requirements. Recent reports indicate that "soldiers who received MRT-led resilience training reported higher levels of resilience and psychological health over time than [those] who did not receive the training. Units that received [the training] at the company level had 60 percent fewer diagnoses of drug [and] alcohol abuse and 13 percent fewer diagnoses of anxiety, depression, [and PTSD]," compared with units that did not receive the training at the company level (Harms et al., 2013).

The costs of war include not only the amount of treasure spent and blood spilled but also the invisible wounds with which service members and their families endure (Vyas et al., 2016; Xenakis, Seamone, & Thomas, in press). Prevention improves mission readiness and protects against expensive personnel loss (Vyas et al., 2016). There is an identifiable cost-benefit to considering the use of an integrated social services model and peer-to-peer education as described in previously stated programs. Continued improvement would allow the DoD to be able to create sustainable systems to aid the development of the holistic resilient service member (Fiksel, 2003).

Conclusion

The DoD openly recognizes the importance of resilience in long-term wellness for service members and their families. The stressors of military service, regardless of whether one deploys into combat (Denning et al., 2014), are potentially severe, and resilience skills can aid resistance to and recovery from these stressors (Vyas et al., 2016). Several DoD-wide and military service-wide frameworks have been implemented to encourage "total fitness" and resilience, but they appear to be inconsistently implemented. These frameworks build upon an integrated service model, tying together existing physical, mental, spiritual, emotional, and other services to build resilience in the military community.

The air force appears to be the only military service with required resilience training for all personnel at the entry level and at other intervals, while the other services have adopted a "train-the-trainer" model, relying on MRTs to reach troops at all levels through their unit resilience programs.

The updating, re-issuance, and renaming of programs and policies in the DoD make it difficult to acquire a full picture of current resilience programs. Generally, it appears the support for resilience programming at the highest leadership levels in DoD is strong, but whether that support has been sufficient to reduce stigma at lower levels is unknown. Also largely unknown is the effectiveness of current programming, an issue DoD is working to correct (Denning et al., 2014).

References

Bartone, P. T. (2006). Resilience under military operational stress: Can leaders influence hardiness? *Military Psychology, 18*(S), S131.

Berman, A., Bradley, J., Carroll, B., Certain, R. G., Gabrelcik, J. C., Green, R., . . . McKeon, R. (2010). The challenge and the promise: Strengthening the force, preventing suicide and saving lives. Department of Defense Task Force on the Prevention of Suicide by Members of the Armed Forces.

Bonanno, G. A., & Mancini, A. D. (2008). The human capacity to thrive in the face of potential trauma. *Pediatrics, 121*(2), 369–375.

Cacioppo, J. T., Reis, H. T., & Zautra, A. J. (2011). Social resilience: The value of social fitness with an application to the military. *American Psychologist, 66*(1), 43.

Connor, K. M. (2006). Assessment of resilience in the aftermath of trauma. *Journal of Clinical Psychiatry, 67*(2), 46–49.

Cornum, R., Matthews, M. D., & Seligman, M. E. (2011). Comprehensive soldier fitness: Building resilience in a challenging institutional context. *American Psychologist, 66*(1), 4.

Denning, L. A., Meisnere, M., & Warner, K. E. (Eds.). (2014). *Preventing psychological disorders in service members and their families: An assessment of programs*. Washington, DC: National Academies Press.

Drummet, A. R., Coleman, M., & Cable, S. (2003). Military families under stress: Implications for family life education. *Family Relations, 52*(3), 279–287.

Fiksel, J. (2003). Designing resilient, sustainable systems. *Environmental Science & Technology, 37*(23), 5330–5339.

Gravitt, C. G., Long, G., & Hutchison, H. L. (2015). *Resilient airmen: Pacific Air Forces' critical enabler*. Montgomery, AL: Air University, Maxwell AFB, Alabama, Air Force Research Institute.

Hardy, L., Arthur, C. A., Jones, G., Shariff, A., Munnoch, K., Isaacs, I., & Allsopp, A. J. (2010). The relationship between transformational leadership behaviors, psychological, and training outcomes in elite military recruits. *The Leadership Quarterly, 21*(1), 20–32.

Harms, P. D., Herian, M. N., Krasikova, D. V., Vanhove, A., & Lester, P. B. (2013). *The Comprehensive Soldier and Family Fitness Program evaluation report #4: Evaluation of resilience training and mental and behavioral health outcomes.* Washington, DC: Department of Defense.

Human Performance Resource Center. (2016). About HPRC. Retrieved from http://hprc-online.org/about-us/about-hprc#about-us

Leslie, S. C. (2014). Comprehensive Airman Fitness: A lifestyle and culture. Retrieved from http://www.af.mil/News/Article-Display/Article/494434/comprehensive-airman-fitness-a-lifestyle-and-culture/

Lester, P. B., Harms, P. D., Herian, M. N., Krasikova, D. V., & Beal, S. J. (2011). *The Comprehensive Soldier Fitness program evaluation. Report 3: Longitudinal analysis of the impact of Master Resilience Training on self-reported resilience and psychological health data.* TKC Global Solutions LLC, Anchorage, Alaska.

Longstaff, P. H., & Yang, S. U. (2008). Communication management and trust: Their role in building resilience to "surprises" such as natural disasters, pandemic flu, and terrorism. *Ecology and Society, 13*(1), 3.

Meichenbaum, D. (2012). *Roadmap to resilience: A guide for military, trauma victims and their families.* Carmarthen, UK: Crown House Publishing Ltd.

Meredith, L. S., Sherbourne, C. D., & Gaillot, S. J., Hansell, L., Ritschard, H. V., Parker, A. M. & Wrenn, G. (2011). Promoting psychological resilience in the US military. *Rand Health Quarterly, 1*(2), 2.

Military Life: The Psychology of Serving in Peace and Combat Thomas W. Britt, ed., Amy B. Adler, ed., Carl Andrew Castro, ed.

Military One Source. (2016). Understanding Confidential Non-medical Counseling for Service Members and Their Families. Retrieved from http://militaryonesource.mil/confidential-help/non-medical-counseling?content_id=282398

Mullen, M. G. (2011). *Chairman's Total Force Fitness Framework* (CJCSI 3405.01). Washington, DC: U.S. Government Printing Office.

Peterson, C., Park, N., & Castro, C. A. (2011). Assessment for the US Army Comprehensive Soldier Fitness program: The Global Assessment Tool. *American Psychologist, 66*(1), 10.

Pietrzak, R. H., Johnson, D. C., Goldstein, M. B., Malley, J. C., & Southwick, S. M. (2009). Psychological resilience and postdeployment social support protect against traumatic stress and depressive symptoms in soldiers returning from Operations Enduring Freedom and Iraqi Freedom. *Depression and Anxiety, 26*(8), 745–751.

Rounds, M. (2010). The principal challenge of realizing total force fitness: Changing our readiness culture. *Military Medicine, 175*(8S), 124–126.

Rutter, M. (1985). Resilience in the face of adversity: Protective factors and resistance to psychiatric disorder. *The British Journal of Psychiatry, 147*(6), 598–611.

Smith, S. L. (2013). Could Comprehensive Soldier Fitness have iatrogenic consequences? A commentary. *The Journal of Behavioral Health Services & Research, 40*(2), 242–246.

Steenkamp, M. M., Nash, W. P., & Litz, B. T. (2013). Post-traumatic stress disorder: Review of the Comprehensive Soldier Fitness program. *American Journal of Preventive Medicine, 44*(5), 507–512.

Teng, E., Hiatt, E., Mcclair, V., Kunik, M., Stanley, M., & Frueh, B. (2013). Efficacy of posttraumatic stress disorder treatment for comorbid panic disorder: A critical review and future directions for treatment research. *Clinical Psychology: Science and Practice, 20*(3), 268–284.

Thomas, K. H., Albright, D., Shields, M., Kaufman, E., Michaud, C., Plummer Taylor, S., & Hamner, K. (2016). Predictors of depression diagnoses and symptoms in United States female veterans: Results from a national survey and implications for programming. *Journal of Military and Veterans' Health, 24*(3), 6–17.

Thomas, K. H., & Plummer Taylor, S. (2015). Bulletproofing the psyche: Mindfulness interventions in the training environment to improve resilience in the military and veteran communities. *Advances in Social Work, 16*(2), 312–322.

Thomas, K. H., Plummer Taylor, S., Hamner, K., Glazer, J., & Kaufman, E. (2015). Multi-site programming offered to promote resilience in military veterans: A process evaluation of the Just Roll With it Bootcamps. *Californian Journal of Health Promotion, 13*(2), 15–24.

Thomas, K. H., Turner, L. W., Kaufman, E., Paschal, A., Knowlden, A. P., Birch, D. A., & Leeper, J. (2015). Predictors of depression diagnoses and symptoms in veterans: Results from a national survey. *Military Behavioral Health, 3*(4), 255–265.

Trump, D. H. (2002). Force health protection: 10 years of lessons learned by the Department of Defense. *Military Medicine, 167*(3), 179.

U.S. Air Force. (2014a). Comprehensive Airman Fitness (CAF). *Air Force Instruction 90–506*.

U.S. Air Force. (2014b). Comprehensive Airman Fitness: A Lifestyle and Culture. Retrieved from http://www.af.mil/News/ArticleDisplay/tabid/223/Article/494434/comprehensive-airman-fitness-a-lifestyle-and-culture.aspx

U.S. Army. (2014). CSF2 Information Sheet. Retrieved from http://armymedicine.mil/Documents/CSF2InfoSheet-Mar2014.pdf

U.S. Department of Defense. (1999). Force Health Protection: Health and Fit Force, Casualty Prevention, Casualty Care and Management. Washington DC: Medical Readiness Division.

U.S. Department of Defense. (2012). Military Family Readiness. Retrieved from http://www.dtic.mil/whs/directives/corres/pdf/134222p.pdf

U.S. Department of Defense. (2015). Department of Defense Strategy for Suicide Prevention. Retrieved from http://www.dspo.mil/Portals/113/Documents/TAB%20B%20-%20DSSP_FINAL%20USD%20PR%20SIGNED.PDF

U.S. Marine Corps. (2011a). Operational Stress Control and Readiness Training Guidance. Retrieved from http://www.marines.mil/News/Messages/Messages-Display/Article/887900/operational-stress-control-and-readiness-training-guidance/

U.S. Marine Corps. (2011b). New DSTRESS Hotline Offers Confidential Counseling. Retrieved from http://www.pendleton.marines.mil/News/News-Article-Display/Article/537321/new-dstress-hotline-offers-confidential-counseling/

U.S. Marine Corps. (2016). DSTRESS Line. Retrieved from http://www.usmc-mccs.org/services/support/dstress-line/

U.S. Navy. (2014). Naval Center Combat and Operational Stress Control. Retrieved from http://www.med.navy.mil/sites/nmcsd/nccosc/Documents/nccosc-strategic-plan-2015.pdf

U.S. Navy. (2016a). Total Sailor Fitness (OPNAV N170). Retrieved from http://www.public.navy.mil/bupers-npc/support/21st_Century_Sailor/readiness/Pages/default.aspx

U.S. Navy. (2016b). Every Sailor, Every Day. Retrieved from http://www.public.navy.mil/bupers-npc/support/21st_Century_Sailor/suicide_prevention/spmonth/Pages/default.aspx

Van der Kolk, B. A. (2014). *The body keeps score: Brain, mind, and body in the healing of trauma*. New York, NY: Penguin.

Vasterling, J. J., Proctor, S. P., Amoroso, P., Kane, R., Heeren, T., & White, R. F. (2006). Neuropsychological outcomes of army personnel following deployment to the Iraq war. *Journal of the American Medical Association, 296*(5), 519–529.

Vyas, K. J., Fesperman, S. F., Nebeker, B. J., Gerard, S. K., Boyd, N. D., Delaney, E. M., . . . & Johnston, S. L. (2016). Preventing PTSD and depression and reducing health care costs in the military: A call for building resilience among service members. *Military Medicine, 181*(10), 1240–1247.

Weinick, R. M., Beckjord, E. B., Farmer, C. M., Martin, L. T., Gillen, E. M., Acosta, J. D., . . . Helmus, T. C. (2011). *Programs addressing psychological health and traumatic brain injury among US military servicemembers and their families*. RAND Corporation, Santa Monica, California, Center for Military Health Policy Research.

Wiens, T. W., & Boss, P. (2006). Maintaining family resiliency before, during, and after military separation. In C. A. Castro, A. B. Adler, & T. W. Britt (Eds.), *Military life: The psychology of serving in peace and combat* (pp. 13–38). Westport, CT: Praeger Security International.

WRAIR Land Combat Study Team. (2006). BATTLEMIND Training I: Transitioning from Combat to home. Retrieved from http://www.ptsd.ne.gov/pdfs/WRAIR-battlemind-training-Brochure.pdf

Point of View—Fostering Veteran-Student Health through Stress Management: Creating Belonging and Success in a College Setting through the Veterans at Ease Program

Robin Carnes and Stephen Kaplan

"I want to say that I am happy and I do not know the last time I was happy for no reason." We heard these words uttered by a Manhattan College student veteran on the last full day of a retreat run by Warriors at Ease at the Sivananda Ashram and Yoga Retreat in the Bahamas. At that moment, we knew this project was special.

Addressing the Unique Needs of Student Veterans

The challenges of returning to civilian/academic life can be made even more difficult by a dis-regulated nervous system that causes symptoms including insomnia, anxiety, depression, chronic pain, difficulty focusing, and mood swings (Church, 2009) and a loss of the intense, intimate, and (sometimes literally) life-saving relational bonds that are a key part of the military experience (Ritchie, 2008). The Veterans at Ease Program at Manhattan College is designed to address these underlying somatic and community concerns in order to make these student veterans' transition to civilian life more successful by enhancing their academic career.

Manhattan College (MC) is located in the northwest corner of the Bronx (NY) and is primarily an undergraduate institution. Committed to student veteran outreach, MC invites all incoming veteran-students to enroll in two special sections of a required first-year course.

Warriors at Ease (WAE) was founded in 2008 with the mission to bring the healing power of yoga and meditation to military communities around the world, especially those affected by combat stress, PostTraumatic Stress Disorder (PTSD), and trauma (Ritchie, 2015). WAE founders, faculty and teachers take every opportunity to educate the military-connected community about the growing body of research highlighting the physical and mental health benefits of yoga and meditation (Khalsa, Cohen, McCall, & Telles, 2016).

Intended Goals and Program Curriculum

As implied in our stated partnership, our overarching goal is the successful integration of veteran-students into academic life and their successful completion of college. As we believe that this success is concomitant with lowering the levels of stress that individuals encounter in their transition from military to civilian life, learning to manage one's stress and the reduction of stress is an immediate goal of our program. Our program is also intended to provide a variety of platforms for veteran-students to bond with each other, which we believe provides valuable support structures emotionally and academically (Whiteman, Barry, Mroczek, & MacDermid Wadsworth, 2013). The retreat program and the on-going campus classes by Warriors at Ease are clearly demarcated events in which veterans have an opportunity to form and develop friendships. In particular, the retreat, in which the group spends 4.5 days together, provides a variety of venues for bonding. Yoga classes followed by didactic and experiential Warriors at Ease program sessions provide veterans six hours a day of shared experiences. In addition, the retreat offers opportunities for the group to relax together in a beautiful tropical venue only feet from a very inviting crystal blue ocean and to enjoy each other's company during meals either on the ashram grounds or in Nassau.

One of the cornerstones of the Warriors at Ease program is iRest® Meditation. This is an evidence-based, 10-stage guided protocol that helps activate the Relaxation Response. Developed by a psychologist and yogic scholar, Dr. Richard Miller, iRest® is very easy to learn and uses everyday, completely secular language. WAE gives iRest ® recordings to students to support their daily practice after the retreat.

The conceptual information WAE faculty present to students is tailored to be as practical, pertinent and personal as possible, avoiding formal PowerPoint and mandates. The real power of the curriculum lies in its emphasis on noticing and trusting individual-level experience of the practices. WAE offers the vets a wide variety of mindful physical movements, breath practices and meditation exercises. We approach each one as an experiment, always encouraging the vets to notice and articulate in the moment how a particular practice is affecting his/her own level of anxiety, clear headedness, pain level, and sense of wellbeing. It is this non-judgmental orientation to personal experience in the moment that gradually builds a powerful sense of agency—"I can notice what I'm feeling. I can respond to myself with care. I can shift my experience, recognize I have choices, and feel better, whether or not the outside circumstances of my life change."

To support participants in their daily lives back at school and work, we give them many resources as take aways: a variety of written, audio and video practices and individualized plans for self-care and a buddy system to help keep them accountable.

In addition, Manhattan College offers two Warriors at Ease classes held on campus every semester. These classes, open to all the veterans at Manhattan College, are a way to refresh and reinforce the lessons of the retreat, strengthen relationships, and include vets who are not able to attend the retreat in the program.

Unexpected Developments

After the third retreat was completed, several veteran participants offered a panel discussion program on Veterans at Ease to the campus at large. Over a hundred people came and listened to the veterans describe their military lives, and the difficult transition to being a civilian and a student. Further, the vets shared how the yoga and meditation practices they learned are supporting them in meeting their challenges. The event was an unqualified success. The vets felt good about being seen by the college community as the strong, capable people they are and for possessing and utilizing stress management skills that were the envy of their peers.

Following the panel discussion, WAE was asked to deliver a mini version of the retreat stress management skills workshop to transfer students (about 10% of whom are veterans) during their orientation to MC. WAE trained 10 MC veterans as assistant workshop leaders in a one day Train-the-Trainer. The vets gave their time, unpaid, to refresh their own skills and to give back what had been so useful to them. In August 2016, WAE presented a 3-hour Stress Management Skills for College Students workshop to 160 transfer students focusing on nervous system basics and evidence-based yoga and meditation practices. The veterans coached small groups of these new students in learning several breathing practices and physical movements and "guarded" while the students did their first guided meditation.

The Manhattan College Veterans at Ease program has witnessed student veterans starting college struggling with a myriad of intense challenges in their transition from military service to civilian life. In classes and on campus, they found it hard to relate to the experiences, interests and concerns of civilian students. Veterans coped the best they could with the transition and with any baggage of their military service. However, some have lost their clarity of purpose, professional structure, and the close, almost-familial bonds that they shared with other service members. A number have felt marginalized, somewhat lost, unseen, and alone—on campus and in their lives.

Then Manhattan College offered them a chance to get away to a beautiful place, address their stress levels, and hang out with one another, at no cost. On retreat, they found that they were seen and embraced fully for who they are; strong, capable, adults, and leaders with wisdom beyond their years. They understood for the first time the neurobiology of their physical and psychological responses to stress and that they could learn new, more functional, patterns of response by using the simple, practical tools presented on the retreat (Kaplan, 2009). They formed friendships, played and explored the workings of their minds and bodies in a curious non-judgmental environment.

Back on campus, they now have deeper relationships with their fellow vets and with the faculty that shared the retreat experience. The campus Valor Club (for veterans only) has grown and offers more opportunities to be together and support one another. There are Veterans at Ease yoga classes to refresh their skills.

Then the veterans stepped into expert leadership roles on campus. They started doing what veterans do—serve others. They offered a panel discussion on what it is like to be a student vet and how the Veterans at Ease program has supported them. Over 100 students and faculty turn out and everyone is impressed with the veterans' powerful stories. Civilian student and faculty want a taste of the grounded strength that the vets embody. At the workshop for transfer students, the vets demonstrate and coach groups of incoming students in evidence-based yoga and meditation skills that they use themselves.

The Veterans at Ease program has facilitated the shift whereby some Manhattan veteran-students who have felt marginalized in the past have become expert leaders on campus—grounded, empowered individuals who are academically successful and ready to give back, yet again.

References

Church, T. E. (2009). Returning veterans on campus with war related injuries and the long road back home. *Journal of Postsecondary Education and Disability, 22*(1), 43–52.

Kaplan, S. (2009). Grasping at ontological straws: Overcoming reductionism in the Advaita Vedānta-Neuroscience dialogue. *Journal of the American Academy of Religion, 77,* 238–274.

Khalsa, S., Cohen, L., McCall, T., & Telles, S. (2016). *The principles and practices of yoga in healthcare.* Edinburgh, Scotland: Handspring Publishing.

Ritchie, E. (2008). Military personnel. In *The encyclopedia of psychological trauma* (pp. 428–430). Hoboken, NJ: John Wiley & Sons, Inc.

Ritchie, E. C. (Ed.). (2015). *Posttraumatic stress disorder and related diseases in combat veterans.* New York, NY: Springer International Publishing.

Whiteman, S. D., Barry, A. E., Mroczek, D. K., & MacDermid Wadsworth, S. (2013). The development and implications of peer emotional support for student service members/veterans and civilian college students. *Journal of Counseling Psychology, 60*(2), 265.

CHAPTER 7

Mental Fitness and Military Veteran Women

Kelli Godfrey, Justin T. McDaniel, Lydia Davey, Sarah Plummer Taylor, and Christine Isana Garcia

Women constitute approximately 15 percent of the armed services and represent a growing segment of the veteran population (Thomas et al., 2016). They are more likely than their male counterparts to report mental health concerns like posttraumatic stress, depression, and suicidal thoughts (Ramsey et al., 2017). Younger women service members and veterans aged 18 to 34 are three times more likely to die from suicide than their civilian counterparts (Beder, 2016). To improve health outcomes for military women, programs grounded in evidence-based psychosocial education and mindfulness-based practices allow providers to address issues unique to women veterans seeking mental health support following military service (Saltzman et al., 2011).

Sources of Stress and Trauma

While the experiences of war can have lifelong impacts on all military service members (Hoge et al., 2008), women veterans often face stressors unique to military service, including relationship challenges, trauma exposure, disruptions of support networks, military sexual trauma and harassment, and transition from military to civilian life (Runnals et al., 2014). For many, the trauma of war may be compounded by military sexual trauma (MST), defined as "physical assault of a sexual nature, battery of a sexual nature, or sexual harassment which occurred while the veteran was serving on active duty or active duty for training" (Barth et al., 2016; U.S. Code, 2006, supplement 5, title 38—Veterans' Benefits, 2012). Currently, Veteran Affairs (VA) data show that 20.5 percent of women veterans report experiencing MST, while a majority of women veterans report enduring ongoing sexual harassment (Barth et al., 2016). Survivors of MST are more likely to experience PTSD and other psychological issues, including alcohol and/or drug abuse, depression, anxiety, and suicidal ideation (Mattocks et al., 2012).

Many women veterans face challenges of single parenting (Gewirtz, Erbes, Polusny, Forgatch, & DeGarmo, 2011), separation from family and social supports during trainings and deployments (Street, Vogt, & Dutra, 2009), frequent moves to duty stations (Shivakumar, Anderson, & Suris, 2015), and transition from military to civilian life (Demers, 2013). Women veterans are three times more likely to be single parents than their male counterparts, which can magnify mental health issues stemming from deployments (Segal, Smith, Segal, & Canuso, 2016).

The VA and Department of Defense (DoD) recognize that supporting the mental health of returning military service members, particularly women veterans, requires long-term intervention programs and mental health support (Runnals et al., 2014).

Types of Care Available

Programs designed specifically for women veterans must account for unique facets of their military experience. Some available mental health services available through the VA include psychological assessments/evaluations, psychotherapy, inpatient/outpatient care, and psychosocial rehabilitation (U.S. Department of Veteran Affairs, 2017). Although there is no consensus on the ideal delivery method for gender-specific mental health services within the VA, several VA facilities have established women-only programs and specialized women's treatment teams (Oishi et al., 2011). Many existing clinical mental and behavioral health services do not include psychosocial and resilience skill-building, though research indicates that such training offers potential for significant positive health outcomes (Pietrzak, Russo, Ling, & Southwick, 2011).

Barriers to Care and Opportunities to Overcome

Many women veterans face real or perceived barriers to care in relation to their military service. These barriers include lack of knowledge of resources or eligibility of resources, lack of gender-specific care, previous poor experiences with the VA, and lack of understanding by personnel of the unique needs of women veterans (Maung, Nilsson, Berkel, & Kelly, 2017).

Gender-specific services that address unique needs of women veterans is a common request (Yano et al., 2010). Along with the lack of specific-care resources for the physical and mental health needs of women veterans, fear of stigma and social isolation are often concerns (Druss & Rosenheck, 1997). Many women veterans avoid treatment because of the associated stigma within military culture (Thomas et al., 2016). Currently, many community organizations are either collaborating with the DoD and VA or providing services privately that seek to meet women veterans' needs (Meredith et al., 2017).

A Solution

The Young Adult and Family Center (YAFC) at the University of California San Francisco (UCSF) developed interventions aimed at meeting the mental health needs of women veterans (UCSF Department of Psychology, 2017). The YAFC offers courses such as Women Warriors and Next Mission, both designed to help women veterans. Active-duty military and veterans can access these unique psychotherapeutic, psychoeducational courses online. The courses focus on posttraumatic growth, resilience-building, and empowering individuals to form healthy lives. These programs are rooted in the YAFC's mission to deliver evidence-based, quality care to those with unmet mental health needs (UCSF Department of Psychology, 2017). YAFC courses are free of charge, and students may earn college credit through the University of California San Diego (UCSD) Extension School.

Women Warriors—Theoretical Basis

A critical hypothesis of each course at the YAFC is that military personnel will be more willing to engage in activities to understand their reactions to extreme stress within the context of a less stigmatizing environment. Additionally, technology-savvy veteran cohorts may appreciate opportunities for interactive learning, computer-based models of information-gathering, and social network sharing.

Strategy behind the Courses

The VA and DoD recognize the mental health of returning service members requires long-term intervention programs and mental health support. During current ongoing conflicts, military service branches shifted perspective on the psychology of the experience of war, from a focus on acute reactions to extreme stress to a broader view that addresses the life cycle of exposure to extreme stress (Rubin, Weiss, & Coll, 2013; Wooten, 2015).

Many mental health treatment efforts target the negative outcomes of exposure to extreme stress, such as posttraumatic stress disorder (PTSD) and traumatic brain injury (TBI; Pietrzak, Johnson, Goldstein, Malley, & Southwick, 2009). Identifying and treating the negative outcomes is essential but only one part of the solution. A growing body of literature documents the positive outcomes that service members experience because of exposure to extreme stress (Spiro, Settersten, & Aldwin, 2016). Schok, Kleber, and Lensvelt-Mulders (2010) discuss the following benefits that service members and peacekeepers have reported from their experience: "Adversity coping"; "developing self-discipline"; "broader life perspective"; "greater independence"; "expanding horizons"; "increasing stress-tolerance"; "better self-worth, assertiveness and ability to take responsibility"; "not taking things for granted"; "learning to cooperate"; "developing stronger friendships"; "valuing life more"; "appreciating peace"; "realizing the importance of family"; and "strengthening faith/spirituality." Some evidence suggests that the experience of growth in the face of adversity can alleviate stress (Schok et al., 2010; Spiro et al., 2016).

One model for understanding the perspective on treating psychological trauma views the development of positive (e.g., growth) and negative (e.g., PTSD) outcomes as separate and distinct pathways (Schok et al., 2010). The model of resilient resources, developed by Schok et al. (2010), posits that functional adaptation is a result of balance between positive and negative outcomes. For example, because of war, a service member may develop negative symptoms (Schok et al., 2010), but the same service member may develop positive outcomes, such as an ability to overcome adversity. In sum, this service member's level of adaptation in response to war experiences may be high, despite negative symptoms. By focusing on both positive outcomes, reintegration programs could enhance individual resilience.

To reach military women, such programs do better in training spaces than clinical treatment (Thomas et al., 2016). Both the VA and the DoD have expended millions of dollars to address barriers to care, including ensuring anonymity of care and using online mediums (www.afterdeployment.org). However, barriers persist. The service members' experience of, and response to, stress may be pathologized (Fala, Coleman, & Lynch, 2016). Military members value strength (Zinzow et al., 2013) while remaining skeptical acknowledging the negative impacts of stress.

In contrast, providers can use the military profession's value of training/education to overcome specific cultural challenges associated with seeking aid from mental health providers (Caforio, 2006). From the basic assumption promulgated by military recruiters that the military is a learning experience to military leaders' belief that service members are trainable for any assignment, training and education are integral parts of the culture of the military (Gagne, 1962). Thus, an intervention that focuses on educating soldiers on stress and a balanced perspective on positive and negative outcomes could be therapeutic and motivate individuals to seek care.

Curriculum Design

The eight-week Women Warriors course is based upon the principles developed in the Next Mission course on posttraumatic growth. YAFC delivers the course through a Health Insurance Portability and Accountability Act (HIPAA)–compliant telemedicine platform allowing students to read course material, submit assignments, and engage each other socially. Students watch video lectures with two course instructors. Lydia Davey, a veteran, and author of this chapter, discusses her experiences on active duty, her return to civilian life, and the ways that these experiences connect to each topic. Dr. Christine Garcia, a clinical psychologist, discusses the neuroscience and psychology behind stress, trauma, resilience, and growth. Students participate in in-class activities such as goal-setting, barriers to goals/growth, homework assignments, and in-class discussions. All content is based on evidence-based practices, including those approved by the DoD for the treatment of PTSD.

The course relies on three principles of healing and posttraumatic growth: (1) stress-focused coping strategies through narrative therapy, cognitive behavioral therapy (CBT), and trauma-based salutogenic exercises; (2) the science behind traumatic stress and its impact on the brain; and (3) community engagement for peer-to-peer support. Understanding the physiological responses to emotional and physical injury is crucial in combating the stigma of brain injury, PTSD, and other illnesses that many veterans carry. Students study brain structure and function (1) as related to normal stress, (2) when undergoing trauma exacted from the war zone, and (3) in relation to the culture of the military.

The course relies on multiple evidence-based modes of healing. Students learn and utilize aspects of (1) acceptance and commitment therapy (ACT; Hayes, Luoma, Bond, Masuda, & Lillis, 2006); (2) dialectical behavior therapy (DBT; Scheiderer, Carlile, Aosved, & Barlow, 2017); and (3) emotion regulation (Rabinak et al., 2014). The instructors use Pennebaker's work on trauma, *Writing to Heal* (2004), heavily throughout the course. The process of writing allows students to "take control of the narratives that control them" (Pennebaker, 2004). Course instructors ask students to journal through collaging, free-writing, and creating trauma maps that describe different trauma points in their lives. Trauma-based salutogenic strategies (Mittelmark et al., 2017) capitalize on exposure-based exercises paired with relaxation work, such as Parnell's bilateral stimulation through resource tapping (Hartung, 2010). This exercise asks participants to activate the right and left hemispheres of the brain through tapping the right and left arms or legs with hands, or tapping the right and left feet on the floor, in rhythmic motion, while experiencing distress. Through exposure to the uncomfortable emotion while utilizing a relaxation or distraction-based activity, individuals become more able to tolerate discomfort (Hartung, 2010). The instructors utilize other body-based exercises that apply mindfulness techniques such as body scan, gratitude practice, yoga for warriors, and breathing exercises.

In the Women Warriors course, students explore coping skills through discussions. As students engage in activities like journaling, relaxation, cognitive behavioral skills, and stress-reduction strategies, they engage with fellow classmates through discussions on course materials and personal experiences that may connect with course topics. Due to the sheer ratio of men to women service members across the years (Segal, 1995), it is likely that women students have not previously had the opportunity to engage with other peers with similarly rare experiences. Their ability to form connections without the barriers of geography provides an extra measure of healing to this course experience.

Curriculum Content

Module One provides an overview of differences in the neuroanatomy and physiology of men and women and explores unique challenges and stressors faced by women in the military. Women veterans learn that they can be active participants in creating stronger, healthier lives for themselves and others.

Module Two examines the link between women's physical symptoms of stress and their emotions. Referencing the Yerkes-Dodson curve (Yerkes & Dodson, 1908), students discover some stress is necessary for optimal performance, while too much stress can be damaging. The instructors discuss ways to decrease stress and introduce a mindfulness exercise to increase awareness of what is happening in the body.

Module Three focuses on choices. It explores what happens in the human brain and body when making choices, how they make these choices, and what strategies may be employed to make the best possible choices based on personal goals. The module examines choice through neuroanatomical, neuropsychological, and psychological lenses. Students learn that brains may remember things and make decisions in a nonlinear fashion after a traumatic event. The concept of "wise mind" (Sakdalan & Gupta, 2012) is introduced as a place from which to make decisions; it takes into account both logic and emotions and produces outcomes with which people are satisfied.

Module Four moves students beyond stress and into conversation about trauma. They learn different types of traumas, including single catastrophic events, sustained intense trauma, and also "small t" (McCullough, 2002) traumas (a constellation of experiences that together can negatively impact a person). Not everyone who experiences trauma will be negatively impacted; however, an intense reaction to trauma is normal (Gold & Wegner, 1995).

Module Five explores how the human brain maps traumatic events, the powerful mind-body connection, and how to rewrite those maps. Students are introduced to the concept of radical acceptance (Chapman, 2006) and learn that it can be united with a growth mind-set (Tan, 2013) to shape a future that is different than the one students always felt was inevitable.

Module Six teaches students about moral injury (Litz et al., 2009), guilt, and resilience (Dekker, 2013). Many service members believe that military service is honorable and good, but they may also recognize that no nation is perfect in its application of force. To begin owning these potentially competing narratives, students follow Pennebaker's writing prompt.

Module Seven allows students to explore pathways to healing as well as concepts of healing throughout history. Instructors discuss the importance of engaging the total person, internal and external, in the healing process and dig into the role forgiveness can have in empowering posttraumatic growth (Schultz, Tallman, & Altmaier, 2010).

Finally, in Module Eight, students learn about the Hero's Journey, a narrative pattern seen in epic stories throughout time (Vecchiolla, 2016). For their final project, students map their own journey against the Hero's Journey.

Why Telemedicine?

Telemedicine is a concept that has received considerable attention in recent years (Morland, Greene, Rosen, & Frueh, 2010; Weinstein et al., 2014). Alternatives to traditional in-person care have emerged as ways to address the limitations of brick-and-mortar services (Egede et al., 2015). Health care has moved more comfortably in this direction as advances in technology have made this type of service more intuitive and accessible (Mermelstein, Guzman, Rabinowitz, Krupinski, & Hilty, 2017). Organizations, health care providers, and patients use HIPAA-compliant platforms to supplement, replace, and allow for collaborative care among providers and patients (Molfenter, Boyle, Holloway, & Zwick, 2015). Patients discussed feeling more secure with the perceived anonymity of telemedicine (Morland et al., 2015). Telemedicine interventions allow patients and doctors to transmit clinical information more easily and unconstrained by time or geographic location.

Reviews of studies examining telemedicine's effectiveness reveal positive outcomes for areas such as diagnosis, assessment, the transmission of information, and communication among providers (Egede et al., 2015; Morland et al., 2015). With specific focus on military veterans with PTSD, patients in rural geographic locations were able to receive services they would otherwise be unable to access (Morland et al., 2015). Further, the scalability of this mode of treatment reduces the cost of service delivery (Egede et al., 2016).

A key step in developing YAFC's intervention was having an information technology platform to support an online, interactive, college-level course.

Core to this strategy was the creation of a social networking platform that embodied privacy protection and security while conforming to HIPAA. The HIPAA-compliant secure social networking platform developed by YAFC, when combined with several emerging technologies, allows information transfer over the Internet (a process known as e-learning). E-learning (Rosenberg, 2001) allows the YAFC instructors to deliver a unique type of therapeutic experience, drawing on synchronous, asynchronous, and social-learning technologies. This allows instructor relationships with students to be interactive while remaining confidential.

YAFC's technology allows instructors to accommodate different learning styles. Beyond the increased capacity to achieve impacts that e-learning technologies provide, they also provide opportunities to establish social networks to facilitate interaction and promote healing (Rovai, 2001). Using homework assignments as community-building exercises capitalizes on the military's strong cultural emphasis on training together, deploying together, and sticking together (Caforio, 2006). Encouraging peer-to-peer interactions allows students to develop agency, competence, and expertise—processes that counteract the debilitating effects of trauma. Because many veterans often believe that only other veterans can understand them (Demers, 2010), peer-to-peer interaction allows them to maintain their "expert status" while providing peer-level support.

Recruitment and Engagement efforts

Important aspects of the success of the courses include recruitment and engagement efforts. Creating a safe environment to share personal experiences is essential from initial recruitment to graduation. YACF recruits via word of mouth, e-mails to veterans organizations, posts on social media platforms, and connections with veterans student organizations. Weekly, instructors send students course material with discussion prompts and homework assignments. Instructors respond to homework assignments and engage with students through discussion postings. Homework assignments are designed to increase contact between students. To this end, students post reactions to items such as coping strategies, readings, videos, and films that correspond to course topics. Instructors also enable the women participating to harness their own resilience by encouraging them to think about and share the positive coping strategies they have used in the past or currently use.

Current and Future Research

The YAFC courses are part of a voluntary study examining the impact of online delivery and healing through a psychoeducation package. At the beginning and end of each course, students complete a questionnaire that asks them about their history of trauma, mental health, and overall health. While YAFC staff are presently unable to share data, some anecdotal evidence suggests that the course is impactful and can be as good as, if not better than, in-person models for reaching women veterans. Preliminary data show decreases in somatization, levels of fear, and sadness. Increased levels of joy and authenticity have also emerged. Students have reported that the course has replaced and/or supplemented the therapy they were receiving or that the course has placed them on a path that makes them feel more amenable to receiving mental health services.

References

Barth, S. K., Kimerling, R. E., Pavao, J., McCutcheon, S. J., Batten, S. V., Dursa, E., & Schneiderman, A. I. (2016). Military sexual-trauma among recent veterans: Correlates of sexual assault and sexual harassment. *American Journal of Preventive Medicine, 50*(1), 77.

Beder, J. (Ed.). (2016). *Caring for the military: A guide for helping professionals.* New York, NY: Routledge.

Caforio, G. (2006). *Handbook of the sociology of the military.* New York, NY: Springer.

Chapman, A. L. (2006). Acceptance and mindfulness in behavior therapy: A comparison of dialectical behavior therapy and acceptance and commitment therapy. *International Journal of Behavioral Consultation and Therapy, 2*(3), 308–313.

Dekker, S. (2013). *Second victim: Error, guilt, trauma, and resilience.* Boca Raton, FL: Taylor and Francis Group.

Demers, A. (2010). When veterans return: The role of community in reintegration. *Journal of Loss and Trauma, 16*(2), 160–179.

Demers, A. (2013). From death to life: Female veterans, identity negotiation, and reintegration into society. *Journal of Humanistic Psychology, 53*(4), 489–515.

Druss, B. G., & Rosenheck, R. A. (1997). Use of medical services by veterans with mental disorders. *Psychosomatics, 38*, 451–458.

Egede, L. E., Acierno, R., Knapp, R. G., Lejuez, C., Hernandez-Tejada, M., Payne, E. H., & Frueh, B. C. (2015). Psychotherapy for depression in older veterans via telemedicine: A randomized, open-label, non-inferiority trial. *The Lancet Psychology, 2*(8), 693–701.

Egede, L. E., Gebregziabher, M., Walker, R. J., Payne, E. H., Acierno, R., & Frueh, B. C. (2016). Trajectory of cost overtime after psychotherapy for depression in older veterans via telemedicine. *Journal of Affective Disorders, 207*, 157–162.

Fala, N. C., Coleman, J. A., & Lynch, J. R. (2016). Anticipatory anxiety in the treatment of combat veterans with posttraumatic-stress disorder. *Journal of Aggression, Maltreatment & Trauma, 25*(2), 210–229.

Gagne, R. M. (1962). Military training and principles of learning. *American Psychologist, 17*(2), 83–91.

Gewirtz, A. H., Erbes, C. R., Polusny, M. A., Forgatch, M. S., & DeGarmo, D. S. (2011). Helping military families through the deployment process: Strategies to support parenting. *Professional Psychology Research and Practice, 42*(1), 56–62.

Gold, D., & Wegner, D. (1995). Origins of ruminative thought: Trauma, incompleteness, nondisclosure, and suppression. *Journal of Applied Social Psychology, 25*(14), 1245–1261.

Hartung, J. (2010). Tapping in: A step-by-step guide to activating your healing resources through bilateral stimulation. *Journal of EMDR Practice and Research, 4*(2), 96.

Hayes, S. C., Luoma, J. B., Bond, F. W., Masuda, A., & Lillis, J. (2006). Acceptance and commitment therapy: Model, processes, and outcomes. *Behavior Research and Therapy, 44*(1), 1–25.

Hoge, C. W., McGurk, D., Thomas, J. L., Cox, A. L., Engel, C. C., Castro, C. A. (2008). Mild traumatic brain injury in US soldiers returning from Iraq. *New England Journal of Medicine, 358*, 453–463.

Litz, B. T., Stein, N., Delaney, E., Lebowitz, L., Nash, W. P., Silva, C., & Maguen, S. (2009). Moral injury and moral repair in war veterans: A preliminary model and intervention strategy. *Clinical Psychology Review, 29*, 695–706.

Mattocks, K. M., Haskell, S. G., Krebs, E. E., Justice, A. C., Yano, E. M., & Brandt, C. (2012). Women at war: Understanding how women veterans cope with combat and military sexual trauma. *Social Science & Medicine, 74*(4), 537–545.

Maung, J., Nilsson, J. E., Berkel, L. A., & Kelly, P. (2017). Women in the National Guard: Coping and barriers to care. *Journal of Counseling & Development, 95*(1), 67–76.

McCullough, L. (2002). Exploring change mechanisms in EMDR applied to "Small-t Trauma" in short term dynamic psychotherapy: Research questions and speculations. *Journal of Clinical Psychology, 58*(12), 1531–1544.

Meredith, L. S., Wang, Y., Okunogbe, A., Bergman, A. A., Canelo, I. A., Darling, J. E., & Yano, E. M. (2017). Attitudes, practices, and experiences with implementing a patient-centered medical home for women veterans. *Women's Health Issues, 27*(2), 221–227.

Mermelstein, H., Guzman, E., Rabinowitz, T., Krupinski, E., & Hilty, D. (2017). The application of technology to health: The evolution of telephone to telemedicine and telepsychiatry: A historical review and look at human factors. *Journal of Technology in Behavioral Science, 1*(1), 1–16.

Mittelmark, M. B., Sagy, S., Eriksson, M., Bauer, G. F., Pelikan, J. M., Lindstrom, B., & Espnes, G. A. (2017). *The handbook of salutogenesis*. New York, NY: Springer.

Molfenter, T., Boyle, M., Holloway, D., & Zwick, J. (2015). Trends in telemedicine use in addiction treatment. *Addiction Science and Clinical Practice, 10*(14), 1–9.

Morland, L. A., Greene, C. J., Rosen, C., & Frueh, B. C. (2010). Telemedicine for anger management therapy in a rural population of combat veterans with posttraumatic stress disorder: A randomized noninferiority trial. *The Journal of Clinical Psychology, 71*(7), 855–863.

Morland, L. A., Mackintosh, M., Rosen, C. S., Willis, E., Resick, P., Chard, K., & Frueh, B. C. (2015). Telemedicine versus in-person delivery of cognitive processing therapy for women with posttraumatic-stress disorder: A randomized noninferiority trial. *Depression and Anxiety, 32*(11), 811–820.

Oishi, S. M., Rose, D. E., Washington, D. L., MacGregor, C., Bean-Mayberry, B., & Yano, E. M. (2011). National variations in VA mental health care for women veterans. *Women's Health Issues, 21*(4), S137.

Pennebaker, J. W. (2004). *Writing to heal*. Oakland, CA: New Harbinger Publications.

Pietrzak, R. H., Johnson, D. C., Goldstein, M. B., Malley, J. C., & Southwick, S. M. (2009). *Psychiatric Services, 60*(8), 1118–1122.

Pietrzak, R. H., Russo, A. R., Ling, Q., & Southwick, S. M. (2011). Suicidal ideation in treatment-seeking veterans of Operations Enduring Freedom and Iraqi Freedom: The role of coping strategies, resilience, and social support. *Journal of Psychiatric Research, 45*, 720–726.

Rabinak, C. A., MacNamara, A., Kennedy, A. E., Angstadt, M., Stein, M. B., Liberzon, I., & Phan, K. L. (2014). Focal and aberrant prefrontal engagement during emotion regulation in veterans with posttraumatic stress disorder. *Depression and Anxiety, 31*(10), 851–861.

Ramsey, C., Dziura, J., Justice, A. C., Altalib, H. H., Bathulapalli, H., Burg, M., . . . Brandt, C. (2017). Incidence of mental health diagnoses in veterans of Operations Iraqi Freedom, Enduring Freedom, and New Dawn, 2001–2014. *American Journal of Public Health, 107*(2), 329–335.

Rosenberg, M. (2001). *E-learning: Strategies for delivering knowledge in the digital age*. Columbus, OH: McGraw-Hill Companies, Inc.

Rovai, A. P. (2001). Building classroom community at a distance: A case study. *Educational Technology Research and Development Journal, 49*(4), 35–50.

Rubin, A., Weiss, E. L., & Coll, J. (2013). *Handbook of military social work*. Hoboken, NJ: John Wiley & Sons.

Runnals, J. J., Garovoy, N., McCutcheon, S. J., Robbins, A. T., Mann-Wrobel, M. C., Elliott, A., & Strauss, J. L. (2014). Systematic review of women veterans' mental health. *Women's Health Issues, 24*(5), 485–502.

Sakdalan, J. A., & Gupta, R. (2012). Wise mind—risky mind: A reconceptualisation of dialectical behavior therapy concepts and its application to sexual offender treatment. *Journal of Sexual Aggression, 20*(1), 110–120.

Saltzman, W. R., Lester, P., Beardslee, W. R., Layne, C. M., Woodward, K., & Nash, W. P. (2011). Mechanisms of risk and resilience in military families: Theoretical and empirical basis of a family focused resilience enhancement program. *Clinical Child and Family Psychology Review, 14*(3), 213–230.

Scheiderer, E., Carlile, J. A., Aosved, A. C., & Barlow, A. (2017). Concurrent dialectical behavior therapy and prolonged exposure reduces symptoms and improves overall quality of life for a veteran with posttraumatic stress disorder and borderline personality disorder. *Clinical Case Studies, 16*(3), 216–233.

Schok, M. L., Kleber, R. J., & Lensvelt-Mulders, G. J. L. M. (2010). A model of resilience and meaning after military deployment: Personal resources in making sense of war and peacekeeping experiences. *Aging & Mental Health, 14*(3), 328–338.

Schultz, J., Tallman, B. A., & Altmaier, E. (2010). Pathways to posttraumatic growth: The contributions of forgiveness and importance of religion and spirituality. *Psychology of Religion and Spirituality, 2*(2), 104–114.

Segal, M. W. (1995). Women's military roles cross-nationally: Past, present, and future. *Gender and Society, 9*(6), 757–775.

Segal, M. W., Smith, D. G., Segal, D. R., & Canuso, A. A. (2016). The role of leadership and peer behaviors in the performance and well-being of women in combat: Historical perspectives, unit integration, and family issues. *Military Medicine, 181*(Suppl 1), 28.

Shivakumar, G., Anderson, E. H., & Suris, A. (2015). Managing posttraumatic stress disorder and major depression in women veterans during the perinatal period. *Journal of Women's Health, 24*(1), 18–22.

Spiro, A. I., Settersten, R. A., & Aldwin, C. M. (2016). Long-term outcomes of military service in aging and the life course: A positive re-envisioning. *The Gerontologist, 56*(1), 5–13.

Street, A. E., Vogt, D., & Dutra, L. (2009). A new generation of women veterans: Stressors faced by women deployed to Iraq and Afghanistan. *Clinical Psychology Review, 29*, 685–694.

Tan, S.-Y. (2013). Resilience and posttraumatic growth: Empirical evidence and clinical applications from a Christian perspective. *Journal of Psychology and Christianity, 32*(4), 358–364.

Thomas, K. H., Albright, D. L., Shields, M. M., Kaufman, E., Michaud, C., Taylor, S., & Hamner, K. (2016). Predictors of depression diagnoses and symptoms in United States female veterans: Results from a national survey and implications for programming. *Journal of Military and Veterans Health, 24*(3), 6–16.

University of California San Francisco (UCSF) Department of Psychology. (2017). Young Adult and Family Center. Retrieved from http://psych.ucsf.edu/yafc

U.S. Code, 2006 edition, supplement 5, title 38—Veterans' Benefits, U.S. Code U.S.C. (2012).

U.S. Department of Veteran Affairs. (2017). Mental Health. Retrieved from https://www.mentalhealth.va.gov

Vecchiolla, L. (2016). The Freedom to Live: Finding Empowering Connections between the Hero's Journey and Trauma Recovery. Available from

Dissertations & Theses @ Chicago School of Professional Psychology. Retrieved from http://search.proquest.com/docview/1783996034

Weinstein, R. S., Lopez, A. M., Joseph, B. A., Erps, K. A., Holcomb, M., Barker, G. P., & Krupinski, W. A. (2014). Telemedicine, telehealth, and mobile health applications that work: Opportunities and barriers. *The American Journal of Medicine, 127*(3), 183–187.

Wooten, N. R. (2015). Military social work: Opportunities and challenges for social work education. *Journal of Social Work Education, 51*(1), 6–25.

Yano, E. M., Hayes, P., Wright, S., Schnurr, P. P., Lipson, L., Bean-Mayberry, B., & Washington, D. L. (2010). Integration of women veterans into VA quality improvement research efforts: What researchers need to know. *Journal of General Internal Medicine, 25*(1), 56–61.

Yerkes, R. M., & Dodson, J. (1908). The relation of strength of stimulus to rapidity of habit-formation. *Journal of Comparative Neurology and Psychology, 18,* 459–482.

Zinzow, H., Britt, T., Pury, C., Raymond, M., McFadden, A., & Burnette, C. (2013). Barriers and facilitators of mental health treatment seeking among active-duty army personnel. *Military Psychology, 25*(5), 514–535.

Point of View—Fitting In and Finding Me

Jessica Wilkes

Separating from the military was like going through high school in reverse order. I started my transition from the military feeling that I knew who I was and what I had to offer to the workforce. I felt confident in my abilities to learn and adapt quickly. After all, I had learned how to skin and cook a rabbit and build a shelter in the snow in survival school. When I hit the job market, I quickly discovered that my years of hard work, discipline, and professional achievements meant very little in the corporate world. Over the next four years I went from feeling like a senior to realizing I had to start over as a freshman; I'm now working my way back up.

I enlisted in the Air Force on February 23, 2000. I was 21 at the time and didn't have much direction in life. I found purpose in the military—I gained financial security, structure, discipline, and most importantly I knew what was expected of me. I never planned to serve more than four years, but military life was a good fit for me. Instead of four years, I stayed for 12.

It's impossible for me to talk about the difficulty I had transitioning out of the military without explaining a time period that changed me forever. I deployed to Iraq for the first time on September 11, 2006, not knowing I would return a different person. Before leaving for deployment I wasn't sure what I would be doing there, or whether I should be concerned about making it back. The thought of not coming back might sound ridiculous to other members of the military (particularly Marines and Army soldiers) because

I was a small female in the Air Force (or as every other branch calls us, the "chair force"). Everything about me said I should be as safe as one could be. As soon as I arrived at my forward operating base (FOB) I knew this deployment wasn't going to be about shooting video of ceremonies and holiday greetings. We were going outside the wire, where improvised explosive devices (IEDs) and sniper attacks were a daily occurrence. Over the months I spent in Iraq, my province went from quiet to nightmarish. Hatred, violence, and death were part of daily life in Iraq, and after a month or two I became numb to it. Each mission I went on, I got closer to becoming a casualty myself. I don't know if I was lucky (from a combat videographer standpoint) or cursed (from a normal human being standpoint) because I always ended up on the missions where something happened and/or I almost died. By the end of my tour my commander gave me a nickname—"bullet magnet."

When it was time to go back stateside, I didn't want to go home. I felt that what I was doing was important and, to be honest, life is simple when you're deployed. You live every day in the present and compartmentalize all of the bad things you don't have time to process or deal with. What I didn't know was that this compartmentalization would drive me straight into the clutches of post-traumatic stress disorder (PTSD). Once home, I worried obsessively about everything I couldn't control. I watched everything I could about what was happening in "my" province. Then the deaths started; I started to see the names of people I knew showing up on the casualty list. Not just one or two, but several at a time. All I wanted was to go back and be with my team.

I began to have nightmares about being wounded in the middle of a firefight. I could see the medics crouching over me trying to save me, but it was always too late. In my head I kept yelling that I wasn't dead, but they never heard me. Everything would go black and I would wake up. What was so upsetting about these dreams wasn't that I died in them, but that they were so vivid and so real. Several years later I still shiver thinking about them.

After a few months of this I went to the mental health clinic and laid it all out to the psychologist. When I was done, he told me that it was too soon for me to have PTSD and that I didn't have all of the symptoms on the checklist. I was diagnosed with Adjustment Disorder, an all-encompassing and meaningless diagnosis, though I didn't know that at the time. I accepted the diagnosis and hoped that it meant that at some point, it would pass and I would move on. It didn't pass. I drank more than I did before, and all I could think about was my tour.

My mind felt like a broken record. I had the same thoughts and memories over and over again. I didn't realize that my personality had changed and I'd become louder and moody. I felt like the other people around me didn't "get" me and looked at me as if they were afraid of me. I don't think they knew what to say to me. I'd come back to a place where only a few people could even remotely understand what I'd been through.

The Nut House

Less than a year later I got orders to a new unit. This unit was well known around the Air Force and some of the most talented Airmen in my career field were stationed there. It was also a combat unit that deployed often. When I arrived I knew that this was where I needed to be. Everyone in my unit understood me, because they'd been there too. They had the same dark sense of humor as I did, and we connected immediately. They didn't look at me like I was a ticking time bomb, as people had at my previous base. Four months after arriving I deployed again. I was looking forward to it because I thought it would be a chance to get closure—I could finish what I started.

It didn't happen that way. As soon as my boots hit the tarmac in Baghdad something changed in me. I was angry but I didn't know why. Wasn't this what I wanted, to put it all to rest and say good-bye to this mission? I spent the next seven months getting angrier each day. After all I'd given and all the lives that were lost, we still weren't anywhere near ready to leave the country or hand over control to the Iraqis.

Coming home, I felt worse. I was angry and anxious all the time. One day when I was in the car, screaming like a maniac at the driver in front of me, I realized that this wasn't just anger. It was rage.

One night I was watching television and something came on about post-traumatic stress disorder and a few of the symptoms described really resonated. One was that I always felt disorganized and out of sorts—I couldn't keep things straight in my head and I couldn't remember anything. The second was an inability to feel loved or feeling disconnected from others. I felt like crying because suddenly it all made sense. I couldn't understand why my head knew what I felt, but emotionally and physically, I felt nothing. My daughter was four or five at the time and I knew I loved her more than anything in the world, but I didn't feel anything. I was numb. The only feelings that felt real were anxiety and anger.

New Diagnosis

Another visit to a mental health provider was hard to do, but I made it into the office. It took me a few visits to muster up the courage to ask him what he thought was wrong with me. When I did, he replied, "Jessica, you have PTSD and I knew it in the first five minutes of meeting you." It was a relief to know that I wasn't going crazy and that how I felt wasn't abnormal.

An Outsider

I left the military and got a civilian job, but I knew from my first day of work that I didn't belong there. It was like being the weird new kid on the first day of school. I didn't connect with anyone and my sense of humor and sarcasm were not well received. I tried my best to fit in but it seemed like I could never get anything right. I'd never felt more alone and now I had no one to talk to about it. I didn't want to be *that* friend who always dumped her problems on others. I found another way to let it out: I started a blog and wrote about everything. Some days I would write more than one entry and didn't stop writing until I got it all out of my head I wrote about not fitting in, about nightmares, and about the things I'd been through. It felt weird to me that I could write a blog that complete strangers read but I couldn't express any of this to most of the people I knew. I was tired of talking about it. Writing kept me sane.

I started adding physical training to my daily regimen. Some days I did cardio, which left me tired but clear-minded. Other days I did yoga and Pilates and found that during those workouts my mind never wandered. I was focused on form and not falling down and when it was time to cool down I almost always fell asleep on my mat. It was easy for me to stay focused and just be in the moment. Being able to just "be" and quiet the noise in my mind was a lifesaver.

What the military either doesn't know or doesn't tell you is that the transition from the military to civilian life doesn't just take a few months. It can take years, and if you're lacking the tools to keep your mind healthy during the tough times, the experience can be catastrophic. Having an outlet is what kept me from falling over the edge. I went from writing, to therapy, to yoga and fitness. I think the combination helped me keep my head above water and to some extent, I think it helped me change the way I look at the ups and downs I've endured. It's become a teaching tool for me.

This coming year will mark five years since leaving the military and I consider myself a "sophomore" in my transition back to civilian life—just now starting to feel like I'll survive it. For some people it may be easy, but others, like me, will struggle to pull it together and make it through.

Looking back on all of the hardships I experienced after leaving the military, I now see that there was a purpose to it all. It was terrible and I never thought it would end while it was happening, but it was valuable life experience. In my job, I talk to veterans transitioning out of the military who want to head back to school. Some of them are struggling with the same things I did—finances, employment, mental health, and just generally finding a place to belong. I can almost always relate with the challenges they are facing, and tell them they're not alone. It feels good to have a purpose again.

CHAPTER 8

Learning from Example: Resilience of Service Members Who Identify as LGBT

Katharine Bloeser and Heliana Ramirez

Lesbian, gay, bisexual, and/or transgender LGBT[1] service members showcase resilience in the face of threat. Historically, LGBT people were banned from serving in the U.S. military. Between 1993 and 2011, LGB people were permitted to serve provided they concealed their sexual orientation. The transgender ban remained in place until 2016. As of the writing of this chapter, the president has advocated for its reinstatement. This has been countered by 56 retired generals and admirals who feel it will degrade readiness and compromise the integrity of the armed forces (Palm Center, 2017).

What can we learn from these service members who exemplify dedication and service in spite of institutionalized discrimination? How can we ensure that all service members thrive in the military and discharge with pride and optimal health and wellness? This chapter addresses resilience among LGBT service members in two distinct ways. The first part examines the notion of LGBT military resilience, and the second portion explores policy level changes.

A Brief History of LGBT Service in the U.S. Military

LGBT individuals have served in the armed forces since the United States was established (Sinclair, 2009). In 1984, the Alexander Hamilton Post 448 of the American Legion was founded in San Francisco for LGBT veterans. Historians' reading of Hamilton's letters to John Laurens suggests that the two were lovers (Aubrecht, 2012).

Homosexuality was first deemed a criminal act in the military during World War I (Shilts, 1993). World War II, however, saw the first discussions of homosexuality in military psychiatry. Draftees entering service were deemed unfit to serve for mental health reasons by psychiatrists (Sinclair, 2009). Policies calling for the designation as *unfit for duty* continued through the 1970s and 1980s. These policies dictated that service members who self-identified as gay or lesbian, engaged in same-sex sexual acts, or attempted to marry persons of the same sex be discharged from military service (National Defense Research Institute, 2010). Beginning in the 1980s, activists called for the U.S. government to lift the LGB military service ban. President Clinton initiated a series of congressional hearings in the face of opposition from the Joint Chiefs of Staff and members of Congress (Frank, 2009). The resulting compromise became known as Don't Ask, Don't Tell (DADT). Under DADT, entering service members were not asked about their sexual orientation or sexual behavior. However, mere suspicion of a service member being LGB led to investigation and subsequent military discharges (National Defense Research Institute, 2010).

For LGB members, service under DADT entailed fear of harassment, violence, investigation, and discharge in addition to the stresses of military service (Burks, 2011; Cameron et al., 2011; Estes, 2007; Frank, 2009; Shilts, 1993). While LGBT veterans reported general satisfaction with military service (Moradi, 2009), concealment of sexual orientation was a constant stressor (Cochran, Balsam, Flentje, Malte, & Simpson, 2013; Moradi, 2009). Service members feared being discovered in routine activities. Phones were tapped, mail opened, conversations overheard, and mental health practitioners and chaplains breached confidentiality (Trivette, 2010).

The effects of discrimination, prejudice, stigma, violence, and harassment are strong among the LGBT population (Meyer, 2003). Research comparing veterans who identify as sexual and gender minorities to heterosexual and/or cisgender veteran populations shows physical and mental health disparities (Pelts, Rolbiecki, & Albright, 2014). Lesbian and bisexual female veterans report poorer physical health (Blosnich & Silenzio, 2013), higher rates of intimate partner violence (Kimerling et al., 2016) and sexual assault (Booth, Mengeling, Torner, & Sadler, 2011), physical violence, depression, posttraumatic stress disorder (PTSD), and alcohol misuse (Mattocks et al., 2013). Sexual minority veterans report greater suicidal ideation (Blosnich, Mays, & Cochran, 2014) and higher smoking rates (Blosnich & Silenzio, 2013) and are more likely to screen positive for PTSD (Cochran et al., 2013). Veterans who identify as transgender are more likely to report suicidal ideation, depression, PTSD, homelessness, incarceration (Brown & Jones, 2015), and military sexual trauma (MST; Lindsay et al., 2016) as compared to cisgender veterans.

This brief literature review on LGBT military is sobering. Yet, like the literature on nonmilitary connected LGBT people, the focus is on illness and disparity. There is little discussion of the majority of LGBT people who do not have mental health challenges (Cochran & Mays, 2013; Herek & Garnets, 2007). This literature largely does not speak to the resilience of LGBT veterans who served and often thrived despite bans on their service (Ramirez & Sterzing, 2017; Riggle, Rostosky, & Horne, 2009; Russell & Bohan, 2005; Savin-Williams, 2008).

What Is Resilience?

There are two closely related concepts in the study of people's ability to *bounce back*, grow, and even thrive in the face of adversity. Resilience is characterized as a dynamic trait that allows a person to return to their baseline functioning after a traumatic event (Herrick, Stall, Goldhammer, Egan, & Mayer, 2014). Resilience can mediate the effects of stigma, prejudice, violence, and harassment on LGBT people (Frost & Meyer, 2015). The second is posttraumatic growth (PTG), a concept developed in response to individuals' ability to grow after coping with trauma (Calhoun, Cann, & Tedeschi, 2000; Calhoun & Tedeschi, 1999). Many argue that because research is problem-focused, clinical practice is hindered (Kwon, 2013). This focus also perpetuates stereotypes of LGBT people as sick and pathological (McWhorter, 1999).

PTG is described in LGBT populations. Literature examining stress-related growth (SRG) in LGBT people suggests that growth is often coupled with social consciousness and activism (Bonet, Wells, & Parsons, 2007; Riggle, Whitman, Olson, Rostosky, & Strong, 2008). One study notes several themes related to the positive aspects of identity. Choosing new and supportive families, serving as role models, and involvement in activism and promoting social justice were all intricately related to identity as sexual minorities (Riggle et al., 2009). Similar concepts were established in a study where SRG was associated with lesbian women's intentions to prepare the way for a new generation as was involvement with activism in the LGBT community. Of note is the finding that lesbians of color reported higher levels of SRG than white women, despite the racism they face in addition to homophobia (Bonet et al., 2007). In terms of older transgender veterans, one study found military service is associated with greater resilience and positive mental health outcomes among veterans as compared to transgender civilian older adults (Hoy-Ellis et al., 2017).

While research suggests that individual traits can foster resilience (Elliott et al., 2015; Southwick, 2012), one must exercise caution when examining resilience in oppressed and marginalized populations such as those who identify as LGBT. When examining resilience, we cannot categorize individuals as either *resilient* or *not resilient* (Meyer, 2015). This can devolve into victim blaming. Instead, we should focus on both individual and communal resources and structural inequality and barriers (Meyer, 2015).

An essential component to resilience is community and social support (Elliott et al., 2015; Southwick, 2012). A sense of belonging has been found to mitigate postdeployment depression in military personnel (Bryan & Heron, 2015) and bolster resilience among injured veterans (Eakman, Schelly, & Henry, 2016). Community-level resilience for LGBT populations can take many forms, including presence of positive role models and a sense of belonging (Kwon, 2013). Community support and belonging have also been found to mitigate the effects of LGBT-related violence and harassment in nonmilitary populations (Meyer, 2015).

LGBT veterans offer numerous examples of resilience. Under military service bans, LGBT service members organized underground support networks; enacted everyday forms of strength, resistance, and resilience in response to the bans; advocated for social change in the military and civilian society; and rose throughout the ranks (Ramirez & Sterzing, 2017; Shilts, 1993; Sinclair, 2009).

How Do We Build upon This Resilience?

Protocols that build upon resilience include individual and community-based interventions. Burgeoning research supports individual-level mind-body interventions, including mindfulness, yoga, and acupuncture (Gayner et al., 2012; Keng & Liew, 2016) as well as affirmative interventions (Alessi, 2014). At the community level, fostering development of and participation in support and cooperative groups can promote resilience (Frost & Meyer, 2015).

To understand how individual and community-level interventions contribute to resilience, we must first examine how they fit into a historical and theoretical perspective. Historically, the medical community described homosexuality and transgender identity as pathological (Zucker & Spitzer, 2005). Until 1973, homosexuality was considered a disorder in the *Diagnostic and Statistical Manual of Mental Disorders* (American Psychiatric Association, 2013). The minority stress model explains LGBT people's elevated rates of health disparities as compared to heterosexual people, instead of damaging and fundamentally incorrect labeling of LGBT identities themselves, as the cause of health disparities (Meyer, 2003). This model describes the cumulative effect of stressors on the lives of LGBT people. Victimization, both covert (e.g., employment discrimination) and overt (e.g., hate crimes), related to one's sexual orientation or gender identity combines with internalized homophobia and/or transphobia and the stresses of daily life. This culmination of stressors is described as minority stress. The result is higher rates of physical and mental health problems (Hendricks & Testa, 2012; Meyer, 2003, 2010, 2014). In one study of veterans who identify as LGB, experiences under DADT resulted in symptoms of PTSD and depression (Cochran et al., 2013).

Individual-Level Interventions

The literature describes two types of individual-level interventions to address the effects of minority stress in clinical practice. The first is the integration of supportive or affirmative practices in psychotherapy (Alessi, 2014). The second is somatic in nature (Gayner et al., 2012; Thomas & Taylor, 2015). We can extrapolate from the existing literature to support future research and inform current practice.

Affirmative Practices

Professional ethics call practitioners to incorporate affirmative principles in their clinical practice. Mental health providers in general do not feel prepared or trained to work effectively with LGBT clients (Bidell, 2013; Bidell & Whitman, 2013). Many clients fear that their therapist will make assumptions that their sexual orientation is a problem requiring treatment. Others express concern when their therapist disrespects their same-sex relationship or avoids discussion of their identity (King, Semlyen, Killaspy, Nazareth, & Osborn, 2007). Therapists should listen and respond to clients' disclosures about LGBT military experiences of minority stress, respecting the range of client reactions to prejudice and stigma, including anger (Alessi, 2014).

Examples can be seen in group psychotherapy with LGBT veterans (Maguen, Shipherd, & Harris, 2005; Ramirez et al., 2013). In one LGBT veteran group, steps were taken to integrate veteran and LGBT identity, help veterans feel safe participating in the group, and empower members developing a sense of community. Participants' safety was facilitated through group ground rules, an emphasis on security, and group facilitation that included challenging homophobia, transphobia, sexism, and racism. Veterans expressed a desire to discuss the residual impacts of DADT on their lives postdischarge (Ramirez et al., 2013). In a second group therapy example, transgender women veterans were invited to an adapted cognitive behavioral therapy (CBT) group. Topics including those related to discrimination and harassment were paired with key steps to empower group members. For example, at the direction of members, the group was called a women's identity group and preferred gender pronouns were used in all documentation (Maguen et al., 2005).

Providers of both mental health and medical care should be receptive to and affirming of their clients' or patients' identity. Affirmative practice requires training. Fortunately, both the Department of Veterans Affairs (VA; www.patientcare.va.gov/lgbt) and organizations like the Fenway Institute (www.lgbthealtheducation.org) and the Human Rights Campaign (www.hrc.org/hei/hei-training-on-the-cal) offer free online trainings.

Somatic Interventions

Somatic interventions show increasing evidence of efficacy in managing stress. Mindfulness, yoga, and acupuncture show promise, in conjunction with evidence-based protocols such as exposure-based treatment for PTSD and other deployment-health-related conditions (Thomas, & Taylor, 2015). Research examining the effects of somatic interventions with LGBT military-connected populations is needed. We can extrapolate from existing research on somatic interventions.

Mindfulness is focused attention to the present moment. This skill entails a focus on breathing rather than following thought patterns associated with posttraumatic stress (e.g., intrusive thoughts) or depression (e.g., negative self-talk). Mindfulness appears effective in managing symptoms and has been integrated into contemporary cognitive behavioral therapy protocols (see Hunot et al., 2013). Research suggests that measures of mindfulness can predict posttraumatic or deployment-related stress reactions (Call, Pitcock, & Pyne, 2015; Glück, Tran, Raninger, & Lueger-Schuster, 2015). The Mindfulness-Based Mind Fitness Training protocol used in two studies taught Marines to regulate the autonomic nervous system's reactions. In one study, after stressful combat training, those who received a mindfulness-based intervention showed reductions in key stress biomarkers (Johnson et al., 2014). In a second study, training was associated with improvements in self-reported perceived stress (Stanley, Schaldach, Kiyonaga, & Jha, 2011).

Can these skills translate to reductions in stress related to LGBT identity? The evidence for mindfulness-based interventions among LGBT people is growing. Among gay men living with HIV, those who participated in mindfulness-based stress attenuation training reported a reduction in depression (Gayner et al., 2012). Lesbian and bisexual women who participated in a mindfulness intervention noted improvements in nutrition and mental-health-related quality of life (Ingraham et al., 2016). The notion that mindfulness can moderate the relationship between minority stress and health has also been demonstrated in non-U.S. LGBT populations (Keng & Liew, 2016; Lyons, 2016).

Standing against Violence and Harassment

Concern existed that lifting the DADT ban may lead to an increase in violence and harassment targeted at LGBT service members (Johnson et al.,

2015). It is important to note that early research about the impact of the repeal of DADT suggests that *out* service has not led to an increase in violence and harassment perpetrated against LGBT service members; however, "harassment, discrimination, and bias remain problems in the wake of DADT repeal" (Belkin et al., 2012, p. 23). Reducing prejudice, stigma, violence, and harassment is the responsibility of all ranks of the military; however, military leaders can have a significant impact (Wang, Glover, Rhodes, & Nightingale, 2013). Leaders' tolerance of violence and harassment has been associated with increased incidences of MST (Murdoch, Pryor, Polusny, Gackstetter, & Ripley, 2009; Sadler, Booth, Nielson, & Doebbeling, 2000). Interventions aimed at decreasing tolerance of LGBT-directed violence and harassment among leaders may reduce its prevalence.

Training to reduce violence and harassment among military personnel may require a change in procedures and military culture. Military trainings targeted at sexual harassment and MST may not be taken seriously or are not comprehensive enough. Many service members do not pay attention to training or see training as only a means to "check the box" on requirements (U.S. Government Accountability Office, 2008, p. 32). Roughly 8–10 percent of service members in all five branches reported not receiving any training directed at MST prevention. Half of the officers and the enlisted ranks reported receiving thorough sexual assault prevention training, including how to intervene if one witnesses an assault (Holland, Rabelo, & Cortina, 2014). This is critical due to concerns that incidences of harassment of sexual and gender minority service members are underreported (Trivette, 2010). Violence and harassment prevention programs should be evaluated to ensure that they are taken seriously by and universally provided to all military personnel.

Supporting LGBT Military Leaders and Families

Exposure to leaders who identify as LGBT is also important for service members and veterans. Service members' opinions of DADT were directly related to individual contact with LGB individuals both inside and outside the military. Those with more contact with sexual minorities reported fewer heterosexist attitudes. Contacts within the military were associated with positive attitudes toward LGB service (Harwood, 2015). One of military culture's most revered tenets is the chain of command (Murdoch et al., 2009). Exposure to more LGBT service members in leadership positions may help to decrease heterosexism and transphobia and in turn perpetration of minority stress.

Supporting LGBT service members and veterans also means supporting their families. To date, there are no published studies that have examined military-connected families with LGBT members. Military children and families with sexual- or gender-minority members should feel supported and embraced in military-connected communities. Research shows that anti-LGBT policies and discrimination reach the children of LGBT parents who often feel that they need to overperform at school or suppress challenges to prove that they are the same as their peers in heterosexual families (Garner, 2005; Wescott & Sawyer, 2007). These families can teach us a great deal, as LGBT parents provide their children with strength and resilience (Stacey & Biblarz, 2001).

Often, clinical practice with LGBT people assumes they are individuals when in fact they are part of families. Mallon (2009) focuses on the need to educate families about gender identity to help dispel myths and improve communication. This fosters the goal of keeping families together as they work through the process of coming out or transitioning (Mallon, 2009).

Antiviolence and harassment policies are an important first step in protecting LGBT service members; however, the environment surrounding the military base is also critically important. For many LGBT military families and individuals, military bases may be a supportive island in a less-accepting region. Different parts of the United States and the world have different levels of hate crimes against LGBT people (Swank, Fahs, & Frost, 2013). Legislators on national and local levels need to take a stance against hate. Marines in North Carolina leaving Camp Lejeune enter a very hostile environment (Tucker & Meier, 2016).

Conclusion

We can learn a great deal about resilience from LGBT service members and veterans. The ability to face the stress of military service as well as daily threats of violence and discrimination is tremendous indeed. PTG is integral to posttraumatic stress, and the two should not be separated in research, clinical practice, or policy development. In fact, active participation in communities, both among veterans and LGBT individuals, is associated with growth from trauma and stress. We are learning that resilience is associated with both individual- and community-level factors. The use of LGBT affirmative and somatic practices can foster resilience and mitigate the effects of stress associated with prejudice, stigma, and discrimination. While as practitioners we can use these interventions at the individual and group levels to support resilience in the face of minority stress, it is critical that we also advocate for LGBT-affirming and protective military policies and management practices among leadership. Further, policy changes are important both in the military and throughout the United States to ensure the safety of LGBT service members. This includes retaining changes permitting open LGBT military service. Through research examining LGBT-affirming and strengths-based clinical care with service members and veterans, much will be learned about resilience in the face of risk.

References

Alessi, E. J. (2014). A framework for incorporating minority stress theory into treatment with sexual minority clients. *Journal of Gay & Lesbian Mental Health, 18*(April), 47–66.

American Psychiatric Association. (2013). *Diagnostic and statistical manual of mental disorders* (5th ed.). Arlington, VA: American Psychiatric Publishing.

Aubrecht, M. (2012). Alexander Hamilton's smoking gun. *The Gay and Lesbian Review Worldwide*, May/June, 17–19.

Belkin, A., Ender, M., Frank, N., Furia, S., Lucas, G. R., Packard, G., . . . Segal, D. R. (2012). *One year out: An assessment of DADT repeal's impact on military readiness*. Los Angeles, CA: The Palm Center at the University of California Los Angeles.

Bidell, M. P. (2013). Addressing disparities: The impact of a lesbian, gay, bisexual, and transgender graduate counselling course. *Counselling & Psychotherapy Research, 13*(4), 300–307.

Bidell, M. P., & Whitman, J. S. (2013). A review of lesbian, gay, and bisexual affirmative counseling assessments. *Counseling Outcome Research and Evaluation, 4*(2), 112–126.

Blosnich, J. R., Mays, V. M., & Cochran, S. D. (2014). Suicidality among veterans: Implications of sexual minority status. *American Journal of Public Health, 104*(Suppl. 4), 535–537.

Blosnich, J. R., & Silenzio, V. M. B. (2013). Physical health indicators among lesbian, gay, and bisexual U.S. veterans. *Annals of Epidemiology, 23*(7), 448–451.

Bonet, L., Wells, B. E., & Parsons, J. T. (2007). A positive look at a difficult time: A strength based examination of coming out for lesbian and bisexual women. *Journal of LGBT Health Research, 3*(1), 7–14.

Booth, B. M., Mengeling, M., Torner, J., & Sadler, A. G. (2011). Rape, sex partnership, and substance use consequences in women veterans. *Journal of Traumatic Stress, 24*(3), 287–294.

Brown, G. R., & Jones, K. T. (2015). Health correlates of criminal justice involvement in 4,793 transgender veterans. *LGBT Health, 2*(4), 297–305.

Bryan, C. J., & Heron, E. A. (2015). Belonging protects against postdeployment depression in military personnel. *Depression and Anxiety, 32*(5), 349–355.

Burks, D. J. (2011). Lesbian, gay, and bisexual victimization in the military: An unintended consequence of "Don't Ask, Don't Tell"? *American Psychologist, 66*(7), 604–613.

Calhoun, L. G., Cann, A., & Tedeschi, R. G. (2000). A correlational test of the relationship between posttraumatic growth, religion, and cognitive Processing. *Journal of Traumatic Stress, 13*(3), 521–527.

Calhoun, L. G., & Tedeschi, R. G. (1999). *Facilitating posttraumatic growth: A clinician's guide*. Mahwah, NJ: Lawrence Erlbaum Associates, Inc.

Call, D., Pitcock, J., & Pyne, J. (2015). Longitudinal evaluation of the relationship between mindfulness, general distress, anxiety, and PTSD in a recently deployed National Guard sample. *Mindfulness, 6*(6), 1303–1312.

Cameron, R. P., Mona, L. R., Syme, M. L., Cordes, C. C., Fraley, S. S., Chen, S. S., . . . Lemos, L. (2011). Sexuality among wounded veterans of Operation Enduring Freedom (OEF), Operation Iraqi Freedom (OIF), and Operation New Dawn (OND): Implications for rehabilitation psychologists. *Rehabilitation Psychology, 56*(4), 289–301.

Cochran, B. N., Balsam, K., Flentje, A., Malte, C. A, & Simpson, T. (2013). Mental health characteristics of sexual minority veterans. *Journal of Homosexuality, 60*(2–3), 419–35.

Cochran, S. D., & Mays, V. M. (2013). A systematic review of sexual orientation and the prevalence of mental health disorders: Implications for research and mental health services. In C. J. Patterson & A. R. D'Augelli (Eds.), *Handbook of psychology and sexual orientation* (pp. 204–222). New York, NY: Oxford University Press.

Eakman, A. M., Schelly, C., & Henry, K. L. (2016). Protective and vulnerability factors contributing to resilience in post-9/11 veterans with service-related injuries in postsecondary education. *The American Journal of Occupational Therapy : Official Publication of the American Occupational Therapy Association, 70*(1), 1–10.

Elliott, T. R., Hsiao, Y.-Y., Kimbrel, N. A., Meyer, E., DeBeer, B. B., Gulliver, S. B., . . . Morissette, S. B. (2015). Resilience, traumatic brain injury, depression and posttraumatic stress among Iraq/Afghanistan War veterans. *Rehabilitation Psychology, 60*(3), 263–276.

Estes, S. (2007). *Ask and tell: Gay and lesbian veterans speak out.* Chapel Hill, NC: The University of North Carolina Press.

Frank, N. (2009). *Unfriendly fire: How the gay ban undermines the military and weakens America.* New York, NY: St. Martin's Press.

Frost, D. M., & Meyer, I. H. (2015). Minority stress and physical health among sexual minority individuals. *Journal of Behavioral Medicine, 38*(1), 1–8.

Garner, A. (2005). *Families like mine: Children of gay parents tell it like it is.* New York, NY: HarperCollins.

Gayner, B., Esplen, M. J., DeRoche, P., Wong, J., Bishop, S., Kavanagh, L., & Butler, K. (2012). A randomized controlled trial of mindfulness-based stress reduction to manage affective symptoms and improve quality of life in gay men living with HIV. *Journal of Behavioral Medicine, 35*(3), 272–285.

Glück, T. M., Tran, U. S., Raninger, S., & Lueger-Schuster, B. (2015). The influence of sense of coherence and mindfulness on PTSD symptoms and posttraumatic cognitions in a sample of elderly Austrian survivors of World War II. *International Psychogeriatrics/IPA, 28*(3), 435–441.

Harwood, J. (2015). Intergroup contact, prejudicial attitudes, and policy preferences : The case of the U.S. military's "Don't Ask, Don't Tell" policy. *The Journal of Social Psychology, 155*, 57–69.

Hendricks, M. L., & Testa, R. J. (2012). A conceptual framework for clinical work with transgender and gender nonconforming clients: An adaptation of the minority stress model. *Professional Psychology: Research and Practice, 43*(5), 460–467.

Herek, G. M., & Garnets, L. D. (2007). Sexual orientation and mental health. *Annual Review of Clinical Psychology, 3*, 353–375.

Herrick, A. L., Stall, R., Goldhammer, H., Egan, J. E., & Mayer, K. H. (2014). Resilience as a research framework and as a cornerstone of prevention research for gay and bisexual men: Theory and evidence. *AIDS and Behavior, 18*(1), 1–9.

Holland, K. J., Rabelo, V. C., & Cortina, L. M. (2014). Sexual assault training in the military: Evaluating efforts to end the "invisible war." *American Journal of Community Psychology, 54*(3–4), 289–303.

Hoy-Ellis, C. P., Shiu, C., Sullivan, K. M., Kim, H. J., Sturges, A. M., & Fredriksen-Goldsen, K. I. (2017). Prior military service, identity stigma, and mental health among transgender older adults. *The Gerontologist, 57*(Suppl. 1), S63–S71.

Hunot, V., Moore, T. H. M., Caldwell, D. M., Furukawa, T. A., Davies, P., Jones, H., Honyashiki, M., Chen, P., Lewis, G., & Churchill, R. (2013). "Third wave" cognitive and behavioural therapies versus other psychological therapies for depression (review). *Cochrane Database of Systematic Reviews*, (10), Art. No.: CD008704.

Ingraham, N., Eliason, M. J., Garbers, S., Harbatkin, D., Minnis, A. M., McElroy, J. A., & Haynes, S. G. (2016). Effects of mindfulness interventions on health outcomes in older lesbian/bisexual women. *Women's Health Issues, 26*, S53–S62.

Johnson, D. C., Thom, N. J., Stanley, E. A., Haase, L., Simmons, A. N., Shih, P.-A. B., . . . Paulus, M. P. (2014). Modifiying resilience mechanisms in at-risk individuals: A controlled study of mindfulness training in Marines preparing for deployment. *American Journal of Psychiatry, 171*, 844–853.

Johnson, W. B., Rosenstein, J. E., Buhrke, R. A., & Haldeman, D. C. (2015). After "Don't Ask Don't Tell": Competent care of lesbian, gay and bisexual military personnel during the DoD policy transition. *Professional Psychology: Research and Practice, 46*(2), 107–115.

Keng, S.-L., & Liew, K. W. L. (2016). Trait mindfulness and self-compassion as moderators of the association between gender nonconformity and psychological health. *Mindfulness, 8*(3), 1–12.

Kimerling, R., Iverson, K. M., Dichter, M. E., Rodriguez, A. L., Wong, A., & Pavao, J. (2016). Prevalence of intimate partner violence among women veterans who utilize veterans health administration primary care. *Journal of General Internal Medicine, 31*(8), 888–894.

King, M., Semlyen, J., Killaspy, H., Nazareth, I., & Osborn, D. (2007). *A systematic review of research on counselling and psychotherapy for lesbian, gay, bisexual & transgender people.* Leicestershire, UK: British Association for Counseling and Psychotherapy. Retrieved from http://www.bacp.co.uk/docs/pdf/9352_lgbt_web.pdf

Kwon, P. (2013). Resilience in lesbian, gay, and bisexual individuals. *Personality and Social Psychology Review, 17*(4), 371–383.

Lindsay, J. A., Keo-Meier, C., Hudson, S., Walder, A., Martin, L. A., & Kauth, M. R. (2016). Mental health of transgender veterans of the Iraq and

Afghanistan conflicts who experienced military sexual trauma. *Journal of Traumatic Stress, 29*(6), 563–567.

Lyons, A. (2016). Mindfulness attenuates the impact of discrimination on the mental health of middle-aged and older gay men. *Psychology of Sexual Orientation and Gender Diversity, 3* (Advance online publication), 1–9.

Maguen, S., Shipherd, J. C., & Harris, H. N. (2005). Providing culturally proficient care for transgender patients. *Nursing, 45*(2), 58–63.

Mallon, G. P. (2009). *Social work practice with lesbian, gay, bisexual, and transgender people within families.* New York, NY: Routledge.

Mattocks, K. M., Sadler, A., Yano, E. M., Krebs, E. E., Zephyrin, L., Brandt, C., . . . Haskell, S. (2013). Sexual victimization, health status, and VA healthcare utilization among lesbian and bisexual OEF/OIF veterans. *Journal of General Internal Medicine, 28*(Suppl. 2), 4–7.

McWhorter, L. (1999). *Bodies and pleasures: Foucault and the politics of sexual normalization.* Indianapolis, IN: Indiana University Press.

Meyer, I. (2003). Prejudice, social stress, and mental health in lesbian, gay, and bisexual populations: Conceptual issues and research evidence. *Psychological Bulletin, 129*(5), 674–697.

Meyer, I. (2010). Identity, stress, and resilience in lesbians, gay men, and bisexuals or color. *Journal of Counseling Psychology, 38*(3), 1–9.

Meyer, I. H. (2014). Minority stress and positive psychology : Convergences and divergences to understanding LGBT health. *Psychology of Sexual Orientation and Gender Diversity, 1*(4), 348–349.

Meyer, I. H. (2015). Resilience in the study of minority stress and health of sexual and gender minorities. *Psychology of Sexual Orientation and Gender Diversity, 2*(3), 209–213.

Moradi, B. (2009). Sexual orientation disclosure, concealment, harassment, and military unit cohesion: Perceptions of LGBT military veterans. *Military Psychology, 21*(4), 513–533.

Murdoch, M., Pryor, J. B., Polusny, M. A., Gackstetter, G. D., & Ripley, D. C. (2009). Local social norms and military sexual stressors: do senior officers' norms matter? *Military Medicine, 174*(October), 1100–1104.

National Defense Research Institute. (2010). *Sexual Orientation and U.S. Military Personnel: An Update of RAND's 1993 Study.* Retrieved from http://www.rand.org/content/dam/rand/pubs/monographs/2010/RAND_MG1056.pdf

The Palm Center. (2017). *Fifty-Six Retired Generals and Admirals Warn That President Trump's Anti-Transgender Tweets, If Implemented, Would Degrade Military Readiness.* San Fransisco, CA: The Palm Center. Retrieved from http://www.palmcenter.org/fifty-six-retired-generals-admirals-warn-president-trumps-anti-transgender-tweets-implemented-degrade-military-readiness/

Pelts, M. D., Rolbiecki, A. J., & Albright, D. L. (2014). Wounded bonds: A review of the social work literature on gay, lesbian and bisexual military service members and veterans. *Journal of Social Work, 15*, 207–220.

Ramirez, M. H., Rogers, S. J., Johnson, H. L., Banks, J., Seay, W. P., Tinsley, B. L., & Grant, A. W. (2013). If we ask, what they might tell: Clinical assessment lessons from LGBT military personnel post-DADT. *Journal of Homosexuality, 60*(2/3), 401–418.

Ramirez, M. H., & Sterzing, P. R. (2017). Coming out in camouflage: A queer theory perspective on the strength, resilience, and resistance of lesbian, gay, bisexual, and transgender service members and veterans. *Journal of Gay & Lesbian Social Services, 29*(1), 68–86.

Riggle, E. D. B., Rostosky, S. S., & Horne, S. G. (2009). Marriage amendments and lesbian, gay, and bisexual individuals in the 2006 election. *Sexuality Research and Social Policy, 6*(1), 80–89.

Riggle, E. D. B., Whitman, J. S., Olson, A., Rostosky, S. S., & Strong, S. (2008). The positive aspects of being a lesbian or gay man. *Professional Psychology: Research and Practice, 39*(2), 210–217.

Russell, G. M., & Bohan, J. S. (2005). The gay generation gap : Communicating across the LGBT generational divide. *The Policy Journal of The Institute for Gay and Lesbian Strategic Studies, 8*(1), 1–8.

Sadler, A., Booth, B. M., Nielson, D., & Doebbeling, B. N. (2000). Health-related consequences of physical and sexual violence: Women in the military. *Obstetrics and Gynecology, 96*(3), 473–480.

Savin-Williams, R. C. (2008). Then and now: Recruitment, definition, diversity, and positive attributes of same-sex populations. *Developmental Psychology, 44*(1), 135–138.

Shilts, R. (1993). *Conduct unbecoming.* New York, NY: Ballantine Books.

Sinclair, G. D. (2009). Homosexuality and the military: A review of the literature. *Journal of Homosexuality, 56*(6), 701–718.

Southwick. (2012). The science of resilience: Implications for the prevention of treatment of depression. *Science, 338*(October), 79–82.

Stacey, J., & Biblarz, T. J. (2001). (How) does the sexual orientation of parents matter? *American Sociological Review, 66*(2), 159–183.

Stanley, E. A., Schaldach, J. M., Kiyonaga, A., & Jha, A. P. (2011). Mindfulness-based mind fitness training: A case study of a high-stress predeployment military cohort. *Cognitive and Behavioral Practice, 18*(4), 566–576.

Swank, E., Fahs, B., & Frost, D. M. (2013). Region, social identities, and disclosure practices as predictors of heterosexist discrimination against sexual minorities in the United States. *Sociological Inquiry, 83*(2), 238–258.

Thomas, K. H., Plummer Taylor, S. (2015). Bulletproofing the psyche: Mindfulness interventions in the training environment to improve resilience in the military and veteran communities. *Advances in Social Work, 16*(2), 312–322.

Trivette, S. A. (2010). Secret handshakes and decoder rings: The queer space of don't ask/don't tell. *Sexuality Research and Social Policy, 7*(3), 214–228.

Tucker, J. D., & Meier, B. M. (2016). Bigotry, bills, and medicine: lessons from the USA. *The Lancet, 388*(10046), 756–757.

U.S. Government Accountability Office. (2008). *DOD's and the coast guard's sexual assault prevention and response programs face implementation and oversight challenges highlights.* Washington, DC.

Wang, J. Y. H., Glover, W. J., Rhodes, A. M., & Nightingale, D. (2013). A conceptual model of the psychological health system for U.S. active duty service members: An approach to inform leadership and policy decision making. *Military Medicine, 178*(6), 596–606.

Wescott, K., & Sawyer, R. (2007). Silent sacrifices: The impact of "Don't Ask, Don't Tell" on lesbian and gay military families. *Duke Journal of Gender Law and Policy, 14,* 1121–1139.

Zucker, K. J., & Spitzer, R. L. (2005). Was the gender identity disorder of childhood diagnosis introduced into DSM-III as a backdoor maneuver to replace homosexuality? A historical note. *Journal of Sex & Marital Therapy, 31,* 31–42.

Note

1. The authors have chosen the term "LGBT" to describe those who identify as sexual and gender minorities. While this term can be limiting, the majority of research on service members and veterans uses this term. It is our hope that the reader will extend this term to include all those who identify as sexual and gender minorities.

CHAPTER 9

Resilient Military Families

Charles R. McAdams III

Introduction

There can be little doubt that the willingness and ability of individuals to accept and overcome their life challenges are often grounded in the support and security provided by their families. The importance of families to soldiers' fitness for navigating the complexity and uncertainty of the modern military environment cannot therefore be underestimated. At the same time, the demands of military service create unique and extraordinary stressors for families who are called upon to relocate frequently, to endure extended separations, and to live with the constant knowledge that one or more of their members could be seriously injured or killed in the future. It has become increasingly clear in recent years that the well-being of military families is directly related to the well-being of the military force as a whole and with that realization has come increased emphasis within the military enterprise on ensuring the readiness or fitness of military families for their critical role.

Families as Systems

Like all living systems, family systems tend to be distinguished by unique relational rules, a shared sense of purpose among family members, and a tendency to uphold family integrity against intrusions from outside influences (Nichols, 2016). Additionally, family systems are usually comprised of a number of smaller subsystems, each of which makes a distinct contribution to the family unit as a whole. For example, adults in a family may be members of both the *parental subsystem* with specific tasks related to child-rearing and the *spousal subsystem* with specific tasks related to family leadership and the modeling of intimacy and commitment. Within the *sibling subsystem*, comprised of the children in a family, brothers and sisters experience their first and often their longest lasting peer group through which they acquire skills in negotiation, cooperation, and mutual support (Cicirelli, 1995).

Healthy or "enabled" family systems are those in which needs of the family system as a whole and the individual needs of family members are being simultaneously fulfilled (Constantine, 1986). Conversely, unhealthy or "disabled" family systems are unable to balance system and individual member needs and thus are more likely to satisfy *either* system or individual needs at the expense of neglect to the other (Constantine, 1986). When imbalances between family member and family system needs occur in enabled families, family members are able to recognize the problem and respond in a way that restores a mutually acceptable state of balance. Conversely, families that are depleted and disabled by internal or external stress may lack the necessary resources for recognizing and addressing threats to their family's stability and, consequently, may respond to stress in ways that result in unstable and chaotic family patterns.

Family Structure

Family structure refers to the complex of repetitive and enduring transaction patterns that occur among members of a given family and uniquely distinguish that family from all others (Minuchin, 1974). Some transaction patterns define the specific rules of engagement or *boundaries* that exist among individual family members and subsystems and between the family as a whole and the outside world. Other transaction patterns define the *hierarchy* of influence or power that various family members have on family decisions, while still others define various *alignments* that have been formed between select family members in order to collectively exert more influence on family decisions than they could exert individually.

In enabled families, the transactional boundaries between family members and between the family as a whole and the outside world are *clear*; that is, they are unyielding enough to maintain a necessary distinction between the various system components yet flexible enough to permit communication among system components that is necessary for maintaining healthy system balance. Transactional boundaries that are excessively unyielding or *rigid* threaten family stability by stifling communication that is needed for coordinated system operation, while excessively flexible or *diffuse* boundaries threaten the family's hierarchical structure as well as its distinct identity by rendering the system overly vulnerable to external influences.

The hierarchy of power or influence can vary greatly among different family systems; however, it is generally agreed that enabled families are hierarchically organized with parents or adult members holding the most influence on family decisions and children having lesser degrees of influence in order of their chronological age. In disabled families, hierarchical problems can include (but are not limited to) the relinquishment by parents of appropriate family leadership, the assumption of excessive leadership responsibility by children, and confusion surrounding the involvement of extended family members in the family leadership structure.

Alignments among family members are considered necessary and beneficial to the family system. For example, an alignment among adults in the parental role of the family is seen as essential to coordinated family leadership and decision making. Similarly, alignment among the siblings can ensure that family leadership hears their less powerful individual voices and that children's interests are considered in critical family decisions. Alignments can also be problematic, especially when they cross generational boundaries or they involve coercive unions or *detouring coalitions* between all or some family members against a third member. Alignments between a parent and older child or a parent and grandparent are examples of cross-generational alignments that can be harmful if they confound the clarity of boundaries, roles, and responsibilities within the family's hierarchical structure. Conflict avoidance through detouring coalitions (i.e., blaming one family member for system conflict) is almost always harmful to family stability, because avoided family conflicts are less likely to be resolved and, thus, more likely to continue or worsen in the future.

The Military Family

From the previous sections, it can be seen that *all* family systems are an intricate and balanced complex of interconnected individuals and subsystems that, in order to be fully enabled, must create conditions of appropriate hierarchical organization, clear rules of interaction both internally and with the environment, and necessary alignment among various members to ensure the satisfactory completion of vital tasks. To remain enabled, families must also be able to maintain these required conditions in the face of continual internal and external (environmental) changes occurring with the passage of time. In effect, it seems that in a complex and rapidly changing world, remaining healthy can be a daunting task for families under even the best of circumstances and for military families there are additional challenges. In fact, research suggests that military families face unique and substantial challenges in maintaining each of the hierarchy, boundary, and alignment conditions considered necessary to family health.

Challenges to the Family Hierarchy

It should come as no surprise that military deployment can be profoundly disruptive to the leadership structure of a family. The extended absence of one parent requires the remaining parent to assume parenting roles and responsibilities that were formally shared, sometimes (and understandably) leading to fatigue and frustration and impaired ability to exert the level of family leadership that is needed (Rosetto, 2015). This additional leadership burden along with grief over the absence and anxiety over the well-being of the deployed partner has shown to have generally negative effect on the mental health, parenting effectiveness, and emotional well-being of nondeployed spouses across service disciplines (Mansfield et al., 2010). The simultaneous deployment of both parents often requires the involvement of extended family members, thereby disrupting the normal family leadership structure to varying degrees depending upon whether children remain in their home or move into the home of the extended family member where they must adapt to a completely new family environment. Whether one or both parents are deployed, it is evident that the often transitional and variable leadership structure in military families can be a contributing factor to adverse outcomes for developing children, particularly adolescent-aged children (Lucier-Greer, Arnold, Mancini, Ford, & Bryant, 2015).

A parent's return from deployment alone may not be synonymous with a return of the family's leadership structure to its predeployment state. During the deployment, the family at home has necessarily assumed new roles, priorities, and routines, such that returning members sometimes struggle to reestablish their role and even may come to feel out of place in their own homes (Sayers et al., 2007). Reintegration into the family may be further disrupted if the returning member is experiencing physical or psychological impairment following the deployment. Research suggests that over a quarter of military personnel have returned from recent conflicts with disabling physical and/or psychological injuries, often with co-occurring depressive disorder and substance abuse (Sandoz, Moyer, & Armelie, 2015). In such cases, it becomes less certain as to when, if ever, the hierarchy of leadership in a military family will be able to return to its predeployment state.

Challenges to Family Boundaries

Change in a family's hierarchical structure invariably necessitates concurrent change in its internal and external boundaries (Gurman & Kniskern, 1981). Internally, boundaries between the parental and sibling subsystems may become more open or diffuse when older children are, by necessity, called upon by the parent at home to assume greater roles in family decision making and the care of younger children. On the other hand, boundaries between the parent at home and younger children may become more closed or rigid if the shift in parenting responsibilities to older children results in the younger children having less access to direct parent-child interaction. Boundaries between the parent at home and other family members generally may become more rigid if that parent is consumed with the fear, fatigue, emotional distress, and grief that have shown to be commonly experienced by military spouses during their partner's deployment (Larsen, Clauss-Ehlers, & Cosden, 2015).

Externally, the boundaries between the nuclear and extended families can be expected to become more diffuse when extended family members are called upon to assist in family leadership and parenting responsibilities during the military deployment of one or both parents. During the period of the deployment, the previous rules of engagement with extended family must be relaxed to enable a shift of extended family members from a primarily supportive role to a role with more direct involvement in family affairs. Lack of clarity in transactional changes stemming from this nuclear-extended boundary diffusion can lead to confusion and conflict unless the changes are clearly specified for all family members (Noriega, Lopez, Dominiquez, & Velasco, 2016).

A family member's deployment may result in increased rigidity in the boundaries between the family and the external community at large, as internal demands on family members at home leave less opportunity for engagement with external social support systems. Tasked with additional work and parental responsibilities, spouses at home may have less time to utilize available military and civilian support services or interact socially with friends, while added chores and childcare responsibilities may limit opportunities for older children to engage as readily in extracurricular school and community activities. It is ironic that at a time when social support may be most needed by a military family, its members may be least open and receptive to receiving it.

Challenges to Family Alliances

Extended physical separation has shown to be a significant stressor to marital or otherwise committed partnerships (Negrusa, Negrusa, & Hosek, 2014), and physical separation due to military deployment is no exception. Despite technological advances that have enabled more frequent communication between a deployed service member and his or her partner at home, family separation, day-to-day stress from limited information, and inability to be fully engaged from a distance can severely and sometimes fatally stress the spousal and parental alliances that are vital to family direction and stability. The prolonged involvement of extended family members or other adults in the family leadership structure can exacerbate the challenge to those alliances as well as to parent-child alliances. When deployed service members return with physical or psychological impairment, the effects of new and existing challenges to the spousal and parental alliances may be felt in the family long after the deployment period has ended.

A unique additional threat to alliance between the adult partners in military families can be postdeployment service member's divided loyalty between his or her natural family and the military unit. During military deployment, soldiers can form intimate bonds with teammates that will last a lifetime (Castro, Kintzle, & Hassan, 2015). Often born from shared struggle, unyielding trust, and commitment to unconditional sacrifice, bonds between military teammates may be deeper than friendship and may rival the significance of bonds with their natural families at home (Lindsay, 2013). Whereas the spouse or partner at home is likely to desire and expect the postdeployment service member' full commitment to family reintegration, the returning service member may feel pulled between shared loyalties and obligations to family members and military teammates. The potential significance of a soldier's postdeployment relationship with teammates may be difficult for family members to understand (Castro et al., 2015); however, until it is acknowledged, understood, and accepted by the family, it may serve as a direct threat to key family alliances and thus to family unity.

Structural Elements of Military Family Fitness

The vital importance of enabled military families to the effective function of the military enterprise as a whole was formally recognized in the early 1980s by former Army chief of staff, General John Wickham, who, in a seminal white paper, identified the supports available to military families at that time as being piecemeal and called for increased efforts to promote family readiness to deal future military challenges (Wickham, 1983). Family readiness, more recently referred to as family fitness, has been defined as "the ability of families to effectively cope with the challenges posed by military service" (Bowles et al., 2015, p. 247). Fit military families are aware of the potential challenges they may face, and these families are equipped with the resources they will need to be resilient and remain enabled in the face of adversity. In effect, they are families with hierarchical, boundary, and alliance structures that can withstand, adapt to, and overcome the unique challenges posed by contemporary military life.

Family Fitness and Family Hierarchy

Fitness in terms of the family hierarchy depends strongly on the assurance of an enabled parental subsystem. Despite the aforementioned challenges of military deployment, the parental subsystem must continue to be able to model and provide family direction, unity, and stability. Research to date suggests that there are several proactive steps that military parents can take to maintain both a committed alliance and effective family leadership, given the challenging circumstances of military separation. They include developing and maintaining a shared commitment to the military service and lifestyle, forming consistent channels of communication for the sharing of information, and establishing mutual agreement on revisions to parenting responsibilities and practices that will occur during a deployment period.

The challenges of military lifestyle, and the stressors of deployment in particular, can be especially problematic for military parents when they do not share a mutually strong commitment to the military mission and lifestyle (Bowles et al., 2015). On the other hand, when parents share a commitment to being a military family, they are more apt to have a mutual understanding of the unique challenges of military life and the need for advance planning to face its challenges. It appears that couples who take the time to examine and resolve possible differences in their respective appraisals of being a military family and who periodically renew their mutual commitment to the military lifestyle will be more willing and better equipped to adjust to the consequences of that lifestyle, whatever they may turn out to be.

Parenting children can be a challenging task for all families (Bradley, 2007). Inasmuch as new parents commonly rely upon their own parents as models of parenting, it stands to reason that couples may bring different and potentially conflictual views to the relationship about parenting and the way that families are "supposed" to function. Avoidance of conflict around parenting and family management is best achieved when parents have established communication channels that enable both parents to regularly express their thoughts and feelings and to be heard. Current research in military family communication suggests that military parents tend to be most successful when these communication channels involve multiple modalities (e.g., e-mail, telephone, letters) that permit them to remain open and active during extended periods of physical separation (Merolla, 2010).

Well-established communication channels between a deployed parent and parent at home may be of limited value to coordinated family leadership if necessary changes in parenting roles and responsibilities during the deployment period have not been agreed upon and addressed with all family members in advance. Family routines have shown to strengthen and stabilize family connections, whereas military relocations and deployments disrupt normal family routines and, consequently, pose a threat to family stability (Patterson, 2002). The impact of military transitions on family stability can be lessened when, prior to a transition period, parents (a) identify and mutually agree on the changes in the parenting and other routines that will be necessary during the transition period and (b) introduce the anticipated changes in routine to all family members to ensure their understanding and to reassure them of the continued involvement of *both* parents in their lives despite the absence of one parent during transition period.

Family Fitness and Family Boundaries

Theories of family therapy suggest that the specific configuration of boundaries between individuals and subsystems in a family is less important to family health and stability than is boundary clarity (Goldenberg & Goldenberg, 2013). Boundary configurations can change in families as long as the key functions of the involved family system components remain intact. For example, during deployment in a military family, older children who assist in parental roles, such as the care of younger children, can do so without detriment to family system stability as long as the transactional rules distinguishing the parental subsystem from the sibling subsystem (e.g., respect for parental authority) are not compromised. Similarly, the younger children will be less threatened by decreased parental presence and availability (i.e., more rigid parental boundaries) during deployment when time has been taken by parents to help them understand the upcoming changes and to assure them that the changes are temporary. In short, advance parental planning for internal boundary changes that will be required during a military transition, including advance analysis of their impact on the family as a whole, will allow a military family to make the necessary adjustments to member roles and responsibilities without undue threat to family system integrity.

Careful advance planning is also the recommended strategy for minimizing the boundary confusion that can occur when external family members (or other individuals external to the family) are called upon to assist a family during deployment. Clear and specific understanding by all internal and external family members as to *who* from the extended family will be entering the family leadership structure, *how* or in what ways the external family member(s) will be involved in family leadership and parenting, and *when* the external family member(s) will be involved (and when they will stop being involved) can help to safeguard the overall integrity of internal-external family boundaries during a necessary but temporary period of internal-external boundary diffusion.

Belonging to a supportive social group such as church, social groups, and community organizations has shown to be helpful to children, adolescents, and adults at home in coping with a parent's military deployment (Johnson, Sherman, & Hoffman, 2007). However, it has been previously noted that increased demands on internal family resources in the absence of a deployed parent can result in more rigid family boundaries with the community, because family members simply have less time to be involved in external support activities. As family leaders plan for the future military deployment of their members, it is important for them to not lose sight of the important role that community support systems can play as sources of connection, information, continuity, and emotional support for family members of all ages who are experiencing various levels of loss, anxiety, and grief. Willingness and effort to develop and/or maintain family members' involvements in social support activities despite constraints imposed by increased internal family system demands can separate enabled from disabled families at times of upheaval due to military transitions.

Family Fitness and Family Alliances

No aspect of the family system may be more critical to the consideration of a family's fitness for facing adversity than the aspect of family alliances. The alliances between the individuals and subsystems are essentially the "glue" that holds a family system together, and the integrity of the system in periods of duress will depend upon the ability of the alliances to withstand the pull of intrusive environmental demands. Most crucial to the maintenance of family integrity at any given time may be the solidarity of the alliance between partners in the spousal subsystem. Distance alone does not truly appear to "make the heart grow fonder" as an old adage suggests; maintaining closeness and connection in committed relationships during extended separation appears to take both advance planning and conscious effort. Couples who put conscious effort into maintaining a close and satisfying relationship generally have shown to be the couples whose relationships are also best equipped to withstand adversity (Halford, Petch, & Creedy, 2015). They tend to be couples who share and regulate their emotions through open, regular, and honest communication; who have devised mutually acceptable strategies for parenting and problem solving; and perhaps most importantly, who have made the ongoing nurturance of love, closeness, and shared vision that initially brought them together a mutual priority (Beavers, 1985).

The loss or diminishment of parents' presence in the day-to-day lives of their children can undoubtedly be expected to place stress on the critical parent-child alliance. It is to the parent-child alliance that children typically refer in describing what "family" means to them and from the parent-child alliance that children are likely to develop their foundational sense if identity (Satir & Bitter, 2000). The parent-child alliance is formed and nurtured through a history of positive interactions between parents and their children (Tissot, Favez, Udry-Jorgensen, Frascarolo, & Despland, 2015), and when through such a history the alliance is strong, its integrity is unlikely to be compromised by the temporary absence or diminished availability of parents during a military deployment period. Military families can proactively reduce the risk of harm to the parent-child alignment during a deployment or other transition period through purposeful and consistent efforts to engage as a family in positive experiences at times when all family members *are* together. Through such efforts, it is anticipated that the alliances of children to their parents and, consequently, a key aspect of family integrity will be more resilient to the stressors of military life.

The potential threat of a service member's bond to his or her military unit and teammates to the solidarity of the spousal or other family alliances can be a particularly formidable threat, because it centers around a bond that has been described by some as one that cannot be fully understood by those who have not experienced it personally (Ringel & Brandell, 2012). As such, it is a bond that may be neither be anticipated nor prepared for by a family prior to a service member's deployment. Although to date, no specific strategies to prepare military families for this threat have been presented in the professional literature, the family systems literature regarding the dynamics of blended family systems offers some useful insight. As recommended for the integration of two families through remarriage, two primary steps in successful integration of a service member's "family" of military teammates into the lives of his or her family at home appear to include anticipating changes and making a plan (Carter & McGoldrick, 2005). The degree to which family members at home can (or cannot) fully comprehend a soldier's bond to teammates and unit may actually be less important to family stability than the realization by all family members that changes *will* have occurred during a deployment, both in the returning soldier and in themselves. Families that anticipate postdeployment changes are less likely to be caught off guard and to respond reactively when actual changes are observed. Spared the element of surprise, all family members are better positioned to try to understand postdeployment changes in family members and the family system as a whole and to explore mutually acceptable strategies for responding to them.

Supporting Military Family Fitness

It can be seen in the preceding section that family resilience to stressful conditions can be strengthened when families acknowledge that they are under duress and take specific preemptive measures to minimize its negative impact on family structure and function. There is also evidence to suggest that military and civilian families alike can benefit from community interventions aimed at promoting their structural resilience to environmental adversity. Following is an overview of the nature and impact of one such promising intervention.

The New Directions for Family and Youth Development Program

The New Directions for Family and Youth Development program is a grant-funded university-community partnership program designed to promote fitness among military and civilian families who are facing substantial internal and/or external challenges. Through attention to the impact of the challenges on the stability of internal family structures, the program attempts to promote family adaptability, unity, and resilience in the face of adversity by introducing and applying knowledge and applications of family systems theory described in the previous sections. All activities in the program curriculum are intended to increase the effectiveness of family leadership, to clarify the boundaries between the family system components and between the system and its environment, and to strengthen key family alliances. Program sessions are 10 weeks in duration, include 8–10 families per session, and involve weekly family participation in family counseling, group counseling for children and adolescents, and parent group education and counseling. Participating families are drawn from local and regional public schools and from multiple military installations in the surrounding area. All family, child, and parent services are provided by advanced doctoral students in counselor education under the supervision of licensed faculty directors, one of whom is a veteran of Naval Special Warfare service.

The curriculum. Central to the New Directions curriculum is a uniform focus among the family, child, and parent program components during each of the 10 sessions. Each week, families, children, and parents participate in guided exploration of the same topic area, enabling family members well as activity leaders to discuss and compare each other's perspectives on the topics between each session. The weekly topic areas are generally as follows: (a) Being a Family, (b) Being a Military Family, (c) Being a Parent in Our Family, (d) Being a Child/Adolescent in Our Family, (e) What We Do That Makes Our Family Special? (f) How We Communicate, (g) When Things Change in Our Family, (h) Who Is There to Help Us? (i) What Have We Learned? and (j) Celebrating Our Family.

Key program assumptions. The curriculum of the New Directions program is grounded in several key assumptions about the needs of families, military and otherwise. They include assumptions that (a) families tend to share more similarities than differences, (b) families cannot function effectively in isolation from their environment, (c) families often fail to utilize their full resources in problem solving, and (d) maintaining an enabled family system in the 21st century is a challenging task at best.

The first assumption that families are more alike than different underlies the program's intention to bring struggling families and family members together into groups. Experience suggests that challenges tend to feel more manageable when families realize that others are experiencing them as well and that they are not alone.

The second assumption that families cannot succeed in isolation underlies the program's intentional inclusion of *both* military and civilian families in the three component groups. Inclusion of military and civilian families in programming has shown to increase mutual understanding of each other's challenges and to facilitate the development of supportive interfamily relationships that afford sources of mutual support long after the program has ended.

The third assumption that families fail to use all the problem-solving tools they have underlies the New Directions program's strong focus on improving communication throughout the family system. Program activities aimed at improving the quantity and quality of communication among members of all family system components have shown to promote more effective family problem solving by ensuring that the ideas and support of all family members are included in the family's development and implementation of problem-solving strategies.

The final assumption that the job of families today is a challenging one underlies an attitude of honoring families that the facilitators of each program component *must* possess and convey in order for the program to succeed. Families are most likely to seek and accept help with their problems when they feel that others will respect them for their problem-solving efforts, no matter how ineffective those efforts might have been.

Outcomes. For the past five years, the New Directions program has provided services to 155 military and civilian families. Throughout that period, combination of standardized and nonstandardized measures have been used to determine program effectiveness in terms of family interactional, organizational, and emotional health; children's internalizing and externalizing behaviors across multiple domains; and parent perceptions of change in family communication, problem solving, and parenting effectiveness.

Pretest-to-posttest scores on the Global Assessment of Relational Functioning (GARF; *DSM-IV*; American Psychiatric Association, 2000), a standardized clinical measure of family health, indicate that significant positive changes have occurred for participating families in terms of each of their interactional, organizational, and emotional aspects of family well-being. Posttest scores on the Clinical Assessment of Behavior (CAB; Bracken & Keith, 2004), a standardized measure of children's problematic behaviors, indicate that participating children's internalized behaviors (i.e., anxiety and depression) and externalized behaviors (i.e., anger and aggression) have moved on the average from mild clinical risk levels to normal levels following their participation in the program. Average participant ratings on the Parent Survey, a program-specific instrument, indicate parent perceptions of substantial improvement on all three of the instrument's family communication, family problem solving, and parenting effectiveness indices.

In summary, it is evident that the focus of the New Directions program on strengthening family structural components and communication has had a positive impact on the military and civilian families who have taken part in it. Longitudinal analysis is currently in progress to determine the resilience of the positive outcomes of the program over time and to assess the effectiveness of the program in its overall goal of helping families more successfully navigate the formidable future challenges that confront them in both the military and civilian contexts.

Conclusion

The structure of all families is complex and constantly evolving, and there is a need for an effective balance among multiple working parts in order for families to be healthy and able to effectively survive a host of challenges they encounter in the social, political, and economic environments of the 21st century. Family fitness to face adversity is not a guarantee—it takes proactive planning and conscious effort from family members as well as support from extended family and community members. Specialized support programs such as the New Directions for Youth and Family Development program can further enhance the readiness of military and civilian families for anticipating and facing formidable challenges to their stability and integrity. Engagement in family practices and community support programs to build family fitness must not be viewed as a sign of pathology or weakness by military families facing the prospect or reality of deployment or other stressful military transitions. On the contrary, such engagement should be viewed as a sign of a military couple's love and commitment to keep their family strong and available to all its members during the most challenging of times.

References

American Psychiatric Association. (2000). *Diagnostic and statistical manual of mental disorders* (4th ed., Test Revision). Washington DC: Author.

Beavers, W. R., (1985). *Successful marriage: A family systems approach to couple therapy.* New York, NY: W.W. Norton & Company Inc.

Bowles, S. V., Pollock, L. D., Moore, M, Wadsworth, S. M., Cato, C., Dekle, J. W., . . . Bates, M. J. (2015). Total force fitness: The military family fitness model. *Military Medicine, 180*(2), 246–258.

Bracken, B. A., & Keith, L. K. (2004). *Clinical assessment of behavior professional manual.* Lutz, FL: Psychological Assessment Resources.

Bradley, R. H. (2007). Parenting in the breach: How parents help children cope with developmentally challenging circumstances. *Parenting: Science and Practice, 7*(2), 99–148.

Carter, B., & McGoldrick, M. (2005). Overview: The expanded family life cycle: Individual, family, and social perspectives. In B. Carter and M. McGoldrick (Eds.), *The expanded family life cycle: Individual, family, and social perspectives* (4th ed.). Boston, MA: Allyn & Bacon.

Castro, C. A., Kintzle, S., & Hassan, A. M. (2015). The combat veteran paradox: Paradoxes and dilemmas encountered with reintegrating combat veterans and the agencies that support them. *Traumatology, 21*(4), 299–310.

Cicirelli, V. G. (1995). *Sibling relationships across the life span.* New York, NY: Plenum Press.

Constantine, L. L. (1986). *Family paradigms: The practice of theory in family therapy.* New York, NY: Guilford Press.

Goldenberg, I., & Goldenberg, H. (2013). *Family therapy: An overview* (8th ed.). Pacific Grove, CA: Brooks/Cole.

Gurman, A. S., & Kniskern, D. P. (1981). Family therapy outcome research: Knowns and unknowns. *Handbook of Family Therapy, 1,* 742–775.

Halford, W. K., Petch, J., & Creedy, D. (2015). *Clinical guide to helping new parents: The couple CARE for parents program.* New York, NY: Springer.

Johnson, S. J., Sherman, M. D., & Hoffman J. S. (2007). The psychological needs of US military service members and their families: A preliminary report. American Psychological Association Presidential Task Force on Military Deployment Services for Youth, Families and Service Members. Retrieved from http://www.ptsd.ne.gov/publications/military-deployment-task-force-report.pdf

Larsen, J. L., Clauss-Ehlers, C. S., & Cosden, M. A. (2015). An exploration of Army wives' responses to spousal deployment: Stressors and protective factors. *Couple and Family Psychology: Research and Practice, 4*(4), 212–228.

Lindsay, P. (2013). *The spirit of Gallipoli: The birth of the Anzac legend.* London, UK: Hardee-Grant Books.

Lucier-Greer, M., Arnold, A. L., Mancini, J. A., Ford, J. L., & Bryant, C. M. (2015). Influences of cumulative risk and protective factors on the adjustment of adolescents in military families. *Family Relations, 64,* 363–377.

Mansfield, A. J., Kaufman, J. S., Marshall, S. W., Gaynes, B. N., Morrissey, J. P., & Engel, C. C. (2010). Deployment and the use of mental health services among U.S. Army wives. *The New England Journal of Medicine, 36*(2), 101–109.

Merolla, A. J. (2010). Relational maintenance during military deployment: Perspectives of wives of deployed US soldiers. *Journal of Applied Community Research, 38*(1), 4–26.

Minuchin, S. (1974). *Families and family therapy.* Cambridge, MA: Harvard University Press.

Negrusa, S., Negrusa, B., & Hosek, J. (2014). Gone to war: Have deployments increased divorces? *Journal of Population Economics, 27*(2), 473–496.

Nichols, M. P. (2016). *Family therapy: Concepts and methods.* Hoboken, NJ: Pearson Education.

Noriega, C., Lopez, J., Dominiquez, R., & Velasco, C. (2016). Perceptions of grandparents who provide auxiliary care: Value transmission and child rearing practices. *Child and Family Social Work, 22*(3), 1–10.

Patterson, J. M. (2002). Understanding family resilience. *Journal of Clinical Psychology, 58*(3), 233–246.

Ringel, S. S., & Brandell, J. R. (Eds.). (2012). *Trauma: Contemporary directions in theory, practice, and research*. Thousand Oaks, CA: Sage Publications.

Rosetto, K. R. (2015). Developing conceptual definitions and theoretical models of coping in military families during deployment. *Journal of Family Communication, 15*, 249–268.

Sandoz, E. K., Moyer, D. N., & Armelie, A. P. (2015). Psychological flexibility as a framework for understanding and improving family reintegration following military deployment. *Journal of Marital and Family Therapy, 41*(4), 495–507.

Satir, V. M., & Bitter, J. R. (2000). The therapist and family therapy: Satir's human validation process model. In A. M. Horne & J. L. Passmore (Eds.), *Family counseling & therapy* (3rd ed.). Itasca, IL: Peacock.

Sayers, S. L., Farrow, V., Ross, J., Beswick, C., Sippel, L., Kane, V., & Oslin, D. W. (2007, November). The importance of family readjustment problems among Iraq and Afghanistan veterans referred for behavioral health evaluation. In S. L. Sayers (Chair), *Couple and family adjustment and reintegration issues for Iraq and Afghanistan military veterans*. Symposium conducted at the annual meeting of the Association of Behavioral and Cognitive Therapies, Philadelphia, PA.

Tissot, H., Favez, N., Udry-Jorgensen, L., Frascarolo, F., & Despland, J. (2015). Mothers' and fathers' sensitive parenting and mother—father—child family alliance during triadic interactions. *The Family Journal, 23*(4), 374–380.

Wickham, J. A. (1983). The Army Family: White Paper 1983. Washington, DC: U.S. Army.

CHAPTER 10

The Promotion of Well-Being in Older Veterans

Kari L. Fletcher, Mariah Rooney O'Brien, and Kamilah A. Jones

This chapter highlights the promotion of well-being among older veterans. It is divided into three overarching sections. First, we describe unique characteristics and considerations of older veterans as a cohort. Second, we introduce tools that may promote well-being. Third, we discuss holistic practices found in complementary and alternative medicine (CAM). Vignettes in each section capture older veterans' respective journeys, from their time of military service to the present.

Older Veterans

Today, 9.4 million veterans—or approximately 45 percent of the 22 million total veteran population (U.S. Department of Veterans Affairs [VA], 2014b)—are ages 65 and over (U.S. Census Bureau, 2012a). In the next 25 years, more than half of veterans will be ages 65 or older (VA, 2011).

In the United States, veterans ages 65 and older constitute 12.8 percent of the older adult population (U.S. Census Bureau, 2012a; VA, 2014a). They are more often male (97%) than female (3%; U.S. Census Bureau, 2012a, 2012b; VA, 2014a) and more often white (91.4%) than black or African (5.9%), Hispanic or Latino (3.1%), Asian (1%), or American Indian/Alaska Native (0.4%; U.S. Census Bureau, 2012b). Most older veterans served during one or more periods/eras: 1,981,000 (8.74%) during World War II (December 7, 1941–December 31, 1946); 2,448,000 (10.8%) during the Korean Conflict era (June 27, 1950–January 31, 1955); 7,526,000 (33.2%) during the Vietnam War era (February 28, 1961–May 7, 1975); or during peacetime years (Torreon, 2017; U.S. Census Bureau, 2012b).

Military Experience: Considerations in Veterans' Subsequent Lives

Military service factors into older veterans' lives as they grow older (Settersten, 2006). In this section, we consider (1) era, cohort membership, and historic events; (2) military service and its subsequent effects; and (3) aging and health.

Vignette 1: "Jessica"

Jessica is a 70-year-old, white (non-Latina), married, retired veteran who served as an Army nurse during Vietnam War (1969–1971). Stationed near Tokyo, Jessica worked in a neurosurgery post-op hospital unit that treated soldiers with both combat and non-combat-related spinal cord or traumatic brain injuries. Many, considered too injured for transport from Vietnam to the larger military hospital located in Hawaii, were air-evac'd or jet-transported to her base either to be stabilized or to say good-bye to family (if at risk for not surviving their injuries).

Era, Cohort Membership, and Historic Events

Jessica largely attributes her decision to join the military to her friend Sherrie, who enlisted during college and then received orders to go to Japan upon graduation. Once there, she wrote Jessica encouraging her to apply: "The patients here are in such need. They really need our help."

When Jessica joined the Army, she felt "ready to fly out of my nest, [to] be in a different place." She was excited to be stationed in Japan, which she found culturally interesting and safe. Living there, she had novel experiences and learned new things in a supportive environment.

With regard to her military/veteran identity, Jessica identifies as a nurse who served during the war. She believes other nurses who served during her time felt similarly. "Nurses were treated as nurses even though we had to find our way." Though serving on the helping end of the war, Jessica is thankful she did not serve in direct combat. Had she been, she is "not so sure that her psyche would have done so well."

Though less connected to today's military where "service members' experiences are different [than mine were]," today Jessica feels quite connected to her own experience, both as a military child (her father served in the Army during World War II) and with regard to her own service. She notices all things military more than she feels she would have had she not served. In church when her minister asks those who have served to identify themselves, Jessica always feels proud to stand up. Also, she supports veteran and police causes, which remain "near and dear to her heart."

Though she thinks fondly upon her service, Jessica rarely talks about her military experience. Occasionally, she and two nurses she served with reminisce over pictures about their experiences together. And upon occasion at home, Jessica's husband refers to her (rank) lightheartedly as "Captain."

Today's older veterans (ages 65 and older) were born in 1952 or earlier. Their early lives may have been influenced by historic events such as the Great Depression (1929–mid-1930s), the Cold War (1947–1991), and Executive Order 998 (issued in 1948), which led to the integration of the armed forces (McFarland, 2012). Older veterans may have served under conscription (the military draft, enforced from 1940 to 1973) and/or within an all-volunteer force (in place from 1973 to the present; Rostker, 2006). They may have received benefits such as guaranteed housing loans and educational benefits, through the Servicemen's Readjustment Act of 1944 and G.I. Bill, respectively (McFarland, 2012).

Military Service and Its Effects

As a turning point versus a disruption. *When asked whether her military service disrupted in her subsequent life, Jessica promptly answered, "It wasn't for me, but it was for my parents. Don't get me wrong, my parents think positively of the military, but I think my choice to join was hard on them."*

When asked whether her life post-military service was a turning point, Jessica responded, "I'm not sure whether or to what end my service in the military influenced my subsequent future decisions." Upon discharge from the military, she toured Europe with a friend, then worked part-time at a university, and eventually returned to school to earn an advanced degree in clinical nursing practice. Jessica sees her military service as connected to her nursing career, before and after. After returning home, Jessica was very comfortable working at the VA.

The military may serve as a frame of reference, dividing life events that took place before, during, or after (Tedeschi & Calhoun, 2006) one's service. Older veterans' life trajectories may be positively and/or negatively impacted by their military service (Fletcher, Albright, Rorie, & Lewis, 2017). Military service can be a turning point that redirects or disrupts their life in a positive manner and/or negatively affect established trajectories and later-life outcomes (Wilmoth & London, 2011).

As contributing factors to subsequent impacts. *Prior to joining the army, Jessica had worked briefly after completing her bachelor's degree as a licensed registered nurse. Then in the military, she completed basic training, and she obtained more "hands on training." Her work was intense. Jessica recalls, "Working one 3–11 pm shift as the only nurse on duty the night 15 patients were admitted to a 50-bed unit, some on stretchers."*

As an Army nurse, Jessica's work duties included drawing blood, using Betadine scrubs to clean out wounds, and helping turn over injured, bedridden patients. She recalls that while very injured "patients [she worked with] in Japan were very much wanting to get better—either to go back home or to return to their unit."

Jessica views her military service as largely positive. "It was a great experience." Both during and after she served, Jessica has "carried a lot of faith that God is with me/us no matter what is going on." In addition to being stationed on the same base as Sherrie, she had good co-coworkers, an "accepting, calm, and good at teaching" head nurse supervisor, as well as a great network of support in the bachelor/officer's quarters where she lived.

Older veterans may experience ongoing stressors that are physical (e.g., pain), cognitive (e.g., rationalization of experience), emotional (e.g., depression), social (e.g., isolation), and/or spiritual (e.g., existential) in nature (Nash, 2006). Long after their military service, they may struggle to navigate separations, readjustment, and transitions (e.g., managing illness, grief, loss, and bereavement; Fletcher, Mankowski, & Albright, 2018; Kulka et al., 1990; Zoli, Maury, & Fay, 2015). Older veterans' resilience—the ability to recover from and rise above setbacks/difficult circumstances (Ginsburg, 2006)—may influence the degree to which risk factors (e.g., combat exposure, age, prior mental health history, military service, or obstacles faced postdeployment; Wilcox, Finney, & Cedarbaum, 2013) and protective factors (aspects that mediate risk, such as perceptions of support; Nock et al., 2013) are present.

Aging and Health

When asked whether military service has affected her health in the long term, Jessica says she feels it has not. She says that her current physical health concerns (e.g., cardiovascular concerns) were influenced by a preexisting childhood condition (which did not keep her from serving) more so than by her military service. With regard to mental health, Jessica says that she was not traumatized by her military experience or the many injuries she witnessed for two main reasons: her faith and the support she received while deployed. She acknowledges, "This might have been a different experience for others."

With aging, deterioration is ongoing and transpires over time (Kane, Ouslander, Abrass, & Resnick, 2013). For veterans and nonveterans alike, aging happens differently and at different rates (Kane et al., 2013). In general, older veterans are thought both to age faster than nonveterans (Damron-Rodriguez, 2011) and to be more prone to disease and disability (Fletcher et al., 2017). In general, factors such as longevity, genetics, and lifestyle choices may contribute positively or negatively to the aging process (McReynolds & Rossen, 2004).

Health-related effects of military service may appear later in life among older veterans (VA, 2009). Susceptible to disease and disability, older veterans often experience physical and mental morbidities and functional impairment at higher rates than nonveterans (Sherwood, Shimel, Stolz, & Sherwood, 2004). Overall, the main causes of death among older veterans remain largely unknown (Maynard & Boyko, 2006).

Possible implications for exposure during service. Today, "older veterans may still be managing injuries they incurred while in the service" (Fletcher et al., 2017). Many who served in combat did so during a time when health care (e.g., mobile Army surgical hospitals) and transportation (e.g., helicopters) technologies had improved in comparison to prior wars, helping them survive injuries incurred while in the service (Boettcher & Cobb, 2006).

Physical. During their service, older veterans may have been exposed to hazardous conditions, to the detriment of their future physical health (VA, 2015b). Exposures may be linked to era of service: mustard gas (World War II); cold injuries (World War II and Korean War); hepatitis C and Agent Orange, the latter of which is linked to certain cancers, congenital effects, nervous disorders, and skin diseases (Vietnam War era; Institute of Medicine [IOM], 2014; VA, 2015b). Older veterans may have been exposed to additional contaminants within or outside combat zones: herbicide tests/storage (1944–1969); classified medical studies (e.g., Edgewood Arsenal/Aberdeen, 1955–1975); contaminated water supplies (e.g., Camp Lejeune, 1950s–1980s); chemical and biological warfare risks (e.g., Project 112/Project Shipboard Hazard and Defense, 1960s–early 1970s); and waste incinerators (e.g., Atsugi, Japan, 1985–2001; VA, 2015b). And like those who served during all eras, older veterans may experience physical concerns common across all eras of service: service-related hearing loss and/or tinnitus (ringing in the ears from excessive noise [American Tinnitus Association, n.d.]) and/or chronic pain (due to the impact of physical work and/or wearing heavy equipment over time [VA, 2015a]).

Psychological. Psychologically, military service impacts older veterans to varying degrees over the course of their lives (Jennings, Aldwin, Levenson, Spiro, & Mroczek, 2006). According to the National Health and Resilience in Veterans Study, most report having successful aging experiences (81%; Pietrzak, Kirwin, & Southwick, 2014). Relative to nonveterans, however, older veterans' rates of depression are twice as high (11%; VA, 2015d) and their substance use concerns are more prevalent (Tanielian & Jaycox, 2008).

Tools That May Promote Well-Being among Older Veterans

Because experiences vary widely, the promotion of well-being—in terms of its applicability, presence, meaning, and integration—looks different among older veterans. Our next section highlights strategies that can be used to promote well-being among older veterans: (1) metaphors; (2) meaning and meaning-making; and (3) stories and storytelling.

Vignette 2: "Sailor"

Sailor is a 70-year-old, married, white (non Latino), partially disabled Vietnam Navy veteran who recently retired from his long-term, successful career in business. He's now returned to school to pursue something both "entirely different" and grounded in his unwavering commitment toward, and passion for, supporting older veterans.

Use of Metaphors

When reflecting upon his life course, Sailor uses a naval metaphor to describe navigating its vicissitudes: "Life for me has been like a gyroscope and a compass." Sailor's life has needed both: the gyroscope "has kept the compass level" and the compass "has helped me keep sight of true north."

Sailor developed this metaphor during basic training. Once out of the military or in the face of life transitions, Sailor notes, "It becomes easy to lose that." To regain a sense of direction, it is important—both for him and for veterans in general—to consider what to do "if facing rough seas and the gyroscope's not working." In his opinion, "if you are used to doing it on your own (compass and gyroscope), asking for help is the biggest hurdle. It is hard when you're vulnerable physically, mentally, and/or chemically." One thing he knows is "at some level we all need help" and "the other side of the coin is an inability to ask for help."

In the service of promoting well-being among older veterans, metaphors can be effective tools that facilitate discussing difficult, even traumatic, events (Foley, 2014). Metaphors—figures of speech "through which we describe one thing in terms of another (Landau, Robinson, & Meier, 2014, p. 4)"—can help convey thoughts (Beckett, 2003) and reach answers (Seiden, 2004) in an economical/compressed and culturally/historically understood manner (Maday, 2007). As a common form of expression, metaphors help organize/make sense of concepts, give words to the previously unknown/unnamed (Maday, 2007), teach moral principles (Loue, 2008), and "approach, apprehend, and give order to experience" by way of indirect situations (Seiden, 2004, p. 487). Used in everyday life (e.g., texts, songs, stories), metaphors offer a strengths-based way (Loue, 2008) to address problems, develop resources, and experience improved outcomes in addressing obstacles such as intimidation, self-doubt, grief, fear, unhappiness, and distress (Burns, 2012).

Thematically relevant metaphors may be universal, military, and gerontological in context. Universal or general metaphors (e.g., "life is a journey") reflect upon one's life experiences (Verstynen, 2011, p. 9). Military metaphors—which may be tactical and/or battle/war-oriented—describe health concerns or illness (e.g., fighting disease; Sablod & Fuks, 2012); obstacles currently faced (e.g., an uphill battle); and/or strategies by which to address problems (e.g., "a new line of attack is needed" or "gain ground"; Maday, 2007, p. 22). Gerontological or aging metaphors—which articulate the strengths and challenges of growing old—may describe life's journey (e.g., "over the hill"), time's "isotropic" characteristics (Maday, 2007, p. 25), "indefinite duration," or impermanent nature (e.g., "old age as the last chapter in the story of life"; Maday, 2007, p. 17).

Use of Meaning and Meaning-Making

> Structure is another important tool Sailor uses to guide his life. Sailor finds structure meaningful. He leans against it when he needs it. For himself and for other older veterans, he feels that "routine, rules, and regulations [can] give us a sense of structure in our lives we might not otherwise have. It can give us a sense of purpose." For him, he knows that "there is a hierarchy of values, a hierarchy of rank."

Just as Sailor's physical well-being, relationships, and religion help him maintain the perspective needed to stay on course/maintain true north, other older veterans' perspectives regarding how they maintain health both within the context of their military service and over the long term vary. Psyche translates from Greek as "life" and includes the ideas of "soul," "spirit," "ghost," and "self" (Psyche, n.d.). Historically, psyche has been loosely explored/applied within the context of "warrior psyche" (Hall, 2007), which considers both what being a warrior entails and what the warrior way of life looks like (Shay, 2002).

Meaning and meaning-making may offer insights into aspects of our psyche and contribute positively toward the promotion of well-being in older veterans. In addition to sharing one's "purpose, value, efficacy, and self-worth," meaning and meaning-making honor our "accomplishment(s), contribution(s), family, friends, health, peace, livelihood, partner(s), and self-worth" (Kolva, 2004, p. iii). And for those who have gone through hard times, insights into others' experiences of self-transcendence and attitudes toward suffering can be made through meaning and meaning-making (Frankl, 1984).

Meaning and meaning-making appear to be a nonlinear, circular, and continuing journey. According to Linz (1990), older veterans (like other older adults) derive meaning in ways such as "being of service to the community, family ties, companionship, spiritual values, religion expressed in terms of prayer meditation, or attending church, continuing education, health, and positive attitude" (Kolva, 2004, p. 29). Meaning and meaning-making may have positive or negative implications in later life (Ebersole & DePaola, 1987).

The Importance of Stories and Storytelling

> Sailor shares that, in life, "it is easy [for anyone] to get off course or to get lost. When there is not land in sight, life can be the seas tossing your boat around." Reflecting upon what has helped him stay centered in the midst of turbulence, Sailor indicates, "My true north is my physical well-being. My sanctum. I bring in others. And my religion. [To maintain] perspective." The importance of his

> *physical well-being cannot be overstated:* "When I lose physical centeredness, I begin to get off course."

Despite messages older veterans may have received that they should forget and/or not talk about their experiences (Hunt & Robbins, 1998), veterans like Sailor may believe that sharing experiences promotes well-being over time. According to Sewell and Williams (2002) and Shaw and Westwood (2002), they may choose to not talk about their experiences for reasons such as a lack of supportive contexts in which to tell these stories (Vincent, 2010). Older veterans' stories—which often contain both pleasant and difficult memories—may be therapeutic and facilitate coping with losses and finding meaning in their accomplishments (Vincent, 2010). Sharing can both "promote improved functioning" and offer an alternative to (often) "negative, medicalized, and pathology-based focused support" (Hunt & Robbins, 1998, p. 58). As Coleman (1999) notes, sharing stories when ready and making one's experiences explicit (e.g., by way of categorizing, understanding) help lessen its ability to impact our lives (Vincent, 2010).

Reflection/reconstruction of stories—commonly referred to as autobiography, life review, reminiscence, narratives (Vincent, 2010)—can help older veterans make sense of their lives (Walker-Birckhead & Davison, 1995). With age, it may be increasingly important to make peace with one's life and what may have transpired because of military service and/or what happened during times of war (Scaturo & Hardoby, 1988). According to Shaw and Westwood (2002), further reviewing, reevaluating, and retelling one's life story may help older veterans integrate their military and/or wartime experiences into their lives (Vincent, 2010). The process of reevaluation can be powerful and may help facilitate healing (Hunt & Robbins, 1998) and integrate difficult experiences (Vincent, 2010) into one's life story.

The process of storytelling may help older veterans make sense of their difficult experiences (Vincent, 2010). This is all the more important as trauma, by its very nature, can be as painful in later life as it was when it occurred (Hunt & Robbins, 1998). For some, processing events may give "meaning to the traumatic events of the war" and play a role in "taking the trauma out of their traumatic memories" (Hunt & Robbins, 1998, p. 63). As a result, older veterans may develop greater capacity to navigate their trauma and feel in control of their experiences (Hunt & Robbins, 1998).

In addition to being of benefit to older veterans, stories and storytelling can be of benefit to their loved ones. In the process of listening to the stories, an array of themes, such as perseverance, motivation, love, and forgiveness (Burns, 2012), can be uncovered. In turn, these themes can facilitate better understanding of the "emotions and experiences," "frustrations and achievements," "joy and sadness," and "pain and pleasure" (Burns, 2012, p. 16) experienced by older veterans. Ultimately, loved ones may learn more about what holds meaning for, has challenged, and has enriched the journeys of the older veterans.

Complementary and Alternative Medicine

The importance of promoting well-being among veterans of all ages through resilience- and community-based interventions has been increasingly articulated (Thomas & Plummer Taylor, 2015). The appeal of this intervention approach is compelling: it offers a responsive and holistic approach to supporting physical and mental health in a way that respects one's spiritual, personal, and economic beliefs/needs (Barnes, Powell-Griner, McFann, & Nahin, 2004). Generally speaking, older adults' mental and physical health outcomes improve when "environmental, cultural, and religious factors are taken into consideration" (Behrman & Tebb, 2009, p. 129).

Complementary and alternative medicine (CAM) addresses "physical, mental, emotional, and energetic or spiritual factors of health and disease" (Mackenzie & Rakel, 2006, p. 3). In practice, CAM employs holistic, multidimensional approaches that both facilitate healing and help prevent illnesses/ailments. Though unconventional by mainstream standards, CAM has been practiced for thousands of years across many cultures and groups (National Center for Complementary and Integrative Health [NCCIH], 2016). CAM practices provide *complementary* (used with) or *alternative* (used in lieu of) care to conventional— also known as Western or allopathic—medicine (NCCIH, 2016). CAM approaches are often grouped into two primary subgroups: natural products and mind/body practices. Natural products may include vitamins/minerals, herbs, and probiotics, while mind and body practices include yoga, meditation, massage therapy, chiropractic, acupuncture, tai chi, and qi gong (NCCIH, 2016). Additional complementary approaches that fall outside of these two subgroups include Ayurvedic medicine, Chinese medicine, naturopathy, homeopathy, and traditional healing practices (NCCIH, 2016).

CAM offers both person-centered/individualized and holistic/integrative approaches to working with older adults who honor their "subjective and interpretative dimensions" and diverse experiences (Richardson & Barusch, 2006, p. 52). In this section, we will highlight CAM approaches that may facilitate the promotion of well-being among older veterans.

Vignette 3: "Richard"

Richard is a 65-year-old, married, white (non-Latino), disabled Vietnam veteran who retired several years ago from a successful career owning a consulting business. While motivated by his father's military service to enlist in the Army at the age of 17, Richard looks back upon his years in the Army—especially during Vietnam—as "the most horrific years of my life." Often Richard wishes he could "turn back the clock" to where he did not enlist and "prayed like hell my number didn't get called [in the draft]." During his two tours in Vietnam, Richard served as an infantryman who saw heavy combat while in country.

Despite his success—great business career, stable financial life, and close family relationships—Richard's day-to-day life is filled with regret, a troubled mind, and a heavy heart. "I saw things no 18- or 19-year-old should have to see." Despite the burden he carries due to his time in Vietnam, Richard acknowledges his gratitude to be alive.

CAM Usage among Veterans

Richard's military service evokes painful memories, which he has spent his life postservice trying to avoid. Casual VA encounters aside, Richard holds back from developing relationships with other veterans. Instead, he focuses on being the best husband, father, grandfather, and business owner possible.

Over the past five years, Richard has been battling two different forms of cancer linked to Agent Orange exposure. He attributes beating the odds on several occasions to his marriage and his family: "[they] keep me strong and trucking along."

His wife has long encouraged Richard to see a therapist: "She thinks I'm depressed, but I'm really doing OK." After two failed therapies, at his oncologist's urging, Richard has agreed to give therapy another try. His new therapist knows his preferences: discussing Vietnam is "off limits," but talking about "anger issues" is acceptable.

Richard's chronic-pain nurse thinks his anger may be his pain trying to escape his body. This resonates with Richard, who has agreed to try acupuncture "to see" if it will help. Richard hopes managing his physical pain will also help him address his anger/overall mental health.

Roughly half of older veterans ages 65 and older report using CAM (Baldwin, Long, Kroesen, Brooks, & Bell, 2002; Clarke, Black, Stussman, Barnes, & Nahin, 2015), a number that continues to rise. CAM utilization—similar across veteran age cohorts (Baldwin et al., 2002)—is higher than among civilians (Goertz et al., 2013).

Increased CAM utilization among older veterans like Richard may be motivated by several factors. First, they may be dissatisfied with certain aspects of conventional care, prescription side effects, perceived shortcomings in clinician drug monitoring, distrust of the pharmaceutical industry, and a lack of holism (e.g., which may not emphasize nutrition, exercise, or preventive medicine; Baldwin et al., 2002; Kroesen, Baldwin, Brooks, & Bell, 2002). Second, CAM use may be associated with high daily stress, perceived negative impact of military life on physical or mental health, and chronic illnesses (Baldwin et al., 2002). Third, CAM offerings and programs have become more available within VA facilities in recent years—specifically with regard to mind-body modalities (Hammond & Vandenberg, 2011). Clinics with ongoing CAM programs have become popular, well utilized, endorsed, and found to help improve physical and mental health symptoms (Hull et al., 2014) across veteran cohorts. Fourth, research findings increasingly support the use of broad-spectrum interventions targeting multiple biological systems (e.g., meditation, acupuncture) to address the complex symptomatology of veterans (Hull et al., 2014).

Using CAM Approaches to Promote Well-Being

Like many Vietnam veterans, Richard attributes his physical problems (e.g., limited mobility, arthritis, and chronic pain from an amputated limb) to his depressive symptoms and tendencies toward social isolation. Richard feels that his providers' medication-based pain-treatment approach exacerbates both his chronic pain and psychological concerns (Mackenzie & Rakel, 2006). For Richard, adjunctive CAM interventions have finally helped him address the root causes of his issues, reduce his symptoms, and mitigate interactions and side effects of his prescribed medications (Mackenzie & Rakel, 2006). Attending chair yoga classes at his local VA helps Richard manage his pain, reduce his social isolation, improve his mobility and flexibility, and obtain tools that help him manage his chronic pain symptoms.

Like Richard, as veterans grow older, many live with complex, chronic conditions that exacerbate their psychological and/or physiological health. CAM offers an important treatment alternative to Western/allopathic medicine, a disease-and-pathology-driven medicine that offers acute treatments for complex issues (Mackenzie & Rakel, 2006). CAM offers nondrug approaches to pain management and associated health concerns such as drug abuse and addiction, sleep issues, and PTSD (NCCIH, 2014), which is also quite promising. Using somatic health treatments in conjunction with other modalities is important since "no single discipline can effectively meet the myriad of issues that emerge in later life" (Richardson & Barusch, 2006, p. 17).

A Brief Introduction to iRest Yoga Nidra

For years postmilitary service, talking about war memories in therapy left Richard feeling agitated, physiologically aroused, and doubtful that he would ever be able to talk about his experiences in way that would be helpful. This belief shifted after several months of working with his current therapist. When his therapist expressed that he believed Richard's "anger issues" would only improve once he addressed his trauma, Richard reluctantly agreed there may be some connection between his anger and his Vietnam experience and expressed that he was "willing to try anything at this point." As an alternative to talk therapy, Richard's therapist referred him to an Integrative Restoration (iRest) Yoga Nidra group at the VA.

After attending the full course, Richard was shocked to find that his anxiety had decreased and that he had experienced fewer moments of irritability and explosive anger. Despite initial skepticism, Richard found himself increasingly enjoying the group and the iRest practice. He had a number of profound experiences during the practices and was relieved to hear that other veterans who had similar combat experiences did as well. It was the first time in Richard's adult life that he found himself enjoying connecting with other veterans and willing to be vulnerable when sharing about his personal experiences.

"I felt like I had just taken the best nap of my life after the practice, but it was more than that. It was as if someone has given me a magical relaxation pill that allowed my whole body and mind to relax. I felt less physical pain, was less irritable, and more willing to embrace the day and whatever came with it on the days I attended group." Richard returned to his therapy sessions during those weeks reporting an increased sense of hope that he may eventually see some relief from his PTSD symptoms. Richard had gained the skills needed through the iRest Yoga Nidra practice to safely begin trauma therapy. His therapist had understood the importance of a stable foundation from which Richard could do the difficult therapy work needed to treat his PTSD. Richard continues to practice iRest on his own several days a week and will occasionally attend an open iRest group at the VA when he is there for treatment.

Programs mentioned in the first section of this anthology such as iRest Yoga Nidra are becoming increasingly popular as adjunctive treatment for PTSD in older veterans; the U.S. Army surgeon general has now endorsed the practice (Integrative Restoration Institute, n.d.). In addition to the demonstrated efficacy of the practice, iRest's accessibility makes it appealing to older veterans and providers working with older veterans alike. The practice can be done in a chair or while comfortably lying down. Additionally, once participants learn the practice and experience it with a qualified teacher or clinician, it can be practiced individually or in groups using CD or MP3 recordings (Stankovic, 2011). Thus, iRest Yoga Nidra can be easily integrated into daily self-care rituals in both a cost-effective and sustainable way.

Implications and Conclusions

Our chapter has considered the promotion of well-being among older veterans. We have highlighted (1) unique characteristics and considerations of older veterans, (2) tools that may promote well-being among this cohort, and (3) how CAM practices may be applied to this population.

References

American Tinnitus Association. (n.d.). *Demographics*. Retrieved from https://www.ata.org/understanding-facts/demographics

Baldwin, C. M., Long, K., Kroesen, K., Brookes, A. J., & Bell, I. R. (2002). A profile of military veterans in the southwestern United States who use complementary and alternative medicine: Implications for integrated care. *Archive Internal Medicine, 162*, 1697–1704.

Barnes, P., Powell-Griner, E., McFann, K., & Nahin, R. (2004). *Complementary and alternative medicine use among adults: U.S. 2002*. Bethesda, MD: National Institutes of Health and the National Center for Complementary and Alternative Medicine.

Beckett, C. (2003). The language of siege: Military metaphors in the spoken language of social work. *The British Journal of Social Work, 33*(5), 625–639. Retrieved from http://www.jstor.org/stable/23720064

Behrman, G., & Tebb, S. (2009). The use of complementary and alternative interventions as a holistic approach with older adults. *Journal of Religion & Spirituality in Social Work: Social Thought, 28*(1–2), 127–140.

Boettcher, W. A., & Cobb, M. D. (2006). Echoes of Vietnam? Casualty framing and public perceptions of successes and failures in Iraq. *Journal of Conflict Resolution, 206*(50), 831–854. doi:10.1177/0022002706293665

Burns, G. W. (2012). *101 healing stories for kids and teens: Using metaphors in therapy*. Hoboken, NJ: John Wiley & Sons.

Clarke T. C., Black, L. I., Stussman, B. J., Barnes, P. M., & Nahin, R. L. (2015). Trends in the use of complementary health approaches among adults: United States, 2002–2012. *National Health Statistics Reports, 79*, 1–9. Hyattsville, MD: National Center for Health Statistics.

Coleman, P. G. (1999). Creating a life story: The task of reconciliation. *The Gerontologist, 39*(2), 133–139.

Damron-Rodriguez, J. (2011). *Aging veterans and their caregivers*. National Center for Gerontological Social Work Education. Retrieved from https://www.cswe.org/Research-Statistics/Research-Briefs-and-Publications

Ebersole, P., & DePaola, S. (1987). Meaning in life categories of later life couples. *The Journal of Psychology, 121*(2), 185–191.

Fletcher, K. L., Albright, D. L., Rorie, K. A., & Lewis, A. M. (2017). Older veterans. In J. Beder (Ed.), *Caring for the military: A guide for helping professionals*. New York, NY: Routledge.

Fletcher, K. L., Mankowski, C. M., & Albright, D. L. (2018). The challenges posed by the mental health needs of military service members and veterans. In J. Rosenberg & S. Rosenberg (Eds.), *Community mental health: Challenges for the 21st century* (3rd ed.). Florence, KY: Routledge.

Foley, P. S. (2014). *The metaphors they carry: Exploring how veterans use metaphor to describe experiences of PTSD and the implications for social work practice*. Master of Social Work Clinical Research Papers. Paper 316. Retrieved from http://sophia.stkate.edu/msw_papers/316

Frankl, V. (1984). *Man's search for meaning*. Washington, DC: Washington Square Press.

Ginsburg, K. R. (2006). *A parent's guide to building resilience in children and teens*. Elk Grove Village, IL: American Academy of Pediatrics.

Goertz, C., Marriott, B. P., Finch, M. D., Bray, R. M., Williams, T. V., Hourani, L. L., . . . Jonas, W. B. (2013). Military report more complementary and alternative medicine use than civilians. *Journal of Alternative & Complementary Medicine, 19*(6), 509–517. doi:10.1089/acm.2012.0108

Hall, J. (2007). The warrior psyche: Gun carriers, whether armed professionals or competitors, all argue about what is best. *Tactical-life*. Retrieved from http://www.tactical-life.com/military-and-police/the-warrior-psyche/

Hammond, M. C., & Vandenberg, P. (2011). *2011 complementary and alternative medicine*. Washington, DC: Department of Veterans Affairs. Retrieved from http://www.research.va.gov/research_topics/2011cam_finalreport.pdf

Hull, A., Reinhard, M., McCarron, K., Allen, N., Jecmen, M. C., Akhter, J., . . . Soltes, K. (2014). Acupuncture and meditation for military veterans: First steps of quality management and future program development. *Global Advances in Health and Medicine*, 3(4), 27–31. http://doi.org/10.7453/gahmj.2013.050

Hunt, N., & Robbins, I. (1998). Telling stories of the war: Ageing veterans coping with their memories through narrative. *Oral History*, 26(2), 57–64.

Institute of Medicine. (2014). *Veterans and Agent Orange: Update 2012*. Washington, DC: The National Academies Press.

Integrative Restoration Institute. (n.d.). *Overview of iRest in the Military*. Retrieved from https://www.irest.us/projects/veterans

Jennings, P. A., Aldwin, C. A., Levenson, M. R., Spiro, A., & Mroczek, D. K. (2006). Combat exposure, perceived benefits of military service, and wisdom in later life: Findings from the Normative Aging Study. *Research on Aging*, 28(1), 115–134.

Kane, R. L., Ouslander, J. G., Abrass, I. B., & Resnick, B. (2013). *Essentials of clinical geriatrics* (7th ed.). New York, NY: McGraw Hill.

Kolva, J. L. (2004). *Life story telling by older adults to elucidate the meaning of their lives* (Doctoral dissertation). ProQuest Dissertation Publishing. (3121780)

Kroesen, K., Baldwin, C. M., Brooks, A. J., & Bell, I. R. (2002). US military veterans' perceptions of the conventional medical care system and their use of complementary and alternative medicine. *Family Practice*, 19(1), 57–64.

Kulka, R. A., Schlenger, W. E., Fairbank, J. A., Hough, R. L., Jordan, K., Marmar, C. R., & Weiss, D. S. (1990). *Trauma and the Vietnam War generation: Report of the findings from the National Vietnam Veteran's Readjustment Study*. New York, NY: Routledge.

Landau, M. J., Robinson, M. D., & Meier, B. P. (2014). Introduction. In M. J. Landau, M. D. Robinson, & B. P. Meier (Eds.), *The power of metaphor: Examining its influence on social life* (pp. 3–16). Worchester, MA: American Psychological Association. Retrieved from http://dx.doi.org/10.1037/14278-001

Linz, R. (1990). *Meaning in old age* (Unpublished doctoral dissertation). California School of Professional Psychology, Berkeley, CA.

Loue, S. (2008). *Transformative power of metaphor in therapy*. New York, NY: Springer.

Mackenzie, E. R., & Rakel, B. (2006). *Complementary and alternative medicine for older adults: A guide to holistic approaches to healthy aging*. New York, NY: Springer.

Maday, R. (2007). *Metaphors of aging* (Doctoral dissertation). ProQuest Dissertation Publishing. (3258126)

Maynard, C. M., & Boyko, E. J. (2006). Differences in cause of death of Washington State veterans who did and did not use Department of Veterans Affairs healthcare services. *Journal of Rehabilitation, Research, and Development, 43*(7), 825–830.

McFarland, S. L. (2012). *A concise history of the Air Force.* Maxwell Air Force Base, AL: Air University, U.S. Air Force Jeanne M. Holm Center for Officer Accessions and Citizen Development.

McReynolds, J. L., & Rossen, E. K. (2004). Importance of physical activity, nutrition, and social support for optimal aging. *Clinical Nurse Specialist, 18*(4). Retrieved from http://www.medscape.com/viewarticle/484344_2

Nash, W. P. (2006). The spectrum of war stressors. In C. R. Figley & W. P. Nash (Eds.), *Combat stress injury, research, and management* (pp. 18–69). New York, NY: Routledge. Retrieved from www.ncdsv.org/images/RPSBS_Combat-stress-injury-theory-research-and-management_4-24-2006.pdf

National Center for Complementary and Integrative Health. (2014). *NIH and VA address pain and related conditions in U.S. military personnel, veterans, and their families: Research will focus on nondrug approaches.* Retrieved from https://nccih.nih.gov/news/press/09232014

National Center for Complementary and Integrative Health. (2016). *Complementary, alternative, or integrative health: What's in a name?* Retrieved from https://nccih.nih.gov/health/integrative-health

Nock, M. K., Deming, C. A., Fullerton, C. S., Gilman, S. E., Goldenberg, M., Kessler, R. C., . . . Ursano, R. J. (2013). Suicide among soldiers: A review of psychosocial risk and protective factors. *Psychiatry: Interpersonal & Biological Processes, 76*(2), 97–125.

Pietrzak, T. J., Kirwin, P. D., & Southwick, S. M. (2014). Successful aging among older veterans in the United States. *American Journal of Geriatric Psychiatry, 22*(6), 551–563.

Psyche. (n.d.). *Online Etymology Dictionary.* Retrieved from Dictionary.com website http://www.dictionary.com/browse/psyche

Richardson, V., & Barusch, A. S. (2006). *Gerontological practice for the 21st century: A social work perspective.* New York, NY: Columbia University Press.

Rostker, B. (2006). *The evolution of the all-volunteer force.* Thousand Oaks, CA: RAND. Retrieved from http://www.rand.org/content/dam/rand/pubs/monographs/2007/RAND_MG265.pdf

Sablod, D., & Fuks, A. (2012). Military metaphors and friendly fire. *Canadian Medical Association Journal, 184*(1), 144.

Scaturo, D. J., & Hardoby, W. J. (1988). Psychotherapy with traumatised Vietnam combatants: An overview of individual, group, and family treatment modalities. *Military Medicine, 153*(5), 262–269.

Seiden, H. M. (2004). On relying on metaphor: What psychoanalysts might learn from Wallace Stevens. *Psychoanalytic Psychology, 21*(3), 480–487.

Settersten, R. A. (2006). When nations call: How wartime military service matters for the life course and aging. *Research on Aging, 28*(1), 12–36.

Sewell, K. W., & Williams, A. M. (2002). Broken narratives: Trauma, metaconstructive gaps, and the audience of psychotherapy. *Journal of Constructivist Psychology, 15*, 205–218.

Shaw, M. E., & Westwood, M. J. (2002). Transformation in life stories: The Canadian War Veterans Life Review Project. In J. D. Webster & B. K. Haight (Eds.), *Critical advances in reminiscence work* (pp. 257–274). New York, NY: Springer.

Shay, J. (2002). *Achilles in Vietnam and Odysseus in America.* New York, NY: Schibner.

Sherwood, R. J., Shimel, H., Stolz, P. & Sherwood, D. (2004). Aging veterans: Re-emergence of trauma issues. *Journal of Geronotological Social Work, 40*(4), 73–86. doi:10.1300/J083v40n04_06

Stankovic, L. (2011). Transforming trauma: A qualitative feasibility study of integrative restoration (iRest) yoga nidra on combat-related post-traumatic stress disorder. *International Journal of Yoga Therapy, 21*, 23–37.

Tanielian, T., & Jaycox, L. H. (Eds.) (2008). *Invisible wounds of war: Summary and recommendations for addressing psychological and cognitive injuries.* Thousand Oaks, CA: RAND.

Tedeschi, R. G., & Calhoun, L. G. (2006). Expert companions: Posttraumatic growth in clinical practice. In L. G. Calhoun & R. G. Tedeschi (Eds.), *Handbook of posttraumatic growth: Research and practice* (pp. 291–310). New York, NY: Lawrence Erlbaum Associates.

Thomas, K. H., & Plummer Taylor, S. (2015). Bulletproofing the psyche: Mindfulness interventions in the training environment to improve resilience in the military and veteran communities. *Advances in Social Work, 16*(2), 312–322.

Torreon, B. S. (2017, October 7). *U.S. periods of war and dates of current conflicts.* Congressional Research Service Report for Congress: Prepared for Members and Committees of Congress. Retrieved from https://fas.org/sgp/crs/natsec/RS21405.pdf

U.S. Census Bureau. (2012a). *Table 521. Veterans Living by Period of Service, Age, and Sex: 2010.* Retrieved from https://www.census.gov/topics/population/veterans.html

U.S. Census Bureau. (2012b). *Table 522. Veterans Living by Period of Sex, Race, and Hispanic Origin: 2010.* Retrieved from https://www.census.gov/library/publications/2012/acs/acsbr11-22.html

U.S. Department of Veterans Affairs. (2011). *2010 National Survey of Veterans: Reported Plan to Use VA Healthcare in the Future, for Selected Group of Veterans.* Retrieved from http://www.va.gov/vetdata/docs/QuickFacts/2010NSV_Quick_Fact_Final.pdf

U.S. Department of Veterans Affairs. (2014a). *National Center for Veterans Analysis and Statistics.* Retrieved from http://www.va.gov/vetdata/Veteran_Population.asp

U.S. Department of Veterans Affairs. (2014b). *National Center for Veterans Analysis and Statistics: Department of Veterans Affairs Statistics at a Glance.* Retrieved from http://www.va.gov/vetdata/docs/Quickfacts/Stats_at_a_glance_12_31_14.pdf

U.S. Department of Veterans Affairs. (2015a). *National Center for Veterans Analysis and Statistics*. Retrieved from http://www1.va.gov/vetdata/

U.S. Department of Veterans Affairs. (2015b). *Public Health: Military Exposures*. Retrieved from http://www.publichealth.va.gov/exposures/

Verstynen, P. (2011). *Exploring the language of older adult learners as they discuss beginning a bachelor's degree program* (Doctoral dissertation). ProQuest Dissertation Publishing. (3461010)

Vincent, W. L. (2010). *Telling stories in a veterans' life review group: Design, pilot study, and evaluation program* (Doctoral dissertation). ProQuest Dissertation Publishing. (3401910)

Walker-Birckhead, W., & Davison, B. (1995). "You'd be very surprised at what the war has done to people": Veterans talk about the war. *Australian Journal on Ageing, 14*(3), 124–127.

Wilcox, S. L., Finney, K., & Cedarbaum, J. A. (2013). Prevalence of mental health problems among military populations. In B. A. Moore & J. E. Barnett (Eds.), *Military Psychologists' Desk Reference* (pp. 187–196). New York, NY: Oxford University Press.

Wilmoth, J. M., & London, A. S. (2011). Aging veterans: Needs and provisions. In R. A. Setterson & J. L. Angel (Eds.), *Handbook of sociology and aging (Handbooks of sociology and social research)* (pp. 661–672). New York, NY: Springer Science and Business Media. https://doi.org/10.1007/978-1-4419-7374-0_28

Zoli, C., Maury, R., & Fay, D. (2015). Missing perspectives: Servicemembers' transition from service to civilian life—Data-driven research to enact the promise of the post-9/11 GI Bill. Institute for the Veterans and Military Families, Syracuse University. Retrieved from http://vets.syr.edu/wp-content/uploads/2015/11/Missing-Perspectives-Report.pdf

PART THREE

Collaborating to Provide Mental Fitness Programming for Military-Connected Populations

CHAPTER 11

Faith-Based Programming for Spiritual Fitness

Rev. Sarah A. Shirley, Rev. Elizabeth A. Alders, Howard A. Crosby Jr., Kathleen G. Charters, and Rev. John Edgar Caterson

In the fourth century CE, a French soldier named Martin encountered a poor man begging for bread. The weather was frigid, and the beggar had no coat. Martin's comrades urged him to ignore the beggar and continue with their mission, but his conscience prevented compliance. Compounding his seemingly insurmountable dilemma, Martin's military obligation precluded him from giving up his own coat lest he freeze and become a casualty. Unwilling to behave uncharitably, he was at grave risk for dereliction of duty. Inspired by soldierly ingenuity and the Holy Spirit, he cut his cloak in half to share its lifesaving warmth with the stranger.

War is fertile territory for moral conflicts like the one Martin faced. In *A Terrible Love of War*, Hillman (2004) criticized the religious community for shirking its responsibility to take on the challenge of thinking deeply about violent conflict. "Philosophy and theology," he wrote, "the fields supposed to do the heavy thinking for our species, have neglected war's overriding importance" (p. 2). Theology, understood as the study of faith, God, or religion, and philosophy, the study of ideas about knowledge, truth, and the meaning of life, are more than academic disciplines. They offer ways of thinking and talking about things that matter deeply to individuals, families, and communities. Delving into life's contradictions, explicating its complexities, and challenging war's apparent intractability are daily tasks for theologians and philosophers alike. Reflecting on who we are to be and how we are to live in light of imperfect solutions such as war are the heartbeat of theology and philosophy.

Practical theology and philosophy are best done in conversation with other people who challenge our assumptions, expand our limited experiences, and help us wrestle with big questions that inform lives well lived (Greitens, 2016). Healthy, religious congregations provide conversational space for working out the big questions of life and growing spiritually. Faith-based communities emerge from and participate in religious traditions that are rich in rituals and beliefs. These traditions, rituals, and beliefs can help prepare warriors for battle, ease them back home, and reintegrate them into their families and communities (Brock & Lettini, 2012; Tick, 2014). In civilian houses of worship and military chapels, warriors and veterans find communities in and with which to have hard and fruitful conversations about faith, meaning, war, values, and purpose: the stuff that is life itself.

Spiritual Fitness

Spiritual fitness has emerged over the past decade as an important concept in human performance optimization and is included among holistic approaches to developing and maintaining fit fighting forces. Spirit has etymological roots in *pneuma* (Greek), *ruach* (Hebrew), and *spiritus* (Latin), evoking images of life-giving breath. In Hindu tradition, breath, life, and spirit are synonymous (Prashna Upanishad 2:3). In Judeo-Christian tradition, the first human is brought to life by God's breath blown into a dirt figure's nostrils (Gen. 2:7). The Veterans Administration (VA) chaplaincy refers to the linguistic relationship among spirit, inspire/expire, and inhale/exhale to explain spirituality as that which is and is not life-giving (Department of Veterans Affairs, 2016, p. 9).

Australia's elite 2nd Commando Regiment captured the idea of breath in its discussion of human performance and spiritual fitness. The commandos define "spirituality" as a "sense of aliveness" and regard spiritual health as "an essential line of operation" that undergirds health, well-being, intra- and interpersonal connectedness, purpose, and personal values. The commandos associate this with participation in something that transcends one's self, contributing to acceptance of human foibles, celebration of diversity, ability to maintain personal integrity, and be at peace (Koss & Holder, 2015, pp. 6–7). Distinct from yet interrelated with emotional well-being and psychological health, "spiritual fitness" has proven difficult to define. Early attempts to clarify the concept led to circular definitions, such as "fitness of the spirit or soul, especially from a religious aspect" (Hufford, Fritts, & Rhodes, 2010, p. 75) and "an individual's overall spiritual condition" (Sweeney, Rhodes, & Boling, 2012, p. 37).

Spirituality is unique to each person, is often related to religious beliefs and practices, and is oriented toward growth throughout a person's lifetime.

Spiritual fitness is about wellness instead of pathology and resists clinical measurement (Mason, 2014). These characteristics challenge institutional efforts to define, assess, and improve spiritual fitness. A workable definition will be broad enough to accommodate a variety of spiritual experiences while specific enough to be useful in efforts to strengthen individual military community members' spiritual fitness.

Examining and defining spiritual fitness from a relational perspective can move us beyond a circular and unhelpful approach to spirituality and well-being. Defining spiritual fitness as relational examines spirituality as the feeling of connection to something greater than one's self—a purpose, a movement, an organization, a mission, a belief system, a family—that is, experienced through intentionally developing relationships with self, others, one's environment, and one's source of ultimate meaning (Koss & Holder, 2015; Van Epp, 2016). Many service members and veterans find their source of ultimate meaning in the God of their personal faith. For these, encouraging spiritual fitness through faith-based programming supports overall well-being and performance.

Faith-Based Programming

"Faith-based" implies emerging from religious traditions or institutions, and "program" denotes the government has authorized and appropriated funds to facilitate service delivery. Most civilian congregations and other private sector religious organizations are rooted in particular faith traditions with theological or ethical guidelines that help inform and shape their programs. Federally organized faith-based programs, however, have a different set of ground rules stemming from religious freedom provisions set forth in the First Amendment of the Constitution. The "free exercise clause" guarantees Americans the right to freely exercise (or not exercise) religious beliefs and practices of their own choosing without undue interference from the government. This is the aspect of the First Amendment that permits and may in fact require the federal government to provide religious support to persons whose freedom of movement it limits through military service or incarceration. The "non-establishment clause" denies the government the right to establish religion. Nonestablishment precludes the United States from having an official religion and is the intellectual foundation for the pluralistic environment in which faith-based programming is made available to military service members and veterans.

The federal government has established chaplaincies in the military services and the VA as the authorized vehicles through which faith-based programming is delivered to service members and veterans. Military chaplaincy is primarily workplace ministry, although military hospitals as well as some outpatient clinics have staff chaplains to provide pastoral care and religious support to patients as well as staff. VA chaplaincy is designed as clinical health care ministry, and VA chaplains are trained and equipped to care for veterans in the same ways chaplains in civilian hospitals minister to their patients.

Title 10, U.S. Code (USC), Sections 3073, 5142, and 8067, provide for appointment of officers as chaplains in the each of the military services. "Chaplain" is the term applied to the clergy who minister in an institutional or community environment rather than in the context of a religious community or organization. Although schools, prisons, corporations, and other organizations employ chaplains, the term itself originates from the military and from the potential spiritual conflict inherent in fulfilling military and religious duties simultaneously. To remember the sacrifice by the French soldier who became St. Martin of Tours, priests carried *capellas*, or symbolic cloaks, into battle. The title "chaplain" is derived from *cappellanus*—custodians of St. Martin's cloak (Bergen, 2004, pp. 45–46).

The first recorded U.S. military chaplain was Samuel Stone, a pastor who joined his congregants and fellow settlers when they responded to an Indian raid in 1637. The Continental Navy, established in 1775, required divine services to be conducted shipboard, which implied the need for and existence of chaplains. Seventeenth- and 18th-century chaplains were, like Stone, local clergy who picked up their weapons along with their prayer books to join the fight or were already in the ranks and given supplemental pay to function as chaplains. The Navy informally required its chaplains to be ordained ministers as early as 1823 but did not formally require such credentials until 1842 (Budd, 2002).

Clarification and modification of chaplains' roles and functions are a theme in the history of military chaplaincy. In addition to their religious duties, they have functioned as intelligence officers, supply clerks, morale officers, education officers, and commanders' secretaries (Herspring, 2001). During the Civil War, the chaplaincy underwent historic changes. Until 1864, many chaplains were active combatants and intelligence gatherers, roles that came to be seen as incompatible with their primary pastoral role. President Abraham Lincoln advocated protecting the pastoral role as part of the Lieber Code, the antecedent of the Law of Armed Conflict and parts of the Geneva Conventions. The Lieber Code included the provision that captured chaplains were to be retained persons to care for fellow prisoners and were not to be classified as prisoners of war; neither were they bound to resist and escape (Odom, 2002).

Today, military chaplains are unequivocally noncombatants set apart to provide religious support. Chaplains are commissioned officers, attend military schools, deploy to combat zones, and meet general readiness requirements. They must have specific educational credentials, in most cases be ordained clergy, and be certified by a recognized religious body. They are ineligible to act as commanders or function outside of their pastoral role. The religious support chaplains provide includes worship, sacraments, religious education, pastoral counseling, spiritual care, relationship enhancement services, and ethical advice to leaders.

VA chaplains meet the same educational and certification standards as their military counterparts and provide religious, pastoral, and spiritual care in medical centers and clinics. The Veteran's Health Administration directive governing spiritual care is explicit that patients determine the sort of chaplaincy care to be provided: "the type and extent of spiritual and pastoral care provided must be commensurate with the needs, desires, and voluntary consent of the individual Veteran" (Department of Veterans Affairs, 2016, p. 2). This is consistent with a VA-wide emphasis on patient-centered care that makes the patient the primary expert about his or her own care plan.

Military and VA chaplains provide similar services in health care settings, participating in ethics committees and processes, offering sacraments and pastoral offices to patients and families, advising clinicians and administrators on how religion and spirituality may affect patient care, and facilitating communication among patients, family members, and medical staff. They offer educational programs, worship services, prayers, blessings, and community programs. VA and military chaplains alike are interested in having excellent relationships with their behavioral health colleagues and informing spiritual care with evidence-based practices, and more and more chaplains are engaging in interdisciplinary research examining relationships between spirituality and health outcomes.

Case Examples: Three Structured Programs for Spiritual Fitness

Providing structured faith-based programs is one approach to developing spiritual fitness and harnessing spirituality and religion for healing. Such programs can offer ways to develop resiliency, assess moral injuries, and address moral injuries' impact on life. The military services and VA hospitals and clinics use a variety of programs, some evidence-based and some not, some locally developed and others from outside vendors, in adopting this approach. Following are three sample programs employed to support service members and veterans in their path to develop, retain, and restore wholeness and well-being: Moral Injury Reconciliation, Building Spiritual Strengths, and Ultimate Spiritual Resiliency and Relationships.

Focus on Forgiveness: Moral Injury Reconciliation

War literature is replete with portrayals of men and women directly involved in or facing moral injury as a result of war's violence. The preponderance of scholarly work concerning spiritual, moral, and psychological effects of war focuses on trauma, usually experienced in direct combat or as a victim of military sexual assault. Traumatic experiences such as killing, failing to prevent one's friends from being killed, or being victimized whether by trusted comrades or strangers can damage one's spiritual well-being (Harris, Park, Currier, Usset, & Voecks, 2015; Rosenheck & Fontana, 2004). This damage to one's spiritual well-being may result in moral injury.

One aspect of moral injury is psychic wounding that disrupts confidence in one's own ability to make moral decisions or in the justness or morality of society or social institutions. It is a wound that damages the sufferer's ability to trust self, God, others, institutions, and ideas and manifests emotionally, socially, spiritually, and physically (Brock & Lettini, 2012; Harris et al., 2015; Jensen & Childs, 2016; Litz et al., 2009, 2015 Shay, 2013; Sherman, 2015).

Trusting is a dangerous business. It implies certainty, expectation, confidence, and reliance. Individuals disappointed in love or swindled in commerce are often derided as fools for having taken others at their word: "trust but verify" is a military maxim; "expectations are premeditated resentments" is a wisdom saying from the recovery community. Trust placed in individuals and institutions to navigate complex and ambiguous situations without causing unintended harm or transgressing implicit shared values creates the context in which moral injuries occur.

A U.S. Navy SEAL who became a clinical chaplain as well as therapist following 25 years of military service designed Moral Injury Reconciliation (MIR) based on his experiences caring for fellow veterans. He wanted to provide a spiritually and clinically sound program to address the fractured trust and broken spirits of his morally injured patients. Inability to trust self, others, and God may be related to an inability to give or receive forgiveness. Barriers to giving or receiving forgiveness together with the potentially therapeutic efficacy of pardon underlie MIR's theoretical framework.

MIR addresses the capacity to forgive through a three-phased, holistic treatment process over the course of nine weeks. The target population is service members, veterans, and others suffering from trauma-related episodes. Using evidence-based therapies, psychoeducation, experiential exercises, communication skills development, and self-care techniques, MIR empowers the individual to discern where forgiveness of self and others is needed and then practice forgiveness in daily life.

Reconciliation is intended to happen within the individual and, when appropriate to the person's belief system, with God or other source of meaning. Reconciliation with the person, persons, or institution whose actions caused the breach requiring forgiveness is not required for healing. Forgiveness implies a change in feeling and/or attitude on the part of the injured party and may or may not involve reconciliation with the offending party. Results from the six pilot MIR groups are promising and indicate that classic understandings of forgiveness facilitating healing continue to be valid (L. Lee, personal communication, July 25, 2016).

Resolving Spiritual Concerns: Building Spiritual Strengths

Building Spiritual Strength (BSS) utilizes a format of eight sessions and a workbook and takes an interfaith and experiential approach to facing trauma. The goal of the program is to reduce trauma's negative effects on spiritual fitness and focus on full optimization of positive spiritual practices and resources. Through this optimization, spiritual fitness becomes a means of meaning-making and reframing trauma. The program focuses on utilizing spirituality in a community setting of fellow trauma survivors, facilitating recovery through both personal and social resources (Meredith et al., 2011).

In the first session, members of the group build rapport through sharing personal history. For military communities, this specifically focuses on sharing both spiritual and military histories. Once rapport is built, goals for spiritual fitness are developed and recorded in the workbook. This not only creates a cohesive support group but also provides achievable goals to set as targets and thus build spiritual strength over time. After completing rapport building and goal setting, the program moves into second and third sessions focusing on experiential practices of spirituality. Over the course of a couple of sessions, the group prays and meditates together and individually and maintains individual logs of reactions to the exercises. Once these exercises are complete and reflections recorded in the members' logs, the fourth session brings the group together to discuss and expand their understanding of theodicy, such as why evil exists or why trauma occurs.

From this point onward, the program transitions from rapport building and spiritual exercises to developing resources for building and maintaining spiritual strength. In the fifth session, the logs are examined to see where avoidant spiritual coping practices are occurring, and members work with the group to discern spiritual practices that are active coping instead of avoidant. By discerning and naming these spiritual practices, the group members are then able to move forward to the next session with new tools and skills to address trauma. The sixth and seventh sessions take the spiritual practices and discernments of the previous session and implement them to address the need for forgiveness and resolving conflict. As this is a key component of moral injury, the strength of this program is that it develops the practices and spiritual fitness needed for forgiveness as an ongoing act of self-care and healing. After implementing the spiritual practices in the forgiveness process, the program concludes with the eighth and final session. Debriefing and planning for future spiritual strength building are vital to the continued success to this program and provide an avenue for trauma survivors to engage future moral injuries (Harris et al., 2011).

Developing Personal Spirituality: Ultimate Spiritual R&R

Ultimate Spiritual Resiliency and Relationships (R&R) is a four-lesson spiritual growth program using John Van Epp's Relationship Attachment Model (RAM). R&R focuses on helping participants develop a clear understanding of their own spiritual beliefs and how these beliefs help them navigate relationships at work and at home. This approach is multidomain and accommodates diverse learning and processing styles. R&R teaches how relationships with self, sources of meaning, others, and the environment can be conceptualized through knowing, trusting, and relying (cognitive and emotive processes). Participants put this into action through committing and touching (behavioral processes). Normally taught by chaplains in a group setting, R&R's outcomes include the ability to articulate one's personal beliefs, increased interest in spiritual matters, and use of the RAM as a tool to assess and improve relationships with self, God (or other transcendent source of meaning), others, and the environment.

The RAM is a model for considering, monitoring, and adjusting thoughts, feelings, and actions relating to self, others, circumstances, and God or other focus of spirituality. It can explain the connections in four key relationships of life: how one relates with oneself, others, circumstances, and spirituality. The model proposes five distinct and interrelated systems of self that occupy unique spaces in the functioning of self and relationships. First, the sensory system contributes awareness within the self of knowing others. Second, the cognitive system contributes beliefs within the self of trusting others. Third, the emotional system produces emotions within the self of relying on others. Fourth, the volitional system produces a will within the self to make and strive to keep commitments to others. Finally, the tactile system contributes actions and expressions within the self that touch others. The first two, knowing and trusting, relate mostly to cognitive processes (thinking). The third, relying, relates to emotive processes (feeling). The last two, committing and touching, relate primarily to behavioral processes (acting/behaving).

R&R invites military members and veterans to identify and consider how they think, what they feel, and what they do in their relationships with self, others, and transcendent sources of meaning. This invitation creates opportunities for conversation among service members and veterans as well as with their chaplains. It creates intentional space to engage in meaning-making and can give both religious and nonreligious people a new language for talking with one another about spirituality. R&R also exposes participants to 12 classic spiritual disciplines: solitude, silence, fasting and abstaining, celebration, sacrifice, service, worship, prayer, confession, submission, fellowship, and study. These or similar spiritual practices are found in most religious traditions as well as some secular programs. R&R's format for introducing spiritual disciplines encourages seeking and finding common ground among diverse participants. Since R&R is presented as an educational, personal development program, it functions as an invitation to spiritual growth that can open the door to lifelong well-being (Van Epp, 2016).

Case Examples: Spiritual Fitness in the Field

Many of us assume that all moral human beings despise war and that every person who must take part does so with some degree of regret. Yet chaplains meet and work with faithful and religious service members who have planned battles, ordered killing, killed enemy combatants, and have felt no agony. Chaplains also serve warriors who thought they would kill without regret yet found they needed to repent of doing violence to fellow humans who were labeled "enemy." No two situations are alike, and none of the people involved in them are spiritually or emotionally identical, making hard-and-fast rules regarding war and peace impossible. One thing is certain: as long as societies engage in violent conflict and employ men and women to wage war on their behalf, they are obligated to provide faith-based programs to develop spiritual fitness, prevent as much moral wounding as possible, and help spirits heal when harmed.

Focus on Forgiveness: Coffee and Confession; Coffee without Conversion

Holy Joe's Café is a ministry developed and managed almost single-handedly by a member of a congregational men's ministry in Wallingford, Connecticut. Holy Joe's mission is to make sure every chaplain in a combat zone has a good cup of coffee to share with the troops in his or her care, because meaningful conversations happen over coffee. Over the years, chaplains have shared Holy Joe's coffee and tea in most deployed locations around the world, many garrisons in the United States and abroad, as well as in some VA hospitals and clinics.

In one of those deployed locations, an army squad engaged in a firefight, and the squad leader and a subordinate soldier were wounded. The younger soldier was seriously injured, and his leader felt responsible, guilty, and just plain bad. A faith with a tradition of confession and absolution might have been helpful to him. Many religions and other spiritual programs include some kind of ritual confession of shortcomings and misdeeds, often leading to an absolution or forgiveness pronounced by clergy or fellow penitent. This soldier did not have such a tradition and was seeking a means of finding forgiveness. He talked with the chaplain who suggested they go together to have a cup of coffee with the younger, more seriously injured soldier.

The squad leader held the coffee pot and three cups in his lap, while the chaplain pushed his wheelchair to the young man's hospital room. The threesome drank coffee and talked over what had happened. In the end, the soldiers agreed that decisions had been made correctly, and they began to talk about what military service was going to be like for the younger of the two, who now had only one leg. He continued to look to his sergeant for leadership, and the sergeant continued to provide it. In the middle of all that, they talked of forgiveness even though no one was at fault. Mutual respect, the chaplain's expertise, and a good cup of coffee facilitated spiritual fitness through a secular form of confession, repentance, and absolution.

Thousands of miles from that bedside, a severely disabled veteran had come to resent many chaplains over the years. He was tired of them pretending to be interested in him when they really "just wanted to shove Jesus down his throat" (Anonymous, personal communication, December 11, 2011). The new chaplain didn't know this about the veteran and visited him several times a week, enjoying his acerbic observations and dry sense of humor. She never talked about religion and didn't offer to pray; she just visited him. She got some coffee from Holy Joe's and asked if her new friend would like some. He hesitated, so the chaplain asked if he would prefer something else. "No," he said, "I like coffee. I'm just wondering if this is when you try to get me to be religious." The chaplain was stunned. It hadn't occurred to her to do anything but be his friend. It was obvious he wasn't interested in traditional religious, spiritual, or pastoral care. When she shared her dismay with the patient, he was equally surprised. They drank their coffee in silence, pondering what these disclosures might mean to their relationship.

The following week, the chaplain was called to the same veteran's ward. The nurse who had cared for the patient for almost a decade asked the chaplain, "What did you do to him? He actually asked to see you! Before he's always told us to keep the chaplains away." The veteran wanted to talk about how to improve his marriage, how to forgive his wife for not visiting him as much as he wanted, and how to ask her forgiveness for not being the best husband in the world. Something about not being evangelized over that cup of coffee opened that veteran to forgiving and seeking forgiveness. Holy Joe's seems to have it right—meaningful conversations happen over coffee.

Resolving Spiritual Concerns: Caring for the Enemy

Tim O'Brien has a great story about a soldier who doesn't like church but thinks about becoming a pastor because he just wants to be nice to people (O'Brien, 1990). Is a pastor the only category of person permitted to treat others with kindness? Perhaps, if the context is war.

One lovely day almost 10 years after 9/11, a helicopter touched down outside a combat hospital. Four black-clad soldiers nimbly jumped out, faces covered and automatic weapons at the ready. It was such an incongruous sight that some of the hospital staff—those who weren't running to pull the inbound patient off the chopper—chuckled. After their patient was safely inside the trauma bay, the soldiers nervously settled on their haunches outside the Emergency Department doors. The chaplain brought them cold water and folding chairs and encouraged them to get comfortable.

One of the soldiers spoke English and so became the spokesperson for his team. After 15 minutes or so of cajoling by their hosts, the team pulled down their baklavas and allowed their faces to be seen while they drank water, ate cookies, and sipped tea. The patient, an "Enemy Prisoner of War," survived and spent several weeks in the hospital. The apprehending forces were responsible for providing guards for the duration of the prisoner's stay, so the soldiers were stuck at the hospital too. Over time the visitors' wariness toward the hospital staff melted into warmth and friendship. Many times they said, "You can't be military! You're too nice! You're too nice. Not military!" The soldiers wanted badly to get back out and hit the streets. There were bad guys to find and capture. They had joined the military to fight, they said, reiterating that the hospital staff couldn't possibly be military—they were too nice! Their worldview did not allow for nice people in the military. These medics and chaplains simply did not fit in their system.

While the hospital personnel were indeed kind, many found taking care of detained persons and enemy prisoners of war exceptionally stressful. In some cases, the same team cared for both a wounded comrade and the person who had done the wounding. Workshops on caring for the enemy, healing and forgiveness rituals, and individual pastoral counseling helped resolve the spiritual conflicts naturally created by working in the midst of active combat.

Developing Personal Spirituality: South Park Sunday School, Theodicy Group

Supporting and encouraging spiritual growth among the military and veteran population require openness, diversity, and flexibility beyond any one chaplain's ability. There are as many spiritual paths as there are individuals; even people who practice the same faith in exactly the same way experience it differently. In one deployed location, in addition to traditional chapel-based ministries, unit-based worship services and Bible studies, and chapel-hosted Alcoholics Anonymous (AA) meetings, two unusual group activities notably fostered spiritual growth.

The first, South Park Sunday School, was developed and led by a chaplain-layperson team. They selected *South Park* episodes with religious and theological themes, wrote discussion questions for each episode, watched one per week with a group of 20–30 deployed service members and civilians, and led discussion based on the questions they had prepared. People who never went to any chapel or chaplain-sponsored activities attended faithfully and participated actively. They shared stories of religious and spiritual struggle in a safe space, and about a third of the group sought personal spiritual direction from the chaplain. *South Park*, a television series known for religious satire and somewhat crude humor, became a vehicle for effective faith-based programming for spiritual fitness (D. Christiansen, personal communications, February 20, 2011, and March 6, 2011).

The second, a theodicy study group, chose to tackle the tension in which its members were living and working. Theodicy engages the question of how evil can exist in the face of an all-powerful and good God. The group's chaplain selected scholarly articles on theodicy and related topics such as just war theory and led a small group in discussion. The group was organized because of requests from service members who wanted to give deep thought to their own beliefs and practices in light of war and other evils that plague humanity. The theodicy study group was a powerful spiritual fitness program for its half dozen members (J. Johannigman, personal communication, May 24, 2011).

Faith and Humanness

Faith is not something that bulletproofs us. Rather, it makes us open to the joys and pains of living and allows us to grow from both. Humans seem to have been created breakable and invincible in equal measure, making us needful of care as well as able to care for others. For many, it is the God of our understanding that chose to create us that way. For others, it is just the way it is and there are no supernatural factors or powers involved in the natural world or in human affairs. Whatever our personal belief system, life is mysterious and painful and sometimes, when human or divine love enters the mix, beautiful. We may be God-created, but as Solovy (2016) reminds us, we and our souls are on a human journey:

> My soul needs a human journey.
> Sometimes, I wish it weren't so.
> Sometimes I wish that pain and suffering
> Had no purpose and no meaning.
> Or—if nothing else—G-d would
> Share that purpose with me.
> But, no, I must find that meaning
> Myself.
> Sickness and health.
> Disaster and trauma.
> The steady drumbeat of death
> From the moment of birth.
> My soul needs a human journey.
> I embrace my fear
> With an open heart.
> I embrace my hope and my yearning
> Never knowing G-d's answers,
> Releasing the vain notion that
> G-d will show up to explain
> How the foundations of earth were built.
> My soul needs a human journey.
> Here is where love resides.

Here is where holiness and the mundane dance.
Here is where I encounter you, my friends.
Here is where I encounter You, my G-d.
Yah, Shecinah, Makor Hayiim,
Source of All,
Fountain of mystery,
Bless the hidden and the revealed.
Bless our moments and our years.
Bless this human journey of souls.

The human journey is beset with conflict, and sometimes conflict erupts into the violence of war. In all conflict, violent or nonviolent, the spirit suffers and struggles. Fortunately, the human spirit, even under the most extreme distress, can endure. Faith-based programming for spiritual fitness manifests hope that the military and veteran spirit can and will endure, grow, and flourish.

Life is in delicate balance
Here on a spinning ball
Blue-green algae growing
On a sea-cliff wall
Man too is a mortal substance
Bound to a hurtling rock
How can the fragile suffer
Shock on shock?
What is it of the spirit
That clings to any ground
Enduring as dark cliff algae
Sea waves pound   ("Blue-Green Algae," by J. Allan Lind, 1960)

References

Bergen, D. L. (Ed.). (2004). *The sword of the Lord: Military chaplains from the first to the twenty-first century.* Notre Dame, IN: University of Notre Dame Press.

Brock, R. N., & Lettini, G. (2012). *Soul repair: Recovering from moral injury after war.* Boston, MA: Beacon Press.

Budd, Richard M. (2002). *Serving two masters: The development of American military chaplaincy, 1860–1920.* Lincoln, NE: University of Nebraska Press.

Department of Veterans Affairs. (2016). *VHA directive 1111: Spiritual and pastoral care in the Veterans Health Administration.* Washington, DC: Department of Veterans Affairs.

Greitens, E. (2016). *Resilience: Hard-won wisdom for living a better life.* Boston, MA: Mariner Books.

Harris, J. I., Erbes, C. R., Engdahl, B. E., Thuras, P., Murray-Swank, N., Grace, D., . . . Le, T. (2011). The effectiveness of a trauma-focused spiritually integrated intervention for veterans exposed to trauma. *Journal of Clinical Psychology, 67,* 425–438. doi:10.1002/jclp.20777

Harris, J. I., Park, C. L., Currier, J. M., Usset, T. J., & Voecks, C. D. (2015). Moral injury and psycho-spiritual development: Considering the developmental context. *Spirituality in Clinical Practice, 2,* 256–266.

Herspring, Dale R. (2001). *Soldiers, commissars, and chaplains: Civil-military relations since Cromwell.* Landham, MD: Rowman and Littlefield Publishers, Inc.

Hillman, J. (2004). *A terrible love of war.* New York, NY: Penguin Books.

Hufford, D. J., Fritts, M. J., & Rhodes, J. E. (2010). Spiritual fitness. *Military Medicine, 175*(8), 73–87.

Jensen, W. A., & Childs, J. M., Jr. (2016). *Moral warriors, moral wounds: The ministry of the Christian ethic.* Eugene, OR: Cascade Books.

Lind, J. A. (1960). *Poems.* Evanston, IL: Schori Press.

Litz, B. T., Lebowitz, L, Gray, M. J., & Nash, W. P. (2015). *Adaptive disclosure: A new treatment for military trauma, loss, and moral injury.* New York, NY: The Guilford Press.

Litz, B. T., Stein, N., Delaney, E., Lebowitz, L., Nash, W. P., Silva, C., & Maguen, S. (2009). Moral injury and moral repair in war veterans: A preliminary model and intervention strategy. *Clinical Psychology Review, 29,* 695–706.

Mason, K. (2014). *Preventing suicide: A handbook for pastors, chaplains, and pastoral counselors.* Downers Grove, IL: InterVarsity Press.

Meredith, L. S., Sherbourne, C. D., Gaillot, S. J., Hansell, L., Ritschard, H. V., Parker, A., & Wrenn, G. (2011). *Promoting psychological resilience in the U.S. military.* Santa Monica, CA: RAND Corporation. Retrieved from https://www.rand.org/pubs/monographs/MG996.html

Newport, F. (2016). *Five key finding on religion in the U.S.* New York, NY: Gallup. Retrieved from http://news.gallup.com/poll/200186/five-key-findings-religion.aspx

O'Brien, T. (1990). *The things they carried.* New York, NY: Mariner Books/Houghton Mifflin Harcourt.

Odom, J. G. (2002). Beyond arm bands and arms banned: Chaplains, armed conflict, and the law. *Naval Legal Review, 49,* 1–67. Retrieved from https://papers.ssrn.com/sol3/papers.cfm?abstract_id=1622899

Rosenheck, R., & Fontana, A. (2004). Trauma, change in strength of religious faith, and mental health service use among veterans treated for PTSD. *The Journal of Nervous and Mental Disease, 192,* 579–584.

Shay, J. (2014). Moral injury. *Psychoanalytic Psychology, 31*(2), 182.

Sherman, N. (2015). *Afterwar: Healing the moral wounds of our soldiers.* New York, NY: Oxford University Press.

Solovy, A. (2016). *My Soul Needs a Human Journey.* Jerusalem, Israel: To Bend Light. Retrieved from http://tobendlight.com/2016/12/a-human-journey/

Sweeney, P. J., Rhodes, J. E., & Boling, B. (2012). Spiritual fitness: A key component of total force fitness. *Joint Force Quarterly, 66,* 35–41

Tick, E. (2014). *Warrior's return: Restoring the soul after war.* Louisville, CO: Sounds True, Inc.

Van Epp, J. (2016). Ultimate Spiritual R&R Research Overview. San Clemente, CA: Love Thinks, LLC. Retrieved from http://www.lovethinks.com/research/rr-program-research/

CHAPTER 12

The Role of Individual Placement and Support (IPS) in Military Mental Fitness

Lori L. Davis and Richard Toscano

Introduction

Meaningful purposeful activity is essential to individuals' identity and sense of vitality. Generativity promotes resiliency, whereas stagnation can lead to emptiness. A life-threatening trauma can shake the core of one's sense of self and identity, making it difficult to stay on track in relationships and work goals. Military deployment can disrupt service members' career paths, and readjustments can be a challenge for many reentering the civilian workforce. Why is work so important in one's recovery from trauma and sense of well-being? This chapter reviews the impact of joblessness on health, the impact of posttraumatic stress on occupational functioning, the evolution of vocational rehabilitation, how Individual Placement and Support (IPS) supported employment can facilitate reengagement in work and recovery from trauma, and how employment can bulletproof the psyche.

Post-Traumatic Stress, Occupational Functioning, and the Impact of Joblessness on Health

A military veteran's ability to obtain and maintain gainful employment is essential to successful reintegration into civilian life. Symptoms of posttraumatic stress disorder (PTSD) can substantially impede a veteran's reintegration and ability to sustain employment. PTSD has profound effects on occupational functioning, significantly impairing time management and work output. Losses in productivity in veterans with PTSD are on average four times higher than nonveteran employees with no psychiatric disorder. Both depression and PTSD are associated with financial difficulties, absenteeism, job turnover, deterioration in work functioning, losses in productivity, lower income, lower occupational status, difficulties with coworkers, and/or nonsupport of their military affiliation by coworkers and employers (Erbes, Kaler, Schult, Polusny, & Arbisi, 2011; Kimerling et al., 2009; Murdoch, van Ryn, Hodges, & Cowper, 2005; Riviere, Kendall-Robbins, McGurk, Castro, & Hoge, 2011).

Many of the symptoms of PTSD can interfere with job performance, particularly somatic symptoms involving anxiety, hypervigilance, increased startle response, irritability, and difficulty concentrating. As the posttrauma brain is busy scanning the environment for signs of threats and processing rather than filtering incoming sounds and sensations, the person is less able to focus on the task at hand in the job setting. Poor performance at work leads to supervisory consequences and further lowers the individual's confidence in his or her ability to do the job. A job loss can undermine self-esteem and exacerbate ambivalence about or fear of pursuing competitive work. This downward spiral ultimately collides with family goals and relationships. Isolation and avoidance lead down a path that seems easiest to pursue yet is a dead end that leads to greater impairments and job loss.

Joblessness is significantly associated with poor physical health, anxiety and depression, low self-esteem, and suicide (Comino, Harris, Silove, Manicavasagar, & Harris, 2000; Korpi, 2001; Martikainen & Valkonen, 1996; Yur'yev, Värnik, Värnik, Sisask, & Leppik, 2012). Conversely, returning to work is associated with improved psychological health, self-esteem, quality of life, and physical health (Ferrie, 2001; Vinokur, van Ryn, Gramlich, & Price, 1991). Employment is strongly associated with positive health outcomes. Compared to the unemployed, individuals in the workforce are less vulnerable to physical and mental health problems (Marwaha & Johnson, 2004; Schennach, Musil, Möller, & Riedel, 2012).

The Evolution of Vocational Rehabilitation and IPS

As vocational rehabilitation services evolved leading up to the Vocational Rehabilitation Act of 1954, the lessons learned from the physical, mental, and emotional scars of war also influenced how our society treated injured or unemployed persons in the general population. The 2003 president's New Freedom Initiative revealed a glaring inadequacy of supports and services to persons with significant mental health concerns. Simultaneously, a shift in practice through IPS was conceived and refined (Becker & Drake, 2003) to address the gap in perceived "readiness" of persons living with the symptoms of a serious mental illness to reenter the workplace.

Based on the robust results of IPS (Luciano et al., 2014; Modini et al., 2016), IPS was rolled out broadly in the Veterans Health Administration in 2004. Simultaneously, research began to apply the core principles of IPS to veterans with PTSD. In a study of veterans with PTSD (Davis, Parker, Kashner, & Drake, 2012), 76 percent of the IPS participants gained competitive employment compared with 28 percent of those in usual-care vocational rehabilitation programs. Compared to the control group, veterans assigned to IPS gained employment more quickly; worked more weeks, days, and hours; and earned higher income, and 40 percent of IPS participants became steady workers compared to 16 percent of the usual-care participants.

What is IPS and how does employment help "bulletproof the psyche" for persons living with PTSD? IPS establishes the tools necessary to combat the triggers that inevitably surface when entering a new environment filled with expectations and challenges. More traditional approaches to vocational rehabilitation presume "readiness" as a requisite to competitive employment. But how do we define readiness when educated, trained, and mission-driven soldiers with PTSD enter the civilian arena? How does one become "ready" when the injury or trauma has shaken one's confidence and self-esteem to the point of insecurity and hypervigilance? Employment outside the safety net of military structure means new people, new situations, and a different definition of "service" than what the military fostered. To effectively reenter the workplace with dignity and success, the veteran with PTSD must overcome the fear of the unknown and maneuver through a civilian workplace that has no instruction manual and is not based on a clear chain of command. The employment marketplace of the 21st century is not always recognizable as mission driven to the trained service member leaving the military and transitioning to the civilian workplace. Add uncertainty, stress, and anxiety-related symptoms of PTSD, and the odds are stacked against the new employee. This may be best understood through a case example.

> Elliott served multiple deployments to Iraq and Afghanistan prior to his honorable discharge from the Marines. He was trained in electronics and communications and wanted to pursue that type of work in the civilian world. Soon after discharge, he had trouble keeping jobs and maintaining his relationships with friends and family, and he started drinking and using substances excessively to cope. Upon the urging of a friend, Elliot reached out to the VA for help and was diagnosed with PTSD. After some initial counseling, he was enrolled in a VA IPS program that helped him access employment in a small electronics store and repair shop. Elliott immediately thrived in this setting. The owner/employer recognized his skill set and gave him more responsibility in managing the store and

The Role of Individual Placement and Support 199

overseeing operations. One day, after several months of a good pattern of success in his new employment, two customers entered the store, browsed refurbished cell phones, and abruptly grabbed some off the rack and ran out of the store. Elliott saw this and pulled his registered handgun out of his backpack and ran after the two men. He jumped on the hood of their car as they tried to escape and as the police arrived. Fortunately, no one was hurt in the incident.

A dramatic scene evolved, and Elliott and the suspects were taken to the police station for questioning. The electronics storeowner, although shocked to hear the sequence of events and possible consequences of handling the situation so aggressively, appreciated Elliott's commitment to the business and defense of the store. He chose to continue to support Elliott's employment but wanted some guidance for both himself and Elliott to ensure more appropriate and safe responses to such events in the future.

The therapist who supported Elliott's PTSD treatment thought Elliott should resign and not pursue work until he became more "ready" to handle civilian employment. The IPS employment specialist was called in to help guide and support Elliott, the employer, and the therapist in finding remedies, both short and long term, for Elliott's safety, continued insight into treatment for the symptoms of PTSD, and success in the workplace.

After negotiating a few days leave from work for Elliott, the IPS specialist worked with all parties in a consensus planning process. Elliott agreed there might be other ways to more safely address conflict situations that arise in the workplace. The employer recognized that his small but growing business might need to establish a personnel plan and orientation for all employees to address a range of potential issues, and the therapist agreed that a return to work was appropriate given the safeguards and supports that were in place through the IPS intervention.

Elliott's story highlights the importance of supporting a veteran with PTSD to make choices about jobs and illustrates how IPS can identify tools and resources for the veteran to "bulletproof the psyche" against triggers that are frequently present in the workplace. The common symptoms of defensiveness, hypervigilance, anxiety, and irritability often signal a misguided response to social, interpersonal, and workplace interactions. In extreme circumstances, these signals can have life-threatening consequences. Employment support, interpretation, and guidance can be crucial to moving beyond the fear and frustration.

IPS is a practice that is most effective when paired early in the treatment cycle with other medical and mental health care rather than at the end of treatment, which is more typical of traditional vocational rehabilitation. Like with early intervention in treating disease and traumatic injuries, integrating return to work early after the diagnosis of mental health conditions such as PTSD can dramatically enhance recovery and substantially improve quality of life. IPS helps to build insight into the triggers of PTSD; establishes an interim support system to address one's identity, self-worth, and self-esteem through employment; and significantly advances the resilience-building work of recovery from trauma. Let us look more closely at the core principles of IPS.

1. *Choice.* The desire to enter or reenter the workplace is the only readiness criterion for access to IPS supports, whereas traditional vocational rehabilitation tends toward prevocational activities or work hardening training to demonstrate ability to return to work. A common coping mechanism to address the symptoms of anxiety, depression, sleep deprivation, anger outbursts, and flashbacks is self-medication with drugs or alcohol. IPS does not exclude access to services based on substance use but rather works with the individual and his or her treatment team to use the motivation to work as leverage to engage in substance use treatment and find other means to manage the symptoms.
2. *Competitive employment.* Meaningful competitive employment, either part-time or full-time, depending on the veteran's life circumstances and financial needs, is the goal of IPS. Introducing employment while still in active treatment can be a very powerful way to regain confidence, a sense of self, and the satisfaction of once again contributing to family, community, and society.
3. *Integration with treatment.* The holistic approach to treatment and recovery incorporates employment planning and support with treatment planning consistent with the individual's goals and aspirations. Essential to the integrated approach is regular communication between the IPS employment specialist and the primary treatment provider or treatment team. By prioritizing coordination between the treatment plan and the employment plan, the veteran with PTSD benefits from a unified message of hopefulness for his or her future and a safeguard to see and respond to symptoms in a timely fashion. The team of a veteran, IPS specialist, MH provider, and sometimes family members and/or employers can rapidly recognize and remediate symptoms and the associated triggering events of the trauma experience. Let us visit the story of Marilyn to illustrate the *choice* and *integrated team* principles.

> Marilyn is a veteran of the army who was stationed in Germany during her service. Although she was not deployed to a combat zone, her trauma, military sexual trauma (MST), was no less debilitating. She tried to start a career after the military but was unable to sustain her employment due to perceived threats, some harassment in the workplace, and perceived advances that increased her anxiety and resulted in her quitting. Marilyn was engaged in treatment on and off but was averse to taking medications for her symptoms; instead, she used marijuana and described herself as a "naturalist." Her therapist, at the time of her referral to IPS services, perceived this as a convenient excuse for smoking pot. During the vocational assessment intake process, the IPS specialist learned that Marilyn was raised in a family from the 1960s. She was opposed to medications

and used natural remedies for everything from the common cold to topical treatments for cuts and bruises.

After getting to know Marilyn and building some trust, the IPS specialist met with her treatment team to discuss strategies for her employment and treatment plan. The primary therapist appreciated the insight into Marilyn's personal history and preferences and recommitted to working on a new plan that included employment. After unsuccessful attempts at working as an office clerk, the IPS specialist helped network Marilyn with a local business that sold gems, stones, and crystals owned by a woman who also believed in the healing power of all things natural. On days when Marilyn was particularly anxious at work, she would assign herself to work in an area with specific crystals to help herself calm down. Her employer also supported her by helping connect her to support groups in the community. Like in this example, an effective IPS program meets the person where he or she is in his or her life and listens carefully to his or her preferences, aspirations, and desires as well as fears and challenges. The power of the integrated team is that the treatment provider and the IPS specialist can learn from the veteran and each other to maximize everyone's buy-in to a plan that works most effectively for that veteran.

IPS pays special attention to the client's preferences. IPS specialists search for competitive jobs that are aligned with the interests and desires of the participant (person-centered). IPS also involves detailed personalized benefits planning in that IPS specialists help veterans obtain personalized and accurate information about their VA, Social Security, and other government entitlements. At the core of IPS are the principles of rapid job search, systematic job development, and follow-along support. IPS specialists use a rapid job search approach to help veterans obtain jobs directly rather than providing lengthy preemployment assessment, training, and counseling. IPS specialists evaluate needs and deliver individualized support in the workplace for as long as needed.

IPS Has Positive Impact on Health Services Utilization

Another positive impact of IPS is that patients with serious mental illness who participate in IPS services have a substantial reduction in health care services utilization (Drake et al., 2013; Hoffman, Jäckel, Glauser, Mueser, & Kupper, 2014; Knapp et al., 2013; Salkever, Gibbons, & Rann, 2014). In addition to superior employment outcomes, IPS participation is associated with fewer hospital days, fewer hospital readmissions, annual inpatient hospital treatment cost savings, and better social return on investment. The long-term vocational and nonvocational trajectories of participants with serious mental illness in IPS are positive (Bond et al., 2001; McHugo, Drake, Xie, & Bond, 2012; Mueser et al., 1997). Work reduces long-term health services utilization, especially steady employment (Kukla, Bond, & Xie, 2012). Employment is consistently associated with reduced utilization of outpatient mental health services and psychoactive medications and lower psychiatric service costs. Longitudinal studies suggest that a meaningful period of competitive employment is associated with improvement over time in symptoms, quality of life, self-esteem, and social functioning as compared to not working (Bond et al., 2001).

Given almost universal acknowledgment that making meaningful contributions through employment will have a positive impact on health, wealth, self-esteem, and improved relations with coworkers, family, and friends, why do the employment rates of veterans with PTSD continue to significantly lag behind the general population? The IPS experience informs the field that employment and health outcomes improve when supports are coordinated between the person, family, clinical supports, and employer, but that coordination is not possible without the consent of the individual with PTSD. Consent means that individuals with PTSD are willing to expose themselves to both perceived and actual stigma against mental illness in our society.

A common response from persons entering an IPS is the reluctance to disclose anything about their mental health challenges. A common refrain is: "If I disclose my disability, no one will hire me." For veterans, that reluctance is magnified based on a military culture that instills the message of strength and invincibility started in boot camp, reinforced in service and deployments, and cemented at the honorable discharge. The message is that showing weakness endangers you and all those around you. However, in the civilian employment world, accommodations for symptoms cannot occur without disclosure. Without disclosure, the individual is vulnerable to coworkers, supervisors, and employers not recognizing interactions and behaviors in the workplace as a function of their trauma and easily remedied by reasonable accommodations or education.

PTSD and Workplace Disclosure and Accommodation

PTSD may qualify as a medical condition that can result in a disability under the Americans with Disabilities Act (ADA) and is covered under the Family Medical Leave Act. However, an applicant is not required to disclose his or her disability unless he or she needs an accommodation to assist him or her in the application or interview process, or once employed, need an accommodation to perform the essential of the job. People with PTSD (or any disability) do not have to undergo a medical exam or answer any medical questions until after they are conditionally offered a job. Requests for medical examinations prior to the job offer are illegal under the ADA. An employee with PTSD can provide documentation of his or her disability and ask for an accommodation when he or she needs an accommodation to perform the essential functions of the job. An employer can discipline an employee with PTSD who fails to meet performance standards or violates conduct standards, even if the behavior is caused by the PTSD disability. However, an employer must consider reasonable accommodations to help the employee with PTSD meet the conduct or performance standards.

What type of job accommodations can be requested by employees with PTSD or considered by employers? Common suggestions for accommodations include a work schedule that allows for clinical appointments, work environments that minimize loud or unexpected noise, and an avoidance of shift work so that the individual can maintain a stable sleep-wake cycle. Concentration can be difficult for individuals with PTSD, and simple workplace accommodations can include tactics to reduce distractions in the work area, such as use of white-noise sound machines, sound absorption panels, or noise cancelling headsets. Persons with PTSD benefit from clear expectation of responsibilities, open communication, and advanced notice of meetings, deadlines, and changes in schedules. Employer-employee agreements on conflict resolution, strategies to use if tensions or anxiety surface, permission to take time-outs to process new or unexpected information, and relating to coworkers are encouraged. People with PTSD do not like to work with their back toward others, so forward-facing work spaces are best. Employees should be aware that employees with PTSD may jump to conclusions that a called meeting is a "conflict" rather than a "conversation." Reassurance prior to beginning a discussion may decrease defensiveness. Stigma is often a problem faced by people with PTSD, so confidentiality is highly important to protect individuals from coworker pressures. However, providing sensitivity training to the entire workgroup can benefit everyone.

The U.S. Department of Labor and affiliates created *America's Heroes at Work* toolkit to help assist and educate employers on how to hire veterans with combat-related PTSD and help them successfully return to the workplace (U.S. Department of Labor, n.d.). These recommendations provide a step-by-step toolkit for employers to use as guidance on employing veterans, especially those with disabilities. Needs for accommodations vary widely depending on an individual's limitations; and it is important to keep in mind that not all veterans with PTSD will need or ask for accommodations.

Well-implemented IPS programs educate clients, employers, and community support resources on the benefits of disclosure and reasonable accommodations. Disclosure can be dignified and nonstigmatizing. Disclosure can define for the individual and the employer how the potential employee can be supported and accommodated to function at optimal performance and sustain that performance over long periods of time to the benefit of the company or organization.

How Employment Can Bulletproof the Psyche

Three key attributes cultivate the traits of worker passion in the workforce: (1) *commitment to domain*—the desire to have a lasting and increasing impact on a focused domain; (2) *questing*—a searching drive to go above and beyond core responsibilities; and (3) *connecting*—seeking out others to find solutions to the challenges (Hagel, Brown, & Samoylova, 2013). Military culture is steeped in these three elements, referred to as a strong commitment to the mission, tendency to go above the call of duty, and disciplined teamwork. A veteran who is matched in a postcombat civilian job that aligns with his or her preferences and abilities in an environment that promotes commitment, questing, and connecting can reclaim his or her passion for work that ultimately maximizes occupational functioning, restores self-reliant behaviors, and builds resiliency within a team. Most success stories resulting from IPS interventions can be encapsulated by commitment to domain, questing, and/or connecting. *Commitment to domain*, for those distracted by the symptoms of their mental health challenges, is the ability to focus and make a meaningful contribution through a job match based on interests, skills, passions, and desires—a core element of IPS. *Questing*, for those living with trauma histories, is the search for environments and relationships that are safe—a prerequisite for job development and placement within IPS. Finally, *connecting* is the employer development and negotiations that lead to the person with PTSD feeling welcomed and part of the team. Jake's story illustrates elements of these attributes in practice.

> *Jake is a former air force mechanic. After years of getting and losing jobs, and finally giving up, he was introduced by his therapist to an IPS program and encouraged to give employment one more try. After going through the individualized assessment process, it was clear that his machinist skills were a source of personal pride, confidence, and sense of identity. After a month of networking in his local community, the IPS specialist met an employer who owned a medium-sized tool-and-dye shop. The owner was interested in hiring veterans and agreed to meet Jake. Jake and the IPS specialist met the next week. After a brief introduction, the employer offered to take Jake on a tour of the factory. As they walked into the plant with loud machines and the hustle and bustle of the workplace, Jake froze. He quickly escalated into panic and could not continue the tour. After discussing the situation, and in the moment, self-disclosing that he had PTSD, the employer said "no problem." They went outside and the employer suggested to Jake and the IPS specialist that they set up another visit for the next day at lunchtime when the plant was relatively quiet. This simple accommodation allowed Jake to have a successful interview and to receive a job offer. Jake later shared that the ability to enter the space and engage with the employer that way made him feel connected and welcomed. Jake, the employer, and the IPS specialist*

developed a plan to gradually increase his work hours over several weeks allowing him to develop a job and mission he valued (*commitment to domain*), to recognize that his skills were valued and see he was making a meaningful contribution (*quest*), and to find a safe way to seek out others toward a common goal and purpose (*connecting*). Jake worked at the company for several years and continued to grow in his career and recovery.

Work can also stabilize individuals and reconnect them with their family and friends. Having to show up at a family gathering and face the onslaught of suggestions about how to get a job can leave the unemployed person with PTSD feeling estranged and embarrassed, which contributes to more social isolation. For veterans who have a strong sense of self-reliance, asking their family for financial help is often out of the question. For many IPS clients, employment restored their sense of dignity and gave them the courage to go to a family gathering and rekindle broken ties.

One of the core symptoms of PTSD is avoidance as a means for the individual with PTSD to not be exposed to triggers that cause anxiety, nightmares, or intrusive memories. Avoidance can lead to social isolation and may be the root cause of work absenteeism. Indeed, a job can serve as a mandated form of behavioral therapy, in that it can be the driving force to prevent an individual from getting housebound or reclusive. When provided with supportive counseling, encouragement from family or the IPS employment specialist, and a job that has some relevance to individual preferences or abilities, the person with PTSD can benefit therapeutically from the work experience. As one IPS client stated, "My work is my therapy."

Conclusion

Reintegration for recently deployed veterans requires finding mainstream competitive employment that provides the veteran with identity, structure, income, daily activity, friends, and other benefits. Without employment, many veterans become enveloped by preoccupation with symptoms, social isolation, economic instability, familial disintegration, substance abuse, legal problems, homelessness, and wayward lifestyles. Recovery includes employment and should be a primary treatment aim. Recovery is a multifaceted process in which people with illnesses or disabilities move beyond preoccupation with illness, become hopeful about the future, and pursue their own journeys and goals. Functional and social recovery involves maintaining valued societal roles and responsibilities, including employment, education, stable housing, and meaningful relationships with family and community (Whitley & Drake, 2010). Reduced reliance on acute-care health systems and more appropriate use of outpatient services are perhaps two of the most important potential impacts of IPS at a systems level. Individuals who gain steady employment report increased self-esteem, decreased psychiatric symptoms, reduced social disability, and greater overall quality of life (Burns et al., 2007). For those who become steady workers, mental health treatment costs decline dramatically over the long term after adjusting for morbidity/needs (Bush, Drake, Xie, McHugo, & Haslett, 2009). Employment helps people escape from the disabled patient role, experience a sense of purpose and accomplishment, and establish a new identity as a working, contributing citizen and family member.

References

Becker, D. R., & Drake, R. E. (2003). *A working life for people with severe mental illness*. New York, NY: Oxford University Press.

Bond, G. R., Resnick, S. G., Drake, R. E., Xie, H., McHugo, G. J., & Bebout, R. R. (2001). Does competitive employment improve nonvocational outcomes for people with severe mental illness? *Journal of Consulting and Clinical Psychology, 69*(3), 489.

Burns, T., Catty, J., Becker, T., Drake, R. E., Fioritti, A., Knapp, M., . . . White, S. (2007). The effectiveness of supported employment for people with severe mental illness: A randomised controlled trial. *The Lancet, 370*(9593), 1146–1152.

Bush, P. W., Drake, R. E., Xie, H., McHugo, G. J., & Haslett, W. R. (2009). The long-term impact of employment on mental health service use and costs for persons with severe mental illness. *Psychiatric Services, 60*(8), 1024–1031.

Comino, E. J., Harris, E., Silove, D., Manicavasagar, V., & Harris, M. F. (2000). Prevalence, detection and management of anxiety and depressive symptoms in unemployed patients attending general practitioners. *Australian and New Zealand Journal of Psychiatry, 34*(1), 107–113.

Davis, L. L., Parker, P. E., Kashner, T. M., & Drake, R. E. (2012). A randomized controlled trial of supported employment among veterans with posttraumatic stress disorder. *Psychiatric Services, 63*(5), 464.

Drake, R. E., Frey, W., Bond, G. R., Goldman, H. H., Salkever, D., Miller, A., . . . Milfort, R. (2013). Assisting social security disability insurance beneficiaries with schizophrenia, bipolar disorder, or major depression in returning to work. *American Journal of Psychiatry, 170*(12), 1433–1441.

Erbes, C. R., Kaler, M. E., Schult, T., Polusny, M. A., & Arbisi, P. A. (2011). Mental health diagnosis and occupational functioning in National Guard/Reserve veterans returning from Iraq. *Journal of Rehabilitation Research & Development, 48*(10), 1159–1172.

Ferrie, J. E. (2001). Is job insecurity harmful to health? *Journal of the Royal Society of Medicine, 94*(2), 71–76.

Hagel, J., Brown, J., & Samoylova, T. (2013). Unlocking the passion of the explorer: A report in the 2013 shift index series. Deloitte University Press. Retrieved from https://dupress.deloitte.com/dup-us-en/topics/talent/unlocking-the-passion-of-the-explorer.html

Hoffmann, H., Jäckel, D., Glauser, S., Mueser, K. T., & Kupper, Z. (2014). Long-term effectiveness of supported employment: 5-year follow-up of a randomized controlled trial. *American Journal of Psychiatry, 171*(11), 1183–1190.

Kimerling, R., Alvarez, J., Pavao, J., Mack, K. P., Smith, M. W., & Baumrind, N. (2009). Unemployment among women: Examining the relationship of physical and psychological intimate partner violence and posttraumatic stress disorder. *Journal of Interpersonal Violence, 24*(3), 450–463.

Knapp, M., Patel, A., Curran, C., Latimer, E., Catty, J., Becker, T., . . . Rössler, W. (2013). Supported employment: Cost-effectiveness across six European sites. *World Psychiatry, 12*(1), 60–68.

Korpi, T. (2001). Accumulating disadvantage. Longitudinal analyses of unemployment and physical health in representative samples of the Swedish population. *European Sociological Review, 17*(3), 255–273.

Kukla, M., Bond, G. R., & Xie, H. (2012). A prospective investigation of work and nonvocational outcomes in adults with severe mental illness. *The Journal of Nervous and Mental Disease, 200*(3), 214–222.

Luciano, A., Drake, R. E., Bond. G. R., Becker, D. R., Carpenter-Song, E., Lord, S., Swarbrick, P., & Swanson, S. J. (2014). Evidence-based supported employment for people with severe mental illness: Past, current, and future research. *Journal of Vocational Rehabilitation, 40,* 1–13.

Martikainen, P. T., & Valkonen, T. (1996). Excess mortality of unemployed men and women during a period of rapidly increasing unemployment. *The Lancet, 348*(9032), 909–912.

Marwaha, S., & Johnson, S. (2004). Schizophrenia and employment. *Social Psychiatry and Psychiatric Epidemiology, 39*(5), 337–349.

McHugo, G. J., Drake, R. E., Xie, H., & Bond, G. R. (2012). A 10-year study of steady employment and non-vocational outcomes among people with serious mental illness and co-occurring substance use disorders. *Schizophrenia Research, 138*(2), 233–239.

Modini, M., Tan, L., Brinchmann, B., Wang, M. J., Killackey, E., Glozier, N., . . . Harvey, S. B. (2016). Supported employment for people with severe mental illness: Systematic review and meta-analysis of the international evidence. *The British Journal of Psychiatry: The Journal of Mental Science, 209*(1), 14–22.

Mueser, K. T., Becker, D. R., Torrey, W. C., Xie, H., Bond, G. R., Drake, R. E., & Dain, B. J. (1997). Work and nonvocational domains of functioning in persons with severe mental illness: A longitudinal analysis. *The Journal of Nervous and Mental Disease, 185*(7), 419–426.

Murdoch, M., van Ryn, M., Hodges, J., & Cowper, D. (2005). Mitigating effect of Department of Veterans Affairs disability benefits for post-traumatic stress disorder on low income. *Military Medicine, 170*(2), 137.

Riviere, L. A., Kendall-Robbins, A., McGurk, D., Castro, C. A., & Hoge, C. W. (2011). Coming home may hurt: Risk factors for mental ill health in US reservists after deployment in Iraq. *The British Journal of Psychiatry, 198*(2), 136–142.

Salkever, D., Gibbons, B., & Ran, X. (2014). Do comprehensive, coordinated, recovery-oriented services alter the pattern of use of treatment services? Mental health treatment study impacts on SSDI beneficiaries' use of inpatient, emergency, and crisis services. *The Journal of Behavioral Health Services & Research, 41*(4), 434–446.

Schennach, R., Musil, R., Möller, H. J., & Riedel, M. (2012). Functional outcomes in schizophrenia: Employment status as a metric of treatment outcome. *Current Psychiatry Reports, 14*(3), 229–236.

U.S. Department of Labor. (n.d.). America's Heroes at Work—Veterans Hiring Toolkit. Retrieved from https://www.dol.gov/vets/ahaw/

Vinokur, A. D., van Ryn, M., Gramlich, E. M., & Price, R. H. (1991). Long-term follow-up and benefit-cost analysis of the Jobs Program: A preventive intervention for the unemployed. *Journal of Applied Psychology, 76*(2), 213.

Whitley, R., & Drake, R. E. (2010). Recovery: A dimensional approach. *Psychiatric Services, 61*(12), 1248–1250.

Yur'yev, A., Värnik, A., Värnik, P., Sisask, M., & Leppik, L. (2012). Employment status influences suicide mortality in Europe. *International Journal of Social Psychiatry, 58*(1), 62–68.

CHAPTER 13

Adapting the Collective Impact Model to Veteran Services: The Case of AmericaServes

Nicholas J. Armstrong, Gillian S. Cantor, Bonnie Chapman, and James D. McDonough Jr.

Navigation: A Central Barrier to Veterans' Access to Services and Care

Today, a gap in services persists across America for our nation's 20.1 million veterans, 1.4 million service members, and their families. This gap does not appear to stem from a lack of resources or capacity. In fact, the Department of Veteran Affairs (VA) budget climbs, and philanthropic giving to military and veteran-serving nonprofits has remained steady since 2001 (Carter & Kidder, 2015). Rather, this gap reflects inadequate ground-level coordination and collective purpose among public, private, and social sector organizations serving this community.

The federal government offers a range of health services, educational programs, and transition supports to the military and veteran communities. The 2017 budget request for the VA alone nears a record $182 billion. However, few veterans experience transition challenges in isolation; the wellness challenges they face are often multiple, interrelated (i.e., comorbid), and social in nature. Social determinants of health—employment, education, housing, relationships, and the like—are strongly correlated with health outcomes

(Bartley & Plewis, 2002; Berkman & Syme, 1979; Marmot & Wilkinson, 2006; Moser, Fox, & Jones, 1984; Stansfeld & Marmot, 2002). Yet, the solutions to these challenges often lie beyond the purview of traditional government and private health systems.

Through elevated public support for veterans, the nonprofit sector has supplemented government reintegration and wellness services through more than 40,000 organizations dedicated to supporting military-connected individuals and countless more serving all Americans. Even so, veterans consistently cite difficulty knowing where to turn due to the diversity and fragmentation of actors across the veterans' services landscape. Consider, for example, a recent survey of more than 8,500 transitioning service members who rank "navigation of benefits and services" as the top challenge in the transition from military to civilian life—even ahead of finding a job or adjusting to civilian culture (Zoli, Maury, & Fay, 2015).

When seeking support, veterans often require assistance identifying reputable services that meet their specific needs and eligibility requirements. The recent Chicagoland Veterans Study found that the many veteran-supporting services in greater Chicago area are not organized to provide holistic support (Kintzle, Rasheed, & Castro, 2016). Notably, the report recommended the creation of a community support network through which organizations work together to meet the most pressing needs of veterans in their community. Various regional needs assessments and research reports over the past decade have raised similar recommendations around facilitating greater access and navigation of services through "high-touch" client-centered engagement and improved collaboration between clinical and social-service organizations (e.g., Berglass & Harrell, 2012; Kidder, Schafer, & Carter, 2016; Schell & Tanielian, 2011).

Recent signs show that collaboration[1] is rising between public, private, and nonprofit organizations serving military-connected individuals (Armstrong, Van Slyke, Isbester, & Chapman, 2016; Carter & Kidder, 2017). The models through which these communities collaborate vary widely by factors such as size, geographic coverage, service domains, and degree of public versus philanthropic sector involvement. These models also vary in their governance, from loose coalitions of the willing to highly structured networks enabled by a central actor coordinating activities through a shared technology.

There remains much to learn from these initiatives as more communities across the country respond to the wellness needs of transitioning service members, veterans, and their families. Above all, understanding the extent to which these initiatives address the challenges of access, navigation, and holistic care is paramount to fostering positive impact on this population.

This chapter highlights the case of AmericaServes, an expanding collective impact (Kania & Kramer, 2011) initiative in multiple communities across the country. The mission of AmericaServes is "to empower a coordinated network of veteran services in the United States, and equip them with the technological and informational resources needed to efficiently and effectively guide service members, veterans, and their families to the most appropriate services and resources" (AmericaServes, n.d.).

In the sections that follow, we describe collective impact as a unique type of public-private collaboration with defining characteristics and necessary preconditions for success. From this discussion, we illustrate how AmericaServes works, explain the underlying logic and measures that inform its design and performance, and highlight recent experiences and lessons bridging theory and practice in supporting its implementation in different communities over the past two years. We conclude with a prospective discussion of AmericaServes' potential for further research, evaluation, and innovation around access to comprehensive services and mental health outcomes.

Collaborative Governance and Communities

Over the past three decades, the public sector has increasingly moved away from traditional, top-down approaches to policymaking and implementation by introducing more collaborative forms of policy governance that involve greater private and social sector involvement (Ansell & Gash, 2008). Collaborative governance refers to decision making and management that occurs when government agencies and nongovernment entities work together toward mutually beneficial outcomes (Emerson & Nabatchi, 2015).

Public-private partnerships are a widely used form of collaborative governance. Yet, while effective in many circumstances, public-private partnerships are often confined to the delivery or production of a single public good or service (Bel, Brown, & Marques, 2015; Brown, Potoski, & Van Slyke, 2013; Osborne, 2000). In more complex policy areas involving multiple stakeholders, however, partnership strategies have improved through the adoption of collaborative governance principles that bridge political and institutional boundaries down to the local level (Ansell & Torfing, 2015; Booher, 2004; Brenner, 2001; Kooiman, 1993). Community-based partnerships, in particular, have employed a mixture of collaborative and cooperative strategies, both formal and informal, but it is not clear how important these have been to the actual work that has taken place or the subsequent outcomes.

While improved understanding of governance and collective-action strategies have helped these strategies gain traction, those employing them often neglect many of the relevant findings from previous research and work within actual communities (Christens & Tran Inzeo, 2015). The terminology used is not as important as finding the best way to drive progress at the local level. It is also important to recognize that the word "community" means different things to different people. It is a catchall phrase used without consideration of its ambiguity (Mulligan et al., 2016). Community can mean everything from a big city to a suburb, a small town, rich or poor, and all in between. Moreover, cities, towns, and small villages function like living organisms with complex, adaptive systems and interacting components that cannot be itemized, controlled, or fully anticipated (Batty, 2005; Berry, 1964; Gershenson, 2013; Portugali, 2000). Ground-level circumstances are also far less ordered than typically assumed. Community-based nonprofits are constantly challenged with regard to issues such as power and conflict, funding deficits, and building local partnership toward a shared mission.

Collective Impact

In the midst of rising public-private collaboration, the public and social sectors are also increasing emphasis on the combined social value—the collective impact—that their collaborative activities generate (Austin & Seitanidi, 2012; Edmondson & Hecht, 2014; Kania & Kramer, 2011; Weaver, 2014). Collective impact is a type of collaborative governance arrangement that engages a wide range of stakeholders and organizations (e.g., diverse missions and sectors) into long-term commitments and a common agenda to address a specific social problem (Kania & Kramer, 2011, p. 39). Collective impact models have built upon collaborative governance and planning models by providing a methodical planning and implementation framework through which public-private partnerships can address complex issues of great need (Hanleybrown, Kania, & Kramer, 2012). Collective impact assumes that its alternative—the isolated impact of one or a few organizations—is often insufficient to solve complex social problems that demand continuous learning and adaptation (Kania & Kramer, 2011, pp. 38–39).

Preconditions for collective impact. Experts suggest that three necessary conditions must precede a collective impact initiative prior to its launch (Hanleybrown et al., 2012, p. 3). First, there must be an influential local champion. This individual(s) or organization(s) must possess the legitimacy, leadership qualities, and altruism required to unite and sustain the commitment of a critical mass of local stakeholders around a common problem. Ensuring local ownership is a widely established, albeit thorny, maxim in community and international development practice. The second precondition is a sufficient reserve of financial resources to sustain the initiative for two to three years, typically generated through a lead funder willing to provide capital for initial planning and implementation. The third precondition is urgency for change. There must be enough agreement among stakeholders that a pressing need requires collective attention and that current efforts are insufficient.

Defining characteristics of collective impact versus collaboration. Collective impact initiatives demonstrate five characteristics that distinguish them from other forms of collaboration (Kania & Kramer, 2011, pp. 39–40). The first trait is a shared commitment to a common agenda. Individual organizations have their own visions of the world around them and their own interests to pursue. For collective impact to work, however, all participants must find consensus around a set of shared goals, objectives, and actions.

Second, the group must develop a common performance measurement system. Defining collective success and developing a set of measures and data for collection and monitoring safeguard both long-term goal alignment and accountability within the group (Provan, Veazie, Staten, & Teufel-Shone, 2005).

Third, the activities of participating individual organizations must be mutually reinforcing. That is, shared data and evidence must inform a common plan or framework that, in turn, guides participants' activities in an integrated and coordinated way (Hanleybrown et al., 2012, p. 8).

Fourth, continuous communication is essential for the collective impact initiative to function effectively. Constant interaction and exchange of information are necessary to (1) build and sustain trust, a well-established element of network success (Klijn, Edelenbos, & Steijn, 2010); and (2) foster group learning and problem solving, also known as "communities of practice" (Wenger, 1998, 2015; Wenger, McDermott, & Snyder, 2002). Communication and evidence-based learning are critical to group innovation and finding new solutions to complex and evolving problems (Kania & Kramer, 2013).

The fifth and final key to achieving collective impact is the central administrative, or "backbone," organization that governs collaboration and coordination across the group (Provan & Kenis, 2008, p. 236). Backbone organizations provide the necessary staffing and infrastructure to facilitate continuous communication, planning, data collection and evaluation, and related administrative tasks to function effectively. Driven by the common agenda, backbone organizations guide vision and strategy, support aligned activities, establish shared measurement practices, build public will, advance policy, and mobilize funding for the group as whole (Turner, Merchant, Kania, & Martin, 2012).

AmericaServes: Program Overview

This section introduces AmericaServes, a collective impact initiative that helps local communities meet the diverse needs of military-connected individuals through a coordinated network of human and social service providers spanning 15 service domains.[2] The aim is for military-connected clients to receive timely, appropriate, and comprehensive access to the resources they need, where they are. The Institute for Veterans and Military Families (IVMF) at Syracuse University administers the initiative in close partnership with a diverse group of public and private partners, including Accenture and Unite US, a veteran-owned software technology firm.

In less than three years, 11 AmericaServes networks have launched across New York, North Carolina, South Carolina, Pennsylvania, Rhode Island, Texas, and Washington State. To date, these networks include more than 600 network providers and 1,500 practitioners from the public and private sectors and have fielded more than 22,000 service requests. More than $9 million in philanthropic investment has been raised to stand up these community networks, and additional support and planning for future networks are underway.

How AmericaServes Works

Analogous to health care coordination models (e.g., accountable care organizations), each AmericaServes network seeks to strengthen how nonprofits operate together by providing initial funding for a coordination center and the technology to manage a referral-based system of care. Community networks are typically comprised of 40–50 (on average) human service organizations from the public, nonprofit, and health care sectors. Prior to launch, interested organizations are brought together through a series of strategic planning sessions (detailed further later) over four to six months designed to build momentum behind a collective impact approach and familiarity with the finer details of network coordination. In this process, members adopt a common intake form to screen clients for social determinants of health and obtain consent for referral within the network to address needs that may arise beyond their own organization's capacity or expertise. Providers also receive training on a secure technology platform, provided by Unite US, Inc.,[3] through which they are able to safely share protected (i.e., Health Insurance Portability and Accountability Act [HIPAA] compliant) client information through case referral.

From this collective group, a committee selects one organization among their peers to serve as the network's backbone administrative organization. These organizations are provided philanthropic resources to staff a coordination center that manages referrals between organizations. Staff members are licensed social workers who screen, triage, assign, and monitor case referrals to other participating organizations based on factors such as urgency, client eligibility criteria for specific services, and known provider capacity to accept case referrals. The result is a more integrated and transparent system of local support and care, enhanced through streamlined referral and active case management.

Military-connected clients may access the network through two primary channels (see Figure 13.1). First, clients are able to self-refer to the coordination center online or by phone. Each network (e.g., NYServes-New York

Adapting the Collective Impact Model to Veteran Services

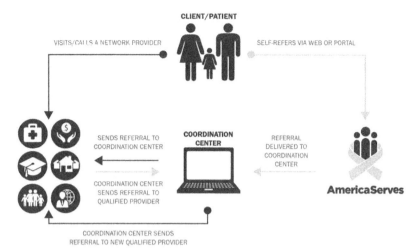

Figure 13.1 Client referral experience

City) has its own web page and is search-engine optimized for those seeking services online within their region of service delivery. Alternatively, clients may access the network in person through any participating organization. For example, a veteran seeking employment support at a participating jobs center will be screened for other needs (e.g., financial assistance and housing) and offered the opportunity to be referred to other network providers for appropriate support. In both scenarios, clients provide electronic consent to share their information in order to receive services offered within the network.

Technology-enabled measurement and evaluation. In both health care and human service delivery, measurement focused on continuous quality improvement is critical to test and implement changes that address the complex or changing needs of the client. Through Unite US, a validated care coordination technology platform, in partnership with the IVMF research and evaluation team, AmericaServes, is able to capture full lifecycle service provision of all clients in each network—from point of entry and referral throughout service delivery to specified outcome. AmericaServes collects a range of data including demographic information; service type and demand; referral tracking statuses; case notes; and time stamps of workflow, appointments, and specific outcomes across an entire community.

Utilizing these data, IVMF, coordination centers, and the communities they serve are able to gain understanding and introduce benchmarks around demand for specific services by specific client demographics (e.g., housing requests by female post-9/11 veterans). Additionally, the technology allows the IVMF and other stakeholders to gauge demand across multiple networks and better understand resource availability and supply of services.

Communities meet regularly to address questions and insights raised by the data and to adapt processes to tackle common challenges. These meetings typically take three forms: focus groups with providers in similar service categories, outreach events targeting specific populations and needs, and quarterly in-progress reports. The measurement and evaluation team at the IVMF, with assistance from Unite US, provides the data to support these conversations.

AmericaServes' network implementation. With every new community, the IVMF has refined the process of building a network. The approach from planning to launching follows five phases—Socialize, Validate, Demonstrate, Prepare/Participate, and Train—that are explained further later.

The goal of the Socialize phase is to ensure the underlying conditions are present to support a coordinated network. These conditions include the buy-in of local leaders, an informal commitment from providers offering a comprehensive range of services, and a willingness to share data. Additionally, there must be resources available to fund the initial two years of the network and the potential for long-term financial sustainability. Activities during this stage typically include small-group strategy meetings with key stakeholders to sketch out next steps.

Once these conditions have been met, the IVMF facilitates a series of planning conversations among the community and with Unite US. During this planning period—the Validate, Demonstrate, and Prepare/Participate phases—the network is created both in person and in the technology platform. Strategy Session 1 confirms the community's understanding of the core problem and AmericaServes' collective impact approach, identifies a service coverage area, and lays out the expectations for providers and the coordination center.

In Strategy Session 2, the Unite US team demonstrates the nuts-and-bolts functionality of the software and how it enhances existing workflows and coordination within and between providers. In this session, the community also establishes the prospective list of service providers to ensure the full range of client needs will be met by the network.

In the 90 days that follow, a request for proposals (RFP) for a coordination center is opened, a local committee selects a winner, and the process to establish the coordination center begins. During this period, the third and final Strategy Session is held to fast-track provider registration, firm up coverage areas, and finalize the service offerings and their categorizations.

In the fifth and final phase, the IVMF monitors launch readiness as participating organizations are onboarded and trained, and the newly minted coordination center strengthens its relationships with providers and stakeholders. Ongoing engagement is critical to the steady-state success of networks and begins well before the official launch date.

AmericaServes' Theory of Change and Measurement

AmericaServes has a two-stage theory of change. The first stage is a system-level intervention among human and social services organizations. At this stage, the focus is on the successful implementation of a collective impact initiative to improve access and navigation to services for local military-connected individuals.

When considering the measurement and evaluation of a collective impact model like AmericaServes, it is important to note that the primary intervention is focused on outcomes associated with the collective *system* as opposed to outcomes associated with individual actors within the system. Systems theory and its application in everything from complex global supply chains to the delivery of human services and health care are based on the assumption that the attributes of throughput (i.e., to what scale and how efficiently and effectively the system navigates a product or person from point A to point B) represent the outcome of the system. In other words, the performance of the system (the causal outcome) is represented by the extent to which the system efficiently and effectively *manages throughput*. To that end, the most generally accepted and widely adopted metrics to capture the performance *outcomes* associated with complex systems relate to the following:

- *Speed:* Has the system expedited throughput (increased the speed associated with moving product/person from point A to B)?
- *Accuracy:* Has the system reduced defects associated with throughput (improved the error rate of moving product/person from point A to B)
- *Scale:* Does the system support increased throughput resulting from efficiencies of *speed* and *accuracy*?

For this reason, speed, accuracy, and scale represent central performance metrics for AmericaServes. We measure network outcomes: (a) Did the network effectively support an expedited connection between the service-seeker and the provider (speed)? (b) Did the network reduce the error rate associated with "bad referrals" (accuracy)? (c) Did the network foster increased capacity to accommodate service-seekers resulting from efficiencies of speed and accuracy?

AmericaServes' second and more tenuous stage of change is at the level of participating organizations and the individual military-connected clients they serve. A fully functional AmericaServes network provides clients unprecedented access—a "no wrong door" entry point—to a comprehensive suite of care, resources, and services. This access results in more timely and appropriate service delivery and better quality of care. A relative improvement in overall military-connected population well-being would thus follow.

Nevertheless, the second-order effects of a networked system on individuals and a broader population are extremely difficult to isolate. We argue that client-centric outcomes (i.e., veteran found a job and received treatment) are incrementally improved because the system efficiently and effectively managed throughput (speed, accuracy, and scale). There are strong arguments and evidence to suggest that this is the case, but ultimately the collaborative is only as good as the providers that compose the network. Thus, we assert that a strong collective impact model is one in which the system both efficiently and effectively manages throughput and provides the consumer transparent information about provider performance. In turn, this creates a free market effect positioned to elevate stronger performance among service providers.

Development of Key Performance Indicators

Although the purpose of AmericaServes is the second-order effect of providing individuals with better care and thereby enhancing quality of life, measuring only this aspect (to the degree possible) would provide little information about the upstream processes and outcomes of the system. The utility of AmericaServes would be questioned if it were not possible to demonstrate effectiveness on some level. However, the IVMF team developed a set of measures and means to gather the necessary data by applying logic model and balanced scorecard frameworks. These tools were used to help the team members dissect the intricacies and dependencies within the program and to prioritize the most meaningful measures and outcomes.

In sketching out the AmericaServes logic model, the IVMF team wanted a cross-section of measures that would be representative of the program in its entirety. They aligned many of the program implementation stages with the phases of the network life cycle—essentially, AmericaServes' theory of change.

- *Network cultivation:* Is the community receptive, and does it have enough resources to support a network?
- *Strategy/preplanning:* Did the team take the right steps to include the right providers in the network, and have the providers been trained appropriately?
- *Steady state:* How is the network operating? How healthy is it?
- *Long-term sustainability:* How are the clients doing? Is the community able to perpetuate the network and continue serving clients?

Next, the team outlined the logic model components at each stage. Representatives from the program contributed to brainstorming sessions as ideas for measurement were collected. Drawing from a broad list of measures, the team organized performance measures using the balanced scorecard categories: financial, process, learning, and customer satisfaction. Finally, the most important measures in each category were elevated as key performance indicators (KPIs). These KPIs represent the most important outputs, outcomes, and impacts identified in the AmericaServes logic model. The remaining measures in the logic model are also tracked and reported regularly to monitor and guide operations at all program levels.

AmericaServes: Bridging Theory and Practice

While every AmericaServes community shares a common goal, software platform, measurement system, and basic activities, there are variables that manifest differently from network to network. The theory and performance indicators outlined above preserve the core of the initiative as it scales but allow for flexibility in its application. This growth and adaptability have afforded the IVMF opportunities for innovation and learning at each stage in the network life cycle.

Network Formation

One area of continuous refinement during network planning has been the classification of service domains (e.g., housing and education). Initially, the IVMF deferred to communities to define appropriate domain categories and map available services to them. As more networks came online and the categories were in active use in the software, the IVMF, Unite US, existing communities, and new communities worked in concert to redefine, add, and ensure proper use of these categories. In late 2016, this discussion informed a comprehensive revision of service domains for the updated version of the Unite US platform.

While some categories are straightforward (e.g., health care, mentoring), many are more complex than may be apparent. For example, if a client reports a pending eviction, she may require emergency support to prevent immediate homelessness. Should the coordination center classify that need as a financial or a housing assistance request? What if Metrolina prefers to define it as the former and Greater Pittsburgh as the latter? These granular, evolving decisions have effects on data and processes well downstream of the network formation stage, requiring substantial consideration when analyzing trends in individual networks, making cross-network comparisons, and managing business processes across AmericaServes as a whole.

Another component of network formation that is complex in practice is the selection of a qualified coordination center to manage referrals between clients and providers. While the IVMF has incorporated lessons into every subsequent RFP, the organizations and operating models for our network backbones remain diverse and have different advantages. Currently, coordination centers roughly fit into one of two categories:

1. A local, often smaller nonprofit organization seeking to dedicate a portion of its mission and resources to the AmericaServes collective impact goal. This model is currently in effect in SCServes (Augusta Warrior Project); NYServes-Upstate (Veterans Outreach Center); and three of our NCServes networks, Metrolina (Charlotte Bridge Home), Coastal (Eastern Carolina Human Service Agency), and Western (Asheville-Buncombe Community Christian Ministry).
2. A larger health care, governmental, or military-connected organization operating in the region seeking to enhance its veteran-oriented care initiatives. This model is currently in effect in NYServes-New York City (Northwell Health), WAServes-Greater Puget Sound (WestCare), NCServes-RDU/Fayetteville (USO of North Carolina), PAServes-Greater Pittsburgh (Pittsburgh Mercy), TXServes-San Antonio (Alamo Area Council of Governments), and RIServes (Office of Veterans Affairs).

AmericaServes has yet to assess which models lead to better system outcomes, in part because it is only beginning to have enough data points (in this case, coordination centers) to make meaningful comparisons and in part because "right" may be highly dependent on community and organizational conditions.

One key determination after several years of learning relates to launch readiness. In order to maximize effectiveness out of the gate, AmericaServes now aims to have at least 40 providers onboarded and trained prior to official launch. In networks that began with fewer providers, the coordination centers spent their initial months with a split focus, conducting outreach to bring additional organizations into the fold as well as acclimating to referral management. Early establishment of a diverse and reliable bench of providers to ensure supply meets demand accelerates the coordination center's ability to connect clients to appropriate care by freeing up bandwidth to cultivate relationships and become experts in program offerings and eligibility.

Network Growth, Ongoing Operations, and Learning

A major challenge of AmericaServes has been "proving" the second stage of the theory of change: coordinated service delivery improves the quality of care and life for veterans and military families. One of the ways to measure success at the individual level is to capture client feedback. Several versions of web and text message surveys have been attempted, but obstacles have stood in the way of obtaining high-quality results.

One issue has been low response rates, which is common when surveying difficult-to-reach populations. Another problem is actually inherent to referral model. In essence, if the coordination centers do their jobs well, they may actually become less visible or memorable to the client. For example, if an intake specialist conducts a high-quality initial needs assessment and matches the client quickly to an appropriate provider, the client may only recall who assisted them, not how they were connected to that assistance.

Several efforts are underway to find better ways to reach clients. In the fall of 2017, a pilot phone survey will be conducted, allowing for both quantitative and qualitative information to be collected about the client experience. A project has also been initiated with Unite US to integrate survey features into the software so that clients can be reached in real time at key service provision milestones. To support this work, AmericaServes is partnering with the Maxwell X Lab, a new policy and program improvement initiative operating out of the Center for Policy Research at Syracuse University's Maxwell School of Citizenship and Public Affairs. The Maxwell X Lab will apply best practices to AmericaServes survey methods, helping test what surveys should (and should not) include, as well as how and when to send them. Maxwell X Lab's experience conducting field experiments and rapidly analyzing results will ground survey efforts in evidence, allow quick method revisions, and maximize reach.

One of the things the data have revealed is that clients typically have more than one need at a time (co-occurrence). While this fact may have been known anecdotally by providers and generally by researchers, the Unite US platform captures the itemized data needed to analyze the nature and frequency of co-occurrence in detail. Learning about specific need relationships is underway—both which needs are most likely to co-occur (e.g., employment and financial assistance) and which client attributes correspond with co-occurrence (service era, household size, gender, etc.). Ultimately, the aim is to use this information to position providers to work more seamlessly as a system to treat comorbidity and social determinants of health. This holistic approach to serving clients may also effectively address mental health needs by providing a sense of security, increasing access to care, and reducing stigma.

In addition to developing measures at all stages of service and program delivery, AmericaServes is creating formal structures to capture knowledge and innovation across networks. One such structure, the community of practice (CoP), is a national membership group where providers serving veterans and their families are given the resources and support to share experiences, discuss challenges and opportunities, and implement best practices. In May 2017, the CoP convened its first annual conference for existing and prospective AmericaServes coordination center staff members and partners. During the conference, the focus was on two key subjects: advancing military cultural competency and establishing shared goals for provider engagement and data management.

In the future, CoP workgroups will help AmericaServes tackle objectives such as defining and updating standard operating universal procedures, building an inventory of tools to further support service providers, and developing a dictionary for all reports and data fields in the Unite US platform. The aim is to create a culture of transparency and standards that will guide decision making at all levels of the initiative.

Network Sustainment

By the end of 2017, NYServes-New York City, NCServes-Metrolina, and PAServes-Greater Pittsburgh will have passed the initial two-year financial and technical assistance commitment. Efforts to ensure sustainability for these pioneer communities and to determine IVMF's long-term role are ongoing.

Similar to considerations for what "right" looks like for coordination centers, there is no definitive version of the ideal funding model. Securing funding depends heavily on understanding the available resources in each community, both in terms of sector (public, nonprofit, or philanthropic) and geographic scale (local, regional, state, or national) and their respective challenges. For example, governmental support typically requires a lengthy contracting or appropriation process.

As of July 2017, the city of New York confirmed its budgetary agreement to support NYServes-NYC for two more years, NCServes-Metrolina was approved for a recurring grant from Mecklenburg County, and the Heinz Endowments will continue funding a portion of PAServes-Greater Pittsburgh beyond its initial commitment. Newer networks are contemplating long-term sustainability sooner, and prospective coordination centers as well as local and state governments have even been pledging fiscal or in-kind investment at the start. For example, RIServes will be the first AmericaServes network paid for by a government for the first two years, and the coordination center for TXServes-San Antonio coordination center has announced plans to partially fund its network.

The IVMF plans to maintain a strong connection to AmericaServes networks past their first two years. The AmericaServes team will continue to operate in a technical assistance role, supporting coordination center operations, provider engagement, and measurement and evaluation. Perpetual data collection, reporting, and communication will be critical to understand which coordination center and funding models are the most successful, improve based on lessons learned, and evaluate outcomes at the system and individual levels. The institute's involvement will ensure consistency and quality across networks, further research efforts on network evaluation, and provide a platform to share ideas with other health and human service organizations.

Future Research: Connecting Care Coordination to Mental Health Outcomes

Given that AmericaServes is less than three years old, and most community networks are younger, much lies ahead in terms of learning, continuous improvement, and understanding how a system-level intervention contributes to individual outcomes, including mental health. While the bulk of the current measures characterize various aspects of the collective impact system and process, the institute's evaluation and research will constantly drive toward understanding the impact on the individual and on the community at large. One priority will be to evaluate the theory that AmericaServes is a mechanism that supports the mental health of military-connected individuals. By design, AmericaServes promotes individual mental health by fostering individual dignity and access to care, proactive support and responsiveness, security, and supportive partnerships with mental health experts.

Dignity and Access to Care

It is often observed that people, including the military-connected population, are reluctant to seek and use mental health resources available to them. The real and perceived stigma of requesting help for the use of mental health services is commonly to blame. The burden of navigating disparate services, including mental health services, may also be difficult to overcome. AmericaServes removes these barriers and supports individual dignity by offering no wrong door to enter the network and including the ability to self-refer. Once referred in, a single intake can suffice to begin the path to customized care. Furthermore, for those who are located in remote areas, do not wish to connect in person, or have time constraints, the online self-referral option eases access to care.

Proactive Support and Responsiveness

The AmericaServes intake process also ensures that clients are comprehensively evaluated. Clients initially seeking other services may have mental health needs identified during the assessment. Approaching each client holistically helps normalize the expectation for clients and providers that mental health support is one of many ways the network can facilitate care.

Once a referral is made, the receiving service provider actively reaches out to the client. Individuals with mental health challenges may not be able to consistently reach out and advocate for their needs. An intentional effort made by the service provider may be the difference between successful and unsuccessful attempts to initiate care.

AmericaServes' design further supports responsiveness and proactive care in several ways. First, coordination centers are aware of provider capacity and availability. Second, robust service offerings guarantee a variety and depth of resources at all times. Third, the transparency and monitoring aspects of the technology help prevent clients from falling through the cracks.

Security

Once the network is established and well known, a potential effect is a community-wide sense of security. In the same way that the public knows that they can dial 911 in an emergency, a military-connected individual would know that they could contact their local AmericaServes if they ever needed services. Having a permanent safety net of providers could be a profound sense of relief, particularly to those who worry about seeking mental health services.

Partnerships and Mental Health Experts

Most importantly, AmericaServes networks can connect the military-connected community directly with mental health resources that best meet their full set of needs. In every network, the VA and/or other health care agencies are active participants. Additionally, all networks include resources that support general wellness, social connections, and spiritual enrichment.

In summary, the theory and implementation of AmericaServes are both designed to improve the quality of life of the military-connected community. While the individual-level impacts have not yet been established, by continuing to measure and improve system outcomes, the AmericaServes model of collective impact could demonstrate that coordinating care across the social determinants of health does improve mental health and encourages progressive wellness programs for veterans and military families in their communities.

References

AmericaServes. (n.d.). Retrieved from http://americaserves.org

Ansell, C., & Gash, A. (2008). Collaborative governance in theory and practice. *Journal of Public Administration Research and Theory, 18*(4), 543–571. doi:10.1093/jopart/mum032

Ansell, C., & Torfing, J. (2015). How does collaborative governance scale? *Policy & Politics, 43*(3), 315–329.

Armstrong, N.J., Van Slyke, R.D., Isbester, M., & Chapman B. (2016, June). *Mapping collaboration in veteran and military family services.* Working Paper.

Institute for Veterans and Military Families, Syracuse University. Retrieved from https://ivmf.syracuse.edu/wp-content/uploads/2016/06/Mapping-Collaboration-Full-Report.pdf

Austin J. E., & Seitanidi, M. M. (2012). Collaborative value creation: A review of partnering between nonprofits and businesses. Part 2: Partnership process and outcomes. *Nonprofit and Voluntary Sector Quarterly, 41*(6), 929–968. doi:10.1177/0899764012454685

Bartley, M., & Plewis, I. (2002). Accumulated labour market disadvantage and limiting long-term illness: Data from the 1971–1991 Office for National Statistics' Longitudinal Study. *International Journal of Epidemiology, 31*(2), 336–341.

Batty, M. (2005). *Cities and complexity.* Cambridge, MA: MIT Press.

Bel, G., Brown, T., & Marques, R. C. (Eds.). (2015). *Public-private partnerships: Infrastructure, transportation and local services.* Oxfordshire, UK: Routledge.

Berglass, N., & Harrell, M. C. (2012). *Well after service: Veteran reintegration and American communities.* Washington, DC: Center for a New American Security.

Berkman, L. F., & Syme, S. L. (1979). Social networks, host resistance, and mortality: A nine-year follow-up study of Alameda County residents. *American Journal of Epidemiology, 109*(2), 186–204.

Berry, B. J. (1964). Cities as systems within systems of cities. *Papers in Regional Science, 13*(1), 147–163.

Booher, D. E. (2004). Collaborative governance practices and democracy. *National Civic Review, 93*(4), 32–46.

Brenner, N. (2001). The limits to scale? Methodological reflections on scalar structuration. *Progress in Human Geography, 25*(4), 591–614.

Brown, T. L., Potoski, M., & Van Slyke, D. (2013). *Complex contracting: Government purchasing in the wake of the U.S. Coast Guard's Deepwater Program.* Cambridge, UK: Cambridge University Press.

Carter, P. & Kidder, K. (2015). *Charting the sea of goodwill.* Washington, DC: Center for a New American Security. Retrieved from https://s3.amazonaws.com/files.cnas.org/documents/VeteransPhilanthropy_151207_rev.pdf

Carter, P., & Kidder, K. (2017). *A continuum of collaboration: The landscape of community efforts to serve veterans.* Washington, DC: Center for a New American Security. Retrieved from https://s3.amazonaws.com/files.cnas.org/documents/CNASReport-CommunityCollaboration-final.pdf

Christens, B., & Tran Inzeo, P. (2015). Widening the view: Situating collective impact among frameworks for community-led change. *Community Development, 46*(4), 420–435.

Edmondson, J., & Hecht, B. (2014). Defining quality collective impact. *Stanford Social Innovation Review.* Retrieved from: https://ssir.org/articles/entry/defining_quality_collective_impact

Emerson, K., & Nabatchi, T. (2015). Evaluating the productivity of collaborative governance regimes: A performance matrix. *Public Performance & Management Review, 38*(4), 717–747.

Gershenson, C. (2013). Living in living cities. *Artificial Life, 19*(3 and 4), 401–420.

Hanleybrown, F., Kania, J., & Kramer, M. (2012). Channeling change: Making collective impact work. *Stanford Social Innovation Review* [Blog entry]. Retrieved from http://www.ssireview.org/blog/entry/channeling_change_making_collective_impact_work

Institute for Veterans and Military Families (IVMF), Syracuse University. (2017). About AmericaServes. Retrieved from http://americaserves.org/

Kania, J., & Kramer, M. (2011). Collective impact. *Stanford Social Innovation Review, 1*(9), 36–41.

Kania, J., & Kramer, M. (2013). Embracing emergence: How collective impact addresses complexity. *Stanford Social Innovation Review* [Blog entry]. Retrieved from http://www.ssireview.org/blog/entry/embracing_emergence_how_collective_impact_addresses_complexity

Kidder, K., Schafer, A. & Carter, P. (2016). *Needs assessment: Veterans in the Dallas-Fort Worth region.* Washington, DC: Center for a New American Security. Retrieved from https://www.cnas.org/publications/reports/needs-assessment-veterans-in-the-dallas-fort-worth-region

Kintzle, S., Rasheed, J. M., & Castro, C. A. (2016). *The state of the American veteran: The Chicagoland Veterans Study.* Los Angeles, CA: University of Southern California School of Social Work. Retrieved from http://cir.usc.edu/research/research-projects/chicagoland-veterans-study

Klijn, E.-H., Edelenbos, J., & Steijn, B. (2010). Trust in governance networks: Its impacts on outcomes. *Administration & Society, 42*(2), 193–221.

Kooiman, J. (Ed.). (1993). *Modern governance: New government-society interactions.* New York, NY: Sage.

Marmot, M., & Wilkinson, R. G. (2006). *Social determinants of health* (2nd ed.). Oxford, UK; New York, NY: Oxford University Press.

Moser, K. A., Fox, A. J., & Jones, D. R. (1984). Unemployment and Mortality in the OPCS Longitudinal Study. *The Lancet, 324*(8415), 1324–1329.

Mulligan, M., Steele, W., Rickards, L, & Fünfgeld, H. (2016). Keywords in planning: What do we mean by "community resilience"? *International Planning Studies, 21*(4), 348–361.

Osborne, S. P. (2000). *Public private partnerships: Theory and practice in international perspective.* London, UK; New York, NY: Routledge.

Portugali, J. (2000). *Self-organization and the city.* Berlin: Springer-Verlag.

Provan, K. G., & Kenis, P. (2008). Modes of network governance: Structure, management, and effectiveness. *Journal of Public Administration Research and Theory, 18*(2), 229–252.

Provan, K. G., Veazie, M. A., Staten, L. K., & Teufel-Shone, N. I. (2005). The use of network analysis to strengthen community partnerships. *Public Administration Review, 65*(5), 603–613.

Schell, T. L., & Tanielian, T. (2011). *A needs assessment of New York State veterans: Final report to the New York State Health Foundation.* Santa Monica, CA: RAND Corporation.

Stansfeld, S. A., & Marmot, M. G. (2002). *Stress and the heart: Psychosocial pathways to coronary heart disease*. London, UK: BMJ Books.

Turner, S., Merchant, K., Kania, J., & Martin, E. (2012). Understanding the value of backbone organizations in collective impact: Part 2. *Stanford Social Innovation Review* [Blog entry]. Retrieved from https://ssir.org/articles/entry/understanding_the_value_of_backbone_organizations_in_collective_impact_2

Weaver, L. (2014). The promise or peril of collective impact. *The Philanthropist*, 26(1), 11–19. Retrieved from https://thephilanthropist.ca/original-pdfs/Philanthropist-26-1-15.pdf

Wenger, E. (1998). *Communities of practice: Learning, meaning, and identity*. New York, NY: Cambridge University Press.

Wenger, E. (2015). *Learning in landscapes of practice: Boundaries, identity, and knowledgeability in practice-based learning*. Oxford, UK; New York, NY: Routledge.

Wenger, E., McDermott, R. A., & Snyder, W. (2002). *Cultivating communities of practice: A guide to managing knowledge*. Boston, MA: Harvard Business School Press.

Zoli, C., Maury, R., & Fay, D. (2015). *Missing perspectives: Servicemembers' transition from service to civilian life. Data-driven research to enact the promise of the post-9/11 GI Bill*. Syracuse, NY: Institute for Veterans and Military Families, Syracuse University.

Point of View—Setting the Bar: Mental Fitness and Performance

Kate Germano

When I walked up the stairs and into the tired-looking compound of 4th Recruit Training Battalion at the Marine Corps Recruit Depot in February 2014, I was surprised at how dark and dirty it appeared. The compound was located in a rather remote corner of the base—right across from family housing and the theater, and a quarter of a mile from the male training battalions. There were weeds everywhere, and dead palmetto bugs—famed super-sized roaches endemic to South Carolina—had been squashed into the catwalks by countless recruit feet. The place looked like it hadn't been painted in at least a decade, and the brass bell on the command's sign out front was corroded and tarnished from lack of care.

I didn't want to judge; after all, I was the new guy, just visiting the battalion for a few days of turnover before heading back to my job at the Pentagon. I wasn't slated to take command of the battalion until June but I wanted to get a head start on the challenges I would face once I arrived. The state of the battalion's grounds and bell pretty much told me everything I needed to know before I even sat down with the current battalion commander.

I was trying hard to keep an open mind about the unit, but it was tough. After all, I was taking command of the only all-female unit in the Department of Defense, and the only place where female Marines are made. I was about to begin two years of working solely with women and had no idea what to expect.

As it turned out, the flying cockroaches would be the least of my problems.

The Marine Corps was the last hold out for gender integration: the Army, Navy, and Air Force had all integrated their boot camps decades before. When pushed by Congress in the 1990s to explain why segregation was necessary, the rationale provided by Marine leaders for a practice considered unacceptable anywhere else in America was that female recruits needed the confidence boost that came from seeing female drill instructors in positions of leadership and authority. But as I quickly found out, simply having female drill instructors would not in and of itself result in strong, resilient young female Marines crossing the parade deck on graduation day. It would take much, much more, starting with the expectation that the female Marines and recruits be held to higher standards.

On the recruit depot, the total segregation of the women at Fourth Battalion was convenient for the Marine Corps as it made them an out-of-sight, out-of-mind problem. The women were simply expected to fail because they had been failing for so long; hence, there was little incentive to change recruiting and training methods. This then created the perception in the minds of male Marines and recruits that it was somehow easier to become a Marine if you were a woman, which bred resentment and a lack of respect for both the female drill instructors and the recruits. And there was some truth to this. Evidence of double standards for performance and conduct for women was everywhere—starting with the sorry state of the battalion grounds.

When I sat down and really started taking a look at our manning numbers and other demographic data, what I discovered was that what was happening at Fourth Battalion should have been expected. Manpower shortages within the battalion were causing quick burnout in the female drill instructors.

My drill instructors were simply exhausted—mentally, physically, and emotionally. Because of staffing shortages, they were guaranteed to suffer from a significant deficiency in quality sleep, and more likely to get sick with upper respiratory infections during each 13-week training cycle. The further they got into their three-year assignments, the more drained they became. Unfortunately, when the drill instructors were tired and angry, bad things happened. Drill instructors who operated in a sleep deficit were more likely to be involved in recruit abuse. Because they were not able to exercise good judgement, these women struggled to control their tempers and moderate their reactions to routine recruit mistakes.

A few months into my tour at Parris Island, I began paying out of pocket for weekly yoga classes for my drill instructors. I did not make the classes mandatory because the training schedule required that we always have drill instructors with the recruits, but I strongly encouraged my company commanders to free up as many women as possible to attend the classes. At first, there was a lot of grumbling from the drill instructors about it. But by the end of the first class, most of my Marines recognized that yoga provided an uninterrupted hour for them to focus on themselves—a rare occurrence at Fourth Battalion. Recognizing the level of exhaustion in the battalion, the instructor used the last 15 minutes of each class to allow the participants to lie on their yoga mats to practice deep breathing techniques. By the end of the first class when I looked around, all of my Marines were sleeping, many resting so deeply that they were snoring.

The fact was that for decades, the female battalion had failed to meet the male battalion averages for any graduation requirement. These requirements included the written test, practical examination, close order drill, the physical and combat fitness tests, and the rifle range. The negative perception the male recruits and drill instructors had of my battalion began to make more sense when I saw the dismal numbers. It was readily apparent that the female drill instructors had bought into the notion that women were somehow less capable than men. Their own tacit acknowledgement that the female recruits would never be able to rise to the level of performance of the men not only perpetuated the cycle of low expectations, but made the recruits more susceptible to emotional instability and physical injury.

Shortly after I took command, I began pulling data to gauge the historical performance of the female recruits at Fourth Battalion. What I found was striking, especially for the rifle range. Despite the slogan "Every Marine a rifleman," since female Marine recruits were first allowed to shoot the M-16A2 service rifle in the 1980s, a full third of every class failed to qualify at the rifle range the first attempt. Historically, the female battalion had a 68–72 percent qualification rate, compared to the high 80s to low 90 percent averages for the male battalions. And the first time I visited the rifle range to see how my recruits were doing, I was struck by the number of recruits in tears as a result of their poor results. It seemed that if they took one bad shot, they completely fell apart. This was unacceptable.

When I started asking questions about why the women were performing so poorly on the rifle range, it became obvious that the prevailing view among both men and women was that women couldn't handle the pressure of qualifying. They were simply viewed as being less mentally tough as their male counterparts. But when I dug deeper, I quickly realized that the recruits were not struggling because they were biologically more susceptible to cracking under pressure. In fact, physiology and biology had nothing to do with the historically poor results for women on the range. Instead, it had everything to do with self-fulfilling prophecy. Simply put, because the drill instructors were convinced that the recruits would struggle at the range, and the coaches did not believe women could shoot, the female recruits didn't shoot well.

In order to improve the recruits' performance on the range, therefore, I began by focusing my drill instructors on their role as teachers and mentors for the recruits, beginning with range fundamentals. We conducted battalion-wide training where I showed them a decade's worth of statistics for all of the graduation events broken out by battalion. When the female drill instructors were presented with the data, I asked them why they thought that for decades the women had underperformed in every testable category. Although a few of them expressed skepticism about the data, most openly expressed their shock and embarrassment over the numbers. They could not explain why the women had never been able to reach the standards of the male recruits in a single category. But when they became aware of the performance delta between the male and female recruits, they mobilized to change the decades-long trend.

I asked them for feedback on how we could start improving the recruits' performance, starting with the rifle range, since shooting badges are the most visible sign of being a Marine. Based on their suggestions and best practices, we eliminated all yelling by the drill instructors at the range, and stressed the importance of the drill instructors as augment coaches to reinforce the techniques and positions taught during grass week (the week of practice preceding the marksmanship test). Most importantly, we eliminated negative comments by the coaches and drill instructors about women and shooting, and instead focused on conveying the expectation that the women not only qualify, but that they earn Expert badges—the top shooting badge.

In just two months, we saw significant improvements in the results of the female recruits on the range. In less than a year, we had increased our initial qualification rate to just under 92 percent—just a hair below the male battalions' average. More importantly, by holding our female recruits accountable for achieving greater results on the range, we significantly increased their overall confidence. Knowing that they were making their male counterparts nervous about the new competition on the block caused these women to march with their shoulders back and their heads held high.

When we resisted the urge to fall back on physiology as an excuse for poor performance and began demanding excellence from our recruits, the morale and performance of the recruits and drill instructors improved drastically in short order. Although we couldn't change our training environment, we could influence our results. Setting a training standard that encouraged self-care and self-regulation created radical improvements in performance—we were making Marines who were both physically *and* mentally fit.

Notes

1. We define a "collaborative" as a collection of public or private organizations that possess the capabilities and resources to work toward and achieve a specific goal, in this case, referring to a shared mission of serving veterans or military families.

2. Service and care domains include benefits, clothing and household goods, education, employment, food, health care, housing and shelter, individual and family support, legal assistance, money management, social enrichment, sports and recreation, transportation, and utilities.

3. See https://www.uniteus.com/.

CHAPTER 14

The Way Forward

Kelsey L. Larsen and Elizabeth A. Stanley

The consistent theme that emerges throughout this volume is that rewiring our brains and nervous systems after prolonged stress or trauma may effectively combat the wide-ranging negative health outcomes caused or exacerbated by military service. Authors across this anthology have repeatedly connected the dots to suggest a powerful cause-effect sequence for "bulletproofing" the mind-body system in various veteran cohorts. Building on these chapters, this conclusion takes a step back to consider whether the mind-body skills training regimens that successfully treat the wounds of service could be effective at helping to prevent those wounds in the first place. If mind-body skills training recalibrates how the mind-body system recovers from prolonged stress and trauma, could moving similar programs into military training environments mitigate the damaging effects of such stress and, in doing so, protect future service members? To answer this important question, we consider the benefits and challenges of implementing mind-body skills training regimens widely throughout active-duty military populations.

The Benefits of Mind-Body Skills Training Regimens during Active-Duty Service

Increased (and routinized) mind-body skills training offers several important benefits to active-duty military populations, the most important being its generalizability. As prior chapters show, mind-body skills training is a true domain-general skill: it cultivates skill sets in individuals that can be easily applied to many environments across a life span. For veterans, this domain-general nature of mind-body skills training ideally means they both learn to reregulate and heal their own postservice dysregulation as well as improve their adaptability and resilience across their personal and professional lives. For active-duty forces, such training could *also* improve their individual and collective performance during fast-changing, complex, and uncertain military missions and thus could multiply its overall return on investment.

Neuroplasticity—the scientific concept that any repeated experience changes the brain and nervous system—grants humans the essential ability to learn from experience. The more we practice a particular task, the more familiar and efficient the brain and body become at performing that specific task—as significant evidence demonstrates across virtually all perceptual, physical/motor, or cognitive tasks in which individuals may be trained (for reviews, see Green & Bavelier, 2008; Slagter, Davidson, & Lutz, 2011). Most training is domain-specific: individuals improve learning in the specific trained context, with little or no transfer of that learning to other tasks or other contexts, no matter how similar. In other words, with most skills training, the benefits are often exceedingly stimulus- or context-specific.

Though most skills-training paradigms rely upon these domain-specific principles, a handful of training paradigms have been empirically shown to confer domain-general learning, in which an individual not only improves on the trained task(s) but is also able to transfer that learning to additional tasks and to other domains. Such domain-general skills training—observed in athletic training, musical training, action video gaming, and *some* forms of mental training—trains these more generalized skills via three important processes (Green & Bavelier, 2008; Slagter et al., 2011; Stanley, in press-a). First, such trainings vary the stimuli and/or the tasks, forcing individuals to learn at more abstract levels and thus understand the general principles for using the skill in different settings. Second, whether in practice or via visualization, these skills trainings tap into cognitive and physical processes in parallel. In other words, it is *embodied* learning, where the practitioner is engaging and developing several perceptual, cognitive, and motor skills in tandem while they practice, such as eye-hand coordination, selective attention skills, and spatial orienting ability. Finally, domain-general skills training regimens usually utilize task progression, advancing incrementally from one level of difficulty to the next. In the process, they aim for moderate stress arousal during skill practice, which is the zone of stress arousal that best allows the learning and consolidation of new skills for skill retention and employment later.

Though traditional military physical fitness training is a handy example of effective domain-general skills training, most military training favors domain-specific skills training. The majority of preparatory programs rely heavily on checklists, templates, and guidelines, offering clear "do" and "don't" scripts for service members to follow based on a given scenario (Stanley, in press-a). Military organizations favor these kinds of domain-specific trainings precisely because such templates can be quickly taught and learned—sometimes only requiring a simple briefing or training module—and easily assessed and tested (one either does or does not perform according to the required "task, condition, and standard"). Domain-specific training can also be scaled across the force quickly, often via widely distributed digital means. Domain-specific learning is favored because it is believed to make service members more knowledgeable, and thus more effective, in conducting specific military tasks or operations. As a basic example, if troops are preparing to deploy to a conflict zone with an unfamiliar language and culture, with domain-specific learning they might be trained to draw on a list of foreign-language phrases and specific cultural rules to follow in that environment and thereby improve their operational effectiveness in that environment. In contrast, training a domain-general skill such as emotional intelligence might improve the troops' ability to read emotions in themselves and others, thus increasing the likelihood they could recognize nonverbal cues during interactions with the host population, see situations from others' point of view, and regulate their own emotions during these interactions. These emotional intelligence skills may also decrease the likelihood of impulsive or reactive behavior when interacting with the host population. Yet, while specific foreign-language phrases and emotional intelligence may both serve important operational functions in a deployed setting, only the latter skill could be similarly used with family members or colleagues in nondeployed contexts.

The military's domain-specific approach to improving operational effectiveness is most notable in stress inoculation. Stress inoculation training (SIT) is underpinned by the philosophy that humans experience a greater stress response when they perceive an event to be unfamiliar, unpredictable, or uncontrollable (McEwen & Lasley, 2002; Sapolsky, 1994). Military stress inoculation aims to minimize the impact of unfamiliarity/unpredictability/uncontrollability by introducing service members to the specific kinds of stressors they are likely to encounter "downrange" during real-world missions (Kavanagh, 2005). The expectation is that, by reducing the novelty of stressors and habituating service members to their effects, SIT will improve service members' ability to perform specific missions in specific environments (Dienstbier, 1989; Driskell & Johnston, 1998; Kavanagh, 2005; Saunders, Driskell, Johnston, & Salas, 1996; Stanley, 2010). However, while SIT may reduce the perception of novelty in these specific situations, its benefits are often limited to the trained scripts and contexts. For instance, in a study of civilian firefighters, although anxiety and cognitive difficulties decreased across repetitions of the *same* scenario in a live-fire training environment, in new (yet structurally similar) scenarios, firefighters experienced anxiety and cognitive difficulties equal to—or even above—first-exposure levels (Baumann,

Gohm, & Bonner, 2011). In other words, these firefighters were unable to translate the emotion regulation and cognitive skills cultivated over repetitions of the same scenario to other scenarios, even when the script was only slightly different.

Paradoxically, even in scenarios in which scripted SIT might appropriately prepare service members for specific military operations, the stress exposure inherent in such training may undermine their ability to retain—and later access and employ—the trained skill. After all, the common belief is that military combat training should strive to be *as* stressful, if not intentionally *more* stressful, than actual combat (Cone, 2006). Yet, while SIT may help troops adaptively function during stress—and also minimize their anxiety about future missions—SIT's intensity and lack of focus on recovery may exacerbate depletion of executive functioning, thereby contributing to difficulties with physiological and emotion regulation (Heatherton & Wagner, 2011; Hofmann, Schmeichel, & Baddeley, 2012). Indeed, in high-stress professional environments like the military, executive functioning is subject to temporal impairment or depletion from a range of situational factors, including concurrent task load, sleep deprivation, environmental or social stressors, the management of mortality concerns, or the consequence of prior high-intensity engagement (see Hofmann et al., 2012 for a review; Maguen et al., 2009; Stanley, in press-b).

Broad-based evidence from several SIT programs, including military field training exercises (Kavanagh, 2005; Lieberman et al., 2005; Lieberman, Tharion, Shukitt-Hale, Speckman, & Tulley, 2002), military survival training (Morgan, Doran, Steffian, Hazlett, & Southwick, 2006; Morgan et al., 2004; Morgan et al., 2002; Morgan et al., 2001), and military predeployment training (Jha et al., 2015; Jha, Morrison, Parker, & Stanley, 2016; Jha, Stanley, Kiyonaga, Wong, & Gelfand, 2010; Jha, Witkin, Morrison, Rostrup, & Stanley, 2017; Stanley, Schaldach, Kiyonaga, & Jha, 2011), reflects their stressful intensity, with training-related stress exposure linked to mood disturbances and cognitive degradation, including symptoms of dissociation, problem-solving deficits, attention deficits, inaccuracies in visual pattern recognition, and significant declines in working memory capacity (WMC). Declines in WMC may also degrade the broader capacity for emotion regulation (Hofmann et al., 2012; Jha et al., 2010; Pe, Raes, & Kuppens, 2013; Schmeichel, Volokhov, & Demaree, 2008). By undermining such core cognitive and self-regulatory processes associated with executive functioning, SIT may actually inhibit service members' ability to retain and later access the specific military skills they are intending to condition.

Thus, whether because the skills taught are too templated and narrow for the military's increasingly complex, volatile, uncertain, and morally ambiguous missions, or because operating in such stressful training environments (beyond moderate stress arousal levels) may impede service members' ability to learn and retain the trained skills, SIT may not actually deliver its expected operational benefits. As Lieberman et al. (2005, p. 428) note, "The extent and magnitude of the decrements in cognitive performance and mood we observed [in their study during military training] confirm the anecdotal observations that have been made in combat . . . even well-trained leaders exhibit significant degradation in cognitive performance and mood when exposed to severe, multifactorial stress."

In contrast, mind-body skills training may effectively cultivate domain-general skills in active-duty military populations, even during stressful military training. For example, in several studies with active military samples, Mindfulness-based Mind Fitness Training (MMFT)® (Larsen & Stanley, in press; Stanley, 2014b; Stanley et al., 2011) has been associated with improved cognitive performance, better regulation of negative emotions, and better self-regulation of the physiological stress response during stressful predeployment training. MMFT draws from and integrates two lineages: traditional mindfulness skills training (Kabat-Zinn, 2013) and an understanding of the neurobiology of stress and resilience and body-based skills to regulate the autonomic nervous system, drawn from body-based trauma therapies like sensorimotor psychotherapy (Ogden & Fisher, 2015; Ogden, Minton, & Pain, 2006) and Somatic Experiencing® (Levine, 1997; Payne, Levine, & Crane-Godreau, 2015). This blend of mindfulness skills training with body-based self-regulation and resilience skills, relying on a unique sequence of exercises designed to move a participant from dysregulation to regulation, makes MMFT distinct from other mindfulness-based approaches.

U.S. combat troops preparing to deploy to Iraq and Afghanistan who received variants of the eight-week MMFT course (ranging from 8 to 24 hours of classroom training) showed significant benefits on several outcome measures, including protection against working memory degradation (Jha et al., 2017) and improvements in sustained attention (Jha et al., 2015; Jha et al., 2016) and WMC, which was significantly linked to decreased negative emotions (Jha et al., 2010); more efficient physiological stress arousal and recovery, as indexed by neuropeptide Y, heart rate, and breathing rate during stressful combat drills (Johnson et al., 2014); more efficient activation of the insula cortex and anterior cingulate cortex (ACC), brain regions implicated in interoception, emotion regulation, and impulse control, as indexed with fMRI during restricted breathing (Haase et al., 2016) and emotional face processing (Johnson et al., 2014) tasks; and self-reported improvements in sleep (Sterlace et al., 2012), perceived stress (Stanley et al., 2011), and mood (Jha et al., 2010).

The MMFT program trains two domain-general skills that undergird a range of cognitive, emotion regulation, and stress self-regulation capacities, even during stress exposure. First, MMFT develops *attentional control* (the ability to deliberately deploy and sustain attention on a chosen target over time), which may lead to improved focus and concentration; better ability to inhibit distractions; and better ability to access, retain, and update relevant information. Second, MMFT develops *tolerance for challenging experience* (the ability to pay attention to, track, and tolerate challenging experiences without needing for them to be different), whether such experiences are external (e.g., harsh environmental conditions or difficult people) or internal (e.g., physical pain, intense emotions, intrusive thoughts, flashbacks, or nightmares; Stanley, 2014b). Both of these skills may then improve interoceptive functioning, cognitive performance, and resilience, suggesting MMFT's power as a domain-general training.

Interoception is "the process through which the brain monitors and updates the body about its overall physical state, including its ability to recognize bodily sensations, be aware of emotional states, and maintain physiological homeostasis" (Johnson et al., 2014, p. 844). The insula and ACC provide top-level control to the subcortical processes for regulating emotions and stress (Critchley et al., 2003; Critchley, Wiens, Rotshtein, Öhman, & Dolan, 2004; Garfinkel & Critchley, 2013). By improving the functioning of this regulatory loop through attention to interoception rather than cognition, it may be possible to improve the functioning of these subcortical regulatory processes and minimize the depletion and degradation of executive functioning during high-stress contexts (Stanley, in press-a). In fact, previous (nonintervention) studies among "elite performers" (both military and civilian samples) demonstrated activation patterns in both the insula and ACC consistent with more efficient interoceptive processing during stress, relative to healthy controls (Paulus et al., 2012; Paulus et al., 2010; Simmons et al., 2012; Thom et al., 2014). Troops who received MMFT showed altered brain activation during stress post-MMFT (Haase et al., 2016; Johnson et al., 2014), similar to the pattern observed among the "elite performers" in the earlier studies (Paulus et al., 2012; Paulus et al., 2010; Simmons et al., 2012; Thom et al., 2014). In contrast, compromised interoceptive functioning has been shown to play a critical role in the development of mood and anxiety disorders (Avery et al., 2014; Domschke, Stevens, Pfleiderer, & Gerlach, 2010; Paulus & Stein, 2010) as well as addictions (Paulus & Stewart, 2014). Thus, as the MMFT research shows, mind-body skills training to improve interoceptive processes may facilitate improved responses to both stress and emotions, even in high-stress contexts characterized by depleted executive functioning (Heatherton & Wagner, 2011; Hofmann et al., 2012; Norris & Hutchinson, Chapter 3, this volume).

Because improved interoception may facilitate better self-regulatory performance (Friese, Messner, & Schaffner, 2012), developing the domain-general skills of attentional control and tolerance for challenging experience may also improve overall cognitive performance during high-stress contexts. These cognitive improvements may include better sustained attention

(Jensen, Vangkilde, Frokjaer, & Hasselbalch, 2012; Jha et al., 2015; Jha et al., 2016; Zeidan, Johnson, Diamond, David, & Goolkasian, 2010) and increased WMC (Jensen et al., 2012; Jha et al., 2010; Mrazek, Franklin, Phillips, Baird, & Schooler, 2013; Zeidan et al., 2010), which has also been empirically linked to improved skills associated with effective decision making, including better conflict monitoring and task prioritization (McVay & Kane, 2009; Redick & Engle, 2006); better situational awareness (Endsley, 1995, 2000); better abstract problem solving and ability to recall, apply, and use facts (Gray, Chabris, & Braver, 2003; Halford, Cowan, & Andrews, 2007; Kane & Engle, 2002); and better ability to regulate negative emotions (Hofmann et al., 2012; Jha et al., 2010; Pe et al., 2013; Schmeichel et al., 2008).

Finally, attentional control and tolerance for challenging experience may also improve *resilience* by widening individuals' windows of tolerance to stress arousal. Resilience is the ability to function effectively during stressful experience and recover efficiently to baseline afterward (Stanley, 2014b, in press-a). The stress response is expressed in the body as physical sensations via activation of the autonomic nervous system (ANS) (e.g., increased heart and breathing rate, nausea, and sweaty palms), as well as in the mind via increased cortical activity (e.g., racing or distressing thoughts; see DeSteno, Gross, & Kubzansky, 2013; Ogden & Fisher, 2015; Ogden et al., 2006). When individuals use attentional control and tolerance for challenging experience to bring interoceptive awareness to the physical sensations and cognitive activity associated with stress activation, it becomes possible for the mind-body system to neurocept safety and then discharge the mobilized stress activation, complete its process of self-regulation, and return to baseline equilibrium. Over time, individuals can learn to support ANS self-regulation to recover from the dysregulation of prior exposure to chronic stress or trauma and to increase their tolerance for greater stress activation in the future (Ogden et al., 2006; Porges, 2011; Payne et al., 2015; Stanley, 2014b, in press-a).

In contrast, without these two domain-general skills, because stress activation is uncomfortable in the mind-body system, individuals may distract from or suppress this self-regulation process, which over time can lead to ANS dysregulation and allostatic load. To manage symptoms of dysregulation, they then frequently resort to maladaptive coping techniques (i.e., tobacco use, substance use, or adrenaline-seeking behaviors) that create a vicious cycle by adding additional stress to the mind-body system and dysregulating it further (Stanley, in press-a). Stress spectrum disorders (including posttraumatic stress disorder [PTSD]) result from a lack of complete recovery and subsequent dysregulation of the ANS (Levine, 1997; Ogden & Fisher, 2015; Ogden et al., 2006; Payne et al., 2015; Scaer, 2005; van der Kolk, 2015).

In sum, as the empirical evidence from MMFT demonstrates, domain-general mind-body skills training may yield broad-based and important improvements in cognitive performance, distress tolerance, self-regulation, resilience, and recovery.

Challenges in Providing Mind-Body Skills Training Regimens during Active-Duty Service

Of course, while the theory and evidence reviewed present a persuasive case for increased integration of mind-body skills training regimens into active-duty training, there are several important content-related and format-related issues to be considered before widespread implementation can take place.

The first challenge is determining precisely where and when in the overall professional development trajectory such training would be most effective. Each phase of service is associated with distinct stressors (Kavanagh, 2005; Pincus, House, Christenson, & Adler, 2005). During predeployment intervals, service members may face anxiety and family tension over pending deployment and the aforementioned stress associated with stress inoculation and field exercises (Cigrang, Todd, & Carbone, 2000; Jha et al., 2010; Lieberman et al., 2005; Maguen et al., 2008; McNulty, 2005; Stanley et al., 2011). Meanwhile, deployment can subject service members to unfamiliar environments, languages, and cultures; exhaustive physical/mental exertion; the need to manage mortality concerns; and combat exposure (Adler, McGurk, Stetz, & Bliese, 2003; Hoge et al., 2004; Junger, 2015; Killgore et al., 2008; King, King, Vogt, Knight, & Samper, 2006; Maguen et al., 2009; Stanley, 2014b). Finally, postdeployment can introduce stress over reestablishing household relationships and reintegrating into nondeployed daily life (Junger, 2015; Lincoln, Swift, & Shorteno-Fraser, 2008; Pincus et al., 2005). Moreover, as seen following increases in the military's operational tempo since 2001, the stressors inherent in each of these phases are often experienced at faster and more frequent intervals (Bonds, Baiocchi, & McDonald, 2010; Castro & Adler, 2005).

Thus, early integration of domain-general mind-body skills training is key for effective active-duty implementation. The earlier troops are exposed to mind-body skills training, the more effectively they could utilize such skills throughout training and "real-world" missions, ideally to effect complete recovery after each stress exposure and to minimize the enduring effects of such exposure. Indeed, they could then use SIT as the setting in which to practice these domain-general skills associated with recovery and resilience. This early integration could also serve as a social reinforcement of its import: just as basic training seeks to begin refining the military-specific skills that enhance overall performance, early integration of mind-body skills training would signal resilience and mental fitness as foundational capacities for performance, and ones that require a long-term daily commitment. This kind of cultural shift will require command support, from the highest levels down through the non-commissioned officer (NCO) corps. It will also require understanding that mental fitness is not just for "fixing" the "problems" of suicide, psychological injury, and other stress-spectrum disorders. Thus, it is essential that any mind-body skills training not be introduced to leaders and units *only* as a stress resilience training (at which point it is likely to be perceived as remedial training for individuals who cannot deal with stress). Rather, for effective long-term integration of such practices, *it must be framed as the domain-general performance enhancement training it actually is.*

The second major challenge to implementing mind-body skills training programs with active-duty troops is weighing the effects of previous exposure to chronic stress and trauma and selecting programs that are capable of working effectively with such exposure. Prior combat/deployment experiences may lead to adaptive survival-based changes in troops' mind-body systems, which may then manifest as ANS dysregulation and depletion of executive functioning skills (Marx, Doron-Lamarca, Proctor, & Vasterling, 2009; Stanley, in press-a; Vasterling et al., 2006). Indeed, in the MMFT pilot study, approximately 59 percent of troops showed active symptoms of distress and dysregulation, related to prior prolonged stress and trauma exposure, before their predeployment training cycle even started (Stanley et al., 2011). Furthermore, even incoming military recruits do not have "blank slate" nervous systems. For example, adverse childhood experiences (ACEs)—including sexual, physical, and emotional abuse; physical and emotional neglect; and family dysfunction during childhood—have been shown to increase the risk for many mental and physical health problems in adulthood (Brodsky & Stanley, 2008; Bruffaerts et al., 2010; Felitti, 2009; Kessler et al., 2010; Mann & Currier, 2010). ACEs lead to life-long sensitization and dysregulation of the ANS and the hypothalamic-pituitary-adrenal (HPA) axis, which increase the susceptibility to stress-related physical illnesses and mood and anxiety disorders in adulthood (see Neigh, Gillespie, & Nemeroff, 2009, for a review). Importantly, in contrast to the draft era, U.S. military personnel during the All-Volunteer Force (AVF) era are more likely to have experienced ACEs, and disproportionately more ACEs, than their civilian counterparts (Blosnich, Dichter, Cerulli, Batten, & Bossarte, 2014). These findings are consistent with earlier research suggesting ACE prevalence may be higher in military populations because individuals may enlist to escape violent, abusive, or dysfunctional home environments (Iversen et al., 2007; Kelly, Skelton, Patel, & Bradley, 2011; Schultz, Bell, Naugle, & Polusny, 2006; Woodruff, Kelty, & Segal, 2006).

Thus, whether from exposure to ACEs and/or occupational stressors during deployment, overcoming the effects of prior stress and trauma exposure in active-duty populations requires experienced instructors to support and guide the reregulation of the mind-body system. These mind-body practices may stir some deep psychological and physiological processes, and out of a commitment to not causing harm, they must be taught by experienced instructors who have already deeply engaged in the process themselves (Creswell & Lindsay, 2014; Norris & Hutchinson, Chapter 3, this volume; Polusny et al., 2015; Stanley, 2014a, in press-a; Williams et al., 2014).

The third challenge to implementing mind-body skills training effectively with active-duty troops is creating and maintaining a cadre of experienced instructors. Ideally, instructors will come from within the chain of command, as NCOs or junior officers are best capable of leading daily mind-body skills practice sessions and integrating self-regulation skills practice into military SIT. Yet, because of the responsibilities and ethical obligations of not inadvertently causing harm, developing a cadre of uniformed, experienced instructors will necessarily take time. As such, this training may initially require recruiting experienced practitioners from outside of the military to help train uniformed instructors, implement the program, and ensure quality control.

The fourth challenge to implementing mind-body skills training effectively with active-duty troops is recognizing that not all mind-body skills training regimens may be equally effective in helping to reregulate the mind-body system in this high-stress context. For instance, many mindfulness-based training programs were not designed in a dysregulation-informed or trauma-sensitive manner and thus may cause risks for individuals currently suffering from psychopathology or other symptoms of dysregulation (Dobkin, Irving, & Amar, 2011; Folette, Palm, & Pearson, 2006; Larsen & Stanley, in press; Lindahl, Fisher, Cooper, Rosen, & Britton, 2017; Shonin, Van Gorden, & Griffiths, 2014; Stanley, in press-a; Strauss, Cavanagh, Oliver, & Pettman, 2014). Indeed, some mindfulness-based programs are contraindicated for individuals actively suffering from posttraumatic stress or trauma. For example, the University of Massachusetts' Center for Mindfulness explicitly states that mindfulness-based stress reduction (MBSR) courses are not indicated for anyone currently suffering from PTSD or other mental illness and recommends seeking other training or treatment if someone has "a history of substance or alcohol abuse with less than a year of being clean or sober, thoughts or attempts of suicide, recent or unresolved trauma" or if one is "in the middle of major life changes" (Center for Mindfulness in Medicine, 2014; Santorelli, 2014). All of these criteria are notably common in the high-stress, active-duty military context.

In contrast, positive psychology and cognitive reappraisal techniques involve actively reinterpreting stimuli before emotional responses become fully activated in order to modify the emotion's impact and trajectory (Fredrickson, 2003; Seligman, 2002). However, because these techniques rely on top-down (lateral prefrontal) regulation of subcortical emotional and stress arousal systems (Hariri, Mattay, Tessitore, Fera, & Weinberger, 2003;

Ochsner & Gross, 2005; Ogden et al., 2006), they may deplete prefrontal executive functioning resources (Heatherton & Wagner, 2011; Hofmann et al., 2012), especially in high-stress contexts associated with cognitive depletion and that tend to elicit negative emotions. Thus, perhaps it is not surprising that military programs relying on such techniques have not shown much empirical efficacy. For example, the Army's Comprehensive Soldier and Family Fitness (CSF2) program has been criticized for universal adoption without pilot testing (Eidelson, Pilisuk, & Soldz, 2011; Eidelson & Soldz, 2012; Institute of Medicine, 2014) and for lack of subsequent peer-reviewed empirical evidence of its effectiveness (Denning, Meisnere, & Warner, 2014; Institute of Medicine, 2014; Smith, 2013; Steenkamp, Nash, & Litz, 2013). Likewise, a recent evaluation of the Marine Corps' Operational Stress Control and Readiness (OSCAR) program found that while the program increased awareness and peer social support, there was no demonstrable improvement in mental health outcomes (Vaughan, Farmer, Breslau, & Burnette, 2015). Given the theoretical mismatch between cognitively taxing strategies like positive psychology and the cognitively depleting military training environment, service members may be unable to reregulate their mind-body systems using such techniques, which, as several authors suggest, may lead those service members to think something is "wrong" with them (Braswell & Kushner, 2012; Smith, 2013). As Braswell and Kushner (2012, p. 535) note, "The implication of this method is to pathologize not only traumatic life circumstances, but also negative *responses* to those circumstances. . . . Positive Psychology may lead traumatized soldiers to castigate themselves for what, in reality, may be the shortcomings of the therapeutic technique" (emphasis in original).

The final challenge to implementing mind-body skills training effectively with active-duty troops is determining which outcome measures are most appropriate for evaluating the regimens' effectiveness on a large scale. Most evaluations of mind-body skills training programs rely on self-report measures, such as the Army's Global Assessment Tool (GAT) online questionnaire, one component of CSF2. However, such self-report surveys may not be effective in evaluating overall progress in building domain-general skills (Institute of Medicine, 2014; Vaughan et al., 2015), and some of these instruments lack the empirical validation found in the scales used in the broader mental health arena (Eidelson & Soldz, 2012). In addition, because of mental health stigma and privacy concerns, troops may be unwilling to answer completely and honestly—indeed, many Marines in the MMFT pilot study admitted to withholding important information on such self-report surveys administered by the Marine Corps for fear of what their chain of command might do with the information (Stanley et al., 2011).

A more robust evaluation may be possible when self-report measures are supplemented and correlated with performance on cognitive tasks and/or individual biomarkers of resilience. (They could also be correlated with brain activation patterns during fMRI scans, as was done in some MMFT research (Haase et al., 2016; Johnson et al., 2014), although brain imaging for widespread evaluation would be prohibitively expensive.) Cognitive behavioral tasks, such as the Sustained Attention to Response Task (SART; Robertson, Manly, Andrade, Baddeley, & Yiend, 1997) to measure attention skills or the Operation Span task (OSPAN; Unsworth, Heitz, Schrock, & Engle, 2005) to measure WMC, could potentially be used as a cognitive equivalent of the services' physical fitness tests used to assess physical fitness twice annually. Of course, using such behavioral tasks to assess cognitive performance could be confounded by applied mental effort (Jha et al., 2010). While this may pose challenges to teasing out *theoretically* whether the mind-body skills training directly causes functional changes in cognitive processes, it should not present an issue for assessing *practically* the usefulness of the mind-body skills training in cultivating domain-general skills for improved performance.

Moreover, while performing combat drills, troops could wear bio-harnesses to measure heart rates and breathing rates during stress arousal and recovery, as was done in one MMFT study (Johnson et al., 2014). Furthermore, measures such as blood-plasma concentrations of neuropeptide Y, a protein released during stress arousal, may yield additional relevant information about the mind-body system's efficiency in recovering and reregulating after the challenge has passed (Johnson et al., 2014), especially when correlated with self-report measures of resilience, perceived stress, or mood. Likewise, blood-plasma concentrations of insulin-like growth factor (IGF-1) may be an indicator of restful sleep—particularly when correlated with self-report measures of sleep quality or data from simple activity trackers—since IGF-1 is produced when the body is getting restful sleep. For instance, in one MMFT study, self-reported improvements in sleep quality, including longer sleep duration and decreased use of over-the-counter and prescription sleep aids, correlated with significantly higher blood-plasma levels of IGF-1 after combat drills (Sterlace et al., 2012). On the other hand, alternatives such as saliva cortisol levels may be a less useful measure of resilience, because fluctuations in the diurnal cortisol cycle make it extremely challenging to measure and evaluate these levels across time.

Conclusion

Implementing mind-body skills training throughout active-duty forces has the potential to shift the entire "bulletproofing" paradigm of military mental health. Such programs may not only complement and reduce the shortcomings of traditional domain-specific military SIT but may also strengthen domain-general skill sets. As evidence from MMFT with active-duty populations shows, the range of potential benefits to cognitive performance, emotion regulation, and physiological self-regulation is substantial.

Nonetheless, the key question remains: Are the methods, practices, and skills to be implemented aligned with the desired outcome? Implementing mind-body skills training effectively in active-duty military populations will demand intentional program design. The greatest potential lies in early interventions, offered by appropriately experienced trainers, and teaching techniques aligned with the high-stress, cognitively depleting military context and compatible with troops' dysregulation from prior prolonged stress and trauma. Using the chain of command to socialize and integrate these programs into the warrior culture and interweave these mind-body skills into military-specific training will be essential.

Of course, while evidence in favor of such active-duty programs continues to accumulate, we must also remember that no program is a silver bullet solution. There are no shortcuts for rewiring the brain and nervous system, and any approach will necessarily take time, commitment, and patience. The human mind-body system's response to prolonged stress and trauma is not an issue to "solve"; viewing it from this perspective would actually deny the constant interaction between the mind-body system and performance. Therefore, if mind-body skills training is implemented with active-duty forces without consistent, repeated practice of the skills, without a cultural embrace on the part of the chain of command, and without appropriate scientific empirical evaluation of its efficacy, it is unlikely to shift the powerful and enduring rates of dysregulation seen among active-duty and veteran cohorts today. In other words, military leadership faces an important decision point. In order to reap the benefits that mind-body skills training may yield in uncertain and complex scenarios, leaders must commit to the creative integration and consistent practice of mind-body skills on a regular—realistically, daily—basis.

References

Adler, A. B., McGurk, D., Stetz, M. C., & Bliese, P. D. (2003). *Military occupational stressors in garrison, training, and deployed environments*. Paper presented at the NIOSH/APA Symposium Modeling Military Stressors: The WRAIR Occupational Stress Research Program, Toronto, Ontario.

Avery, J. A., Drevets, W. C., Moseman, S. E., Bodurka, J., Barcalow, J. C., & Simmons, W. K. (2014). Major depressive disorder is associated with abnormal interoceptive activity and functional connectivity in the insula. *Biological Psychiatry, 76*(3), 258–266.

Baumann, M. R., Gohm, C. L., & Bonner, B. L. (2011). Phased training for high-reliability occupations live-fire exercises for civilian firefighters. *Human Factors, 53*(5), 548–557.

Blosnich, J. R., Dichter, M. E., Cerulli, C., Batten, S. V., & Bossarte, R. M. (2014). Disparities in adverse childhood experiences among individuals with a history of military service. *JAMA Psychiatry, 71*(9), 1041–1048.

Bonds, T., Baiocchi, D., & McDonald, L. (2010). *Army deployments to OIF and OEF.* Santa Monica, CA: RAND Corporation.

Braswell, H., & Kushner, H. I. (2012). Suicide, social integration, and masculinity in the US military. *Social Science & Medicine, 74*(4), 530–536.

Brodsky, B. S., & Stanley, B. (2008). Adverse childhood experiences and suicidal behavior. *Psychiatric Clinics of North America, 31*(2), 223–235.

Bruffaerts, R., Demyttenaere, K., Borges, G., Haro, J. M., Chiu, W. T., Hwang, I., . . . Nock, M. K. (2010). Childhood adversities as risk factors for onset and persistence of suicidal behaviour. *The British Journal of Psychiatry, 197*(1), 20–27.

Castro, C. A., & Adler, A. B. (2005). Preface to the special issue. *Military Psychology, 17*(3), 131–136.

Center for Mindfulness in Medicine, Health Care, and Society. (2014). FAQ—Stress Reduction. Retrieved from https://www.umassmed.edu/cfm/mindfulness-based-programs/faqs-mbsr-mbct/

Cigrang, J. A., Todd, S. L., & Carbone, E. G. (2000). Stress management training for military trainees returned to duty after a mental health evaluation: Effect on graduation rates. *Journal of Occupational Health Psychology, 5*(1), 48–55.

Cone, R. W. (2006). The changing national training center. *Military Review, 86*(3), 70–79.

Creswell, J. D., & Lindsay, E. K. (2014). How does mindfulness training affect health? A mindfulness stress buffering account. *Current Directions in Psychological Science, 23*(6), 401–407.

Critchley, H. D., Mathias, C. J., Josephs, O., O'Doherty, J., Zanini, S., Dewar, B. K., . . . Dolan, R. J. (2003). Human cingulate cortex and autonomic control: Converging neuroimaging and clinical evidence. *Brain, 126,* 2139–2152.

Critchley, H. D., Wiens, S., Rotshtein, P., Öhman, A., & Dolan, R. J. (2004). Neural systems supporting interoceptive awareness. *Nature Neuroscience, 7*(2), 189–195.

Denning, L. A., Meisnere, M., & Warner, K. E. (2014). *Preventing psychological disorders in service members and their families: An assessment of programs.* Washington, DC: National Academies Press.

DeSteno, D., Gross, J. J., & Kubzansky, L. (2013). Affective science and health: The importance of emotion and emotion regulation. *Health Psychology, 32*(5), 474–486.

Dienstbier, R. A. (1989). Arousal and physiological toughness: Implications for mental and physical health. *Psychological Review, 96*(1), 84–100.

Dobkin, P. L., Irving, J. A., & Amar, S. (2011). For whom may participation in a mindfulness-based stress reduction program be contraindicated? *Mindfulness, 3*(1), 44–50.

Domschke, K., Stevens, S., Pfleiderer, B., & Gerlach, A. L. (2010). Interoceptive sensitivity in anxiety and anxiety disorders: An overview and integration of neurobiological findings. *Clinical Psychology Review, 30*(1), 1–11.

Driskell, J., & Johnston, J. (1998). Stress exposure training. In J. Cannon-Bowers & E. Salas (Eds.), *Making decisions under stress: Implications for individual and team training* (pp. 191–217). Washington, DC: APA Press.

Eidelson, R., Pilisuk, M., & Soldz, S. (2011). The dark side of comprehensive soldier fitness. *American Psychologist, 66*(7), 643–644.

Eidelson, R., & Soldz, S. (2012). *Does comprehensive soldier fitness work: CSF research fails the test.* Working Paper Number 1. Coalition for an Ethical Psychology. Bala Cynwyd, Pennsylvania.

Endsley, M. R. (1995). Toward a theory of situation awareness in dynamic systems. *Human Factors: The Journal of the Human Factors and Ergonomics Society, 37*(1), 32–64.

Endsley, M. R. (2000). Theoretical underpinnings of situation awareness: A critical review. In M. R. Endsley & D. Garland (Eds.), *Situation awareness analysis and measurement* (pp. 3–32). Mahwah, NJ: Lawrence Erlbaum Associates.

Felitti, V. J. (2009). Adverse childhood experiences and adult health. *Academic Pediatrics, 9*(3), 131–132.

Folette, V., Palm, K., & Pearson, A. (2006). Mindfulness and trauma: Implications for treatment. *Journal of Rational-Emotive & Cognitive-Behavior Therapy, 24*(1), 45–61.

Fredrickson, B. L. (2003). The value of positive emotions: The emerging science of positive psychology is coming to understand why it's good to feel good. *American Scientist, 91*(4), 330–335.

Friese, M., Messner, C., & Schaffner, Y. (2012). Mindfulness meditation counteracts self-control depletion. *Consciousness and Cognition, 21*(2), 1016–1022.

Garfinkel, S. N., & Critchley, H. D. (2013). Interoception, emotion and brain: New insights link internal physiology to social behaviour. Commentary on: "Anterior insular cortex mediates bodily sensibility and social anxiety" by Terasawa et al. (2012). *Social Cognitive and Affective Neuroscience, 8*(3), 231–234.

Gray, J. R., Chabris, C. F., & Braver, T. S. (2003). Neural mechanisms of general fluid intelligence. *Nature Neuroscience, 6*(3), 316–322.

Green, C. S., & Bavelier, D. (2008). Exercising your brain: a review of human brain plasticity and training-induced learning. *Psychology and aging, 23*(4), 692–701.

Haase, L., Thom, N. J., Shukla, A., Davenport, P. W., Simmons, A. N., Stanley, E. A., . . . Johnson, D. C. (2016). Mindfulness-based training attenuates insula response to an aversive interoceptive challenge. *Social Cognitive and Affective Neuroscience, 11*(1), 182–190.

Halford, G. S., Cowan, N., & Andrews, G. (2007). Separating cognitive capacity from knowledge: A new hypothesis. *Trends in Cognitive Sciences, 11*(6), 236–242.

Hariri, A. R., Mattay, V. S., Tessitore, A., Fera, F., & Weinberger, D. R. (2003). Neocortical modulation of the amygdala response to fearful stimuli. *Biological Psychiatry, 53*(6), 494–501.

Heatherton, T. F., & Wagner, D. D. (2011). Cognitive neuroscience of self-regulation failure. *Trends in Cognitive Sciences, 15*(3), 132–139.

Hofmann, W., Schmeichel, B. J., & Baddeley, A. D. (2012). Executive functions and self-regulation. *Trends in Cognitive Sciences, 16*(3), 174–180.

Hoge, C. W., Castro, C. A., Messer, S. C., McGurk, D., Cotting, D. I., & Koffman, R. L. (2004). Combat duty in Iraq and Afghanistan, mental health problems, and barriers to care. *New England Journal of Medicine, 351*(1), 13–22.

Institute of Medicine. (2014). *Preventing psychological disorders in service members and their families: An assessment of programs.* Washington, DC: The National Academies Press.

Iversen, A. C., Fear, N. T., Simonoff, E., Hull, L., Horn, O., Greenberg, N., . . . Wessely, S. (2007). Influence of childhood adversity on health among male UK military personnel. *The British Journal of Psychiatry, 191,* 506–511.

Jensen, C. G., Vangkilde, S., Frokjaer, V., & Hasselbalch, S. G. (2012). Mindfulness training affects attention—Or is it attentional effort? *Journal of Experimental Psychology: General, 141*(1), 106–123.

Jha, A. P., Morrison, A. B., Dainer-Best, J., Parker, S., Rostrup, N., & Stanley, E. A. (2015). Minds "at attention": Mindfulness training curbs attentional lapses in military cohorts. *PLoS ONE, 10*(2), e0116889.

Jha, A. P., Morrison, A. B., Parker, S. C., & Stanley, E. A. (2016). Practice is protective: Mindfulness training promotes cognitive resilience in high-stress cohorts. *Mindfulness, 8*(1), 46–58.

Jha, A. P., Stanley, E. A., Kiyonaga, A., Wong, L., & Gelfand, L. (2010). Examining the protective effects of mindfulness training on working memory capacity and affective experience. *Emotion, 10*(1), 54–64.

Jha, A. P., Witkin, J., Morrison, A., Rostrup, N., & Stanley, E. (2017). Short-form mindfulness training protects against working memory degradation over high-demand intervals. *Journal of Cognitive Enhancement, 1*(2), 154–171.

Johnson, D. C., Thom, N. J., Stanley, E. A., Haase, L., Simmons, A. N., Pei-an, B. S., . . . Paulus, M. P. (2014). Modifying resilience mechanisms in at-risk individuals: A controlled study of mindfulness training in Marines preparing for deployment. *American Journal of Psychiatry, 171*(8), 844–853.

Junger, S. (2015). How PTSD became a problem far beyond the battlefield. *Vanity Fair.* Retrieved from http://www.vanityfair.com/news/2015/05/ptsd-war-home-sebastian-junger

Kabat-Zinn, J. (2013). *Full catastrophe living: Using the wisdom of your body and mind to face stress, pain, and illness* (Revised ed.). New York, NY: Bantam.

Kane, M. J., & Engle, R. W. (2002). The role of prefrontal cortex in working-memory capacity, executive attention, and general fluid intelligence: An individual-differences perspective. *Psychonomic Bulletin & Review, 9*(4), 637–671.

Kavanagh, J. (2005). *Stress and performance: A review of the literature and its applicability to the military.* Santa Monica, CA: RAND Corporation.

Kelly, U. A., Skelton, K., Patel, M., & Bradley, B. (2011). More than military sexual trauma: Interpersonal violence, PTSD, and mental health in women veterans. *Research in Nursing & Health, 34*(6), 457–467.

Kessler, R. C., McLaughlin, K. A., Green, J. G., Gruber, M. J., Sampson, N. A., Zaslavsky, A. M., . . . Williams, D. R. (2010). Childhood adversities and adult psychopathology in the WHO World Mental Health Surveys. *The British Journal of Psychiatry, 197*, 378–385.

Killgore, W. D., Cotting, D. I., Thomas, J. L., Cox, A. L., McGurk, D., Vo, A. H., . . . Hoge, C. W. (2008). Post-combat invincibility: Violent combat experiences are associated with increased risk-taking propensity following deployment. *Journal of Psychiatric Research, 42*(13), 1112–1121.

King, L. A., King, D. W., Vogt, D. S., Knight, J., & Samper, R. E. (2006). Deployment Risk and Resilience Inventory: A collection of measures for studying deployment-related experiences of military personnel and veterans. *Military Psychology, 18*(2), 89–120.

Larsen, K. L., & Stanley, E. A. (in press). Mindfulness-based Mind Fitness Training (MMFT): Mindfulness training for high-stress and trauma-sensitive contexts. In I. Ivtzan (Ed.), *The handbook of mindfulness-based programs: Every established intervention, from medicine to education*. Abingdon, UK: Routledge.

Levine, P. A. (1997). *Waking the tiger: Healing trauma: The innate capacity to transform overwhelming experiences*. Berkeley, CA: North Atlantic Books.

Lieberman, H. R., Bathalon, G. P., Falco, C. M., Kramer, F. M., Morgan, C. A., & Niro, P. (2005). Severe decrements in cognition function and mood induced by sleep loss, heat, dehydration, and undernutrition during simulated combat. *Biological Psychiatry, 57*(4), 422–429.

Lieberman, H. R., Tharion, W. J., Shukitt-Hale, B., Speckman, K. L., & Tulley, R. (2002). Effects of caffeine, sleep loss, and stress on cognitive performance and mood during US Navy SEAL training. *Psychopharmacology, 164*(3), 250–261.

Lincoln, A., Swift, E., & Shorteno-Fraser, M. (2008). Psychological adjustment and treatment of children and families with parents deployed in military combat. *Journal of Clinical Psychology, 64*(8), 984–992.

Lindahl, J. R., Fisher, N. E., Cooper, D. J., Rosen, R. K., & Britton, W. B. (2017). The varieties of contemplative experience: A mixed-methods study of meditation-related challenges in Western Buddhists. *PLOS One, 12*(5), e0176239. doi:10.1371/journal.pone.0176239

Maguen, S., Metzler, T. J., Litz, B. T., Seal, K. H., Knight, S. J., & Marmar, C. R. (2009). The impact of killing in war on mental health symptoms and related functioning. *Journal of Traumatic Stress, 22*(5), 435–443.

Maguen, S., Turcotte, D. M., Peterson, A. L., Dremsa, T. L., Garb, H. N., McNally, R. J., & Litz, B. T. (2008). Description of risk and resilience factors among military medical personnel before deployment to Iraq. *Military Medicine, 173*(1), 1–9.

Mann, J. J., & Currier, D. M. (2010). Stress, genetics and epigenetic effects on the neurobiology of suicidal behavior and depression. *European Psychiatry, 25*(5), 268–271.

Marx, B. P., Doron-Lamarca, S., Proctor, S. P., & Vasterling, J. J. (2009). The influence of pre-deployment neurocognitive functioning on post-deployment

PTSD symptom outcomes among Iraq-deployed Army soldiers. *Journal of the International Neuropsychological Society, 15*(06), 840–852.

McEwen, B., & Lasley, E. (2002). *The end of stress as we know it.* Washington, DC: Joseph Henry Press.

McNulty, P. A. F. (2005). Reported stressors and health care needs of active duty Navy personnel during three phases of deployment in support of the war in Iraq. *Military Medicine, 170*(6), 530–535.

McVay, J. C., & Kane, M. J. (2009). Conducting the train of thought: Working memory capacity, goal neglect, and mind wandering in an executive-control task. *Journal of Experimental Psychology: Learning, Memory, and Cognition, 35*(1), 196–204.

Morgan, C. A., Doran, A., Steffian, G., Hazlett, G., & Southwick, S. M. (2006). Stress-induced deficits in working memory and visuo-constructive abilities in special operations soldiers. *Biological Psychiatry, 60*(7), 722–729.

Morgan, C. A., Hazlett, G., Doran, A., Garrett, S., Hoyt, G., Thomas, P., . . . Southwick, S. M. (2004). Accuracy of eyewitness memory for persons encountered during exposure to highly intense stress. *International Journal of Law and Psychiatry, 27*(3), 265–279.

Morgan, C. A., Rasmusson, A. M., Wang, S., Hoyt, G., Hauger, R. L., & Hazlett, G. (2002). Neuropeptide-Y, cortisol, and subjective distress in humans exposed to acute stress: Replication and extension of previous report. *Biological Psychiatry, 52*(2), 136–142.

Morgan, C. A., Wang, S., Rasmusson, A., Hazlett, G., Anderson, G., & Charney, D. S. (2001). Relationship among plasma cortisol, catecholamines, neuropeptide Y, and human performance during exposure to uncontrollable stress. *Psychosomatic Medicine, 63*(3), 412–422.

Mrazek, M. D., Franklin, M. S., Phillips, D. T., Baird, B., & Schooler, J. W. (2013). Mindfulness training improves working memory capacity and GRE performance while reducing mind wandering. *Psychological Science, 24*, 776–781.

Neigh, G. N., Gillespie, C. F., & Nemeroff, C. B. (2009). The neurobiological toll of child abuse and neglect. *Trauma, Violence & Abuse, 10*(4), 389–410.

Ochsner, K. N., & Gross, J. J. (2005). The cognitive control of emotion. *Trends in Cognitive Sciences, 9*(5), 242–249.

Ogden, P., & Fisher, J. (2015). *Sensorimotor psychotherapy: Interventions for trauma and attachment.* New York, NY: W. W. Norton & Company.

Ogden, P., Minton, K., & Pain, C. (2006). *Trauma and the body: A sensorimotor approach to psychotherapy.* New York, NY: W. W. Norton & Company.

Paulus, M. P., Flagan, T., Simmons, A. N., Gillis, K., Potterat, E. G., Kotturi, S., . . . Davenport, P. W. (2012). Subjecting elite athletes to inspiratory breathing load reveals behavioral and neural signatures of optimal performers in extreme environments. *PLoS ONE, 7*(2), e29394.

Paulus, M. P., Simmons, A. N., Fitzpatrick, S. N., Potterat, E. G., Van Orden, K. F., Bauman, J., & Swain, J. L. (2010). Differential brain activation to angry faces by elite warfighters: Neural processing evidence for enhanced threat detection. *PLoS ONE, 5*(4), e10096.

Paulus, M. P., & Stein, M. B. (2010). Interoception in anxiety and depression. *Brain Structure and Function, 214*(5–6), 451–463.

Paulus, M. P., & Stewart, J. L. (2014). Interoception and drug addiction. *Neuropharmacology, 76*, 342–350.

Payne, P., Levine, P. A., & Crane-Godreau, M. A. (2015). Somatic experiencing: Using interoception and proprioception as core elements of trauma therapy. *Frontiers in Psychology, 6*, 1–18.

Pe, M. L., Raes, F., & Kuppens, P. (2013). The cognitive building blocks of emotion regulation: Ability to update working memory moderates the efficacy of rumination and reappraisal on emotion. *PLoS ONE, 8*(7), e69071.

Pincus, S., House, R., Christenson, J., & Adler, L. (2005). The Emotional Cycle of Deployment: A Military Family Perspective. Retrieved from https://msrc.fsu.edu/system/files/The%20Emotional%20Cycle%20of%20Deployment%20-%20A%20Military%20Family%20Perspective.pdf

Polusny, M. A., Erbes, C. R., Thuras, P., Moran, A., Lamberty, G. J., Collins, R. C., . . . Lim, K. O. (2015). Mindfulness-based stress reduction for posttraumatic stress disorder among veterans: A randomized clinical trial. *JAMA, 314*(5), 456–465.

Porges, S. W. (2011). *The Polyvagal Theory: Neurophysiological foundations of emotions, attachment, communication, and self-regulation.* New York, NY: W. W. Norton.

Redick, T. S., & Engle, R. W. (2006). Working memory capacity and attention network test performance. *Applied Cognitive Psychology, 20*(5), 713–721.

Robertson, I. H., Manly, T., Andrade, J., Baddeley, B. T., & Yiend, J. (1997). Oops!: Performance correlates of everyday attentional failures in traumatic brain injured and normal subjects. *Neuropsychologia, 35*(6), 747–758.

Santorelli, S. (2014). *Mindfulness-Based Stress Reduction (MBSR): Standards of practice.* Worcester, MA: The Center for Mindfulness in Medicine and Society, University of Massachusetts Medical School.

Sapolsky, R. M. (1994). *Why zebras don't get ulcers.* New York, NY: W. H. Freeman.

Saunders, T., Driskell, J. E., Johnston, J. H., & Salas, E. (1996). The effect of stress inoculation training on anxiety and performance. *Journal of Occupational Health Psychology, 1*(2), 170–186.

Scaer, R. C. (2005). *The trauma spectrum: Hidden wounds and human resiliency.* New York, NY: Norton.

Schmeichel, B. J., Volokhov, R. N., & Demaree, H. A. (2008). Working memory capacity and the self-regulation of emotional expression and experience. *Journal of Personality and Social Psychology, 95*(6), 1526–1540.

Schultz, J. R., Bell, K. M., Naugle, A. E., & Polusny, M. A. (2006). Child sexual abuse and adulthood sexual assault among military veteran and civilian women. *Military Medicine, 171*(8), 723–728.

Seligman, M. E. P. (2002). Positive psychology, positive prevention, and positive therapy. In C. Snyder & S. Lopez (Eds.), *Handbook of positive psychology* (pp. 3–9). New York, NY: Oxford University Press.

Shonin, E., Van Gordon, W., & Griffiths, M. D. (2014). Are there risks associated with using mindfulness in the treatment of psychopathology? *Clinical Practice, 11*(4), 398–392.

Simmons, A. N., Fitzpatrick, S., Strigo, I. A., Potterat, E. G., Johnson, D. C., Matthews, S. C., . . . Paulus, M. P. (2012). Altered insula activation in anticipation of changing emotional states: Neural mechanisms underlying cognitive flexibility in Special Operations Forces personnel. *Neuroreport, 23*(4), 234–239.

Slagter, H., Davidson, R., & Lutz, A. (2011). Mental training as a tool in the neuroscientific study of brain and cognitive plasticity. *Frontiers in Human Neuroscience, 5*, 1–12.

Smith, S. L. (2013). Could Comprehensive Soldier Fitness have iatrogenic consequences? A commentary. *The Journal of Behavioral Health Services & Research, 40*(2), 242–246.

Stanley, E. A. (2010). Neuroplasticity, mind fitness, and military effectiveness. In M. Armstrong, C. Loeb, & J. Valdes (Eds.), *Bio-inspired innovation and national security* (pp. 257–279). Washington, DC: National Defense University Press.

Stanley, E. A. (2014a). Cultivating the mind of a warrior. *Inquiring Mind, 30*(2): 16–31.

Stanley, E. A. (2014b). Mindfulness-based Mind Fitness Training (MMFT): An approach for enhancing performance and building resilience in high stress contexts. In A. Le, C. T. Ngnoumen, & E. J. Langer (Eds.), *The Wiley-Blackwell handbook of mindfulness* (pp. 964–985). London, UK: Wiley-Blackwell.

Stanley, E. A. (in press-a). *Widen the window: Training the brain and body to thrive during stress, uncertainty, and change*. New York, NY: Avery Books.

Stanley, E. A. (in press-b). War duration and the micro-dynamics of decision making during stress. *Polity*.

Stanley, E. A., Schaldach, J., Kiyonaga, A., & Jha, A. P. (2011). Mindfulness-based mind fitness training: A case study of a high-stress predeployment military cohort. *Cognitive and Behavioral Practice, 18*(4), 566–576.

Steenkamp, M. M., Nash, W. P., & Litz, B. T. (2013). Post-traumatic stress disorder: Review of the Comprehensive Soldier Fitness program. *American Journal of Preventive Medicine, 44*(5), 507–512.

Sterlace, S. R., Plumb, T. N., El-Kara, L., Van Orden, K. A., Thom, N. J., Stanley, E. A., . . . Johnson, D. C. (2012). Hormone regulation under stress: Recent evidence from warfighters on the effectiveness of Mindfulness-Based Mind Fitness Training in building stress resilience. Society for Neuroscience Poster Presentation.

Strauss, C., Cavanagh, K., Oliver, A., & Pettman, D. (2014). Mindfulness-based interventions for people diagnosed with a current episode of an anxiety or depressive disorder: A meta-analysis of randomised controlled trials. *PLOS One, 9*(4), e96110.

Thom, N.J., Johnson, D.C., Flagan, T., Simmons, A.N., Kotturi, S.A., Van Orden, K.F., . . . Paulus, M.P. (2014). Detecting emotion in others: Increased insula and decreased medial prefrontal cortex activation during emotion processing in elite adventure racers. *Social Cognitive and Affective Neuroscience, 9*(2), 225–231.

Unsworth, N., Heitz, R.P., Schrock, J.C., & Engle, R.W. (2005). An automated version of the operation span task. *Behavior Research Methods, 37*(3), 498–505.

van der Kolk, B. (2015). *The body keeps the score: Brain, mind, and body in the healing of trauma.* New York, NY: Penguin Books.

Vasterling, J.J., Proctor, S.P., Amoroso, P., Kane, R., Heeren, T., & White, R.F. (2006). Neuropsychological outcomes of army personnel following deployment to the Iraq war. *Journal of the American Medical Association, 296*(5), 519–529.

Vaughan, C., Farmer, C., Breslau, J., & Burnette, C. (2015). *Evaluation of the Operational Stress Control and Readiness (OSCAR) program.* Santa Monica, CA: RAND Corporation.

Williams, J.M.G., Crane, C., Barnhofer, T., Brennan, K., Duggan, D.S., Fennell, M.J., . . . Von Rohr, I.R. (2014). Mindfulness-based cognitive therapy for preventing relapse in recurrent depression: A randomized dismantling trial. *Journal of Consulting and Clinical Psychology, 82*(2), 275–286.

Woodruff, T., Kelty, R., & Segal, D.R. (2006). Propensity to serve and motivation to enlist among American combat soldiers. *Armed Forces & Society, 32*(3), 353–366.

Zeidan, F., Johnson, S.K., Diamond, B.J., David, Z., & Goolkasian, P. (2010). Mindfulness meditation improves cognition: Evidence of brief mental training. *Consciousness and Cognition, 19*(2), 597–605.

About the Editors and Contributors

Editors

David L. Albright, PhD, MSW, holds the Hill Crest Foundation Endowed Chair in Mental Health Research at the University of Alabama. He is a military veteran and former research fellow with both the Department of Veterans Affairs and the RAND Corporation's Center for Military Health Policy Research. Learn more at davidlalbright.com.

Kate Hendricks Thomas, PhD, MS, ERYT-200, is a behavioral health researcher focused on mental health promotion for service members and military veterans. She served as a Marine Corps officer and is now an assistant professor of health sciences at Charleston Southern University and director of the Public Health program. Thomas is the author of *Brave, Strong, True: The Modern Warrior's Battle for Balance* and is a speaker who teaches resilient leadership, mental fitness, and spiritual development. Learn more at drkatethomas.com.

Contributors

Rev. Elizabeth A. Alders, MDiv, MS, is a member of the Association of Professional Chaplains. Her research focuses on developing spiritual distress assessments for trauma patients. A graduate of Vanderbilt Divinity School and Virginia Commonwealth University, she is committed to integrating research into the chaplaincy profession.

Nicholas J. Armstrong, PhD, MPA, is the senior director for research and evaluation at the Institute for Veterans and Military Families (IVMF) and adjunct professor of public administration and international affairs at Syracuse University's Maxwell School of Citizenship and Public Affairs. He is an Army veteran who served in Iraq, Afghanistan, and Bosnia.

Katharine Bloeser, PhD, MSW, is currently an assistant professor at the Silberman School of Social Work at Hunter College, City University of New York. Bloeser has worked with veterans as a clinical social worker at the Washington, DC, VA Medical Center and the War Related Illness and Injury Study Center.

Gillian S. Cantor, MPA, is on the Research and Evaluation team at the Institute for Veterans and Military Families. In her role as program evaluation manager, she oversees the evaluation and continuous improvement of the AmericaServes initiative.

Robin Carnes, MBA, C-IAYT, is a leader in bringing evidence-based yoga and meditation practice into mainstream settings such as the Department of Defense, VA, and universities. From 2006 to 2012, Carnes was yoga and meditation instructor for a DoD acute PTSD program at Walter Reed Medical Center. She cofounded Warriors at Ease, which has trained 600+ yoga teachers to teach safely and effectively in military communities. Her work has been featured in the *Washington Post, Woman's Day Magazine, Huffington Post*, and *Army Magazine*, as well as the award-winning documentary, *Escape Fire: The Fight to Rescue America's Healthcare*. In 2013, she was honored by the Smithsonian Institution for her pioneering work in bringing yoga to military communities.

Rev. John Edgar Caterson, DMin, M.Div., serves at Joint Special Operations University (JSOU) as codirector of Special Operations Chaplains Graduate Certificate Program and instructor of record for the Spiritual Readiness course. He has served as JSOU's codirector of the Religious Support Team Orientation course, senior advisor to the U.S. military chief of chaplains, and subject matter expert at the Eisenhower Leadership Center at West Point and continues to serve as a senior advisor to Gallup Faith. He has authored a dozen books.

Bonnie Chapman, RN, MPH, is the director of evaluation and innovation at the Institute for Veterans and Military Families. Chapman was previously the director of quality for the SUNY Upstate Cancer Center.

Kathleen G. Charters, PhD, RN, CPHIMS, is a nurse informatician who teams with health care providers and chaplains to create and evaluate programs and services integrating physical, psychological, and spiritual care. Charters currently works for the Henry M. Jackson Foundation for the Advancement of Military Medicine at the Consortium for Health and Military Performance in support of the Spiritual Performance Program. She spent 25 years as a nurse in the U.S. Navy, 6 years as senior consultant to the

About the Editors and Contributors 257

Veterans Health Agency, and 6 years as a nurse consultant to the Defense Health Agency.

Howard A. Crosby Jr., MBA, has served in the Army Chaplain Corps as a reserve chaplain assistant for the past 19 years. He served for 9 years in Florida, Qatar, Jordan, Egypt, Iraq, and Afghanistan while assigned to Central Command and several years at the Pentagon with the Army Chief of Chaplains Office.

Joseph M. Currier, PhD, is an assistant professor and director of Clinical Training in the Combined Clinical & Counseling Psychology Doctoral Program at the University of South Alabama. His research focuses broadly on enhancing the efficacy and availability of mental health services for military veterans and their families.

Lydia Davey is a communications strategist and global content marketing manager at Apple Inc. A Marine Corps veterans, Davey codeveloped *Women Warriors: A Course on Post-traumatic Growth* at the University of California in San Francisco and served as a course instructor there. She is a Defense Council member at the Truman National Security Project.

Lori L. Davis, MD, is a clinical professor of psychiatry at the University of Alabama's School of Medicine and associate chief of staff for Research and Development at the Tuscaloosa VA Medical Center.

Kent D. Drescher, PhD, is a clinical psychologist at the National Center for PTSD, Dissemination and Training Division, part of the VA Palo Alto Health Care System. His current work involves education activities in the areas of trauma and spirituality and moral injury among veterans.

Sanela Dursun, PhD, is a research psychologist and the director of the Personnel and Family Support Research section at Defence Research and Development Canada. She is responsible for managing and delivering research, analysis, and expert advice on strategies to improve the well-being of serving members, veterans, and their families.

Jacob K. Farnsworth, PhD, is a clinical psychologist with the Veteran Affairs Eastern Colorado Health Care System. His clinical services focus primarily on evidence-based treatments for posttraumatic stress disorder and substance use.

Charles R. Figley, PhD, is a former Marine who served in the Vietnam War and went on to become a pioneering researcher in the field of Vietnam veterans and posttraumatic stress disorder. Professor Figley received the VVA Excellence in the Sciences Award at the 2016 National Leadership in Tucson. Figley served in Vietnam as a corporal, voluntarily working with Vietnamese children during his free time. In 1977, he established the Family Research Institute and in 1978 wrote *Stress Disorders among Vietnam Veterans*, which helped recognize PTSD as a psychological condition for the first time. Figley cofounded the Society for Traumatic Stress Studies and the online journal *Traumatology*. In 2004, Professor Figley was awarded a senior Fulbright Research Fellowship to conduct research in Kuwait. He is now the Paul Henry Kurzweg Distinguished Chair and director of the Tulane Traumatology Institute at Tulane University, New Orleans.

Kari L. Fletcher, PhD, MSW, is an associate professor and the coordinator of Area of Emphasis in Military Practice in the St. Catherine University–University of St. Thomas School of Social Work. Her experience working with military/veteran-connected populations across age cohorts within direct practice contexts spans 18 years and includes affiliations with the VA (as a clinical social worker, 2000–2010), Vet Center (as an external consultant, 2014–present), and Military OneSource (as a psychotherapist, 2015–present).

Cate Florenz, MA, is a communication planner, analyst, and veteran Marine Corps officer. Since leaving active duty in 2008, she has worked supporting the Department of Defense and other federal departments in areas of communication, technology, and digital media.

Christine Isana Garcia, PsyD, is a clinical psychologist who specializes in the treatment and understanding of trauma and resiliency. She is the associate and clinical director at the Young Adult and Family Center at the University of California at San Francisco.

Kate Germano was an officer in the U.S. Marine Corps for 20 years, retiring in July 2016. A combat veteran during the war in Iraq, she filled a variety of challenging and high-profile positions, including Marine aid de camp to the Secretary of the Navy, commanding officer of a recruiting station, and commanding officer of Fourth Recruit Training Battalion, the only all-female unit in the Department of Defense. While assigned to the training battalion, she uncovered systemic failures in how women were recruited and trained. After retirement, she served as the chief operating officer of the Service Women's Action Network, the nation's only nonprofit solely focused on supporting and advocating for women in the military and veteran communities. She is the author of *Fight Like a Girl: The Truth behind How Female Marines Are Trained*.

About the Editors and Contributors

Kelli Godfrey, LMSW, is a doctoral student at the University of Alabama's School of Social Work. Godfrey has worked for the U.S. Army, providing services to Army soldiers and their families and as a victim advocate for survivors of military sexual assault.

Matthew J. M. Hendricks, MS, is a retired Marine Corps infantry officer and Purple Heart recipient. He lives in Virginia, where he teaches high school English. His combat experiences in Ramadi, Iraq, and subsequent medical procedures at Bethesda Naval Hospital, helped instill a "Carpe Diem" sense of urgency in all aspects of his life. His mission and purpose are guided by his firm faith in God, which has enabled him to strive to implement the maxim of one of his favorite historical figures, General Thomas "Stonewall" Jackson: "Let the Institute be heard from today."

Kyleanne Hunter, PhD, is a research fellow at the Josef Korbel School of International Studies, University of Denver. Prior to becoming an academic, she spent over a decade as an officer in the U.S. Marine Corps. She flew the AH-1W "Super Cobra" attack helicopter, with multiple combat tours. She is a contributor for gender and foreign affairs to the *New York Times, Washington Post*, CNN, Al-Jazeera, NPR, Fox News, and *Huffington Post*.

Aurora Hutchinson, MA, is a certified meditation teacher and wellness educator at the Mindfulness Center in Bethesda, Maryland, where she teaches group classes; conducts corporate seminars; and works with private clients seeking to learn meditation for stress management, improved health, and career and family support. She is a PhD candidate in psychology with training in neuroscience and pharmacology.

Kamilah A. Jones, PhD, LCSW, is a senior social worker at the U.S. Department of Veterans Affairs in Atlanta. Her clinical training fellowships were completed at Yale University and Emory University.

Stephen Kaplan, PhD, is a professor of Indian and Comparative Religions and director of Veteran Success Programs at Manhattan College, Bronx, New York. He is the author of two books and numerous articles focusing on Hinduism, Buddhism, and the neurosciences. For the past two years, he has been working with the Sivananda Ashram, Warriors at Ease, and Manhattan College, providing stress reduction programs for incoming Manhattan College veteran-students.

Ben King, MA, is a teacher, public speaker, veteran Army psychological operations sergeant, and a community organizer. In 2011, he founded Armor

Down to help veterans thrive as civilians and started Mindful Memorial Day at Arlington Cemetery to help visitors mindfully honor the sacrifice of the fallen. He consults for the Women in Military Service for America Memorial.

Kelsey L. Larsen, MPP, MA, is a PhD candidate at Georgetown University, where she researches political decision-making effects of combat-related nervous system dysregulation in military populations and how specific mindfulness-based trainings might yield health and decision-making benefits in such populations. She works for the Henry M. Jackson Foundation for the Advancement of Military Medicine at the Uniformed Services University of the Health Sciences, providing teaching and research support for the Department of Medicine at the Walter Reed National Military Medical Center.

Jennifer E. C. Lee, PhD, is a researcher within the Canadian Department of National Defence, where she leads a team of health psychologists and epidemiologists. She chairs the Technical Cooperation Program Human Resources and Performance Group (TTCP HUM) Action Group on Resilience.

Charles R. McAdams III, EdD, holds the positions of professor and chair in the School Psychology and Counselor Education department at The College of William & Mary, where he also co-directs the university-based New Horizons Family Counseling Center. Dr. McAdams's interest in addressing the needs of military families stems from his physical location in the Peninsula and Tidewater regions of Virginia, which are home to multiple military installations as well as from his own previous active duty experience with Naval Special Warfare. He is a licensed Professional Counselor and Marriage & Family Therapist, and his research and clinical practice have focused on the promotion of family stability and support to enhance individual well-being in both military and civilian populations.

Wesley H. McCormick, MDiv, MS, is a combined-integrated clinical and counseling psychology doctoral student at the University of South Alabama. A graduate of Asbury Theological Seminary and Huntingdon College, his research examines veteran mental health, trauma, and religious/spiritual struggles.

Justin T. McDaniel, PhD, is an assistant professor of Public Health at Southern Illinois University, Carbondale. Using spatial epidemiological methodologies, he studies the geographic distribution of mental health issues among military veterans. He is also the cofounder of an international nonprofit organization, the International Center for Community Health Promotion and Education.

James D. McDonough Jr., USA (Ret. Colonel), MA, is the managing director of programs and services at the Institute for Veterans and Military Families (IVMF) and oversees the AmericaServes initiative. Before joining the IVMF, McDonough served as senior fellow for veterans affairs at the New York State Health Foundation; president and CEO of the Rochester, New York-based Veterans Outreach Center Inc.; and director of the New York State Division of Veterans' Affairs. He is a 26-year veteran of the U.S. Army, including service in Germany, Korea, and Kuwait in support of Operation Iraqi Freedom.

Deborah Norris, PhD, ERYT-500, C-IAYT, is the founder of the Mindfulness Center based in Washington, DC, and professor and director of the Psychobiology of Healing Program at American University. She has been a psychologist and research scientist at the Veterans Affairs Medical Center is Washington, DC, studying the role of mind-body interventions for the treatment of pain, stress, and neurological disorders.

Sarah Plummer Taylor, MSW, ERYT-500, CHC, is an established leader in the field of resilience-building, holistic health coaching, and yoga for veterans. She is an adjunct professor of health sciences at Charleston Southern University and a city impact manager for The Mission Continues. Plummer Taylor is a former Marine Corps intelligence officer. She is the author of *Just Roll with It: 7 Battle Tested Truths for Building a Resilient Life*.

Heliana Ramirez, PhD, LISW, is a senior social worker at the Veterans Affairs Palo Alto Health Care System, where she serves as the facility's lead LGBT veteran care coordinator. Her work with LGBT veterans includes founding the VAPAHCS LGBT Veteran Support Group; producing the documentary film *The Camouflage Closet* regarding trauma and recovery among LGBT veterans; and providing LGBT veteran clinical care and cultural competence trainings to VA staff, universities, and mental health leadership of the California National Guard. In 2012, she founded the VAPAHCS LGBT Staff and Allies Special Emphasis Program and has led VAPAHCS in achieving the designation as a leader in LGBT Healthcare Equality from the Human Rights Campaign's Healthcare Equality Index.

Mariah Rooney O'Brien, MSW, LCSW, RYT, is a postgraduate social work fellow at the Trauma Center at Justice Resource Institute and is a project Coordinator for the Center for Treatment of Developmental Trauma Disorders in Boston, MA. As a yoga teacher she has worked with veterans through the Department of Veterans Affairs, Warriors at Ease, and Wounded Warrior Project. In her clinical work, she has served veterans at the Department of Veterans Affairs, and the Change Step program Domestic Abuse Project in Minneapolis, MN.

Margaret M. Shields, PhD, MS, is a health researcher focused on stress reduction and self-efficacy as they relate to mental health. She is an assistant professor of Public Health at Charleston Southern University.

Rev. Sarah A. Shirley, MDiv, MAS, is a priest of the Episcopal Diocese of Washington and spiritual director. For the past 25 years, she has served as a community, health care, and military chaplain in Nevada, Texas, Florida, Maryland, Oman, and Afghanistan.

Elizabeth A. Stanley, PhD, MBA, is an associate professor of security studies at Georgetown University. A former U.S. Army intelligence officer, she created Mindfulness-based Mind Fitness Training (MMFT), a resilience training tested through four DoD-funded neuroscience research studies. She has taught MMFT to thousands in military and civilian high-stress environments. She is also a certified practitioner of somatic experiencing, a body-based trauma therapy.

Richard Toscano, MEd, is a national subject matter expert on evidence-based supported employment, called Individual Placement and Support (IPS) and Customized Employment (CE), a highly individualized, career planning process promoted by the Department of Labor/Office of Disability Employment Policy. At the Tuscaloosa VA Medical Center, Toscano is the expert IPS trainer, supervisor, and fidelity monitor on projects to advance the recovery of veterans with posttraumatic stress.

Laura Westley, MBA, is a West Point graduate, former Army Captain and Iraq War veteran. She is also an author, speaker, playwright, veterans' mental health advocate, and technology consultant. Her memoir and musical comedy show, both titled *War Virgin*, have been featured in numerous publications, including NPR, *The Boston Globe*, *Playboy*, and *Broadway World*. Her writing has been published in *Washington Post, Hill, Foreign Policy, Military Times*, and *Huffington Post*.

Jessica Wilkes is the Veteran & Military Student Services program coordinator for the College of Charleston. She is a 12-year Air Force veteran and former combat camera videographer. She deployed to Iraq twice and earned the Bronze Star. She is now a liaison and advocate for veteran and military students during their transition from combat to campus.

Index

Note: *n* following page number represents an endnote.

Acceptance and commitment therapy (ACT), 88, 120
Accommodations, job, 202–3
Adaptive disclosure (AD), 87
Adjustment disorder, 130
Adverse childhood experiences (ACEs), 6–7, 70, 241
Affirmative practices, 137–38
Afghanistan, war in, 3–7, 30, 84
After-action reviews, 86
Agent Orange, 166, 171
Aging. *See* Veterans, older
Air Force resiliency training, 101–2, 106–7
Alcohol. *See* Substance abuse
Alexander Hamilton Post 448, 133–34
Alliances, in families, 148–49, 151–52, 155–56
Allostasis, 48–49, 54–55
Alternative medicine, 170–73. *See also* Mindfulness; Yoga
Americans with Disabilities Act (ADA), 202
America's Heroes at Work, 203
AmericaServes: about, 211, 213–14; challenges, 220–22; coordination centers, 213, 216, 219–20; funding, 222–23; implementation phases, 216; measurement/evaluation, 215–17, 220–21; mental health outcomes, 223–24; network formation, 219–20; performance indicators, 218–19; process of, 214–16; technology of, 215–16; theory of change, 217–18
Anger, 131
Anterior cingulate cortex (ACC), 57–59, 237, 238
Anxiety: and gamma-aminobutyric acid (GABA), 53; and norepinephrine, 51; sexual harassment, 200–201; in workplace, 203. *See also* Mental health
Army resiliency training, 102–3, 106
Assault, sexual, 116–17, 134–35, 139, 200–201
Attentional control, in mindfulness, 58–59, 237–39

BATTLEMIND, 101
Behavioral change theories, 69
Behavioral strategies, mindfulness: attentional control, 58–59; body awareness, 54–57; emotional

regulation, 57–58; pain recovery, 56, 59–60
Belonging, sense of, 32, 38–39
Bible, 23–24. See also Spiritual fitness
Biochemicals: hormones, 49–51; neurotransmitters, 51–54
Blogs, 132
"Blue-Green Algae" (Lind), 193
Body awareness, in mindfulness, 54–57
Boundaries, in families, 148, 150–51, 154–55
Breath: in mindfulness, 55, 56, 59; spiritual, 182
Building Spiritual Strength (BSS), 186–87

Careers, 196–97, 202–4. See also Individual Placement and Support (IPS)
Challenges, tolerance for, 238–39
Chaplains, 86, 97, 183–85
Chemical exposure, 166
Children: behaviors, 158; relationship with during deployment, 155–56; siblings, during parent deployment, 148, 149, 150; trauma for, 6–7, 70, 76–77, 241. See also Families, military
Churches, 182. See also Spiritual fitness
Cingulate cortex, 57
Clergy, 86, 97, 183–85
Cognitive processing therapy (CPT), 88–89
Collaborative governance, 211
Collective impact, 211–13, 216, 219–22. See also AmericaServes
Combat exposure: depression, 9–11; post-traumatic stress disorder (PTSD) risk, 4–8; suicide, 10–11; veterans, older, 166; workplace concerns, 203

Communities of practice (CoP), 213, 221–22
Community-based programming, 211–12
Community support. See Social support
Complementary and alternative medicine (CAM), 170–73. See also Mindfulness; Yoga
Comprehensive Airman Fitness (CAF), 101–2
Comprehensive Soldier and Family Fitness (CSF2), 103, 243
Comprehensive Soldier Fitness (CSF), 102–3
Coordination centers (AmericaServes), 213, 216, 219–20
CoP (communities of practice), 213, 221–22
Corticotrophin-releasing hormone (CRH), 49–50
Cortisol, 49–50, 51
CPT (cognitive processing therapy), 88–89
Cultural resilience, 71–72
Culture, of military. See Warrior culture

Davey, Lydia, 120
Death: responsibility for, 8, 77; training for, 34; witness of, 78, 185
Default mode network (DMN), 58–59
Defense Suicide Prevention Office (DSPO), 96. See also Suicide
Dehydroepiandrosterone (DHEA), 49–50
Department of Defense (DoD) resiliency programs. See Resiliency programs, Department of Defense (DoD)
Depression: cingulate cortex, 57; employment, 197; and estrogen, 50; LGBT, 134, 136, 138; and post-traumatic stress disorder (PTSD),

9–11; resiliency, 72; veterans, older, 166; women, 116–17. *See also* Mental health; Post-traumatic stress disorder (PTSD)
DHEA (dehydroepiandrosterone), 49–50
Discrimination, LGBT, 134–35, 140
DMN (default mode network), 58–59
DoD (Department of Defense) resiliency programs. *See* Resiliency programs, Department of Defense (DoD)
Domain-general skills, 233–35, 237–39
Domain-specific skills, 234–37
Don't Ask, Don't Tell (DADT), 134, 137, 139
Dopamine, 51–52
Drugs. *See* Substance abuse
DSTRESS, 105
Dysphoric mood, 9

Eastern medicine, 170–73
Education, as mental health intervention, 119–20
Efficacy, 70–71
E-learning, 118, 120, 122–23
Emotional: intelligence, 235; regulation, 57–58
Employers, of veterans, 199, 203
Employment, postdeployment, 196–97, 202–4. *See also* Individual Placement and Support (IPS)
Enemy, caring for, 190–91
Estrogen, 50
Executive functioning, 236–38

Faith, 192
Faith-based communities, 182. *See also* Spiritual fitness
Families, military: alliances, 148–49, 151–52, 155–56; boundaries, 148, 150–51, 154–55; challenges, 150–52; extended, 151–52, 154; hierarchy, 148–50, 152–54; LGBT, 139–40; vs. military unit relationships, 152, 156; New Directions for Family and Youth Development, 156–59; parenting, during deployment, 117, 150–53; relocations, 153; resiliency training for, 103; storytelling, 169–70; structure, 148–49; as systems, 147–48
Family, as a stressor, 117
Family Readiness System (FRS), 100–101
Female service members. *See* Women service members
First Amendment, 183
Flexibility, psychological, 84–85
Focused resilience training, 99, 102–5
Force Health Protection and Readiness Program, 100
Force Resiliency, 96
Forgiveness, 88–89, 185–87, 189–90
Free exercise clause, 183

Galanin, 53–54
Gamma-aminobutyric acid (GABA), 52–53
Garcia, Christine, 120
Gender minorities, 146n1. *See also* LGBT service members
Genders. *See* LGBT service members; Women service members
God. *See* Spiritual fitness
Governance, collaborative, 211
Group therapy. *See* Social support
Guilt, 8, 10, 26–27, 78–79. *See also* Moral injury (MI)

Hamilton, Alexander, 133–34
Harassment, sexual, 116–17, 134–35, 139, 200–201
Health care providers training, 87
Health Insurance Portability and Accountability Act (HIPAA), 120, 122

Hierarchies, of families, 148–50, 152–54
Hispanic service members, 6
Holy Joe's Café, 189–90
Homeostasis, 48, 50, 54–55
Homosexuality. *See* LGBT service members
Hormones, 49–51
Humanness, and faith, 192–93
Hypothalamic-pituitary adrenal (HPA) axis, 48–52, 56, 57, 60

Improvised explosive devices (IEDs), 43–44
Individual Placement and Support (IPS): about, 198; benefits, 198, 201–2; and health services, 201–2; importance of, 198–99; principles of, 200–201
In-groups, 34, 36–39
Institute for Veterans and Military Families (IVMF), 213–16
Insula, 57, 238
Integrated social service models (resiliency programs), 99–101
Integrative Restoration (iRest) Yoga Nidra, 172–73
Interoceptive awareness, 54–59
Interoceptive functioning, 238
Iraq, war in, 3–7, 30, 84
IRest® Meditation, 112–13
IRest Yoga Nidra, 172–73

Jobs, 196–97, 202–4. *See also* Individual Placement and Support (IPS)
Journaling, 120, 132

Language, 35–37
Leadership, military: LGBT, 139–40; moral injury, 80–82; prayer, 25; resiliency programs, 105, 240–41; violence, 139
Learned helplessness, 50

LGBT service members: affirmative practices, 137–38; families, 139–40; harassment, 138–39; history, 133–34; interventions, 136–38; military leaders as, 139; mindfulness, 138; resilience among, 135–37, 140; stressors, 134–35, 136–37; term use, 133, 146n1; violence, 138–39
Lieber Code, 184
Lind, J. Allan, 193

Manhattan College, 112
Marine Corps: females, 228–31; Mindfulness-based Mind Fitness Training (MMFT)®, 53; resiliency training, 104–5
Maxwell X Lab, 221
Meaning-making, 168, 187, 188
Mechanisms, physiological, 54
Meditation. *See* Mindfulness
Memories, sharing, 168–70
Memory, 237
Mental health: burdens of, 4–5; care, rejection of, 39, 119–20; and collective impact (*see* AmericaServes); and employment, 196–97, 202–4 (*see also* Individual Placement and Support (IPS)); providers, and LGBT clientele, 137; ripple effect, 11–12; risk factors, 5–9; stigma, 118; and warrior culture, 39–40. *See also* Anxiety; Depression; Post-traumatic stress disorder (PTSD)
Mental health prevention, service members: collective impact, 209–24, 228–32; Department of Defense (DoD) resilience programs, 95–107, 111–14; employment, 196–206; families, military, 147–59; LGBT service members, 133–40; mind-body skills training, 233–45; mindfulness, and

resiliency, 47–60, 66–68; moral injury, and resiliency, 76–89; resiliency theory, 69–73; spiritual fitness, 181–93; veterans, older, 162–73; warrior culture, 29–40, 43–46; well-being issues, 3–13, 18–28; women service members, 116–24, 129–32. *See also* Mental health
Metaphor use, 167–68
Military bases, 140
Military OneSource, 101
Military sexual trauma (MST), 116–17, 134–35, 139, 200–201
Miller, Richard, 113
Mind-body connections, 32–37
Mind-body skills training, 240–44
Mindfulness: behavioral strategies (*see* Behavioral strategies, mindfulness); LGBT, 138; meditation forms, 55–56; Mindfulness-based Mind Fitness Training (MMFT)®, 237–39; neurology of (*see* Neurology, of mindfulness); students, 111–14; training, 34–35, 237–39, 240–44; for women, 120–21; yoga (*see* Yoga). *See also* Yoga
Mindfulness-based Mind Fitness Training (MMFT)®, 53, 237–39
Minority stress, 136–37
Mistrust, 80
Moral injury (MI): about, 8–10, 77–79; civilian life adaptations, 82–83; combat effectiveness, 83–87; deployment adaptations, 80–82; disengagement, 82–83; example of, 76–77; increasing, 84–85; interventions, 87–89; military resilience, 79–80; reconciliation, 185–86, 189–90; situational context, 83–87; therapeutic approaches, 87–88. *See also* Morality

Moral Injury Reconciliation (MIR), 186
Morality: of service members, 34, 39; skepticism of, 81–82; social, 78–79

Naval Center Combat and Operational Stress Control (NCCOSC), 103–4
Neurohormonal balance, 50
Neurology, of mindfulness: about, 47–49; attentional control, 58–59; body awareness, 54–57; emotional regulation, 57–58; hormones, 49–51; mechanisms, physiological, 54; neurotransmitters, 51–54; pain recovery, 56, 59–60; sensory information, 54–57; warning on, 56
Neuropeptide Y (NPY), 53
Neuroplasticity, 33–34, 234
Neurotransmitters, 51–54
New Directions for Family and Youth Development, 156–59
New Freedom Initiative, 197
Non-establishment clause, 183
Nonprofits, service member programs, 210
Norepinephrine, 51

Objects, in warrior culture, 32, 35–37
Online treatments, 118, 120–23
Operation Enduring Freedom/Operation Iraqi Freedom (OEF/OIF), 3–7, 30, 84
Operational Stress Control and Readiness (OSCAR), 104, 243

Pain, 56, 59–60
Parenting. *See* Families, military
Philanthropic giving, 209
Philosophy, 181–82
Postdeployment: college, 111–14; employment, 196–97, 202–4 (*see also* Individual Placement and Support (IPS)); family (*see* Families,

military); parenting, 150; reintegration stresses, 72–73, 82–83, 129–32; warrior culture, 35. *See also* Veterans, older
Posttraumatic growth (PTG), 120, 135
Post-traumatic stress disorder (PTSD): avoidance, 205; cingulate cortex, 57; combat exposure, 4–8; and depression, 9–11; and employment, 196–99, 198, 202–3; examples of, 76–77, 79, 130–32, 170–73, 198–99, 204–5; holistic approach for, 172–73; online treatment, 120; prevalence, 4–5; research for, 6–8, 10–13; risk factors, 5–9. *See also* Depression; Mental health
Potentially morally injurious events (PMIEs), 78
Prayer, 25–27
Proximity, in warrior culture, 31–32
Psychological conditioning, 33–34
Psychological flexibility, 84–85
Public-private partnerships, programming, 211

Race, 6
Referrals, programming. *See* AmericaServes
Reintegration, to civilian life. *See* Postdeployment
Relationship Attachment Model (RAM), 187–88
Relaxation strategies, 120–21. *See also* Mindfulness; Yoga
Religion, 23–28. *See also* Spiritual fitness
Religious freedom, 183
Relocations, 153
Research for post-traumatic stress disorder (PTSD), post deployment, 6–8, 10–13
Resiliency: in children, 70; cultural, 71–72; definitions, 48, 69, 79–80; factors for, 97; families (*see* Families, military); focused, 99, 102–5; in LGBT service members, 135–37, 140; and moral injury (*see* Moral injury (MI)); and neurology of mindfulness (*see* Neurology, of mindfulness); spiritual, 187–88; and stress, 239; theory, 69–73; training (*see* Resiliency programs, Department of Defense (DoD); resiliency training); traits, 71; in veterans, older (*see* Veterans, older); women (*see* Women service members)
Resiliency programs, Department of Defense (DoD): about, 96–97; barriers to, 105; Comprehensive Airman Fitness (CAF), 101–2; Comprehensive Soldier Fitness (CSF), 102–3; DSTRESS, 105; effectiveness of, 106; Family Readiness System (FRS), 100–101; Force Health Protection and Readiness Program, 100; Force Resiliency, 96; Military OneSource, 101; Naval Center Combat and Operational Stress Control (NCCOSC), 103–4; Operational Stress Control and Readiness (OSCAR), 104; Strategy for Suicide Prevention, 98; Total Force Fitness (TFF), 99–100; Total Sailor Fitness (TSF), 103; Young Adult and Family Center, 118
Resiliency training: branch specific, 101–5; family, 99–101; focused, 99, 102–5; theory, 69–73; timing of, 34–35, 40
Resilient Airmen, 101
Reward-motivation, 52
Rituals, 33, 35
R&R (Ultimate Spiritual Resiliency and Relationships), 187–88
Rules of engagement (ROEs), 80–81

Self-efficacy, 70–71
Self-reference, 58
Self-regulation, 72–73
Semiotics, in warrior culture, 31, 32, 35–37
Sensory information, in mindfulness, 54–57
Sexual harassment, 116–17, 134–35, 139, 200–201
Sexual orientation. *See* LGBT service members
Shame, 8, 78–79
Siblings, 148, 150–51, 154
Social isolation, 205
Social support: families, 151, 154–59; LGBT service members, 136–37; post-traumatic stress disorder (PTSD), 7, 10–11, 12; resilience, 85–86; spiritual, 187, 191–92; Warriors at Ease, 111–14; women, 121, 123
Solovy, Alden, 192–93
Somatic interventions. *See* Mindfulness; Mindfulness-based Mind Fitness Training (MMFT)®; Yoga
Somatic sensing, 54–57
Somatosensory information, 55–56
South Park Sunday School, 191
Spiritual fitness: about, 182–83; chaplains, 183–85; humanness, 192–93; reconciliation, 185–86, 189–90; spiritual concerns, 186–87, 190–91; spiritual growth, 187–88, 191–92
Spirituality, 182–83. *See also* Spiritual fitness
Spouses, 148, 151, 155. *See also* Families, military
Stone, Samuel, 184
Storytelling, 168–70
Strategy for Suicide Prevention, 98. *See also* Suicide
Strength, of service members, 39
Stress inoculation training (SIT), 235–37
Stress-related growth (SRG), 135
Stress-sensitization hypothesis, 7
Student-veterans, 111–14
Substance abuse: cingulate cortex, 57; and employment, 198, 200; family reintegration, 150; harassment, 117; and post-traumatic stress disorder (PTSD), 79, 88; prevention, 103; stress, 239; veterans, older, 166
Suicide: cingulate cortex, 57; and joblessness, 197; LGBT service members, 134; post-traumatic stress disorder (PTSD), 8–10; prevention, 96, 98, 105; Vietnam veterans, 38; women, 116, 117
Suicide Prevention Processes, 105
Support groups. *See* Social support
Symbols, of warrior culture, 37

Tapping, 120–21
Technology: in treatments, 118, 120, 122–23; in warrior culture, 30
Telemedicine, 120, 122–23
Testosterone, 50
Thalamic gating, 56–57
Thalamus, 55–57
Theodicy, 191–92
Theology, 181–82
Third-wave resiliency theory, 71
Tolerance, for challenge, in mindfulness, 238–39
Tone of speech, 36
Total Force Fitness (TFF), 99–100
Total Sailor Fitness (TSF), 103
Training: for death, 34; family, 99–101, 156–59; habit creation, 33–34; harassment, 139; health care providers, 87; mindfulness (*see* Mindfulness); moral, 86, 87; stress inoculation training (SIT), 235–37;

warrior culture, 33–35. *See also* Resiliency training

Transgender service members, 134–35, 137

Trauma: childhood, 6–7, 70, 76–77, 241; psychological, 8; sexual, 116–17, 134–35, 139, 200–201; and spirituality, 186–87; storytelling, 169; witnessing, 76–79 (*see also* Moral injury (MI))

Trauma informed guilt reduction therapy (TrIGR), 87

Trust, 185

Ultimate Spiritual Resiliency and Relationships (R&R), 187–88

Unit survival, 80

United US, 214–15, 221

University of California San Francisco (UCSF), 118

Van Epp, John, 187

Variations, in warrior culture, 32

Veterans, older: about, 162–64; complementary and alternative medicine (CAM), 170–73; eras of, 163–64; health, 165–66; meaning-making, 168; metaphor use, 167–68; service factors in postdeployment, 164–65; storytelling, 168–70

Veterans Affairs (VA), 118, 119, 183–84, 183–85, 209

Veterans at Ease, 112–14

Vietnam veterans, 6, 38, 81, 83. *See also* Veterans, older

Vocational rehabilitation, 197–98. *See also* Individual Placement and Support (IPS)

Volunteer military, 30, 241

Vulnerabilities, 11–12

Warrior culture: ancient, 29–30; belief in, 38–39; formation of, 31–33; mental health views, 39–40; modern, 29–31; postmilitary, 35; semiotics, 31, 32, 35–37; training, 33–35; variations in, 37–39; and work cultures, 204

Warriors at Ease (WAE), 111–14

Wickham, John, 152

Women service members: lesbian (*see* LGBT service members); Marines, 228–31; mental health services, barriers to, 117–18; post-traumatic stress disorder (PTSD) risk, 6; story of, 129–32; stressors, 7, 116–17; and suicide, 116; treatment, mental health, 117; Women Warriors (*see* Women warriors)

Women Warriors: course strategy, 118–20; curriculum, 120–23; recruitment for, 123; research, 123–24

Workplace, 196–97, 202–4. *See also* Individual Placement and Support (IPS)

Yoga, 45, 66–68, 112–13, 132, 172–73

Young Adult and Family Center (YAFC), 118